AEROSPACE SCIENCE 100:

MILESTONES IN AVIATION HISTORY

Second Edition

AIR FORCE J.R.O.T.C.

C² Technologies

www.C2TI.com

C² Technologies, Inc.
1921 Gallows Road, Suite 1000
Vienna, VA 22182-3900
703-448-7900
www.c2ti.com

Editorial Credits
High Stakes Writing, LLC, Editorial oversight: Lawrence J. Goodrich
Department of the Air Force Editor: Michael Wetzel

Production Credits
Chief Executive Officer: Dolly Oberoi
President: Curtis Cox
VP, Operations: James E. Threlfall
VP, Services: Jimmy Ruth
Program Manager: Gayla Thompson
Photo Researcher: Rodger Stuffel
Cover Design: Rodger Stuffel and Michael Wetzel
Interior Design and Composition: Mia Saunders

Cover Images: Lt Gen Elwood Quesada, Lt Col James Jabara, Brig Gen William Mitchell, Gen Benjamin O. Davis, Eugene Bullard, SSgt Esther M. Blake, Maj James Ellison and Tuskegee cadets, F-35, heritage flight (F-4, P-47, P-51, F-16), B-2 with B-52, V-22, MQ-1B, C-141B, KC-135 with F-4Cs courtesy US Air Force. Bellanca Pacemaker courtesy Federal Aviation Administration. Blanche Stuart Scott (ggbain 12209) courtesy Library of Congress, Prints and Photographs Division/George Grantham Bain Collection. Igor Sikorsky (cbh 3b40533), Wright brothers' first flight (ppprs-00626) courtesy Library of Congress, Prints and Photographs Division. Montgolfier brothers' balloon © Nicku/Shutterstock. DaVinci's ornithopter © LeoBlanchette/Shutterstock. DaVinci's airscrew © Mar.K/Shutterstock. Boeing 707 © Ivan Cholakov/Shutterstock. Spirit of St. Louis © Martha Dean/Shutterstock. B-17s bombing Dresden © Everett Historical/Shutterstock. Pan American Boeing 307 © Dmitry Morgan/Shutterstock

Printing and Binding: Print Printers Inc.

Some images in this book feature models. These models do not necessarily endorse, represent, or participate in the activities represented in the images.

Jeanne M. Holm Center for Officer Accessions and Citizen Development Credits
Director of Academic Affairs: James Wiggins
Chief, AFJROTC Curriculum: Vickie Helms, M.Ed.
Curriculum Instructional Systems Specialist: Michael Wetzel, M.Ed.

Library of Congress Cataloging-in-Publication Data on file
ISBN 978-0-9984993-1-4

Printed by a United States of America–Based Company
15 14 13 12 11   10 9 8 7 6 5 4 3 2

Contents

Preface

Aerospace Science 100: Milestones in Aviation History is a course that covers the development of flight throughout the centuries. It all starts with an examination of ancient civilizations and flight, then progresses through time to future developments in aerospace, with an introduction into cyber technologies.

Our intent is to bring alive the significant discoveries and inventions that have made flight possible for today and beyond. We will also focus on the people who helped make these discoveries in flight a reality. This book tells the stories of why we are so proud of our Air Force heritage—laying the foundation for future Air Force JROTC aerospace science courses. The mission of AFJROTC is to "develop citizens of character dedicated to serving their nation and community"; our goal with *Milestones in Aviation History* is to stimulate an interest in aerospace technology.

All chapters and lessons contain full-color images, diagrams, or other visual information. Each lesson includes a "Quick Write" exercise at the start of each lesson. A "Learn About" box tells you what you should take away from the lesson. A vocabulary list ensures that you will understand the terms you encounter throughout the text.

At selected points in each lesson, "Waypoints" will highlight useful information, including stories from people who have been successful applying these keys. "The Right Stuff" provides short profiles of famous people who have played significant roles in aviation. Each lesson is followed by "Checkpoints" to allow you to review what you have learned. An "Applying Your Learning" section at each lesson's end presents one or more discussion questions to further reinforce what you have learned. Throughout this course 21st century learning is adopted with readings, video clips, hands-on learner-centered lesson activities, and chapter project-based learning opportunities.

Chapter 1: Exploring Flight discusses ancient flight through the early pioneers of aviation. It includes the tools and imagination used hundreds of years ago by the Chinese and Leonardo da Vinci's vision of parachutes and gliders. A lesson on the early days of flight will cover the discovery of how to fly using hot air balloons, early engines to propel dirigibles, and early flight experiments with gliders.

This chapter also explores the Wright brothers' experiments and designs and their systematic approach to be the first to achieve controlled, manned, heavier-than-air, powered flight. The final lesson examines the contributions of early aviation pioneers and the continued development of aircraft and engines.

Chapter 2: Developing Flight focuses on early days of Army aviation through World War I. You will study how military aviation advanced during World War I, reshaping the way countries would fight future wars. This chapter examines the role barnstormers played in getting America interested in aviation, how Charles Lindbergh captured imaginations with his trans-Atlantic solo flight, and how Amelia Earhart became the first woman to fly across the Atlantic Ocean. You will learn how the development of instrument flying and navigation aids benefited commercial aviation. The chapter ends with an examination of how commercial aircraft builders contributed to the rapid expansion of commercial passenger and airmail services.

Chapter 3: Evolution of the Early Air Force focuses on evolution of the Army Air Corps after World War I through the end of World War II. The first lesson explores the roadblocks the Army Air Corps faced and overcame to establish its own identity, including the court-martial of Brigadier General William "Billy" Mitchell for his harsh criticism of senior military officers. You will also learn about the causes of war during this time and the heroic acts of those who fought the air battles over Europe and Asia.

You will learn about the significance of tactical and strategic air warfare and how it contributed to Allied victory. This chapter explores the challenges of racism that minorities faced during World War II and how they overcame these challenges, establishing a legacy of unwavering patriotism and unmatched aerial dominance. You will learn about the contributions of women in training male aviators and ferrying aircraft to war, even thought they were not allowed to participate in combat. The final lesson explores the contributions of military aircraft during World War II and how Allied air superiority helped win the war.

Chapter 4: Commercial and General Aviation Take Off opens with the expansion of federal oversight of commercial and general aviation. The introduction of regulations and the organizations that enforce them help make the skies much safer than in the early days of aviation. You will also learn about commercial aviation in the early days of flight—how developments in aviation technology positively affected airlines, opening the door for worldwide expansion of passenger and cargo service.

You will examine how general aviation became a popular method of transportation and the pioneers who built the aircraft. You'll also explore why the federal ideal of putting an airplane in every garage failed. The final lesson will discuss the founding of the Civil Air Patrol (CAP) and the extraordinary work done by general aviators during World War II. You will also study the different aircraft and categories that make up general aviation.

Chapter 5: The US Air Force is Born will start off with why the Army Air Forces transitioned to the US Air Force. You will examine military developments after World War II, how the National Security Act of 1947 paved the way for an independent Air Force, and how the Cold War affected US foreign policy and US Air Force priorities. You will also examine the significant contributions of test pilots after World War II and how the dangerous work they accomplished provided data and technology for many of the aircraft flown today.

This chapter also makes an in-depth examination of the role of airpower from the Korean War through the Vietnam War—and the aviators and aircraft that were pivotal to each outcome. You will learn about military operations the US military has conducted to protect national interests and provide humanitarian relief. Throughout the chapter aviators who have demonstrated the "right stuff" are highlighted for their bravery and achievements.

Chapter 6: The Modern Air Force begins with the development and evolution of the helicopter from pre-World War I to modern-day conflicts and operations. You will explore the role of the helicopter use for military and civilian purposes. As you continue through the chapter you will learn how the use of stealth technology helped create the latest, fifth generation of military aircraft and weapons. You will learn how drones and unmanned aerial vehicles (UAVs) have provided the military with unique multi-mission, medium and high-altitude, long-range, surveillance aircraft.

The final lesson will examine military aircraft of the future and how they will help the US Air Force maintain air superiority. You will learn about the history of cybertechnology, the rise of the Internet, and the security and privacy issues you face when computing. You will learn about the measures being taken to defend our government and personal information from cyberattacks.

At the end of the textbook, you will find a glossary defining all the vocabulary words and telling you which page each term appears on. You'll also find an alphabetical index at the end of the text, as well as a list of references.

This textbook and materials have been prepared especially for you the cadet—to increase your knowledge and appreciation of aviation. As you begin your academic journey in high school, hopefully the material presented here will inspire you to seek your own career path in aviation. Just as those men and women of the past used their imagination and engineering to create flight when many thought it was not possible, you can be the technicians, engineers, and scientists designing and building the aircraft of the future—aircraft that we now can only imagine.

Michael Wetzel and Lawrence J. Goodrich

Acknowledgments

This second edition of *Aerospace Science 100: Milestones in Aviation History* was developed based in part on the recommendations from Air Force JROTC instructors, who are responsible for teaching this curriculum.

The Jeanne M. Holm Center for Officer Accessions and Citizen Development (Holm Center) Academic Affairs Directorate (DE) team involved in the production effort was under the direction of Mr. James Wiggins, Director of Academic Affairs for the Holm Center at Maxwell Air Force Base, Alabama, and Ms. Vickie Helms, M.Ed., Chief, AFJROTC Curriculum (DEJ). Special acknowledgment goes to Mr. Michael Wetzel, M.Ed., an instructional systems specialist and Academic Credit Liaison for the Holm Center Academic Affairs, who was the Air Force researcher, editor, reviewer, and significant contributor for the AS 100 textbook. We commend Michael for his persistent efforts, commitment, and thorough review in producing the best academic materials possible for JROTC cadets worldwide.

Our deepest appreciation goes to Master Sergeant William Chivalette (retired), curator, Air Force Enlisted Heritage Hall, Gunter Annex, in Montgomery, Alabama, for invaluable historical expertise and insight. We would like to recognize Air Force JROTC cadet Moriah Graham for earning her private pilot's license and the efforts of the instructors at DE-931 in making this a reality. A special acknowledgement goes to Headquarters, Civil Air Patrol for granting permission to use their curriculum materials.

We would also like to express our gratitude to the C^2 Technologies team for all its hard work in publishing this book. In addition to project manager Gayla Thompson, that team consisted of Lawrence J. Goodrich at High Stakes Writing, LLC, who provided editorial oversight, and Mia Saunders, the designer and compositor. Our appreciation also goes to Erin Kelmereit, chief developer of the Instructor Guide.

All the people identified above came together on this project and combined their efforts to form one great team, providing 21st century learning materials for all our units. We believe this curriculum will continue the precedent of providing "world class" curriculum materials. Our goal is to create materials that provide a solid foundation for educating future members of society able to be productive and responsible citizens.

CHAPTER 1

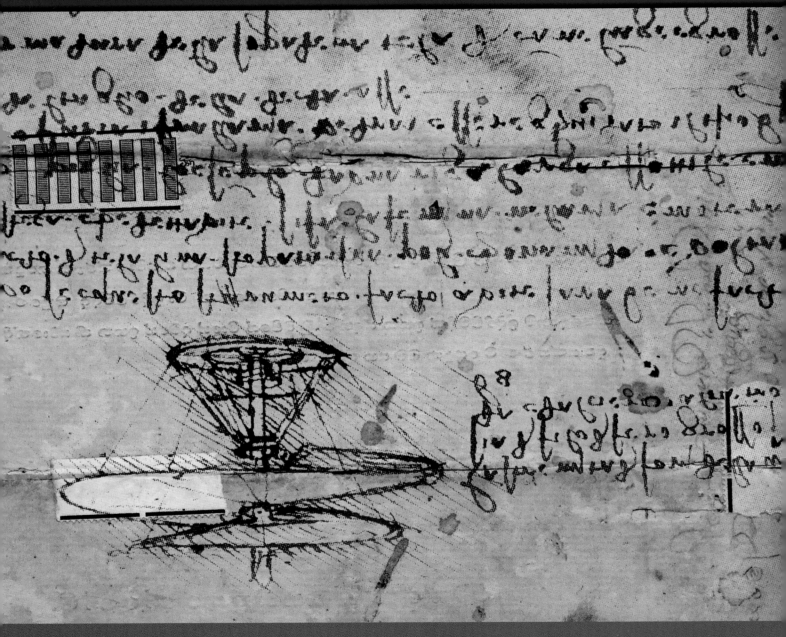

Leonardo Da Vinci's sketch of a flying machine in 1503
Janaka Dharmasena/Shutterstock

Exploring Flight

Chapter Outline

> " The way in which we experience the irregularities of the wind while sliding through the air cannot be learned in any other way except by being in the air itself.... "
>
> Otto Lilienthal, "The Father of Modern Aviation"

Ancient Flight

Learn About

- how humans tried to fly in ancient times
- key aviation devices created during ancient times
- why machines don't fly the way birds do

A STIFF, 27-MILE-AN-HOUR WIND roared across the dunes at Kill Devil Hills, North Carolina. Wilbur Wright reached out to steady the wing of his experimental flying machine. His brother, Orville, lay at the controls. For years the brothers had worked for this moment—both in their bicycle shop in Dayton, Ohio, and on these same coastal dunes. They'd tested kites. They'd tested gliders. They'd even built a small wind tunnel and learned how to control their craft in the air.

Now, on 17 December 1903, they were ready to find out: Would their heavier-than-air craft leave the ground and fly on its own?

Orville gunned the engine, and Wilbur let go of a wire that held the plane in place. _The Wright Flyer_ rolled down a set of tracks on a trolley, with Wilbur's hand still steadying the wing. Suddenly, it happened: The _Flyer_ lifted into the air, dropped the trolley, and flew for 12 seconds. Under Orville's control, it landed 120 feet away from the track's end. The Wright brothers had achieved a milestone: the first controlled, sustained, and powered heavier-than-air flight.

That flight and the three that followed on that raw December day changed the course of human history. After thousands of years of dreaming and trying, humans had mastered flight. But the Wrights' achievement was only the final step in centuries of attempts to learn how to fly. The brothers from Dayton built on the work of hundreds of others before them.

How Humans Tried to Fly in Ancient Times

Humans have dreamed of taking flight—of escaping gravity to fly "free as a bird"—for thousands of years. People told tales about flight—*the act of passing through the air on wings*—around the fire at night. Parents in early societies handed down these stories to their children.

One of the best known is the Greek story of Daedalus and his son, Icarus, who were imprisoned by King Minos on the island of Crete. To escape, they made wings from bird feathers and attached them to their bodies with beeswax. The wings did carry them off the island. But Icarus enjoyed his new freedom so much that he ignored his father's warning and flew too close to the sun. Its heat melted the wax. Icarus fell into the sea and drowned.

The story of Icarus and Daedalus is a myth. It isn't a true story. But people still tell it today because of what it says about the human quest for freedom—and about sons who disobey their fathers. The story, however, doesn't say much about how to build a good flying machine.

The first true stories of human attempts to fly, though, included things that today seem almost as strange as stick-on wings. Some of these early inventors made devices of lightweight material such as cloth or wood, in imitation of birds' or bats' wings. They strapped the devices onto their arms or legs, or both. Then they would jump from the top of a tower or tall building, hoping to glide or flap their way gently to earth.

Unfortunately, none of the devices succeeded. At best, they slowed their wearers' plunge to earth. These early inventors all made hard landings, resulting in serious injury or death.

History credits a Moor named Armen Firman with the first known human attempt to fly. In the year AD 852, he put on a huge cloak and jumped from a tower in Cordoba, Spain.

Vocabulary

- flight
- parachute
- kite
- gunpowder
- rocket
- legend
- helicopter
- streamlining
- glider
- ornithopter

He hoped the cloak would open wide like a bat's wings to slow him on the way down. But it didn't, and Firman fell to his death. His unfortunate experiment might be described as an early attempt at a jump by parachute—*a device intended to slow free fall from an aircraft or another high point.*

Key Aviation Devices Created During Ancient Times

Chinese Kites

A Chinese military observation kite might have looked like something like this.

A lot of ancient scientific progress took place in China. The Chinese invented the kite around 1000 BC. A kite is *a light framework covered with paper or cloth, provided with a balancing tail, designed to be flown in the air.* A kite may seem very different from an airplane, but kites were actually among the first man-made devices to take flight. It's not clear that these early kites actually carried people at first. Evidence suggests, though, that they were quite large and strong. Within a few hundred years, people were using them in warfare.

Around AD 1300 the Italian explorer Marco Polo reportedly saw Chinese sailors attached to kites as "eyes in the sky," observing enemy actions during battle. In the seventeenth century, other Western observers reported seeing Chinese soldiers on kites serving as flying spies.

Waypoints

Using Kites Against an Enemy

In 200 BC, a Chinese general named Han Hsin used kites to scout his enemy's position and movements by air. His soldiers attached long measuring ropes to the kites. They got the kites in the air and then let the wind carry them to a position over the enemy camp. By determining how much rope had been let out, the Chinese soldiers could figure how far away the enemy was. They wanted to tunnel under the enemy's walled fortress. The marks on the rope showed them how far they had to dig to reach it.

Chinese Gunpowder and Rockets

In the AD 800s, the Chinese made another important invention: gunpowder—
*an explosive powder made of potassium nitrate, charcoal, and sulfur, used to shoot projectiles
from guns.* And just 200 years later, the Chinese were using gunpowder to make the first
simple rockets. A rocket is *a large, cylindrical object that moves very fast by forcing burning
gases out one end of the tube.*

The Chinese used these devices mostly for celebrations, such as holiday fireworks.
But they also used their rockets in battle to scare off the enemy.

There's even a Chinese legend, or *unverified story handed down from earlier times*, about a
rocket trip into space. This legend says that a man named Wan Hoo fastened 47 rockets
to a chair. All 47 rockets were lit at the same time by 47 servants. As the servants ran
for cover, there was a huge explosion. After the smoke had cleared, both Wan Hoo and
the chair were gone, never to be seen again. Some believe he went up in a ball of fire,
but legend suggests that perhaps he became the Man in the Moon.

It's obvious that this is just a story. But in a way, the legend foretold history. When the
Apollo astronauts traveled to the moon in the 1960s and 1970s, they were strapped into
special chairs in their spacecraft and then lifted away from Earth by rockets.

The legend of Wan Hoo
Courtesy of NASA

A Parachute and a Helicopter

The first person in the history of aviation who was also a real scientist was Leonardo da Vinci (1452–1519). Da Vinci produced the first known designs for a parachute and a helicopter, *an aircraft that gets its lift from spinning blades.* He apparently made models of both and may even have flown one of his helicopters.

Da Vinci's drawing of an "airscrew" looks a lot like a modern helicopter. And in fact, both devices are based on the same principle: a flat screw that, when turned, produces lift. What's more, today's parachutes are based on principles first described by Da Vinci. His invention, he wrote, would allow someone to "throw himself down from any height without sustaining any injury."

Leonardo DaVinci's self-portrait

Jakub Krechowicz/Shutterstock

The Right Stuff

Leonardo da Vinci

Have you heard the term "Renaissance man?" It refers to someone who has many talents. Leonardo da Vinci was such a man. He's best known today as an artist—for example, he painted the *Mona Lisa*. But he was a scientist, too. He conducted the first scientific experiments in aviation.

A model of DaVinci's "airscrew" helicopter

Mar.K/Shutterstock

Like other scientists, Da Vinci observed the world closely. Also like other scientists, he kept good records. He filled the pages of his notebooks with detailed drawings of things he had actually seen, as well as things he thought up. The notebooks included 160 pages of drawings of his projects for flight. The notebooks show that Da Vinci understood several key concepts in aviation, such as streamlining, which is *designing an aircraft to reduce resistance to motion through the air.*

His orderly way of working did a lot for science. But it could have done much more. Tragically, his notes were lost for about 300 years following his death. He left his drawings and papers in the care of a friend, who never published them. Scientists today wonder how much sooner human flight would have developed had Da Vinci's work been available during those "lost" years.

Gliders

Da Vinci also researched the idea of a glider, *a light aircraft without an engine, designed to glide after being towed aloft or launched from a catapult.* Gliders were the first aircraft that had directional control.

Da Vinci was fascinated with birds, and he experimented with flapping-wing machines. He worked out structures and mechanisms intended to mimic the motions of a bird. These included some designs for ornithopters. An ornithopter is *an aircraft designed to get its upward and forward motion from flapping wings.* (Orni- comes from a Greek word for bird.)

Da Vinci was a careful observer. But even he didn't understand how complex the movements of a bird's wing are. He also didn't realize that human muscle power could never be powerful enough to keep a person in the air. That realization didn't come until about 150 years after Da Vinci's death. At that time, the Italian biologist Giovanni Alfonso Borelli (1608–1679) concluded that a man's muscle power just wasn't great enough to lift his weight.

You may think of birds as "lightweights," and in many ways, they are. But it's relative proportions that matter. Birds are very powerful for their size. Their large wing muscles and hollow bones make them well suited to flight. Unfortunately, when it comes to being able to fly on their own muscle power, humans have more in common with elephants than with birds!

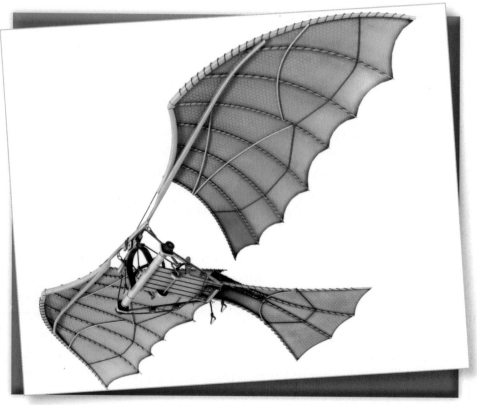

A 3D drawing of DaVinci's ornithopter
Leo Blanchette/Shutterstock

Why Machines Don't Fly the Way Birds Do

The Principles of Bird Flight

A bird's flight is similar to an airplane's in some ways and different in others. Here's how Dr. Paul Fortin, author of *The Fantasy and Mechanics of Flight*, explains it:

> There are two phases of bird flight—a ground phase and a lift phase. The ground phase allows the bird to get started moving forward in order for the wings to provide the necessary lift. To be lifted by its wings, a bird . . . must be moving forward fast enough to make air pass over its wings. A bird can move forward by flapping its wings. Most of the flapping is done by the outer wing. The flight feathers work like the propeller of a plane: i.e., they push downward and backward, thereby driving the air backward and moving the bird forward. Once the bird's speed is adequate, lift over the wing is generated by the same principle as the flow of air over the wing of an airplane.

Dr. Fortin adds:

> Slow-motion pictures of birds in flight show that the wings move downward rapidly. The wing tips trace a figure eight as they move though the air. The downward beat of the wings moves the bird forward as the outer tips push against the air. Wing feathers are arranged much like shingles on a roof. They change position when the bird is flapping. On the downbeat of the wing, the feathers are pressed together so little air can pass through them. On the up stroke the feathers open.

Bird flight and the flight of human-made aircraft rely on two kinds of lift, each named for a famous scientist who never flew, but who made significant contributions to aeronautical science: Daniel Bernoulli and Sir Isaac Newton.

The Swiss scientist Daniel Bernoulli (1700–1782) made an important discovery about the relationship between pressure and fluids (liquids or gases) in motion. A fluid has a constant pressure, he found, but when a fluid starts to move faster, the pressure drops. Wings are designed to make air flow faster over their tops. This makes the pressure drop and the wings move upward, defying the force of gravity. This phenomenon is known as *Bernoullian lift* or *induced lift*.

Sir Isaac Newton, an Englishman who lived from 1643 to 1727, formulated three famous laws of motion. The third law states, "For every action, there is an equal and opposite reaction." This principle comes into play when an airplane is ascending, or flying higher. When a pilot angles the wing of the plane up against the oncoming wind, the action of the wind causes a reaction by the wing. This reaction provides some additional lift, known as *Newtonian* or *dynamic lift*. So with Bernoullian lift pulling from above and Newtonian lift pushing from below, a wing has no choice. It can only go up—whether it's attached to a bird or to an airplane.

By now you're beginning to understand that birds and airplanes don't work exactly alike. Here's another difference: Airplanes are fixed-wing aircraft. They don't flap their wings as birds do. Instead, airplanes rely on their propellers or jet engines to get them off the ground.

Why Ancient Inventors Tried to Mimic Bird Flight

At the beginning of aviation discovery, flapping wings seemed to be what flight was all about. People observed birds, bats, and insects flying this way. As you've now learned, some early inventors thought feathers might possess some lifting power of their own. And even a thinker as brilliant as Leonardo da Vinci got stuck on birds as the model for human flight. Some scientists think that if Da Vinci had focused on fixed-wing gliders, instead of ornithopters, he might have done even more for the progress of aviation than he actually did. Only when people stopped trying to fly as birds did the way open for the Wright brothers' success on the North Carolina dunes.

TABLE 1.1 Timeline of Aviation History

Date	Event
1000 BC	Chinese invent the kite.
200 BC	Chinese General Han Hsin uses kites for military strategy.
In the AD 800s	Chinese invent gunpowder.
AD 852	In an unsuccessful attempt to fly, Armen Firman dons a huge cloak and jumps from a tower in Cordoba, Spain.
AD 1100	Chinese start using gunpowder to make simple rockets.
AD 1300	Explorer Marco Polo reportedly sees Chinese sailors flying on kites as "eyes in the sky," observing enemy actions during battle.
1452–1519	Life span of Leonardo da Vinci, who pioneered the scientific study of aviation.
1643–1727	Life span of Isaac Newton, who formulated three laws of motion.
1700–1782	Life span of Daniel Bernoulli, who discovered the phenomenon of induced lift.
17 December 1903	Wilbur and Orville Wright make the first controlled, sustained, and powered heavier-than-air flight.

✔ CHECKPOINTS

Lesson 1 Review

Using complete sentences, answer the following questions on a sheet of paper.

1. What milestone did the Wright brothers reach in December 1903?

2. Who were Daedalus and Icarus?

3. Who was Armen Firman, and what was his role in aviation history?

4. What were some early military uses of kites?

5. Who made the first rockets? What were they first used for?

6. What kinds of flight devices did Leonardo da Vinci explore?

7. What are the two phases of bird flight?

8. What contributions did Daniel Bernoulli and Sir Isaac Newton make to aviation science?

APPLYING YOUR LEARNING

9. Flying squirrels don't have wings, but they do have flaps of skin between the legs on each side of their body. These flaps allow them to "fly" from tree to tree or from a tree to the ground. To which flying device would you compare a flying squirrel and why?

This page not used

Quick Write

_____

_____

After reading the account of how hot air balloons were used in the Battle of San Juan Hill, how do you think the information the US Army balloonists gathered changed the course of the battle? What lesson can you draw from the fact that the Americans could view the battlefield and the Spanish could not?

Learn About

- historical developments of lighter-than-air flight
- early military contributions of lighter-than-air flight
- early contributors to heavier-than-air flight

IT HAD BEEN A TOUGH TRIP for Lieutenant Colonel Joseph E. Maxfield of the US Army Signal Corps. The year was 1898. The United States was at war with Spain.

Six years earlier, the Signal Corps had formed a balloon section. For the first time since the Civil War, the Army was back in the business of spying from the sky.

Now Colonel Maxfield was in charge of a single balloon. It was the only one the Army had.

Maxfield traveled alone with the balloon from New York to Florida. Then with troops and some equipment, he sailed for Cuba. That country, then a Spanish colony, was one of the major theaters of the Spanish-American War.

Maxfield's party included three officers and 24 enlisted men. Only one man had ballooning experience— Sergeant Will Ivy Baldwin, who had once worked as a stunt balloonist and had built a balloon with his wife the previous year. None of the others, including Maxfield, had ever even seen a balloon go up.

The party sailed into Santiago harbor 22 June. Because they lacked supplies, they would be able to inflate the balloon just once. They wouldn't be able to reinflate it.

The terrain was rugged. It took them a whole day to get from the harbor to their headquarters. And once they unpacked their balloon, they found that parts of it had stuck together in the heat. Other parts had disintegrated.

But somehow, they managed to inflate the balloon using hydrogen cylinders. And they got it into the air several times.

On 1 July 1898 during the Battle of San Juan Hill, Soldiers went aloft to scout the enemy position. They made an initial ascent at some distance from the battle. The leader of the Soldiers, Lieutenant Colonel George M. Derby, then ordered the balloon forward. He got it to within 650 yards of the Spanish infantry trenches. Maxfield feared this was too close to the enemy.

In a way, he was right. By the end of the day, the balloon had been hit by so many enemy bullets that it was useless. But before that, it gave observers aboard a totally different view of the battle. Because of what they'd seen, the balloonists suggested new ways to direct American troops advancing against the Spanish. They also identified new artillery targets.

The battle was a big US victory. Teddy Roosevelt's Rough Riders made a name for themselves in it. The "buffalo Soldiers," members of an all-African-American regiment, got to show what they were made of.

The Battle of San Juan Hill was a milestone in military aviation. The spies in the sky may have decided the battle.

It was a good day for Maxfield's balloon.

The US Army Signal Corps balloon in Cuba
Courtesy US Army

Cuba and the US Gulf Coast
Victor Maschek/Shutterstock

Historical Developments of Lighter-Than-Air Flight

Aviation developments in the 19th century followed two lines: lighter-than-air craft and heavier-than-air craft. Lighter-than-air craft include balloons and dirigibles. The story you've just read shows how far these craft had come by the end of the 19th century. Heavier-than-air machines include gliders, and later, airplanes and jets.

Whether their craft are lighter or heavier than air, all aviators face the same three problems:

- How to get up into the air
- How to stay up in the air
- How to control where they're going, including getting safely back to earth

Principles of Balloon Flight

A balloon operates on the principle of *buoyancy*. If the air or gas inside a balloon is lighter than the air around it, it will float. Hot air takes care of the first challenge of flight—getting up into the air.

A Jesuit priest, Laurenço de Gusmão, gets credit for inventing the hot-air balloon. In 1709 he demonstrated his invention before the King of Portugal. Word soon spread across Europe.

Several people tried out balloons during the 18th century. The work of the Montgolfier brothers, Joseph and Étienne, led to the first balloon flight with humans aboard. On 21 November 1783, Pilatre de Rozier and François d'Arlandes made a historic 25-minute flight over Paris in a Montgolfier hot-air balloon.

Waypoints

Printing Presses and Flying Machines

What do printing presses have to do with flying machines? Quite a bit. During the early years of aviation, the cost of printing fell sharply. Books and papers became cheaper. More people could afford to buy them. For the first time, scientists throughout Europe could read about one another's work. Printing presses were a big help in making the dream of flight come true.

The Montgolfiers' achievement was impressive. But there was still work to do. The brothers hadn't figured out how to achieve the second principle of flight— to keep the balloon up in the air. To do that, you need to keep the air inside the balloon hot. This meant having a fire under the balloon. That was dangerous. It also meant that balloons needed to carry fuel, and fuel was heavy.

While the Montgolfiers were testing their balloons, the young French scientist J.A.C. Charles experimented with hydrogen. This gas is lighter than air. It provided much more lift than hot air, and the balloonists didn't need to carry a fire and fuel aloft to keep the air heated. Lift is *the upward force on an aircraft against gravity.*

The Right Stuff

A Big Idea Sparked in Front of the Fireplace

Joseph and Étienne Montgolfier were the first to achieve manned flight. The brothers were papermakers and amateur scientists in Annonay, France. They kept up with the work of other scientists around Europe.

One day in 1782 Joseph Montgolfier was sitting in front of his fireplace when he happened to notice the sparks and smoke rising.

This got him thinking—and experimenting. He made a small bag out of silk and held the bag upside down. Then he lit a fire under the opening at the bottom. The bag swelled and rose to the ceiling. Soon Joseph and his brother moved their experiments outdoors. They built and flew larger bags made of paper and linen.

The brothers thought they'd discovered a new gas. They even gave it a name: "Montgolfier gas." Today we know that they hadn't discovered a new gas at all. They'd simply observed a principle of physics: Hotter air rises above cooler air.

The Montgolfiers' experiments attracted attention. French King Louis XVI and Queen Marie Antoinette asked to see one of the balloons in action. Eventually this led to the first manned balloon flight on 21 November 1783.

The Montgolfier brothers' balloon
Nicku/Shutterstock

The Montgolfiers achieved a milestone in the history of flight. But Joseph Montgolfier's observation in front of the fire also has a lesson for creative thinkers of all kinds: You never know where you'll find a good idea. It may come as you sit in front of your fireplace.

Steam Engines

Steam engines were the main source of mechanical power in the 19th century—before the invention of the gasoline-powered internal-combustion engine and the electric motor. Water heated by fire (usually fueled by wood or coal) was used to create steam. The steam's force drove a piston or turbine blade that turned a wheel or—as in the case of the Giffard dirigible—a propeller. The discoverer of steam power, James Watt, coined the term *horsepower* as a measurement of mechanical power. One horsepower is 33,000 foot-pounds of work in one minute.

But hydrogen could be risky, too, because it is very flammable—it catches fire easily. Many people were killed before a safer gas, helium, came into use. (Helium isn't as flammable as hydrogen.)

Despite the risks, Charles and a passenger made the first manned hydrogen balloon flight on 1 December 1783. Their flight lasted more than two hours and covered more than 27 miles.

In the years that followed, ballooning attracted interest across Europe. Benjamin Franklin, then an American diplomat in France, saw one of Charles's balloons in 1783. He immediately wrote home, stressing the military importance of the new invention. In 1783 the French Army started using balloons for aerial reconnaissance—*looking over battlefields from the sky.*

Dirigibles

Once balloonists started using lighter-than-air gases, they had solved two of the three problems of flight: getting up into the sky, and staying there. The days of bringing their flying fireplaces along with them were past. But the third problem of flight—control of the craft—was still a problem. It was, that is, until inventors came up with the dirigible—*a steerable airship.*

A balloon in the sky is like an inner tube floating along a river. The inner tube follows the river currents, and a balloon follows the air currents. The balloon rides high or low, depending on how much gas it holds. You can't steer it.

The new dirigible airships had two things that helped pilots steer them. First, they had rudders. A rudder is *a vertically hinged airfoil used for controlling horizontal movement of an aircraft.* Pilots could use the rudder to turn the craft left or right. Second, like steamships or motorboats, the new airships had power sources that drove propellers. Equipped with propellers, the craft could move through the air much as ships move through water.

Scientists also thought an airship with pointed ends would fly better than a round balloon. In 1852 Henri Giffard of France built a cigar-shaped dirigible. It was 114 feet long and 39 feet in diameter. A three-horsepower steam engine pushed it through the sky at about five miles an hour. Most historians give Giffard credit for inventing the first successful dirigible.

Development of dirigibles continued. Some inventors tried out internal keels to improve these aircraft. A keel is *a structure that extends along the center of a craft from the front to the back.* A keel helps keep the craft rigid and fully extended. It also streamlines it.

(A *rigid* craft has a frame that contains several balloons to provide lift. A *non-rigid* ship, on the other hand, holds its shape through gas pressure alone.)

The next breakthrough came in 1872, when German engineer Paul Haenlein built a dirigible with an internal-combustion engine, *an engine in which the fuel is burned inside, rather than in an external furnace.* (A gas-burning car engine is an internal combustion engine.) Two men made their names with these engines: Alberto Santos-Dumont and Count Ferdinand von Zeppelin.

Alberto Santos-Dumont

Santos-Dumont's first dirigible was 82 feet long. A three-horsepower gasoline motor (about half the power of a small lawn mower) powered it. It could reach an altitude of 1,300 feet. A pilot steered it with a rudder. Between 1898 and 1907 Santos-Dumont built and flew 14 of these non-rigid airships.

Santos-Dumont, a Brazilian, became famous in 1901. In that year, he flew an airship around the Eiffel Tower. He completed a nine-mile loop in less than half an hour. This won him a big cash prize from a rich oilman named Henri Deutsch. Santos-Dumont gave the money to his own workers and to the poor of Paris.

Santos-Dumont became a familiar sight in his frequent flights over the rooftops of the French capital. His generous and adventurous spirit won over the French people. He helped spark interest in aviation worldwide.

Count von Zeppelin

Zeppelin's machines were rigid dirigibles. In July 1900 this German inventor built and flew the first successful rigid dirigible, the LZ-1.

This led to the world's first commercial airships. The *Zeppelins*, as they were known, were luxurious. They had roomy, wood-paneled cabins. They carried 20 or more passengers. They flew at speeds exceeding 40 miles an hour. For a few years, they had a good safety record.

But the days of airships were numbered. The first airplanes were beginning to hop off the ground. Within a few decades, airplanes would crowd airships almost completely out of the skies.

The first ascent of the LZ-1, 2 July 1900
Library of Congress, Prints and Photographs Division, cph 3c00556

Balloons in the US Civil War

The US armed forces first used balloons during the Civil War. But it took President Abraham Lincoln to make it happen.

After the Civil War began, many aeronauts—*people who travel in airships or balloons*—volunteered their services for the Union cause. They thought it would be a good idea to use balloons for aerial reconnaissance. After all, the French had done this more than half a century earlier.

One of these aeronauts was Thaddeus Lowe. He tried to interest General Winfield Scott, head of the Union Army, in balloons. But Scott saw no military need for them.

Lowe didn't give up, however. He was a friend of Joseph Henry, the head of the Smithsonian Institution. And Henry knew President Lincoln. Henry convinced the president to let Lowe demonstrate what a balloon could do.

Lincoln's note to General Scott
Courtesy National Air and Space Museum, Smithsonian Institution

Lowe launched a balloon from the National Mall, a short distance from the White House. A telegraph wire ran from the balloon, up into the sky, and down to the White House, where Lincoln could receive messages over it. From his balloon, the pilot described what he saw to the President. This demonstration made Lincoln realize how useful balloons could be for keeping an eye on Confederate forces. Lincoln sent General Scott a note asking him to reconsider Lowe's offer.

Lowe was finally allowed to organize the Balloon Corps of the Union Army, the first air arm of the United States military. The balloonists provided valuable information to Union forces during several battles.

But it was a struggle. Lowe often had to pay for staff and supplies out of his own pocket. It was sometimes hard to get permission to send the balloon aloft. Despite some success, the Army disbanded the balloon service in 1863, before the war ended.

The Confederate Army also tried to start a balloon force. Southern women even donated silk dresses to build a balloon. But the Southern balloon effort never really got off the ground.

The Balloon's Contribution to US Victory in the Battle of San Juan Hill

On 1 October 1890 the US Congress gave the Signal Corps the duty of collecting and transmitting information for the Army. At that point, the military had not conducted balloon operations for nearly 30 years. But several other countries—Britain, France, Germany, Italy, Japan, and Russia—had established balloon corps as part of their armed forces. Brigadier General Adolphus V. Greely, the chief signal officer, interpreted his assignment to include aerial navigation. In 1892 he established a balloon section in the Signal Corps.

Union forces preparing Thaddeus Lowe's balloon at the Battle of Fair Oaks, Virginia
Matthew Brady/Library of Congress, Prints and Photographs Division, 33091v

A few years later, the United States was at war with Spain. The Battle of San Juan Hill gave the Army a chance to see what a balloon could do.

As shown in the story at the beginning of this lesson, Lieutenant Colonel George M. Derby insisted on bringing the Army's single spy balloon as close to the action as possible during the Battle of San Juan Hill on 1 July 1898.

From that position, observers on board could see a new trail leading to the Spanish forces. This let US commanders divide their Soldiers into two forces to advance against the enemy. This relieved congestion on a main road where the Americans were more vulnerable to Spanish attack. The observers also suggested directing artillery fire from El Pozo Hill against the San Juan Hill trenches.

Historians say these actions may have turned the battle into a US victory.

Early Contributors to Heavier-Than-Air Flight

While balloons and dirigibles were enjoying success, other aviators were making progress with heavier-than-air craft.

Gliders

Sir George Cayley (1773–1857) picked up where Leonardo da Vinci left off in developing gliders. This Englishman's gliders resembled today's model gliders. They had the same design as most of today's airplanes, with wings up front and a tail behind.

Cayley also came up with the idea of using a fixed wing for lift and a separate system for propulsion. The fixed-wing idea seems simple now. But it was quite new at a time when many people still had flapping birds' wings as their model for flight.

Cayley identified three important forces in connection with aviation. The first force was lift. The second was drag, *the pull, or slowing effect, of air on an aircraft.* The third was thrust, *the forward force driving an aircraft.* In 1850 Cayley built the first successful full-size manned glider.

Cayley also recognized that a flying machine would need the right kind of engine to propel it. Steam engines were too heavy.

The Right Stuff

Sir George Cayley

Sir George Cayley was nine years old when the Montgolfiers made their first balloon flight. But even at that young age, he started experimenting with small paper balloons. Later he built model helicopters using Leonardo da Vinci's "airscrew" concept. In 1809 Cayley summarized his research in a scientific paper. It contained one sentence that laid the whole foundation for modern aeronautics. That sentence read: "The whole problem is confined within these limits, namely, to make a surface support a given weight by the application of power to the resistance of air." In other words, the problem was how to provide lift using wind resistance.

A drawing of Sir George Cayley's glider

Work on gliders continued, even after the Wright brothers' flights in 1903. Two men were especially important.

The first was Otto Lilienthal of Germany, a famous aviator. In fact, he's often called the "Father of Modern Aviation." Between 1891 and 1896 he made more than 2,000 glides. His abilities as an engineer and mathematician helped with the development of powered flight. Altogether, Lilienthal constructed 18 types of gliders—15 monoplanes and three biplanes. (A biplane is *an aircraft with two main supporting surfaces, usually placed one above the other.*)

On 9 August 1896, he decided to fly his glider one more time. He took off in a gusty wind. His glider stalled at 50 feet up and dropped like a rock. Sadly, Lilienthal was severely injured in the crash and died the next day. But subsequent aviators, including the Wright brothers, made use of his data and experiments.

The second was John J. Montgomery, an American. After witnessing a glider flight in 1869, he began his own aerial experiments in August of 1881. After 20 years of experiments, he unveiled his glider to the public in 1905. He thrilled people by performing sharp dives and turns in the air. His glider reached speeds of 68 miles an hour. Unfortunately, on 18 April 1906, Montgomery's gliders were destroyed in the San Francisco earthquake. He eventually restarted his work in 1911 with new glider called the *Evergreen*. Sadly, on 31 October 1911, while flying at an altitude of less than 20 feet the *Evergreen* glider stalled, came down on the right wing, and Montgomery was killed.

Otto Lilienthal flying his glider
Everett Historical/Shutterstock

Failed Attempts to Construct an Airplane

In 1843, two Englishmen designed an aircraft theoretically capable of carrying a man. They were W. S. Henson, an inventor, and John Stringfellow, an engineer. The two received a patent—*a legal document protecting the rights of an inventor*—for their design. Their aircraft, the *Ariel*, was to be a monoplane—*an airplane with one set of wings.* It would have a 150-foot wingspan. It would be powered by a steam engine driving two six-bladed propellers. As it turned out, however, the *Ariel* was never built. But the plans were engineering masterpieces.

In 1848 Stringfellow built a steam-driven model that did fly. This was the first successful powered flight of a heavier-than-air craft.

The Contributions and Failures of Samuel Langley

Dr. Samuel Pierpont Langley was one of the first Americans to try to build a flying machine with a motor. He started experimenting with aerodynamics in 1885. Rubber bands powered his first models. In 1898 the US government gave him a $50,000 grant to continue his work.

On 7 October 1903 his aircraft, the *Aerodrome*, was ready for a test flight. Langley planned to launch it from a catapult on a barge on the Potomac River. The plane's engine worked well, but the aircraft caught on the launching car on takeoff. It fell into the river.

Two months later, Langley tried—and failed—again. His efforts got a lot of press coverage in Washington. Government officials read about them and withdrew their support. So Langley gave up his project. He donated his *Aerodrome* to the Smithsonian Institution.

Despite his failures, Langley made important contributions to aviation. For example, he explained how birds can soar in the sky with no apparent movement of their wings. (As you read in the last lesson, Bernoullian lift pulls the wings up from above, while Newtonian lift pushes them up from below.) Historians fault Langley for spending too much time on how to power his aircraft and not enough on how to control it. Even so, for his contributions to aviation, Langley Air Force Base in southeastern Virginia is named after him.

Samuel Langley's *Aerodrome* moored on the Potomac River
Library of Congress, Prints and Photographs Division, Harris & Ewing Collection, hec 04223

✔ CHECKPOINTS

Lesson 2 Review

Using complete sentences, answer the following questions on a sheet of paper.

1. What are the two lines of aviation development followed in the nineteenth century?

2. What are the three problems of flight all aviators face?

3. How did inventors solve the problem of steering lighter-than-air craft ?

4. Who was Thaddeus Lowe, and what group did he did he organize during the Civil War?

5. When the US Army Signal Corps established a balloon section, which other countries had already been using balloons as part of their armed forces?

6. How did a balloon help the US Army win the Battle of San Juan Hill in Cuba?

7. Which three important forces did Sir George Cayley identify?

8. Which two men did important work using gliders?

9. What do historians fault Samuel Langley for?

APPLYING YOUR LEARNING

10. Are dirigibles still in use today? What are they called? What are they used for?

LESSON **3**

The Wright Brothers Take Off

Quick Write

_____

_____

The Wright brothers were the first to conduct a manned, controlled, sustained, and powered heavier-than-air flight. Many others had tried unsuccessfully to do this. After reading the paragraphs to the right, list three reasons for the Wrights' success.

Learn About

- the Wright brothers' first flight
- how the principles of airplane flight were applied to the *Wright Flyer*
- the contributions the Wright brothers made to US Army aviation
- how the Wright brothers were the first to succeed in powered flight

IT WAS 14 DECEMBER 1903. Wilbur and Orville Wright stood on the sand dunes of Kill Devil Hills, North Carolina. Beside them was their aircraft, the *Wright Flyer*. It was ready for its first real test. Although their first successful manned flight of this craft would not come until three days later, on 17 December, they had high hopes. The two men had worked for years for this moment. One important question remained: who would fly the craft?

They tossed a coin. Wilbur won. He would pilot the *Flyer* on its first attempt at flight.

Choosing the pilot was a matter of chance. But it wasn't chance that brought the two brothers to this important day. It was years of work and study. Why did they succeed when others had failed?

First, they were intelligent men. They learned from the experiences of others. Second, they were also creative thinkers and great problem solvers. Third, and perhaps most important, they were patient.

A well-known proverb says, "Genius is patience." And the brothers' patience paid off. After making hundreds of flight trials between 1899 and 1903, the Wrights achieved what earlier men had only dreamed of.

The Wright Brothers' First Flight

The *Wright Flyer* that Wilbur and Orville successfully flew in December 1903 was larger than any aircraft the brothers had built earlier. A biplane, it was equipped with an engine and propellers, had a wingspan of 40 feet, 4 inches, and a wing area of 510 square feet. The Flyer was 21 feet, 1 inch long. It stood 9 feet, 4 inches tall. It weighed 605 pounds without a pilot and about 750 with a pilot on board.

The Parts of the Wright Flyer

The *Flyer*'s wings had two main parts—spars and ribs. The spars are *the main, lengthwise pieces of the wing*. Attached to the spars were ribs. The ribs are *the crosswise pieces that give the wings their shape*.

Muslin, a lightweight fabric, covered the wings. It reduced wind resistance and added strength as the wings warped during turns. Struts and bracing between the top and bottom wings further reinforced the plane.

Two propellers sat behind the wings. They rotated in opposite directions and were made of two layers of spruce wood. Their job was to help move the craft forward. The plane also had a front elevator, which was covered by fabric. A rudder at the rear was also wrapped in fabric. The other important part of this plane was, of course, the engine. The *Flyer*'s engine was water cooled like a car engine and fueled by gasoline. The engine and the propellers together weighed about 200 pounds.

Before the *Flyer*, two assistants hand-launched the brothers' gliders. Each assistant would hold a wing and help lift the craft in the air. But the new, powered *Flyer* was too heavy for that. Rather than the wheels that are so common on the airplanes you see today, the brothers used skids—*long, thin runners, like a pair of skis*. Before takeoff, the plane sat on a trolley that rolled along wooden rails.

Vocabulary

- spars
- ribs
- skids
- elevator
- wing warping
- yaw
- airfoil
- center of pressure
- angle of attack
- relative wind
- bid
- strut
- bracing
- lateral
- pitch
- canard configuration
- sateen

Orville Wright (1871–1948)

Orville Wright was the scientist of the family. He loved science and technology. He was also quite shy, although he was never timid about playing practical jokes on his family and friends. Later, he wrote about the support he and his siblings found at home:

> We were lucky enough to grow up in an environment where there was always much encouragement to children to pursue intellectual interests; to investigate whatever aroused curiosity. In a different kind of environment, our curiosity might have been nipped long before it could have borne fruit.

Wilbur Wright (1867–1912)

Wilbur, four years older than Orville, was outgoing. He excelled at writing and public speaking. He loved to read. Both Wilbur and Orville liked to tinker as children.

When they had questions about anything mechanical, they would go to their mother, Susan. She was good at inventing. She made toys for her children and basic appliances for herself. Originally, Wilbur hoped to attend Yale University, but he was needed at home to help care for his mother. So he taught himself by reading a lot.

Orville (*left*) and Wilbur Wright
Library of Congress, Prints and Photographs Division, Cole & Co., cph 3a08822

How the Flyer Worked

The brothers controlled their craft through three main means they developed in their glider experiments:

- The forward elevator, *a small moving section attached to a fixed wing to help control up-and-down movement of the aircraft*
- The use of wing warping, *twisting the tips of the wings with a series of cables*
- A single, movable rear rudder

Surprisingly, the pilot did not sit upright. Instead, he lay on his stomach in a padded cradle on the lower wing. Because the engine was somewhat right of center, the pilot was placed slightly left of center to balance the weight.

To the pilot's left was a lever that he used to control the up-and-down movement of the elevator. By moving the lever with his hand, he could climb or descend.

By moving his hips, he pulled on the cables connected to the wings and rudder. This movement could direct the plane left or right.

Before the brothers invented the single, movable rudder, their gliders often slid sideways rather than turned. A *sidewise movement* is called a yaw. With the new, flexible rudder, the plane finally turned in the intended direction. For instance, if the pilot moved his hips so the cable pulled down on the left wing, the plane would veer left. The cables attached to the wings from the cradle twisted one wing down while forcing the other wing up. If the aircraft began to yaw, the rudder corrected this by reacting to pressure from airflow.

To design the propellers, the brothers drew on their bicycle-shop experience. They made the propellers rotate by attaching them to the engine with bicycle chains. To rotate the propellers in opposite directions, they simply twisted one of the two chains into a figure 8.

Before launch, wires tethered the airplane to earth. Only when the engine had fully revved up did the trolley start to move down the tracks. The plane lifted off the trolley as it rose into the air.

How the Principles of Flight Were Applied to the *Wright Flyer*

To get the *Wright Flyer* off the ground, the brothers had to solve the principles of flight: lift, drag, thrust, angle of attack, center of pressure, airfoil, and relative wind. The combination of solutions they found is still used for modern airplanes.

An engine and propellers gave Wilbur and Orville the ability to use not only lift but also thrust to propel their plane through the air. Both these forces are necessary for powered flight. As you learned in Lesson 2, *lift* is an upward force; *thrust* is a forward, or horizontal, force; and *drag* is the slowing effect of air on an aircraft.

When working on their gliders, the Wrights focused most of their attention on the lift exerted on the wings. Now that they had an engine and propellers, they could start to think more about thrust. They considered the propellers as extra wings on their airplane. But unlike wings, which are stable and horizontal, the propeller "wings" rotated and sat vertically. The propellers on the *Flyer* were eight feet in diameter.

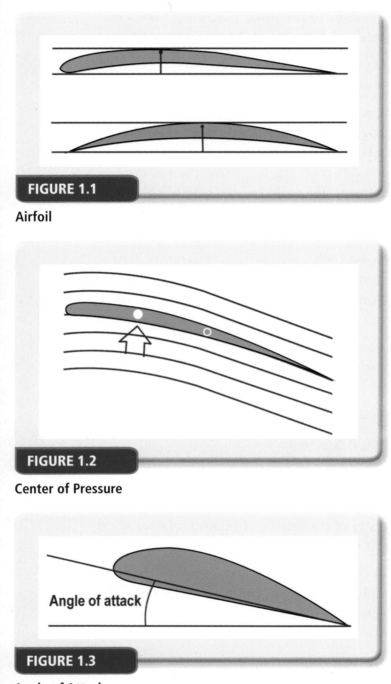

FIGURE 1.1

Airfoil

FIGURE 1.2

Center of Pressure

Angle of attack

FIGURE 1.3

Angle of Attack

If a horizontal, curved wing reacts to lift, the Wright brothers reasoned, vertically mounted propellers could provide the airflow for thrust. They calculated they needed 90 pounds of thrust to propel the *Wright Flyer*. Their 12-horsepower engine and the large propellers proved equal to the task. The fabric with which they coated the wings, elevator, and rudder helped reduce drag.

Airfoil is *a wing's profile* (Figure 1.1). The Wrights experimented extensively with wing shapes to learn which curve worked best. They had moved the center of pressure, or *the focal point of lift*, further forward on the wing than had earlier experimenters (Figure 1.2). They had also learned that a low angle of attack—*the angle between the* relative wind *(the flow of air) and the airfoil*—provided more stability and control during flight (Figure 1.3). You'll read more about how they came to these conclusions while developing their gliders later in this lesson.

The Contributions the Wright Brothers Made to US Army Aviation

After their first success, the Wright brothers continued refining their airplane. Once they had achieved powered flight, they no longer needed the wind conditions of the North Carolina coastline for their tests. In October 1905 they circled a field in Dayton, Ohio, for 38 minutes and traveled 24 miles. They decided it was time to cash in on their remarkable invention.

They'd already started their marketing effort. Back in January 1905 they contacted their representative in Congress, R. M. Nevin, and asked him to try to interest the US government in buying their airplane. Mr. Nevin passed along their letter to the Board of Ordnance and Fortifications, which made military weapons purchases. The board was leery of wasting government money. It turned down the brothers' offer.

The brothers, patient as always, contacted the secretary of war later that year. Again, their offer was rejected. After all, as Lesson 2 related, the government had already invested $50,000 in Samuel Langley's flight experiments. The secretary didn't want to spend more money when the outcome seemed so uncertain.

Why the US Army Purchased the *Wright Flyer*

Meanwhile, the British and French governments got into the act. They were interested in buying the *Flyer*. Representatives from both countries made offers to the Wrights. But the brothers wanted the US government to have first crack at owning a *Wright Flyer*.

A turning point came on 22 May 1906. On that date, after three years of trying, the brothers received a government patent for their invention. This spurred the Aero Club of America, a group of aviation enthusiasts and scientists, to take action. They sent a clipping about the Wrights to President Theodore Roosevelt. The president ordered the Board of Ordnance and Fortifications to look again into the airplane.

After that, things started to happen. On 23 December 1907, Brigadier General James Allen, chief of the Army Signal Corps, sent out a request for bids to build a plane for the government. A bid is *an offer or a proposal, with a price attached*. The brothers received their copy of General Allen's request on 3 January 1908.

The bid set forth the technical requirements for the craft. These requirements stated that the craft must:

- achieve a speed of 40 miles per hour,
- carry two passengers for a total of 350 pounds,
- have a fuel tank large enough to fly 125 miles nonstop, and
- be able to land without damage.

The government also required that the successful bidder train two Army pilots to fly the craft.

The *Wright Flyer* met these requirements. Orville Wright signed a contract on 10 February 1908 selling the *Flyer* to the US government.

Ways the Wright Brothers Contributed to Army Aviation

With the purchase of the *Wright Flyer*, the Army bought not only the military's first plane but also access to the Wright brothers' inventive minds. In the years that followed, the Wrights continued to improve their aircraft. For instance, they created wheels for the *Flyer*. The wheels enabled it to take off and land in a wider variety of settings.

Orville spent much of 1908 and 1909 improving the *Flyer*. He made more test flights and took up military passengers. One such flight tragically ended in a crash that seriously injured Orville and killed 1st Lieutenant Thomas Selfridge—the first US military aviation casualty. Wilbur was often overseas giving demonstrations during this time.

The brothers switched roles in mid-1909. Wilbur trained two pilots for the Army—1st Lieutenant Frank P. Lahm and 2nd Lieutenant Fredric E. Humphreys. In October 1909 both men made their first solo flights with less than a month's training. These were adventurous men: each had barely three hours' instruction in the air before going it alone.

The Wright brothers' Type A airplane flying at Fort Myer, Virginia, in 1909

Library of Congress, Prints and Photographs Division, Harris & Ewing Collection, hec 06070

A third pilot, 1st Lieutenant Benjamin Foulois, got instruction later that month. One of the men initially picked for pilot training, he was delayed because of business in France. He took the *Wright Flyer* to Fort Sam Houston, Texas, where he continued teaching himself to fly. He corresponded with Wilbur and Orville whenever he had a question. On 2 March 1910 he took his first solo flight. By the time of his retirement a quarter-century later, Foulois had achieved the rank of major general. He was also chief of the Army Air Corps.

It took a while for the Army to decide how to use airplanes during war. At first, the Army thought that airplanes would be useful only for aerial reconnaissance, much as hot air balloons were used during the US Civil War and the Spanish-American War. But World War I brought about a change in strategy: soon, the warring sides were employing planes for bombing missions and to support troops on the ground. Before that could happen, however, airplanes needed improvements to make them faster, sturdier, and more reliable.

How the Wright Brothers Were the First to Succeed in Powered Flight

All pilots face three challenges—they must get up in the air, stay up, and control their craft. The choice of craft was up to the pilot. And pilots had three choices to experiment in flight:

- Manned and powered full-size aircraft
- Models
- Full-size gliders

The Wrights chose a glider as their starting point. By using a glider, they could focus first on balancing and controlling their aircraft. Power—an engine—could come later. This approach explains why they succeeded where Samuel P. Langley, who focused on power, failed.

But before they could build a full-size glider, they needed to experiment with other, smaller craft. This was a complicated process. The brothers applied what they learned at each step to make the next one go more smoothly. This step-by-step experimenting was the key to the Wright brothers' success.

Waypoints

Wilbur Writes to the Smithsonian

One reason for the Wright brothers' success was their patience. Another was that they asked lots of questions. They wanted to build on what others had learned. So Wilbur went to the experts. The following is from a letter he wrote to The Smithsonian Institution in Washington, D.C., on 30 May 1899:

Dear Sirs:

I have been interested in the problem of mechanical and human flight ever since as a boy I constructed a number of bats of various sizes after the style of Cayley's and Penaud's machines. My observations since have only convinced me more firmly that human flight is possible and practicable. It is only a question of knowledge and skill just as in all acrobatic feats.... I believe that simple flight at least is possible to man and that the experiments and investigations of a large number of independent workers will result in the accumulation of information and knowledge and skill which will finally lead to accomplished flight....

...I wish to obtain such papers as the Smithsonian Institution has published on this subject, and if possible a list of other works in print in the English language. I am an enthusiast, but not a crank in the sense that I have some pet theories as to the proper construction of a flying machine. I wish to avail myself of all that is already known and then if possible add my mite to help on the future worker who will attain final success....

Yours truly,

Wilbur Wright

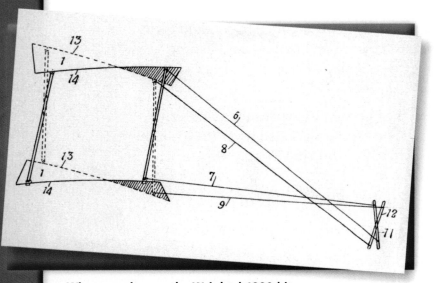

Wing warping on the Wrights' 1899 kite

Library of Congress, Manuscript Division, Wilbur and Orville Wright Papers

Step One: An Unmanned Box Kite

The brothers began in July 1899 with an unmanned box kite. The kite had a five- foot wingspan and a biplane structure. It also had struts that connected the upper and lower wings. A strut is *a vertical post*. The kite also had bracing, or *support*, that was *strung diagonally between the struts*. The Wrights used steel for the bracing.

They adapted their bracing design from a manned glider created by Octave Chanute and Augustus Herring in 1896.

The brothers also had a unique approach to controlling the kite. They discovered that they didn't need to tilt an entire wing to turn the craft: They needed to twist only the ends of the wings. They used the process of wing warping. To warp the wings, they removed the bracing between the front and rear struts. They attached four cords to the top and bottom of the front outer struts. Pulling on these ropes turned the craft.

In the summer of 1899, Wilbur successfully tested the kite in a field. The first step in the experiment for aircraft control was a success. The next step: put a person on a glider.

Waypoints

An Absentminded Invention

Wilbur Wright was talking to a customer in the bicycle shop he owned with his brother in Dayton. As he did so, he toyed with a long, empty carton. Twisting the carton this way and that, he made a discovery: the sides of the box retained their shape and strength. Wilbur figured this same principle would apply to the wings of a biplane kite. In other words, the tip could be twisted, but the wing would remain strong. Thus the brothers' groundbreaking wing-warping theory was born.

Step Two: Manned Gliders

The box kite taught Wilbur and Orville Wright how to control lateral—*sideways*—turns. But building a successful manned glider presented other challenges. Between 1900 and 1902, the brothers built three gliders. Before putting a man aboard, they flew each glider like a kite. They wanted to test it for control and lift. Only after doing this would they put a man aboard.

The early glider experiments were successful. They taught the brothers three important things:

- How to control climb and descent
- The best design for the shape of the wing
- How large the wing area had to be to sustain lift

The First Glider (1900)

With a man on board the craft, knowing how to move up and down was essential. Otherwise, a sudden pitch—*a movement up or down*—could be fatal. For example, the German aviator Otto Lilienthal, whom you read about in the previous lesson, died when his craft made a downward pitch and crashed.

The Wrights studied Lilienthal's data. They used it to design a device that gave them greater control of pitch. In their experiments at Kitty Hawk in 1900, they had placed an elevator at the front of the glider.

This was a unique idea: Earlier designers had mounted elevators behind the wings. But the Wrights found it easier to control climb and descent when the elevator was placed forward. This development saved the Wrights' lives on several occasions.

A canard configuration is another name for *an elevator that sits in front of the wings.* (*Canard* is the French word for duck—early observers thought the canard configuration resembled a flying duck.)

Next, the Wrights tackled the challenge of how to shape the glider's wing. This took a couple years to figure out. In 1900 they focused on airfoil. In particular, they zeroed in on the curve of a wing.

The Wrights' 1900 glider
Library of Congress, Prints and Photographs Division, pppprs-00556

Wings have a lot to do with lift, which, as you've learned, is the upward force on an aircraft. The Wrights tried to design a wing that shifted the center of pressure toward the front edge of the wing—the wing edge nearest the front of the aircraft. Earlier designers thought that the center of pressure should be in the middle of the wing. The Wrights placed the highest point of the wing's arc closer to the outer edge than to its center. They believed this would create greater stability and control.

A Stitch in Time

A glider's wings need to be strong but not heavy. They need to be stiff but not inflexible. In 1900 Wilbur and Orville Wright hit on a way to get all of this: fabric. They covered the top of the glider's wings with French sateen, *a cotton fabric woven like satin with a glossy surface*. Pieces of the wings' framework slid into "pockets" sewn on the underside of the fabric. These skeleton-like pieces of the wings "floated" inside the pockets.

The fabric took the role that heavier wires and bracing would otherwise have taken. The Wrights attached the fabric to the wing's frame on the bias, which is a 45-degree angle. This made the wing stronger.

The brothers test-flew their glider at Kill Devil Hills in 1900. It didn't crash. But clearly improvements were necessary. The Wrights left North Carolina and headed back to Ohio. During the winter, they would tinker with their craft and build the next version of their glider.

The Second Glider (1901)

The Wrights' first glider had a wing area of 165 square feet. That glider didn't have nearly enough lift. So for their 1901 glider, the brothers increased the wing area to 290 square feet. This glider was also a big disappointment. The brothers couldn't control it well when they tested it at Kill Devil Hills. It flew less than 300 feet. Time to return to Dayton.

Wilbur and Orville built a wind tunnel in their bicycle shop in Ohio to test model-size wings. These wings came in many shapes—squares, rectangles, and semicircles. They ranged from perfect curves to arcs with their highest points at the outer edges. The Wrights made them of sheet steel. Over the winter, the brothers cut more than 200 model wings of different shapes.

The Wright Brothers' 1901 wind tunnel
Ken La Rock/Courtesy National Museum of the US Air Force

The Third Glider (1902)

At this point, the brothers could have been tempted to try powered flight. After all, their model-wing tests had answered many questions. But remember—these two men were patient. They didn't want to rush the process. So in preparation for 1902, they applied what they'd learned to build a third glider.

This glider had two fixed, vertical rudders behind the wings. Test flights showed that this resulted in erratic behavior during turns. So the Wrights tried a single, movable, vertical rudder. This improved control. This aircraft, too, had a forward elevator, but it had a more elliptical shape, and longer, skinnier wings. Wing area was 305 square feet. In addition, the glider had a low angle of attack. This also made the glider more stable and easier to control.

This design was a success. The brothers took to the air in the North Carolina dunes more than 700 times in the fall of 1902.

Winter arrived. It was time to head back to Ohio. It was also finally time to put an engine on the glider.

Step Three:
A Manned, Powered Aircraft

One key to the Wright brothers' success was their countless test flights. Another was sticking with a core design. Their kites and gliders evolved from a single design into the manned, powered aircraft they eventually flew in 1903. They tinkered with the details, but didn't get distracted. For instance, they didn't attempt powered flight until they'd perfected other elements, such as the wings.

Wilbur Wright and Dan Tate flying the 1902 glider as a kite
Library of Congress, Prints and Photographs Division, ppprs-00631

Wilbur flying the 1902 glider
Library of Congress, Prints and Photographs Division, ppprs-00603

Once they'd resolved questions about control and lift, the brothers set out to fit their plane with an engine. They hoped they might buy one ready made. They sent out queries to a number of firms. But no one met their needs or price. So the brothers had their bicycle mechanic, Charles E. Taylor, build them a four-cylinder, 12-horsepower engine.

In September 1903 they returned to Kitty Hawk and Kill Devil Hills. The aircraft was ready. But they couldn't take to the skies quite yet. They had to build a trolley track to give their powered aircraft a running start. Bad weather also caused delays. So the first test flight of the *Wright Flyer* didn't take place until 14 December.

The brothers tossed a coin. Wilbur won the toss. He took the pilot's seat for the initial powered flight. He rolled down the trolley, launched into the air, and—crashed. That flight lasted only 3.5 seconds. The crash damaged the elevator.

But the brothers were not discouraged. Quite the opposite—in a note to home, Wilbur wrote, "There is now no question of final success."

It took three days to repair the damaged craft. Then, on 17 December, Orville took the controls for this day's first flight. It was 10:35 a.m. The *Flyer* rose into the air.

It stayed aloft for 12 seconds and traveled 120 feet. He had made the first controlled, sustained, heavier-than-air human flight with a powered aircraft.

On that momentous day, the brothers took turns piloting the *Flyer* for three more flights. Each launch was more impressive than the last. The fourth and final launch lasted 59 seconds. The craft traveled 852 feet.

On that day atop the windswept dunes of North Carolina's Outer Banks, the aviation age had begun.

The Wright brothers' first sustained powered flight, Kitty Hawk, North Carolina
Library of Congress, Prints and Photographs Division, ppprs-00626

✔ CHECKPOINTS

Lesson 3 Review

Using complete sentences, answer the following questions on a sheet of paper.

1. What were the two parts of the *Wright Flyer*'s wings?

2. What did the Wright brothers invent in order to control yaw?

3. What are the principles of flight the Wright brothers had to solve?

4. What kind of force did the *Wright Flyer*'s engine and propellers provide?

5. Who was the first US military aviation casualty?

6. Who was Benjamin Foulois?

7. How did the Wright brothers' approach to building an aircraft differ from Samuel Langley's?

8. What three important points did the Wrights learn from their gliders?

APPLYING YOUR LEARNING

9. What lessons can you learn from the Wright brothers about problem solving?

Pioneers of Flight

Quick Write

_____

_____

Both the Wright brothers and Glenn Curtiss were heavily involved with bicycles before taking up flight. What similarities do you see between bicycles, early motorcycles, and early airplanes?

Learn About

- key individuals and contributions in early aircraft development
- the contributions of early American pioneers in aviation
- the contributions of women in early aviation

GLENN CURTISS, born in Hammondsport, New York, in 1878, sped onto the aviation scene in the early 1900s. But he was riding a motorcycle, not an airplane. At Ormond Beach, Florida, in 1907, he set a world speed record for motorcycles: 136.3 miles per hour (mph). People called him the "fastest man on Earth." This was the same year the Wright brothers received their bid request for a military airplane from the Army Signal Corps chief, Brigadier General James Allen.

Much was happening all at once in the world of transportation. And any advance in one field sparked progress in another. Curtiss's passion for speed began with bicycles. As a teenager, he raced at county fairs and often won. This experience led to his love of fast motorcycles. Curtiss liked to fiddle with the mechanical side of bicycles, motorcycles, and engines as well. Actually, he did more than tinker with them—he built gasoline engines for motorcycles. Barely out of his teens, he started his own motorcycle business, the G.H. Curtiss Manufacturing Company.

His work with motorcycle engines eventually caught the eye of people in the field of flight. Once they introduced Curtiss to aircraft, he was hooked for good.

Key Individuals and Contributions in Early Aircraft Development

In the first decade of the 1900s, when the Wright brothers were making aviation history, other people were also becoming aviation pioneers. Each person made developments in aircraft that earned him or her a place in aviation history.

Glenn Curtiss

Glenn Curtiss pushed aviation forward in several ways. Even before his record-setting motorcycle ride in 1907, Curtiss was dipping his toes into aviation. He'd begun racing with his bike motors in Florida in 1904. It was there that Thomas Baldwin discovered Curtiss.

Baldwin, an American balloonist, owned a dirigible. As you read in Lesson 2, a dirigible is a lighter-than-air, steerable airship. By the early 1900s aviators in France and Germany were using engines to maneuver such aircraft in the sky. But balloonists in the United States hadn't yet taken that step. Baldwin was looking for a lightweight engine for his aircraft when he spotted Curtiss racing in Florida. He saw how well Curtiss's engine performed. He asked if he could buy one. The young mechanic agreed. He tweaked one of his engines for use in an aircraft.

Baldwin's aircraft, equipped with a Curtiss engine, was the first powered dirigible in America. Before long, other balloonists wanted Curtiss motors, too. And in 1908 the US government purchased one of Curtiss's engines for the US Army's first dirigible, SC-1. Later, the military would purchase Curtiss planes and engines for use in World War I. The Army used the Jenny airplane—or JN-4—for training pilots. Curtiss's Wasp engine broke records for speed and rate of climb.

Vocabulary

- aileron
- fuselage
- multiengine plane
- cockpit
- tandem
- porthole
- radial
- crankshaft
- solo
- pylons
- jumpsuit

Glenn Curtis
Everett Historical/Shutterstock

The Aerial Experiment Association

Glenn Curtiss was a busy man in 1907. In addition to working on some of the devices already mentioned, he joined the Aerial Experiment Association (AEA). Alexander Graham Bell, best known as the inventor of the telephone, formed this group. The inventors who belonged made some important design breakthroughs.

First, they built the first American plane equipped with ailerons. An aileron is *a small flap on the wing for controlling turns*. Ailerons replaced the Wright brothers' wing-warping technique, which used cables to pull on the ends of the wings. The aileron was a more effective means to move an aircraft left or right. It also provided lateral balance. This was critical whenever airplanes had rigid metal wings.

The Aerial Experiment Association, including Glenn Curtiss (*left*) and Alexander Graham Bell (*center*)

Library of Congress, Prints and Photographs Division, pppmsc 00852

Although association members get credit for introducing this idea to America, none of them dreamed it up. The aileron was patented in Great Britain in 1868. In 1904 a Frenchman who was flying a glider used ailerons for the first time.

Second, members of the group built and flew the country's first seaplane. Curtiss would later win the first government contract with the US Navy for seaplanes.

Glenn Curtiss winning the Scientific American trophy in the *June Bug*

Library of Congress, Prints and Photographs Division, Ernest L. Jones Collection, cph 3b06819

Curtiss's Fame Grows

Curtiss continued to enter contests. In 1908, piloting an association plane called the *June Bug*, he won the Scientific American trophy. The award was for making the first public flight of more than one kilometer (0.6 miles). At the Rheims Air Meet in France in 1909, Curtiss picked up a prize for speed. He flew the fastest two laps over a triangular, 6.21-mile course. For this feat he took home the Gordon Bennett trophy. Curtiss won the trophy in his *Golden Flyer*. His average speed? An amazing 47 mph.

Never one to rest, Curtiss opened a flight school in 1910, the same year the Wright brothers opened their school. Also in 1910, a pilot named Eugene Ely flew a Curtiss biplane from the deck of a ship off Hampton Roads, Virginia. Later, Ely landed the plane on a wooden platform built on the armored cruiser USS *Pennsylvania*.

Curtiss's effect on aviation can still be felt today. To begin with, motorcycle engines were light and powerful. Aircraft also need light, powerful engines that won't weigh them down. Less weight puts less strain on the aircraft during takeoff, landing, and flight.

Louis Blériot

Across the Atlantic Ocean, the French pilot Louis Blériot was also pushing the limits of flight. He was the first man to cross the English Channel in a heavier-than-air craft. And what an adventure it turned out to be.

He took off on 25 July 1909 from near Calais, in northern France, without a compass. Within 10 minutes, he was lost. He could see nothing but water and sky. He had no coastline in sight to guide him. Blériot piloted his aircraft as best he could toward England. He knew the journey was about 25 miles.

Finally he caught sight of the English cliffs of Dover. But then he encountered another hitch. His engine was overheating, and he was still above water and could not land. Then he spotted a small rainstorm. He veered toward it. The rain cooled his engine, and he landed safely. The flight took 37 minutes.

Louis Blériot starting his monoplane before his cross-channel flight on 25 July 1909
Library of Congress, Prints and Photographs Division, George Grantham Bain Collection, cph 3a35984r

This flight took place in a powered monoplane that Blériot built. (The Wright brothers' aircraft were biplanes.) He was the first man to build a powered monoplane. He named the aircraft that brought him across the English Channel the *Blériot XI* because he'd built 10 others before it. He'd crashed nearly 50 times during test flights of those aircraft. The 11th plane brought him safely to England's shores.

Blériot had many other accomplishments. Like Curtiss, he entered the first international air meet in Rheims in August 1909. While Curtiss won the two-lap contest for speed, Blériot snapped up a trophy for a one-lap contest by flying at 47.8 mph. Also like Curtiss, Blériot built planes for the war effort during World War I. But Blériot built aircraft for his own country, France.

The Names and Anatomy of Period Aircraft

During the years between the Wright brothers' famous flight of 1903 and the start of World War I in 1914, aircraft continued to grow more sophisticated. The first man to use ailerons, Frenchman Robert Esnault-Pelterie, was also the first to fully enclose the fuselage. A fuselage is *the body of an airplane containing the crew and passengers (or cargo).* Enclosed cabins protected pilots and passengers from the wind and rain.

Multiengine Planes

While Louis Blériot was experimenting with monoplanes, brothers Eustace, Howard, and Oswald Short of England were adding engines to their aircraft. A multiengine plane—*a plane with more than one engine*—had greater power, reliability, and safety than a single-engine plane. Just as two heads are supposedly better than one, two (or more) engines upped an aircraft's power. Safety increased, too. If one engine died during flight, the second could provide enough power to get the plane back to earth.

Igor Sikorsky
Library of Congress, Prints and Photographs Division, cbh 3b40533

The Short brothers built the *Triple Twin*, a two-engine, three-propeller aircraft in 1911. They placed one engine in front of the cockpit—*a space inside the fuselage where the crew sits.* They mounted the second engine behind the cockpit. The forward engine ran the two propellers on the wings; the rear engine drove the third propeller.

Meanwhile a Russian pilot named Igor Sikorsky was designing a four-engine aircraft called *Le Grand*. He flew it on 13 May 1913. He used four 100-horsepower engines to lift the 92-foot-wingspan airplane. He mounted the four engines in two pairs in tandem—*two objects with one placed directly behind the other*—on the lower wings. The front engines powered the forward propellers, and the back engines drove the pusher propellers. Because the plane was so big, the landing gear had 16 wheels. The aircraft also had an enclosed cockpit. Each passenger could peer through a porthole—*a small, circular window.*

An early, two-engine version of *Le Grand*
Library of Congress, Prints and Photographs Division, George Grantham Bain Collection, ggbain 17174v

Passenger-friendly inventions such as portholes and enclosed cabins contributed greatly to the development of today's commercial airliners. Flying in a protected body and having viewing windows made air travel more attractive to paying passengers.

Rotary Engines

Strong engines were essential for sustained flight. But the earliest engines were relatively heavy. The engine and propellers on the 1903 *Wright Flyer* weighed about 200 pounds. One reason for this weight was that these early engines used water as a coolant. They also weren't efficient: In 1907 every 10 pounds of engine generated just one horsepower.

Another set of brothers, Laurent and Gustav Seguin of France, set out to reduce the motor weight. Their solution? Rotary engines. Rotary engines used circulating air, rather than water, as a coolant. The Seguins placed the engine's cylinders in a radial, or *round*, pattern. They fitted each cylinder with a fin to draw out the heat as the plane flew.

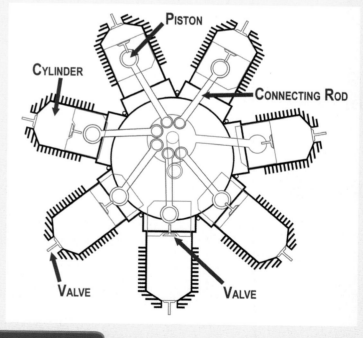

FIGURE 1.4

The Gnome rotary engine

With these changes, engines became more efficient. The number of pounds of engine weight needed to generate one horsepower dropped from 10 to three. The Seguins named their engine the Gnome.

But the Gnome was still a work in progress. The brothers needed to find a way to prevent the engine from overheating when the aircraft was revving up before takeoff. The brothers decided that the crankshaft—*a shaft that turns or is turned by a crank*—should no longer rotate the propeller and engine. Instead, the propeller and engine ought to rotate around the crankshaft. The Seguins bolted the crankshaft to the plane's frame. So even when the plane was at a standstill, air would circulate around the engine and keep it cool.

The Contributions of Early American Pioneers in Aviation

While some aircraft pioneers were achieving fame as inventors, others were breaking barriers as pilots. All these aviation pioneers needed great courage. They were flying in an age when planes were, frankly, quite flimsy. They also had to be very curious. They were exploring a new frontier. And like Glenn Curtiss, they shared a passion for flight and speed—for soaring into the sky. Each one faced challenges—crashes were many, and all pilots knew the possible consequences. But they dared to continue flying.

The *Vin Fiz Flyer*

Could Calbraith Perry Rodgers fly across the United States in 30 days? That was his goal in 1911. Newspaper publisher William Randolph Hearst was offering a $50,000 prize to the first pilot who made the journey in that timeframe. Rodgers wanted to give it a try. But he had no money. Like today's NASCAR drivers, he needed a sponsor.

Rodgers asked soft drink manufacturer Vin Fiz if it would provide financial support for his flight in exchange for nationwide publicity. The company agreed. It bought him a Wright airplane (the *Vin Fiz Flyer*) and made sure he had all the spare parts he'd need. Rodgers hired mechanic Charles Taylor away from the Wright brothers to help him out on his adventure.

Calbraith Rodgers taking off in the *Vin Fiz Flyer*
Library of Congress, Prints and Photographs Division, cph 3a45208r

Rodgers took off on 17 September 1911 from Sheepshead Bay, on New York's Long Island. With publicity in mind, Vin Fiz mapped his route. The flight plan called for stops in major cities such as New York City, Chicago, Kansas City, San Antonio, El Paso, and Yuma. The destination was Pasadena, California.

Rodgers's biggest worry was getting over the Rocky Mountains with a 40-horsepower engine. Headwinds and weather would slow him down. As the journey progressed, his shortest flights were around 40 miles, and his longest was 133 miles. He averaged around 52 mph. He made 68 landings.

The plane needed countless repairs along the way. In fact, by the time it got to Pasadena, the *Vin Fiz Flyer* had only two original parts—the rudder and one strut, the result of crashing 19 times during his trip. The trip turned out to be 4,251 miles long, rather than the anticipated 3,390. It took 49 days. Rodgers didn't win the award because the flight took too long. But he'd earned a place in aviation history—he made the first airplane crossing of the United States from coast to coast.

The First Enlisted Pilot Gets His Wings

US Army Private First Class (PFC) Vernon Burge was the first enlisted man to become a pilot. The Army Signal Corps' Aeronautical Division, created in 1907 to take charge of ballooning and air machines, had a general rule that only officers could be pilots. Enlisted men trained as mechanics. And as late as 1908, the bulk of the "flying" done in the Aeronautical Division was done in balloons. The mechanics had to know how to work with balloon fabric, to control the aircraft, and to prepare the gases for the balloons.

Burge was one of eight enlisted men who joined the division in 1907. In 1909 he and nine other enlisted men joined 1st Lieutenant Benjamin Foulois and a civilian mechanic at Fort Sam Houston in San Antonio, Texas. This was when Foulois was teaching himself how to fly. Burge and another private, Glenn Madole, assisted by the civilian mechanic, built a landing system for Foulois' airplane. During this time, Burge learned as much as he could about repairing and flying airplanes.

Colonel Vernon Burge
Courtesy Airmen Memorial Museum

By the time Burge became a pilot in 1912, the Army Aernonautical Division had 11 aircraft, 14 officer pilots, and 39 enlisted men. But it wasn't until 18 July 1914 that the US House of Representatives passed a bill that authorized enlisted men to fly. The bill limited the number of enlisted pilots to 12. That bill was also important because it gave official status to the Army's aviation arm—it created the Aviation Section of the Army Signal Corps, which replaced the corps' Aeronautical Division.

A Private's Persistence

PFC Vernon Burge knew he wanted to be a pilot from the moment he laid eyes on an airplane. When he volunteered for balloon duty in August 1907, he began a five-year journey as ground crewman, balloon handler, and airplane mechanic. He and his fellow mechanics spent a good deal of those five years at air shows around the country, helping prepare aircraft and keep them fit for flight. Burge absorbed all he could about balloons and airplanes.

In early 1912 Burge, by now a corporal, shipped with a Wright B airplane to the Philippines. Brigadier General James Allen had ordered that an air station be established at Fort McKinley. Burge reported to 1st Lieutenant Frank P. Lahm, who was setting up a flight school at the station. Aware of the shortage of officers, Burge took the plunge. He asked Lieutenant Lahm whether he could train to be a pilot.

Lahm agreed, and Burge began his instruction 8 April 1912. He already knew a good deal about flying. As a mechanic, he'd taxied a good many airplanes along runways to make sure the engines were running right and repairs were correctly done. He passed his flight test 14 June 1912.

Burge's hard work, love of flying, and persistence eventually earned him a place in the Army as an officer. He retired 31 January 1942 at the rank of colonel. He'd spent 35 years in military aviation and had served as a pilot for 30 of those years. He'd logged 4,667 hours and 55 minutes in the air—quite a career.

Sergeant Vernon Burge in Flight Training
Courtesy Airmen Memorial Museum

A working replica of the 14-Bis flown by Alberto Santos-Dumont

Luis Fernando Curci Chavier/Shutterstock.com

Other Male European Pilots and Their Accomplishments

Alberto Santos-Dumont

The first European pilot to fly a powered airplane was Alberto Santos-Dumont—the same Alberto Santos-Dumont from Lesson 2 who was already famous in France for his dirigible flights. Santos-Dumont built the 14-Bis and flew his powered airplane some three years after the Wright Brothers in 1906. His aircraft was a very impractical box kite design, with its fuselage and elevator sticking out front of the pilot. The pilot would stand upright in a wicker balloon basket.

Henri Farman

The son of a British journalist, Henri Farman was raised in France. Although he originally took up the sport of bicycle racing, he progressed to automobile racing—eventually taking his mechanical skills and competiveness to powered flying machines. He soon became one of the most famous pilots in France, becoming wealthy from his accomplishments. In 1912, he partnered with his brother Maurice and soon became France's largest airplane manufacturer. His airplane company produced over 12,000 military aircraft during World War I.

Thomas Octave Sopwith

British aircraft manufacturer Thomas Sopwith learned to fly in 1910. By 1912 he had set up the Sopwith Aviation Company, building Britain's first successful seaplane. His company later manufactured some of the most famous fighter aircraft of World War I, which will be discussed in the next chapter.

M·I·L·E·S·T·O·N·E·S

Europe Versus America

Although the Wright brothers were the first to fly a powered airplane in America, Europe had more pilots than the United States did in those early days. France was the leader; by 1911 it boasted 353 pilots. Great Britain had 57, Germany 46, Italy 32, and Belgium 27. The United States had 26, giving it a sixth-place ranking in the world.

The Contributions of Women in Early Aviation

Besides the obstacles of distance and altitude, other early pilots faced the obstacle of their gender. Women found it difficult to realize their dreams of joining men in the skies. Even the most successful female pilots felt the strain.

Blanche Stuart Scott, the first American woman to solo in a plane, said, "There seemed to be no place for a woman engineer, mechanic, or flier. Too often people paid money to see me risk my neck, more as a freak, a woman freak pilot, than as a skilled flier." Because of this public pressure and a few severe accidents in the air, Scott retired from flight in 1916 when she was only 27 years old.

Despite the obstacles, many women thrived on the thrill of lifting, looping, and diving through the air. They broke records and paved the way for women in the future to enter careers in commercial and military aviation.

Blanche Stuart Scott

Blanche Stuart Scott was used to setting records. She became the first woman to drive a car across America in 1910. And she didn't do it on a highway, or even on a state route. At that time, there were fewer than 300 miles of paved roads in the entire United States.

Blanche Stuart Scott
Library of Congress, Prints and Photographs Division, George Grantham Bain Collection, ggbain 12209

When men started setting records in aviation, Scott wanted to be part of the action. She was Glenn Curtiss's only female student in 1910. In fact, she was Curtiss's first student ever, and he never took on another. In addition, Scott was the only female student pilot in the United States at that time. Curtiss worried about this. If Scott crashed, he feared he'd be blamed for putting a woman in harm's way. What's more, she'd be using a single-engine plane that Curtiss designed, and some people might think the plane was faulty. For these reasons, he did what he could to keep Scott from being able to take off.

Scott would taxi back and forth across the runway in Curtiss's plane. But she could never get into the air. Frustrated, on 2 September 1910, she got out of the plane and took a close look at the engine. She was, after all, a curious person.

She noticed a small piece of wood lodged under the throttle lever. She deduced this hindered the lever's motion. And she also concluded that Curtiss had placed the wood there to make sure the aircraft wouldn't be able to get off the ground when she sat at the controls.

Scott removed the wood, climbed back into the cockpit, and asked a mechanic to crank the propeller. She taxied down the runway, and the plane lifted off. Scott was airborne.

Scott had become the first American woman to solo in a fixed-wing airplane. To solo is *to fly with no one else on board.* She flew with exhibition groups for six years, although she never got her pilot's license. She was known for two stunts. In one, she flew under bridges upside-down. Her other stunt was the "death dive." She would climb to 4,000 feet, then plunge the plane toward earth, leveling off only when she reached 200 feet.

Scott was adventurous, but even daring people get their fill. After a number of accidents, she retired in 1916 at the age of 27. She died in 1970 at the age of 81. She'd lived to see the first man land on the moon.

Bessica Medlar Raiche

Some aviation historians think Bessica Medlar Raiche was really the first woman to go solo. She made that flight on 13 October 1910. They contend Scott got into the air purely by accident. But Raiche herself gave Scott credit for the event.

Bessica Medlar Raiche
Courtesy National Air and Space Museum, Smithsonian Institution, NASM-2007-5475

"Blanche deserved the recognition," Raiche said, "but I got more attention because of my lifestyle. I drove an automobile, was active in sports like shooting and swimming, and I even wore riding pants and knickers. People who didn't know me or understand me looked down on this behavior. I was an accomplished musician, painter, and linguist. I enjoyed life, and just wanted to be myself."

Raiche never got a license. But flying excited her. She and her husband, François, formed a lightweight airplane company called the French-American Aeroplane Company. They did two important things to make their planes better than other lightweight aircraft. They took off some pounds by exchanging heavier fabrics, such as muslin, for silk. They also used piano wires instead of iron wires.

Raiche eventually left flying. She entered medical school and became a doctor. She became one of the first woman specialists in obstetrics and gynecology. She died in 1932.

Harriet Quimby

Harriet Quimby was the first American woman to earn her pilot's license. A journalist, she wrote for a popular magazine called *Leslie's Weekly*. But she wanted to make more money to support herself, her parents, and her ambition to become a creative writer.

In 1910 she watched aviator John Moisant fly around the Statue of Liberty in New York harbor. The sight thrilled her. She signed up for flying lessons. She got her license on 1 August 1911, after completing a two-part test. The first part of the test required her to make five left and right turns around pylons—*tall, thin towers*.

Harriet Quimby
emka74/Shutterstock

She also had to fly five figure eights. Quimby passed this part with ease. For part two, she had to land within 100 feet of her takeoff point. Quimby failed this part the first time around. She took the test again the next day. This time she succeeded. She landed within 7 feet, 9 inches, of her takeoff point. What was so remarkable was that in those days, planes did not have brakes. Quimby set a record with her mark.

Quimby set other records: She was the first woman to fly at night (1911) and the first woman to cross the English Channel in the pilot's seat (1912).

She broke a fashion barrier, too. The long dresses that women wore at that time weren't practical for a pilot. Most of the planes were open to the elements, and long pieces of fabric might get caught in a propeller or other mechanism. Quimby designed an outfit for female pilots. Her tailor sewed a one-piece uniform made of purple satin. Quimby had invented the jumpsuit, *a one-piece outfit*.

Harriet Quimby in the jumpsuit she designed

Library of Congress, Prints and Photographs Division, New York World-Telegram and Sun Newspaper Photographs Collection, cph 3c22868v

Despite the progress, flight was still a dangerous business. Quimby entered the Boston Air Meet on 1 July 1912 in a Blériot monoplane. She and her passenger, William P. Willard, took off over Boston Harbor in hopes of making a record 58 mph flight over a body of water. At 5,000 feet, the plane flipped and nosed downward. As horrified spectators watched, Quimby and Willard fell from the plane and plunged into the waters. Both perished. Amazingly, the monoplane—now with no pilot or passenger—righted itself and landed in the harbor with a light crash.

In 1991, the US Post Office created a stamp in Quimby's honor.

Matilde Moisant

Matilde Moisant didn't buy into the superstition that the number 13 is unlucky. Her achievements proved how wise she was to ignore such beliefs. To begin with, she was born Friday, 13 September 1887. That was a good day for her and her parents.

Nearly 24 years later, on 13 April 1911, Moisant became the second woman in America to get a pilot's license. She won the Rodman Wanamaker Trophy for flying at an attitude of 2,500 feet. This was amazing in a day when planes weren't as stable as they are now. She also got a court to acknowledge it was legal to fly on Sundays. This happened after a sheriff in Long Island, New York, tried to arrest her for flying on a Sunday. Moisant's response was to hop in her plane and fly to another field.

One tragedy did strike: her brother, John Moisant, also a pilot, died in a crash in 1910. Matilde crashed a number of times herself, but she continued flying. Her brother's death deeply affected her, and on 13 April 1912, she said she'd make her last flight the next day. It turned out to be a very dangerous flight. The fuel tank sprang a leak, and by the time Moisant landed, her clothes were on fire.

Fortunately, the thickness of her clothing and her leather helmet protected her. Matilde Moisant died in 1964 at the age of 77.

MILESTONES

Dressed for Success

Harriet Quimby was a good friend of Matilde Moisant, John's sister. The two women decided to sign up for flight training together. When they did, both dressed as men. Why? Women were discouraged from learning how to fly, so they figured they'd need a disguise. Somehow, newspapers found out. They'd uncovered a fascinating story about two determined women.

Matilde Moisant
Courtesy National Air and Space Museum, Smithsonian Institution, NASM-73-3564

WOMEN IN EUROPE also turned their eyes to the sky during the early days of flight. Thérèse Peltier was the first European woman to fly as a passenger in a powered airplane in July 1908. The first European woman to pilot a plane was French baroness Raymonde de la Roche. The date was 22 October 1909. Soon after, she attained another first. On 8 March 1910 she became the first woman to earn a pilot's license.

Raymonde de la Roche
Courtesy National Air and Space Museum, Smithsonian Institution, NASM-81-3423

Julia Clark

On 19 May 1912, Julia Clark was the third American woman to gain her pilot's license. Sadly, she achieved an unfortunate other first: she was the first woman pilot to die in a crash.

Clark had a fascinating life. She immigrated to the United States from London and became an American citizen. She learned to fly at the Curtiss Flying School at North Island in San Diego. After soloing in a Curtiss plane, she joined an exhibition group. On the evening of 17 June 1912, she decided to take a test flight. It was dark, and she couldn't see that one of her plane's wings was about to hit a tree limb. The aircraft crashed. She died only about two weeks before Harriet Quimby.

Katherine and Marjorie Stinson

Flying was a family affair for the Stinsons. Katherine, her two brothers, and her sister Marjorie all became pilots.

Katherine earned her pilot's license on 24 July 1912. She was the fourth American woman to do so. And at age 16, she was also the youngest. She would eventually become one of the most successful women in aviation.

For example, Katherine was the first pilot of either gender to take part in a parade. She covered her plane with roses for the 1913 New Year's Day Tournament of Roses Parade in California and flew over the parade route. Later, she set a distance record for both genders in a nonstop cross-country flight.

Her younger brothers, Eddie and Jack, became pilots. Jack was a test pilot.

Her younger sister, Marjorie, graduated from the Wright Flying School in August 1914. (Wilbur Wright had her mother sign a waiver because of Marjorie's age.) At 17, Marjorie became the first woman authorized to fly the experimental airmail service.

Katherine Stinson

Library of Congress, Prints and Photographs Division, George Grantham Bain Collection, ggbain 18209v

All four siblings had the support of their mother, Emma. She even went so far as to move the family to San Antonio, Texas, so her daughters could open a flying school. When World War I began, the sisters tried to enlist as pilots in the Army, but they were rejected. So they opened a school to train Americans and Canadians as pilots for the war.

Marjorie Stinson with a group of Army officers

Library of Congress, Prints and Photographs Division, Harris & Ewing Collection, hec 11664v

LESSON 4   Pioneers of Flight

A supporter, New York Congressman Murray Hulbert, tried unsuccessfully to get Congress to pass a bill allowing women to join the Flying Corps. But women were allowed to do little more than serve as nurses during the war. Katherine went to France to work as an ambulance driver because, in her own words, "I didn't feel I was doing enough for the war effort."

Katherine retired from aviation after an illness in 1920, and spent many years as an architect in New Mexico. She died in 1977. Marjorie quit flying in 1930 and worked for 15 years as a draftsman at the War Department in Washington, D.C. She died in 1975.

The war the Stinsons tried to join would lead to revolutionary developments in aviation.

✔ CHECKPOINTS

Lesson 4 Review

Using complete sentences, answer the following questions on a sheet of paper.

1. What did Glenn Curtiss build that interested airship owners?

2. What did Curtiss accomplish while flying the *June Bug*?

3. What did Louis Blériot do when his engine overheated as he was crossing the English Channel?

4. What did Calbraith Perry Rodgers accomplish in the *Vin Fiz Flyer*, and how long did it take?

5. Who was the first enlisted man to become a pilot?

6. What was his final rank, and when did he retire?

7. What did Blanche Stuart Scott remove from her plane's engine to get it to fly?

8. Why was it remarkable that Harriet Quimby landed her plane 7 feet, 9 inches from her takeoff point?

9. Who was the fourth American woman to earn a pilot's license?

APPLYING YOUR LEARNING

10. Based on what you have read here, what very basic safety measure might have saved the lives of several early flyers?

CHAPTER 2

An artist's conception of a World War I dogfight between British and German planes
Keith Tarrier/Shutterstock

Developing Flight

Chapter Outline

LESSON 1

Airpower in World War I

LESSON 2

**Expanding the Horizon
from Barnstormers to Mainstream**

LESSON 3

Early Developments in Commercial Flight

"Aviation is proof that given the will, we have the capacity
to achieve the impossible."

Captain Eddie Rickenbacker

Airpower in World War I

Quick Write

_____

_____

Faced with seven German planes against his one, Eddie Rickenbacker knew he must remain calm. Why do you think that was important? What lesson do you think you can learn for use in emergencies you might face?

Learn About

- the contributions of Americans pilots during World War I
- how the airplane revolutionized war
- new developments in aviation during World War I
- how the war sped up aviation development in the United States

EDWARD RICKENBACKER was an American combat pilot during World War I. He shot down 26 German airplanes in just five months. He was the only surviving pilot of that war to receive the Congressional Medal of Honor during his lifetime.

Rickenbacker earned his medal for an act of bravery on 25 September 1918. He was flying alone when he came across seven German planes—five Fokker D-VIIs and two Halberstadt CL-IIs. When facing such situations, he knew a pilot must remain calm. And he certainly must have done so. Defying the huge odds, he shot down two of the seven enemy planes.

Rickenbacker was one of the American "aces" in the war. The French came up with the title of _ace_ for any pilot who had knocked five or more enemy planes out of the sky over the course of the war. The Germans, however, insisted their ace pilots bring down at least 10 aircraft to earn the title. An "ace of aces" was the pilot from each country who had taken down the most enemy aircraft.

Edward Rickenbacker was America's ace of aces. He shot down 26 planes during World War I.

Courtesy US Air Force

France's ace of aces was René Fonck. He had 75 kills, or planes shot down. Edward Mannock, with 73 kills, took the prize in Britain. And Baron Manfred von Richthofen of Germany (known as the "Red Baron") shot down 80 airplanes. Rickenbacker, with 26 kills, was America's ace of aces.

The Contributions of American Pilots During World War I

Despite the contributions of brave pilots on both sides, most World War I battles were fought on land or at sea. Airplanes were still fragile when the war started in 1914. After all, the Wrights didn't make their historic flight until 1903.

But during the war, aviation engineers made tremendous advances. Some American commanders in the field had great faith in the capabilities of the Aviation Section of the Army's Signal Corps. In a few key instances, aircraft contributed to the Allied victory. Aircraft had important functions—from doing aerial reconnaissance to shooting down enemy aircraft.

The Outbreak of World War I

World War I began in Europe when a Serb assassinated Austrian Archduke Franz Ferdinand on 28 June 1914. Ferdinand was next in line to the Austro-Hungarian throne. Because of alliances among different nations in Europe, one country after another soon declared war.

First Austria-Hungary declared war on Serbia. Then Russia entered the fray on Serbia's side. Germany, which had ties to Austria-Hungary, was the next to step into the conflict by declaring war on Russia. Soon *Russia, France, Serbia, and Britain*—the Allies—were at war against *Germany, Austria-Hungary, and Turkey*—the Central Powers. (Many other countries later joined the fight, including the United States and Italy on the side of the Allies. Russia withdrew from the war after the Russian Revolution at the end of 1917.)

When Germany invaded France on 4 August 1914, the war started in earnest.

American President Woodrow Wilson vowed that the United States would remain neutral. But over time, that proved impossible. German U-boats—*short for "undersea boats," the name given to German submarines*—attacked American ships

Vocabulary

- Allies
- Central Powers
- U-boats
- escadrille
- machine gun
- stalemate
- appropriate
- strategic
- dogfight
- strafe

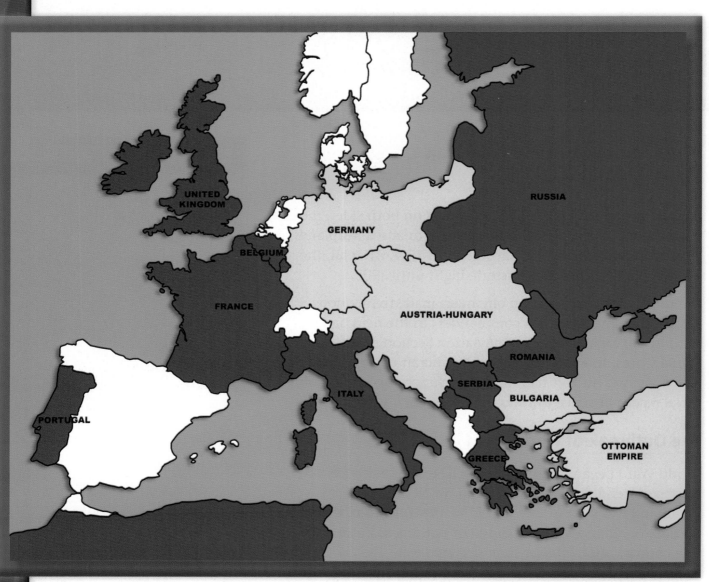

World War I alliances as of 1917—the Allies are in dark red and the Central Powers in yellow.

in the Atlantic because the United States was sending goods to Britain. Wilson asked Germany to stop sinking American ships. And for a while, Germany did.

But in early 1917 two things happened. Germany once again targeted all American ships headed toward Britain. And in a telegram discovered by British intelligence, Germany asked Mexico to make war with the United States if the United States did not remain neutral. If Mexico joined the war and the Central Powers won, Germany promised Mexico it could have Texas, Arizona, and New Mexico.

As a result, President Wilson asked the US Congress to declare war on Germany. Congress agreed. The United States entered World War I in April 1917.

The use of airplanes as weapons took major leaps forward during that war. The heroic central figure in airpower was the pilot.

Four American pilots in particular made their marks during World War I, also known as the Great War. But it all began with a group of US pilots who together formed the Lafayette Escadrille in France.

The Lafayette Escadrille

Some American pilots didn't wait for the United States to join the war. They tried to enter the military services of the Allies. For legal reasons, most countries couldn't accept the men's offers. But France, with its French Foreign Legion made up entirely of fighters from outside France, could sign up these volunteers.

In April 1916 seven American pilots formed a fighting group that they called the Escadrille Américaine. An escadrille is *a small squadron of planes*. The pilots were wealthy young men who had been living in Paris. In the next few days seven more Americans, then serving in French units, joined the squadron.

When the men of Escadrille Américaine began racking up German kills, Germany protested. It said that the United States was breaking its promise of neutrality.

The men had to change their group's name. They decided to call it the Lafayette Escadrille. Its name honored the Marquis de Lafayette, a French nobleman who fought for the 13 American colonies during the Revolutionary War. Now individual Americans were fighting on behalf of France and the Allies in the war against the Central Powers.

In the escadrille's first five months, its pilots fought in 156 air battles and shot down 17 enemy planes. By the time the United States Air Service brought the unit under its supervision in 1918, its pilots had made 199 kills. Six members were aces. Forty died by the war's end. The escadrille included Eugene Bullard, the only African-American to serve as a pilot in the war.

Members of the Lafayette Escadrille in 1915–1916
Library of Congress, Prints and Photographs Division, George Grantham Bain Collection, ggbain 21985

Raoul Lufbery

Raoul Lufbery was the most famous pilot of the Lafayette Escadrille. He had 17 combat victories during the war. A native of France, he came to the United States as a child and became an American citizen. As a young man, he tried the US Army but didn't care for the discipline. During travels abroad, he met Marc Pourpe, a French pilot. Pourpe took him on as his mechanic. Together they traveled to India, China, and Japan.

Raoul Lufbery
R. Soubiran/Library of Congress, Prints and Photographs Division, cph 3c01970

The pair was in France when war broke out. Lufbery followed Pourpe into the military by way of the French Foreign Legion. He continued working as Pourpe's mechanic. No doubt he was also listening to the pilots talk about effective combat maneuvers and flying techniques. When Pourpe died in action in 1914, Lufbery trained to be a pilot. He signed up with the Lafayette Escadrille shortly after it was established.

Lufbery used to give two pieces of advice to new combat pilots. First, he said, don't lunge headfirst into combat. Take stock of the scene before committing yourself. Second, he cautioned that a pilot in a burning plane would have a better chance of survival if he tried to bring it in for a landing. Parachutes were not standard equipment in those days, so pilots couldn't safely jump from a damaged aircraft.

Sadly, Lufbery was not able to follow his own advice. When a German aircraft shot Lufbery's plane on 19 May 1918, his aircraft became engulfed in flames. Lufbery jumped to his death.

Edward Rickenbacker

Edward "Eddie" Rickenbacker, America's ace of aces, started out as a professional racecar driver. He competed in the Indianapolis 500 three times. Rickenbacker learned a lot about automobiles through an engineering correspondence course. He also worked at a car-manufacturing company. Like Glenn Curtiss, who'd broken speed records on motorcycles, Rickenbacker set a record in a racecar. His top speed was 134 mph.

Although he was making excellent money as a racer, Rickenbacker wanted to be a part of the war effort. In 1917, he asked the US Army to consider forming a squadron of pilots made up of racecar drivers. The military didn't take him up on his offer, but they did ask whether he would like to enlist and serve as a staff car driver.

Rickenbacker said yes, and fate stepped in. One day while Rickenbacker was driving a member of General John J. Pershing's staff, they passed the broken-down car of Colonel William "Billy" Mitchell, chief of the US Air Service. Rickenbacker pulled over to the side of the road. Drawing on his expertise in engine repair, he fixed the car. Colonel Mitchell was impressed. Later he asked Rickenbacker to be his driver. Before long, Rickenbacker had Mitchell's permission to train as a pilot.

Rickenbacker rose from an enlisted Soldier to the rank of captain and took command of the 94th Squadron. He did two important things for his men. He got them equipped with parachutes. And he figured out how to keep an airplane's machine gun—*an automatic rifle that uses belt-fed ammunition*—from jamming.

Eddie Rickenbacker rose from an enlisted Soldier to the rank of captain during World War I.

Courtesy US Air Force

From Ace to Airline President

Rickenbacker didn't slow down when World War I ended. He remained in the reserves and worked his way up to colonel. He also returned to one of his first loves—cars. Rickenbacker founded an automobile manufacturing company.

The personal side of his life flourished, too. He got married and had two children. In 1927, the pace picked up. Rickenbacker, who'd once raced in the Indianapolis 500, bought the Indianapolis 500 Speedway. He sold it after World War II.

Rickenbacker remained engaged in engines, cars, and planes in other ways as well. He was an aviation advocate. He managed General Motors Fokker Aircraft Company. Next he took on the job of vice president of American Airlines. He eventually left that job to go back to Fokker, where he became manager of its Eastern Airlines division.

Then in 1938, Rickenbacker bought Eastern Airlines. Friends gave him financial support for the purchase. He worked at Eastern for more than 20 years and retired in 1959 as president. He remained as chairman of the board until 1963. Rickenbacker spent the last 10 years of his life promoting aviation, both military and civilian. He died in 1973.

Frank Luke

Frank Luke was a wild card. He didn't have the discipline of a Rickenbacker or a Lufbery. But he did have their guts. He was tough—he came from the Arizona mountains and had worked in copper mines.

As soon as the United States entered the war, Luke volunteered. He chose the Army Signal Corps and completed his nine-week flight training in seven weeks. In March 1918 he went to France as a 2nd lieutenant. After more training, he began to go out on patrols. But he never saw any German aircraft. Running out of patience, he flew solo over a German airfield in August 1918. He met up with six Albatross fighters (a German biplane) and shot one down.

One month later Luke asked permission to go after a German balloon that another squadron had tried unsuccessfully to shoot down. Balloons were always heavily guarded because they were so vulnerable. Another plane went along with Luke to watch his back. Luke got his balloon, and several others over the next several days.

2nd Lieutenant Frank Luke standing next to one of the German balloons he shot down

Courtesy US Army

Luke still sometimes went off by himself. Once he disappeared overnight. When Luke returned, his commander grounded him. Luke took off again anyway, even though he risked court-martial. This time he went after three more balloons. Observers on the ground saw one go up in flames. But he was never seen alive again. French villagers reported that he was jumped by enemy Fokkers. He shot down two before being wounded in the shoulder. He eluded the other attackers and shot down two more balloons. Then he strafed some German soldiers on the ground. He then landed his bullet-ridden plane to get some water from a stream. A German foot patrol surrounded him. He drew his revolver and killed seven German soldiers before the Germans killed him.

Luke's career as a combat pilot was short: he died just 17 days after his first kill. In that time, he shot down 15 balloons and three airplanes. It was one of the records of the war.

Eugene Bullard

Only one African-American served as a pilot during World War I. His name was Eugene Bullard. Bullard was also one of the few enlisted men to fly an airplane.

Bullard carved his own path throughout his life. When he was only eight years old, he ran away from his home in Georgia. His goal was to get to France. He'd heard France was a wonderful place for people of all races. It took him 11 years, but he finally got there.

Like other Americans wishing to join the fight in World War I, Bullard signed up with the French Foreign Legion in October 1914. He was wounded four times while with an infantry unit whose members called themselves the "swallows of death." After his fourth wound, he transferred to the French Air Service and became a pilot. He was the first black man to get a pilot's license and the first black American fighter pilot. He tried to join the US Air Service, but the Army turned him down. He shot down two German aircraft while in the French Air Service. Finally, he got into a tussle with a French officer— rather than court-martial him, the French military transferred him back to the infantry, where he served the rest of the war.

When Eugene Bullard hung up his infantry boots at the end of World War I, he returned to Paris. This was the city that felt like home to him. Before the war he'd been a boxer. But now he was a war veteran who'd suffered many wounds. He needed work that exercised his mind more than his body. He went into the nightclub business and met many famous people such as authors Ernest Hemingway and F. Scott Fitzgerald. He also got married. His wife was the daughter of a countess. They had two children. Years passed, and another war was brewing—World War II.

Corporal Eugene Bullard
Courtesy US Air Force Enlisted Heritage Hall

Eugene Bullard's pilot's license issued by the Fédération Aéronautique Internationale (France)
Courtesy US Air Force Enlisted Heritage Hall

During all his time in Europe, the former war pilot had picked up language skills. In addition to English and French, Bullard spoke German quite well. Because Bullard had great affection for his adopted country of France, he agreed to help when the French government asked him to spy on Germans living in France. War broke out in 1939, and with the German army about to take the city of Paris in 1940, Bullard knew he had to leave. He did this because if he were captured he'd be charged as a spy and because he wanted to protect his two children. (Bullard and his wife had separated years before, but when she died, Bullard gained custody of their children.)

From War Hero to Elevator Operator

After fleeing Paris, Bullard went with his children to the city of Orleans, south of the French capital. He joined a group of uniformed troops defending that city, and was once again wounded. A woman spy smuggled him and his children into Spain. The family was later sent back to the United States, where Bullard recovered.

Bullard spent the rest of his life in Harlem, New York, working as an elevator operator at Rockefeller Center. The US military didn't recognize his wartime achievements until after his death in 1961, when the US Air Force commissioned him as a lieutenant.

But the grateful French never forgot him. The French government awarded him a Croix de Guerre (War Cross) medal, which it gave to individuals who displayed heroism during fighting with enemy forces. Bullard also received several other medals for his contributions to the war effort, both in the air and in the infantry. In 1954, France asked him to visit to help light the Eternal Flame of the Tomb of the Unknown French Soldier in Paris at the Arc de Triomphe. This was a great honor. French President Charles de Gaulle even praised Bullard on a visit to New York City in 1960.

The Red Baron

Baron Manfred von Richthofen was Germany's ace of aces. He shot down 80 Allied aircraft. Born into a wealthy military family, by age 20, he was a lieutenant in a Prussian Army cavalry regiment. But once the fighting moved to the trenches, the horse cavalry no longer had an important role in combat.

So Von Richthofen joined the German Imperial Air Service. He soon commanded a group with scarlet-colored planes. Because of his record of conquests in the air and the color of his planes, he became known as the Red Baron. Allied fire killed Von Richthofen in 1918, three years after he became a pilot.

Manfred von Richthofen, the Red Baron

Courtesy National Archives and Records Administration, ARC 540163

US Contributions to the Air War

By 1917, after years of bloody fighting that cost both sides millions of casualties, the war in Europe was at a stalemate. A stalemate is *a situation in which further action is blocked*. The French Army was demoralized. The British tried to reinforce France, but inexperienced replacements composed the bulk of British troops by this point. Germany was also weakening. A force was needed to tip the balance one way or the other. The Allies hoped that force would be the United States, which joined the effort in April.

In August 1917 the US Congress vowed to "darken the skies over Europe with US aircraft." It voted to appropriate—*to set aside for a specific use*—$64 million to build airplanes.

Congress had good intentions, but it had made an empty promise. The United States lacked both the engineers to design planes and the manufacturers to assemble them. Even by the end of the war, all American pilots were still flying British or French planes.

Britain and France had entered the war in 1914 with 450 aircraft. Germany at that time had 200. All three countries had working aviation industries in those years. By 1917 France and Germany each boasted more than 2,000 aircraft. Britain was continually flying patrols along the North Sea, but the Allies were running out of steam. At that time, the United States had just one manufacturer: Curtiss Aircraft.

While the United States never built more than a handful of airplanes during the war years, it did provide considerable manpower in the air. It entered the European conflict with 100 pilots and trained 10,000 more before the war's end in November 1918. In all, 781 enemy planes fell to American-piloted aircraft. US pilots also took part in 150 bombing raids.

It may have taken America the better part of a year to ramp up its effectiveness in the war, but its support of the Allies was crucial. In one of the most significant air battles of World War I—the Battle of Saint Mihiel—America's Billy Mitchell led the Allied air attack. As you'll read later, that battle determined the war's outcome.

How the Airplane Revolutionized War

Until World War I, most people thought the role of aircraft in combat was limited to aerial reconnaissance. Countries won wars based on the strength of their infantries and the power of their navies. That's how it had been for centuries.

Enlisted Pilots

The United States entered the war in 1917 with 100 pilots. Billy Mitchell and another officer, Hap Arnold, had done their best to build up the number of pilots by training enlisted men. Both officers thought highly of the enlisted men in the Army's Signal Corps. The enlistees knew aircraft engines inside and out. Mitchell, an outspoken advocate of airpower, helped ensure that the National Defense Act of 3 June 1916 included language that authorized the training of enlisted men as pilots.

When the US Army bought its first *Wright Flyer*, even Brigadier General James Allen didn't think of an airplane as a potential offensive weapon. Dropping bombs from the sky seemed an unlikely idea. Conducting battles between squadrons of planes also seemed far-fetched. After all, planes of those days were built of plywood, and their wings were wrapped in fabric. But World War I would alter the military's views.

While many improvements were still needed to make the airplane the fierce weapon it is today, battlefield strategy evolved dramatically over the course of the Great War. The airplane reshaped the way countries fight wars more quickly than any other weapon in military history. A motto emerged by war's end: "If you control the air, you cannot be beaten; if you lose the air, you cannot win."

The Long-Range Raid and the Machine Gun

In 1915 German airships floated over London and dropped bombs that destroyed buildings and killed many people. Through 1917 the Germans worked on perfecting these long-range strategic raids. Strategic means *designed to strike at the sources of an enemy's military, economic, or political power.* But the British were really the first to attempt a long-range raid. In 1914 they targeted hangars housing German aircraft.

The Germans flew hydrogen-filled zeppelins. But zeppelins had one major weakness: hydrogen is very flammable. So zeppelins easily burst into flames when hit by antiaircraft fire. This led the Germans to develop a twin-engine bomber called the Gotha IV. The Gotha IV went on bombing raids over many British cities in 1917.

New Zealand pilot Lieutenant A. de Bathe Brandon attacks a zeppelin raider over London on 31 March 1916. New Zealand was then part of the British Empire.
Everett Historical/Shutterstock

Bombs on Britain

AT FIRST PILOTS CARRIED SMALL BOMBS in their laps and dropped them by hand. Once aircraft could carry heavier loads, some ferried thousands of pounds of bombs. Accuracy of bombing, however, remained an issue.

It wasn't a zeppelin that dropped the first bombs on Britain. It was a German FF-29 seaplane. The date was 21 December 1914, and the target was Dover, a city in southeast England. The FF-29 missed its target that day. But three days later it raided Britain a second time. Its bombs hit Dover this time, but no one was killed.

The next day the aircraft invaded British airspace a third time. It dropped two bombs on nearby Kent. Over the course of the war, Germany hit London alone with 56 tons of bombs. German aircraft dropped 214 tons of bombs on the rest of the country.

As a result of these raids, Britain had to take new measures to protect its own shores. English fighter squadrons were ordered to return from France so they could guard British soil.

When World War I began in 1914, pilots flew everything from balloons and dirigibles to airplanes. They soared over enemy positions to spot troop movements and artillery positions. They also took photos of what they'd seen.

Each side wanted to do something to counteract this use of aircraft. Both sent up airplanes to shoot down observation aircraft, first with pistols and rifles and later with machine guns.

Whether the enemy was using pistols or machine guns, another countermeasure was now necessary. Each side had to protect its observation aircraft. Aerial combat was born.

Waypoints

The First Independent Flying Force

In response to German air raids on English cities and factories, the British formed their own bombing unit. Although the British were the first to conduct a long-range raid, they hadn't established a new arm of their military to do so. But in 1917 the British Royal Flying Corps (RFC) founded its first bombing wing. Unlike American and other Allied aviation units, the RFC did not answer to an infantry officer. It was independent. In 1918 the RFC merged with the Royal Naval Air Service and became today's Royal Air Force.

The Germans quickly picked up on the airplane-mounted machine gun. Machine guns had been around since the late 19th century, and they were in full use by infantrymen from the start of World War I. They weren't used right away in the air, however. In 1915 French pilot Roland Garros first bolted an automatic rifle to his plane so he could shoot straight through the propeller. To keep from shooting his propeller off, he attached steel plates to the backs of the blades.

The Germans got to see Garros's deadly invention up close when they downed his plane in April 1915. They asked a Dutchman, Anthony Fokker, to take the design a step further. Fokker built an interrupting gear. He hooked the machine gun to the plane's engine. In this way, the gun would not fire while the propeller was in the way. For the next year, the Germans ruled the skies.

But if the Germans could capture and copy Garros's design, it was only a matter of time before the Allies captured a German aircraft and copied Fokker's interrupting gear. In April 1916 the Allies did just that. Soon the Allies and the Central Powers were again on equal footing. The famous dogfights commenced. A dogfight is *a battle between fighter planes.* The fighter aces came out of these aerial battles. Sometimes squadrons with as many as 50 planes faced off.

A French Spad fighter wins a dogfight with a German Albatross in World War I.
Everett Historical/Shutterstock

Furthermore, once machine guns were mounted on planes, pilots could use them to strafe soldiers on the ground. To strafe is t*o attack with a machine gun from a low-flying aircraft.*

The Battle of Saint Mihiel

In September 1918 the Battle of Saint Mihiel in France finally turned the tide in favor of the Allies. Airpower played a tremendous role in this offensive. Brigadier General Billy Mitchell commanded nearly 1,500 Allied airplanes—American, French, British, Italian, and Portuguese—to drive the Germans out of France. This was the largest assembly of aircraft ever gathered for a single mission.

The Allied pilots had two goals. The first was to destroy German planes in the air. The second was to destroy German aircraft in hangars on the ground. Mitchell committed 1,000 planes to this portion of the mission. The rest of the planes protected the Allied ground troops. They scouted out enemy positions. Mitchell wrote that the Allied planes were "to be put into a central mass and hurled at the enemy's aviation, no matter where he might be found, until complete ascendancy had been obtained over him in the air."

The four-day Battle of Saint Mihiel established the role of mass movements of airpower during wartime. It weakened the Central Powers and destroyed enemy supply lines. This offensive helped lead to Allied victory two months later.

The Birth of New Strategies

Airplanes now offered possibilities that challenged age-old warfare strategies. In traditional battles, troops dug trenches. They tried to hold their own lines and break through the enemy's trench lines. Assaults were from the front. But airplanes changed that. Planes could fly over an enemy's trenches, bomb from overhead, and strafe troops. What's more, they could hit important targets behind enemy lines, such as factories. This provided the element of surprise as well.

Planes didn't come into their own until World War II. Nevertheless, their use during World War I set the stage for the next worldwide conflict.

An American pilot takes pictures of enemy ground positions using a Graflex camera circa 1917–1918.
Everett Historical/Shutterstock

A German crewmember drops a bomb on an Allied position on the Western Front.
Everett Historical/Shutterstock

New Developments in Aviation During World War I

Airplanes flew a whopping 64 mph when the first shots of the Great War rang out. Most European nations had a few hundred planes. America had only about 20. But no one had aircraft that were combat worthy.

Over the next four years, the technology of the Allied and Central Powers' airpower would continually leapfrog one over the other. Speeds picked up. Aircraft became stronger and sturdier. Maximum altitudes climbed from 10,000 feet to 24,000 feet.

As the saying goes, "Necessity is the mother of invention." And if survival in war isn't a necessity, what is?

When Louis Blériot crossed the English Channel in 1909, some thought his quick, 37-minute passage from one country to another suggested the face of future wars. If a friendly aircraft could travel that fast from Calais to Dover, couldn't an enemy do the same? Many countries built small armies of planes. Once war broke out, the pace of invention picked up.

By 1918 three specialized types of aircraft had emerged: the fighter, the observation aircraft, and the bomber. Observation aircraft were in use from the start. Most of them were dirigibles and balloons. Some planes even had extra seats for photographers.

The fighter came into its own with the birth of the dogfight. This era had the biggest impact on small-craft development. Once both the Allies and the Central Powers had mounted machine guns with interrupting gear on their airplanes, quick, easy maneuvers became essential. A pilot wanted to get out of the way of the bullet spray.

The British Sopwith Triplane was one of the aircraft designed during the war to engage in dogfights.
IanC66/Shutterstock

A Junkers D-1 replica
IanC66/Shutterstock

These fighter aircraft needed three qualities: they had to be lightweight, fast, and maneuverable. Both sides designed their own memorable fighters. The British built the Sopwith Camel and the SE-5A. The French had the Spad VII and Nieuport 28. The Germans crafted the Fokker Dr-I and D-VII.

Seven months before the war ended, a German designer named Hugo Junkers made a breakthrough. He built an all-metal, low-wing monoplane fighter, the Junkers D1. No longer would a pilot have to fly a plywood-and-fabric contraption that easily caught fire. Fortunately for the Allies, the Germans assembled only 45 of these planes.

During the war, airplanes became faster. By early 1918 fighters zipped along at a cool 130 mph. When Igor Sikorsky flew his four-engine, 92-foot-wingspan *Le Grand* in 1913, he probably couldn't have imagined that in just five years 100-foot-wingspan bombers would be carrying loads that weighed thousands of pounds. As the Germans learned with their zeppelins, bombs were best delivered by planes sturdy and large enough to carry heavy loads. The British, for example, designed the Super-Handley Page bomber. The first model had two engines; later models had four. The four-engine model could carry six men and 30 260-pound bombs.

Any breakthrough in design gave the side that had it an edge. Ground soldiers, pilots, commanders, and engineers—all contributed to the war effort.

How the War Sped Up Aviation Development in the United States

On the eve of the war's outbreak, the US House of Representatives on 18 July 1914 authorized the Army's Signal Corps to create an aviation branch with 60 officers and 260 enlisted men. When in March 1916 the 1st Aero Squadron took to the field to help General John J. Pershing secure the US–Mexico border, the squadron had eight biplanes. But these planes were not nearly powerful enough to get over Arizona's Casa Grande Mountains. Recognizing the need, the Congress appropriated $13.2 million to build up the Aviation Service.

As noted earlier, when Congress appropriated $64 million for airplanes in 1917, the United States was far behind other nations in airpower. Army staff officers still had their eyes focused on the infantry. They had no plans for their aviation section. The United States could never again be so unprepared.

Chief of the Air Service, Brigadier General Billy Mitchell drew up the plan for the 1,500-plane movement in the Battle of St Mihiel.

Courtesy US Air Force

Brigadier General Billy Mitchell believed strongly in the future of aviation as an instrument in warfare. He saw its possibilities, including as a weapon against navies. Mitchell didn't learn to fly until he was 36—that's old for a beginning pilot. But he was one of the freshest thinkers in air warfare.

After consulting with other officers, Mitchell devised a three-pronged theory to fight wars from the sky:

1. Air superiority over the battlefield must be completely assured.

2. Airpower may then be employed offensively against the enemy's ground troops.

3. Finally, aerial bombardment may be directed against the enemy's supplies, railroads, communications, and airdromes.

As chief of the Air Service, Mitchell held great sway with Airmen. But the aviation arm still fell under the command of the Army. And the Army saw airplanes as nothing more than extensions of ground forces. Mitchell, on the other hand, always pushed for an independent air service. He considered new strategies, such as the mass use of airplanes in the Battle of Saint Mihiel. For these reasons, today's US Air Force still considers Mitchell one of its founding fathers. You'll read more about him in a later lesson.

✔ CHECKPOINTS

Lesson 1 Review

Using complete sentences, answer the following questions on a sheet of paper.

1. What was the Lafayette Escadrille?

2. Who was America's "ace of aces?"

3. Who was the only African-American pilot in World War I? Which air service accepted him?

4. What did the British Royal Flying Corps do that separated it from other Allied air forces?

5. What did Anthony Fokker build?

6. What three specialized types of aircraft had emerged by 1918?

7. When did the US House of Representatives authorize the Army Signal Corps to create an aviation branch?

8. What was Brigadier General Billy Mitchell's three-pronged strategy to fight wars from the sky?

APPLYING YOUR LEARNING

9. Explain how the airplane revolutionized war.

Learn About

- the barnstormers' significance
- notable pilots who were barnstormers
- the barnstormers' significant contributions to aviation
- how barnstormers changed public opinion of aviation

BESSIE COLEMAN was an unlikely pioneer. She was one of 13 children born to a former slave in Texas sometime in the 1890s. Her father was part African-American and part Cherokee and Choctaw Indian. Her mother, an African-American, didn't know how to read. But she had big ideas for her little girl. She made Bessie want to "become somebody."

It took a while, but Coleman figured it out. The "somebody" she wanted to become was an airplane pilot.

Coleman managed to graduate from high school. She even had a semester of college in Oklahoma. She loved to read. One of the things she read about was aviation. During World War I, she was living in Chicago, working as a manicurist. The newspapers were full of stories about the air war in Europe.

Coleman decided she didn't want to remain on the ground. She didn't want only to read about aviation. She wanted to fly.

When she went to sign up for lessons, doors closed in her face. Yes, there were a few women pilots—but a black woman? No one she talked to could imagine such a thing.

But she had a powerful friend—Robert S. Abbott. He was the editor of the _Chicago Weekly Defender_. His newspaper had sponsored a contest to find the best manicurist in black Chicago. Coleman won that contest.

So Coleman had an "in" with Abbott. She went to see him. He liked her idea of flight lessons. And he had an idea of his own. Go to Europe, he said. People there will be more accepting of you. He had another tip: Learn French before you go!

So Coleman went back to school—night school this time. She learned French and traveled to Europe.

After a few months, she ran out of money. So she returned to the United States. She went back to work. She saved as much money as she could. Finally she had enough to return to Europe. She looked for the best flight teacher she could find. She ended up studying with the chief pilot for Anthony Fokker, the famous aircraft manufacturer.

Fokker saw Coleman's talent and encouraged her. He became her mentor. A mentor is a *trusted coach or guide*.

On 15 June 1921, Bessie Coleman got her license. She was the first licensed black woman aviator in the world.

Vocabulary

- mentor
- barnstormer
- spectators
- altitude
- aerodynamic
- enthusiasts
- amphibian planes

Bessie Coleman's French pilot's license
National Air and Space Museum, Smithsonian Institution, SI-99-15416

The Barnstormers' Significance

Bessie Coleman's story is inspiring to anyone striving to make a dream come true. Her story is also important because of the kind of aviator she was. Coleman earned fame as a barnstormer—*a pilot who travels around the country giving exhibits of stunt flying and parachuting.* The term *barnstorming* comes from the time pilots would fly over a small rural town to attract attention, then land at a local farm. In the 1920s, the term became attached to stunt flying. Historians give stunt pilots like Bessie Coleman credit for sustaining the aviation industry during its early years.

Barnstorming shows drew crowds of spectators—*people who come to see an event or show*—during and after World War I.

These daredevil pilots, along with the stuntmen and parachutists who worked with them, entertained people in the days before there were theme parks or television. Some pilots worked in teams. Their acts were called "flying circuses." Once the war was over, these pilots became the public face of American aviation.

The aircraft industry had boomed during the war. Britain, France, Germany, and Italy produced tens of thousands of planes. And the United States was catching up. By the war's end, it had almost 4,000 planes and about 9,500 men in the air service.

But on 14 November 1918, three days after the war ended, the US government canceled $100 million worth of airplane contracts. The country's leaders didn't yet see how important aircraft could be for national security in peacetime.

Within three months, 175,000 workers in the aircraft industry lost their jobs. Aircraft production dropped by 85 percent. The Army dumped its surplus warplanes onto the market. That was a big blow to the aircraft companies. Who would buy their new planes when Uncle Sam was selling old ones at bargain prices?

Commercial and private aviation did not yet exist. There were no regularly scheduled flights for business or vacation travelers. Cars weren't yet popular either. Most people traveled from one city to another by train. In fact, even though aviation had been important during the war, by 1918 most Americans had still never seen an airplane.

The barnstormers changed that. Many of them were former Army pilots. Since military aviation had been cut back, a large number lost their jobs. They leaped at the opportunity to keep flying.

These pilots enjoyed showing off the skills they had mastered in combat. They excelled at tight turns and daring maneuvers. And they often flew the same aircraft—planes such as the Curtiss JN-4 ("Jenny")—that they had trained on in wartime.

A replica Curtiss JN 4 "Jenny"
Kletr/Shutterstock

Notable Pilots Who Were Barnstormers

Bessie Coleman was just one of several Americans who gained fame as barnstormers and helped move aviation into the public eye. Like the pilots of World War I, the barnstormers were a special breed.

For the barnstormers, flying was in some ways less risky than it had been for combat pilots. No enemy guns fired on them as they performed maneuvers over fields and county fairgrounds. But flying, especially stunt flying, was still dangerous. Many of the barnstormers died in air accidents. Among them were Bessie Coleman and another pilot named Lincoln Beachey.

Born in San Francisco, Beachey (1887–1915) was one of the top barnstormers. At one point, Orville Wright called him "the greatest pilot of all time." In his Curtiss biplane, Beachey thrilled crowds with his dives. He could snatch a scarf or a handkerchief off the ground using the tips of his wings. On 14 March 1915, Beachey first flew his new plane, a more powerful monoplane. While flying upside down, he pulled too hard on the controls to pull out of the inverted flight. As a result, the wings snapped off and the monoplane crashed in San Francisco Bay, killing him. However, Beachey had many firsts in his short flying career. He was the first American pilot to perform the inside loop, the first to make an airplane tail slide on purpose, the first to figure out how to pull out of a deadly spin, and the first person to fly through a building.

Lincoln Beachey
Courtesy Air Force Historical Research Agency

SOMEONE ON THE GROUND would first notice it as a buzz or a whine. Much too loud for an insect, they said. It sounded like an engine. But what was an engine doing up in the sky? Could it be one of those newfangled flying machines?

Or maybe a farmer would see a shadow fall across his field— a shadow much too big to be that of a bird.

It's an airplane! A barnstormer had come to town!

The pilot would typically circle over a village or a small town to get people's attention. Then he'd land in a nearby field. Word would spread. People would gather to get a look at the aircraft. The pilot would offer rides. Some hardy souls would volunteer to go up. They would typically get a five-minute flight for $5—the equivalent of about $50 today.

Barnstormers liked to show what they could do wherever crowds gathered at places like county fairs and carnivals. Flying circuses, conducted by teams of pilots, became a popular form of entertainment.

Pilots who weren't part of the circuses often teamed up with stuntmen. The stuntmen had an amazing bag of tricks. "Wing walking," for example, was a real crowd pleaser.

With the pilot flying a biplane in a circle, the stuntman would leave the cockpit. He or she would walk out on the edge of the lower wing, then climb to the upper wing and walk back toward the cockpit. To give viewers an extra thrill, some wing walkers would stand on their heads.

Barnstormer Ormer Locklear performing a wing-walking stunt with his Curtiss JN-4D, around 1919–1920

© 2002 National Air and Space Museum, Smithsonian Institution (SI Neg 84-556-D-2)

Waypoints

Omlie's Air Markers

In 1935, Phoebe Fairgrave Omlie made one of her biggest contributions to American aviation when she developed the "air marker" system. This was a network of black and orange navigational markers in which names of towns were painted in 12-foot letters on the roofs of buildings all across the country. These markers identified the location, showed which direction was North, and indicated the distance and direction of the nearest airport. Eventually 16,000 markers—one every 15 miles—guided pilots along every air route in the United States.

Even Charles A. Lindbergh, best known for his 1927 solo flight across the Atlantic Ocean, was a barnstormer at the beginning of his career. (You'll read more about Lindbergh in the next lesson.)

As you read earlier, most barnstormers were former military aviators. But women also were taking to the skies. Among them was Phoebe Fairgrave Omlie.

She ran her own flying circus. She was the first woman in the United States to become a licensed transport pilot. In 1933, she also became the first woman appointed to a federal government job in aviation—special assistant for air intelligence for the National Advisory Committee for Aeronautics, the agency that eventually became the National Aeronautics and Space Administration (NASA).

For pilots such as Coleman and Omlie, as well as for women across the nation, it was an exciting time. Opportunities were widening. With passage of the 19th Amendment to the US Constitution, women won the right to vote. Many cast ballots for the first time in the 1920 presidential election.

Margery Brown, another female barnstormer, wrote about why women wanted to fly: "Halfway between the Earth and sky one seems to be closer to God. There is a peace of mind and heart, a satisfaction that walls cannot give. When I see an airplane flying I just ache all over to be up there."

Phoebe Fairgrave Omlie
Underwood & Underwood, Library of Congress, Prints and Photographs Division, cph 3b43433

The Barnstormers' Significant Contributions to Aviation

Historians call the years between 1919 and 1939 the "golden age of aviation." Pilots set one record after another. They flew faster. They attained greater **altitude**—*the height above Earth's surface.* They served as test pilots. (It's probably fair to say that in those early days, every pilot was a test pilot.)

During this period airplanes evolved from slow-moving, cloth-and-wood structures to faster aircraft made of metal. These planes were more **aerodynamic**—*designed with rounded edges to reduce wind drag.*

Engines became more reliable. This was another key advance. Soon wealthy aviation **enthusiasts**—*strong supporters or fans*—began to offer prizes for the first pilot to achieve a certain goal.

In 1911, for instance, newspaper owner William Randolph Hearst offered $50,000 to the first pilot who could fly across the United States in 30 days or less. As you read in Chapter 1, Lesson 4, Calbraith Rodgers was the first to fly the distance. But he didn't win the prize. He took almost three weeks too long. Engine trouble, among other problems, slowed him down.

Another wealthy aviation enthusiast was Raymond Orteig. In the early 1920s he offered $25,000 for the first nonstop flight from New York to Paris. Again, the engines weren't up to the task.

But within a few years, engines had improved enough to make transatlantic flight possible. Some pilots then turned to a new challenge: polar exploration.

From childhood, Rear Admiral Richard E. Byrd had longed to explore the North and South Poles. Trained as a flier, he advanced both aviation and polar exploration. In 1926 he and his pilot were the first to fly over the North Pole. Their aircraft was a Fokker monoplane with three Wright Whirlwind engines.

In 1926 Byrd flew to the South Pole. His expedition included three Loening **amphibian planes**—*aircraft designed to take off and land on either water or land.*

Rear Admiral Richard E. Byrd: Polar Aviator

After World War I, barnstormers brought the magic of flight to the American heartland. And beginning in the 1920s, Richard E. Byrd helped direct attention to the ends of the earth—the North and South Poles.

Born in 1888 to a famous Virginia family, he graduated from the United States Naval Academy in 1912. He was a naval aviator in World War I. Eventually he rose to the rank of rear admiral in the US Navy.

He developed plans and navigational aids for the Navy's first transatlantic flights. He also helped Charles Lindbergh prepare for his solo flight across the Atlantic Ocean.

Byrd's polar adventures began with an assignment in western Greenland, in the North Atlantic. On 9 May 1926 he and his pilot, Warrant Officer Floyd Bennett, were the first people to fly over the North Pole. For their feat, both men received the Medal of Honor, not usually given in peacetime. Finally, Byrd turned his attention south. For the next three decades, he did more than anyone else to direct exploration of Antarctica.

On 28 November 1929, Byrd and his pilot Bernt Balchen flew to the South Pole.

It was the first of many trips. The team carried out scientific research. They studied meteors, cosmic rays, weather, and Earth's magnetism.

In 1934 Byrd spent five months living alone in a hut 123 miles away from his main base. It was as far south as any human had ever lived.

He was a celebrity, and he liked being famous. He knew that interest in his exploits helped build public support for scientific exploration. He raised a great deal of money for research, too.

By the 1950s he was the senior US government official in charge of South Pole research. He was an active explorer until the last months of his life. He died in 1957 at the age of 68.

Then-Lieutenant Commander Richard E. Byrd (*second from right*) and US Navy Pilot Floyd Bennett (*far left*) on their return from the North Pole in 1926
Courtesy US Navy/Naval History and Heritage Command

How the Barnstormers Changed Public Opinion of Aviation

Since most Americans had never even seen an airplane, whatever ideas they had about flying probably included many fears. The barnstormers' demonstrations didn't do away with people's fears. After all, spectators sometimes saw dreadful accidents. But the barnstormers' air shows certainly created an interest in flight, even in rural areas and small towns. They publicized the airplane and brought romance to flying. Some people believe that without the barnstormers, aviation might have died altogether in the United States.

A 1919 newspaper advertisement for a barnstormer exhibition

© 2002 National Air and Space Museum, Smithsonian Institution (SI Neg 85-12327)

Stanford University historian Joseph Corn describes the importance of the barnstormers in his book, *The Winged Gospel*:

> Crowds assembled at the smallest airfield to watch planes take off and land, while the public voraciously consumed the many stories about aviation in newspapers and magazines.... So central was the airplane in the American imagination, in fact, that many people expected that they would soon take to the sky, flying their own family plane.... But more than anything, the airplane symbolized the promise of the future.

As people around the world would soon find, that future was closer than most of them realized.

✔ CHECKPOINTS

Lesson 2 Review

Using complete sentences, answer the following questions on a sheet of paper.

1. What do historians give stunt pilots like Bessie Coleman credit for?

2. What happened to the US aircraft industry after World War I ended?

3. Who was Lincoln Beachey?

4. Who was the first woman appointed to a federal job in aviation?

5. What did wealthy aviation enthusiasts offer that advanced progress in flight?

6. What were Richard Byrd and his pilot the first to do?

7. What were the effects of the barnstormers' air shows?

8. According to author Joseph Corn, what did the airplane symbolize?

APPLYING YOUR LEARNING

9. Why do you think the barnstormers' air shows changed people's ideas about aviation?

Early Developments in Commercial Flight

Quick Write

_____

_____

Charles Lindbergh did not have modern navigation equipment or another pilot when he made his famous New York-to-Paris flight. After reading the story about his flight across the Atlantic Ocean, name three things that make this solo flight a historical accomplishment.

Learn About

- why Charles Lindbergh's contribution to aviation became famous
- the significance of Amelia Earhart's transatlantic flights
- how early developments benefited commercial aviation
- the consequences of the Airmail Act
- the introduction of passenger service in aviation
- the contributions of aircraft manufacturers to commercial aviation

CHARLES A. LINDBERGH was one of many young men and women learning to fly in 1922.

He toured as a wing walker and parachutist in a barnstorming act, and then as a pilot. He joined the Army in 1924 and graduated first in his flying class in 1925, but did not receive a regular commission. He joined the Army Reserve and returned to civilian life. He then spent a year as a pilot for the new airmail service.

In September 1926 he decided to try to fly across the Atlantic. He had his eye on the Orteig prize— $25,000 for the first pilot to fly solo nonstop from New York City to Paris, France.

Lindbergh knew that other pilots were after the same prize, so he moved fast. He had $2,000 of his own savings, plus $13,000 he'd collected from businessmen in St. Louis. He struck a deal with Ryan Aircraft Inc. to build him a plane. He wanted a high-wing monoplane with a single air-cooled 220-horsepower Wright Whirlwind engine.

Just 60 days after the contract was signed, Ryan delivered the aircraft. After a few weeks of test flights, Lindbergh was ready. He named the aircraft the *Spirit of St. Louis*, in honor of the men who had supported him.

On 10 May 1927, he flew nonstop from San Diego to St. Louis. After a brief stop, he flew on to New York City. He made it in 21 hours and 20 minutes of flying time. No one had ever flown across the country so fast.

He had set a record before he even took off for Paris. On 20 May, after waiting a while for the weather to clear, he took off from a rain-soaked runway at Roosevelt Field.

Lindbergh had no radio. He had only a compass to guide him as he flew above the stormy skies over the North Atlantic. And he was alone.

But 27 hours after taking off, he saw a promising sight: the green western edge of the British Isles. Circling low, he spotted some boats in the water. He leaned out of his plane and called down to the fishermen: "Which way is Ireland?"

He was on course. And he was ahead of schedule. He crossed the Irish Sea and the English Channel. Finally he entered the French skies.

He touched down 21 May 1927 at Le Bourget Airport outside Paris. He'd flown 3,600 miles in 33½ hours and won the Orteig prize.

Lindbergh's route across the North Atlantic

Why Charles Lindbergh's Contribution to Aviation Became Famous

In times past, travelers would often see big stones or slate tablets along the road. These stones marked the distance to the next town. These were called milestones.

Today people use the word milestone to describe *an important event, such as a breakthrough in the advancement of knowledge in a field.*

The Wright brothers' flight on 17 December 1903 was a milestone flight. So was Lindbergh's transatlantic solo flight, which opened the door to the daily international air travel we enjoy today. In the early 20th century, the golden age of aviation, such milestone flights came one after another.

Today, jumbo jets fly from New York to Paris in less than one-third the time Lindbergh took. But his flight—which demonstrated the potential of the airplane as a safe, reliable mode of transportation—still stands as one of the greatest individual achievements of all time.

The minute his plane touched down in Paris, Lindbergh became an international hero. Newspapers and magazines around the world reported on his achievement.

The barnstormers had built public interest in aviation by giving farmers five-minute spins over their cornfields. In July 1927, still piloting the *Spirit of St. Louis*, Lindbergh embarked on a tour of the country. A high-level kind of barnstorming, you might call it. In a little more than three months, he flew 22,350 miles back and forth across the United States. He made speeches in 72 cities. Lindbergh encouraged people to get pilot training.

The Spirit of St. Louis at the National Air and Space Museum in Washington, D.C.

Martha Dean/Shutterstock

His efforts to promote civil aviation led to the construction of hundreds of airports. He was a true goodwill ambassador for aviation.

In December Lindbergh capped off a historic year with a 3,200-mile all-American tour. He began with a nonstop flight from Washington, D.C., to Mexico City.

He then continued southward to a dozen other Latin American countries.

Over the next several years, Lindbergh and his wife, Anne Morrow Lindbergh, worked in civil aviation. They made survey flights to determine the best routes for new airlines.

Charles A. Lindbergh

Charles Lindbergh—"Lucky Lindy"—appeared to lead a charmed life in many ways, but his life was not without controversy or tragedy.

He and his wife suffered personal tragedy when their infant son was kidnapped and murdered in 1932. The case was one of the most sensational crimes of the first half of the 20th century. Weary of life in the public eye, the Lindberghs moved to England.

But Europe wasn't all that peaceful in the 1930s. War was brewing. Lindbergh assessed the strength of the air forces of different countries in Europe. As a result, he called for the United States and its Allies to make an agreement with the Germans that would end the war. He thought the Germans were too strong to defeat in battle.

Charles A. Lindbergh
Library of Congress, Prints and Photographs Division, George Grantham Bain Collection, ggbain 35317

Lindbergh returned to the United States in 1939 and made a survey for the War Department. He gave speeches for the America First Committee, a group that opposed the US entry into World War II. For this, some people branded him pro-Nazi, and he resigned his Army Reserve commission.

But in 1941, when the United States entered World War II, he offered his services to the Army Air Force. Later, he went on several missions as a civilian consultant to the Ford Motor Company and the United Aircraft Corporation. Although officially an "observer," he flew 50 combat missions during a tour of duty in the Pacific.

In 1954, President Eisenhower and the US Senate returned Lindbergh to the Air Force Reserve as a brigadier general. Lindbergh died in 1974.

Anne Morrow Lindbergh: Aviator and Writer

In 1927 Anne Morrow was in Mexico City when Charles Lindbergh showed up for Christmas dinner at her parents' house.

He was on the goodwill tour of Latin American countries that he made after his historic transatlantic flight. Anne's father, Dwight Morrow, was the US ambassador to Mexico. Lindbergh had stopped to spend the holiday with him and his family.

Anne and Charles fell in love, and in 1929 they married. They formed a remarkable partnership. She learned to fly. The sky was the one place they could be alone together, away from hero-worshipping crowds.

She referred to herself as "Charles's faithful page." Her husband said of her, "No woman exists or has existed who is her equal."

Anne Morrow Lindbergh
Library of Congress, cph 3a49159

As an aviator, Anne Lindbergh is best known for her 1931 flight to China via the "Great Circle Route." She accompanied her husband, serving as his copilot, navigator, and radio operator. The Lindberghs showed it was possible to reach Asia from the United States by flying over Canada and the North Pole, rather than across an ocean.

She wrote about the trip in a book called *North to the Orient*. Writing was a way for her to establish her own identity and to step out of her husband's shadow. She also wrote *Listen: The Wind* and *Gift from the Sea*. She lived until 2001.

The Significance of Amelia Earhart's Transatlantic Flights

Amelia Earhart also made two milestone flights across the Atlantic. The story of her achievement sheds light on the state of aviation at the time.

Lindbergh's historic solo crossing did not lead to routine air travel right away. Flying was still dangerous. In 1927, the year Lindbergh achieved fame, 19 men and women died in unsuccessful attempts to fly across the Atlantic.

Amelia Earhart was the first woman to fly across the Atlantic. But she went as a passenger, not a pilot. She'd had some flight training. But Earhart hadn't yet devoted her life to aviation.

In April 1928, however, aviator Wilmer Stultz asked her a favor. He and his navigator, Louis Gordon, wanted Earhart to accompany them as they crossed the Atlantic. They were seeking a prize offered by Pittsburgh heiress Amy Phipps Guest. She wanted to get a woman across the ocean in the air—even if only as a passenger.

The plane Stultz, Gordon, and Earhart flew was the *Friendship*—a Fokker C-2 trimotor with a gold and flame-red paint job. It was a long, cold, dangerous trip. They lost radio contact on the way. They had only a gallon of fuel left when they landed. And they landed in the wrong country—Wales instead of Ireland. But they made it across the Atlantic.

Stultz got a $20,000 award. Gordon got $5,000. Earhart received no money.

After all, she had gone along, as she later indicated in the title of her autobiography, "for the fun of it." But the flight was a great opportunity for her to be an apprentice— *a person who works with a skilled master to learn by practical experience.*

Stultz was one of the best pilots of that day. And Earhart, even though wedged between two gas tanks for most of the trip, didn't miss a thing. She watched every move Stultz made. She saw how he maneuvered through fog and storms. And she got it all down in her notebook.

The press hailed her as "Lady Lindy." Like Lindbergh, Earhart gained fame overnight. And like him, she toured the country.

But not everyone accepted Earhart as a hero. Some critics said she'd gotten a free ride. They said she'd depended on the luck and the skill of her male pilot. She struggled with self-doubt. But finally she proved her courage: she made more milestone flights. She set the altitude record for an autogiro, *an early, helicopter-like aircraft*, reaching 18,415 feet. Then she became the first woman, and second person, to make a transcontinental—*coast-to-coast*—flight in an autogiro.

But Earhart still wasn't content. For her, the milestone that mattered most was a solo crossing of the Atlantic. She wanted to be the first woman to do it.

On 20 May 1932 she took off in her Lockheed Vega from Harbour Grace, Newfoundland. It was the fifth anniversary of Lindbergh's famous flight.

Fifteen hours later, she touched down at a farm outside Londonderry in Northern Ireland. She had covered 2,065 miles, braving storms, heavy clouds, and strong winds. She had coped with iced-up wings, instrument problems, and a broken weld in the exhaust system.

But she made it. No free ride this time. She proved she was a skilled and brave aviator.

Earhart reached another milestone in 1935 as the first pilot to fly from Honolulu to Oakland, California. That trip took 18 hours and 16 minutes.

At that point, she felt the only goal left was a "true" round-the-world flight. Other pilots had flown around the world by that time. But they'd made their circuits in the northern hemisphere, where there is more land. A circuit is *a route that passes through one or more points and then returns to the starting point.* Pilots could make a circuit of the globe by "island hopping"—making periodic stops to refuel. Earhart's goal was to circle the globe as close as possible to the equator—*the imaginary circle that divides Earth into northern and southern halves.*

Earhart took off 2 June 1937. With her was copilot Frederick Noonan. All went well for 40 days. They racked up 22,000 miles. But on the longest leg of the trip, from Lae, New Guinea, to Howland Island in the Pacific, the plane disappeared. President Franklin D. Roosevelt ordered a massive search. It was not successful. On 18 July 1937, the US Navy declared Earhart and Noonan lost at sea.

The Right Stuff

Amelia Earhart: Aviation Pioneer

Amelia Earhart (1897–1937) is one of the most outstanding women in aviation. Had she lived longer, she probably would have accomplished even more. Sadly, she disappeared at the peak of her career.

She was born in Kansas. She learned to fly, but didn't have a clear career goal. She was a teacher and social worker in Massachusetts. She thought about becoming a doctor.

Amelia Earhart sitting in the cockpit of her Lockheed Electra, in which she disappeared in 1937

Everett Historical/Shutterstock

But after becoming the first woman to fly across the Atlantic, she knew what she wanted to do with her life: she wanted to be an aviator.

Earhart encouraged other women pilots. Like some other early aviators, she was also a writer. She published two books and even married her publisher, George Putnam, in 1931. She continued her career under her own name, however.

Earhart's disappearance during her around-the-world flight in 1937 remains one of the 20th century's great mysteries.

How Early Developments Benefited Commercial Aviation

If commercial airlines were to be a part of the nation's commerce and transportation, planes needed to be able to fly at night. They also had to be able to fly during fog and storms as well as in good weather. This problem had to be solved if aviation was to be part of the mainstream—*the current of most people's life and activities.*

This milestone was reached in a flight by 1st Lieutenant James Harold Doolittle on 24 September 1929. His was the first successful blind flight—*the act of taking off and landing relying solely on instruments inside the cockpit for guidance.* He took off, flew five miles, and landed safely—all without looking out of the plane. Because of his work, manufacturers started equipping planes with instruments and two-way radios.

Doolittle's blind flight built on the work of Sergeant William C. Ocker, the third enlisted man in the Army to become a pilot.

Ocker worked with Captain David A. Myers, the flight surgeon at Crissy Field, California, to solve the problem of spatial disorientation. Spatial disorientation is *a condition in which a person's sense of direction does not agree with reality.*

A pilot who is spatially disoriented literally doesn't know which end is up. In the early days, even experienced pilots could get confused when visibility was poor. They sometimes thought they were banking left when they were banking right. This happened because they'd lost sight of the horizon, which they used to orient themselves.

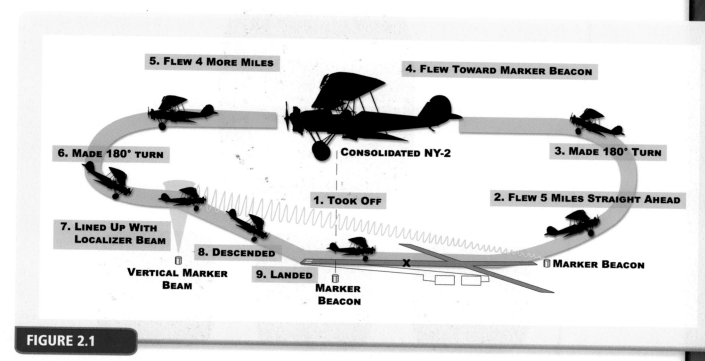

FIGURE 2.1

1st Lieutenant Doolittle's Blind Flight Route

Ocker knew about spatial disorientation. He'd struggled with it himself. For years he had used a turn-and-bank indicator, a device created by his friend Elmer Sperry, to help him stay oriented while flying. But the device never seemed to work in bad weather. At such times, it often gave a reading at odds with what Ocker's instincts were telling him.

Ocker's "lightbulb" moment came when he realized that the times when the indicator seemed wrong were exactly the times when he needed it most. When he was disoriented, the indicator was correct.

Ocker failed an orientation test when Captain Myers spun him around in a special chair designed to simulate the conditions that gave pilots so much trouble.

But Ocker passed when he brought along and used his trusty turn-and-bank indicator.

Many early pilots took pride in their ability to "fly by the seat of their pants." But Ocker and Myers realized that pilots of the future would have to rely more heavily on instruments. Their work led to Doolittle's successful blind flight.

Ocker developed a number of devices that became critical to pilot training and aviation in general. These inventions are forerunners of today's flight simulators. A flight simulator is *a training device that simulates, or imitates, the experience and sensation of flight.* It lets pilots train without having to go up in the air.

FIGURE 2.2

A Turn and Bank Indicator in Three Different Turning Positions

Ivsanmas)/Shutterstock

CHAPTER 2   Developing Flight

Lieutenant General James "Jimmy" Doolittle: Versatile Aviator

Lieutenant General James Harold "Jimmy" Doolittle (1896–1993) was one of the most versatile figures in American aviation. Despite his name, this famous aviator could do just about anything.

He was born in Alameda, California. He attended the University of California and the Massachusetts Institute of Technology. He got flight training during World War I.

He made the first successful blind takeoff and landing in 1929. He left the Army Air Corps in 1930 and entered private business. But first and foremost a Soldier, he returned to the Air Corps in 1940.

Early in WW II, Doolittle led a surprise raid on Tokyo, Japan's capital, on 18 April 1942. It involved 16 twin-engine B-25 bombers. For this daring raid, the planes took off from the aircraft carrier USS *Hornet*. He won the Medal of Honor for his role in this raid.

Later, he served in North Africa and Europe. He became a lieutenant general in 1944. When the war ended in 1945, he returned to private business. In 1989, President Ronald Reagan awarded him a Presidential Medal of Freedom.

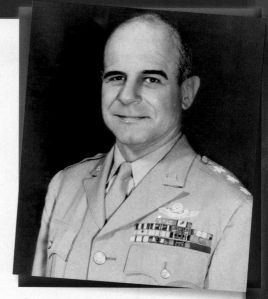

Lieutenant General James Doolittle
Courtesy US Air Force

The Right Stuff

Katherine Sui Fun Cheung: First Asian-American Woman Pilot

Katherine Sui Fung Cheung (1904–2003) left China at 17 to study music in Los Angeles. At age 26, she started flying lessons. She made her first solo flight after only 12$\frac{1}{2}$ hours of instruction. She became the first licensed Asian-American woman pilot in the United States. A member of the exclusive "Ninety-Nines" club—an organization of 99 women pilots, such as Amelia Earhart and Phoebe Fairgrave Omlie, who worked to further women's interest in aviation and aviation in general—she took part in air shows and air races. (The Ninety-Nines organization continues today.) Cheung amazed crowds with her rolls and loops in the air. Cheung planned to go to China to train pilots there. But a tragic crash that killed her cousin ended those plans. At 38, she promised her dying father she would give up flying. She kept her promise and in later years went into the flower business.

Katherine Sui Fun Cheung
Credit: Los Angeles Public Library

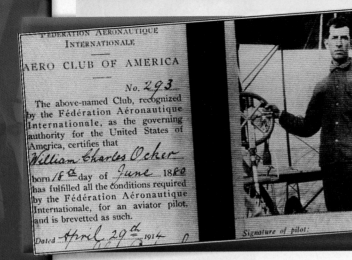

William C. Ocker's pilot's license
Courtesy US Air Force Enlisted Heritage Hall

Sergeant William C. Ocker: A Flying Hero Moves Up Through the Ranks

When William Charles Ocker enlisted in the US Army in 1898, most Soldiers were still on the ground. Ocker helped give the Army wings.

He became an excellent pilot. When he took the test for his license, the examiner wrote, "It was the most remarkable series of landings ever made by a student flying for a pilot's license. Ocker's mastery of the machine was superb...." He got his license on 29 April 1914.

But his great achievements were in laying the foundation for blind flight and developing testing and training equipment.

Ocker was born in Philadelphia. He left school at the end of seventh grade. He enlisted during the Spanish-American War. He saw action in that conflict and the Philippine Insurrection as well.

On guard duty in Fort Myer, Virginia, in 1909, he'd seen the Wright brothers demonstrate their aircraft. From then on, he knew he wanted to fly. He became the third enlisted man allowed to serve as a pilot.

Later Ocker became an officer. Among his many aviation inventions was the 1938 development of a new type of airplane propeller that made less noise and vibrated less. This meant less stress on the propeller blades.

His ambition, he often said, was to be not the best pilot, but the oldest pilot. He was indeed one of the oldest pilots in time of service in the Army Air Corps. He retired as a colonel and died in 1942 at age 62. His contributions to aviation safety helped countless aviators live longer, saving many lives during World War II. In 1955, the Air Force presented the Legion of Merit medal to his widow, Doris Ocker.

Sergeant Ocker in full dress uniform
Courtesy US Air Force Enlisted Heritage Hall

The First Air Refueling of the *Question Mark*

Another hurdle to mainstream aviation was providing enough fuel for long-distance runs. Pilots needed a system for aerial refueling, which is *taking on more fuel in flight*. Two Army lieutenants, 1st Lieutenant Lowell H. Smith and 1st Lieutenant J. P. Richter, achieved this in 1923. They tanked up by running a 50-foot hose from a supply aircraft to a plane making a long trip. They could pump about 50 gallons of fuel each time. They were able to stay aloft for 37 hours and 15 minutes.

On New Year's Day 1929, Major Carl Spaatz took off in the *Question Mark*, a Fokker C-2 Trimotor. By the time he landed—almost a week later—he had set an endurance record. Spaatz and his crew—Captain Ira C. Eaker, 1st Lieutenant Harry Halverson, 2nd Lieutenant Elwood R. Quesada, and Staff Sergeant Roy W. Hooe—stayed up 150 hours, 40 minutes, and 15 seconds. They had refueled 37 times.

Two Douglas C-1 aircraft, each with a three-man crew, provided the fuel for the *Question Mark*. Captain Ross G. Hoyt, 1st Lieutenant Auby C. Strickland, and 2nd Lieutenant Irvin A. Woodring served as one tanker crew. Members of the second crew were 1st Lieutenant Odas Moon, 2nd Lieutenant Andrew F. Solter, and 2nd Lieutenant Joseph G. Hopkins. Their feat demonstrated the practicality of in-flight refueling.

Refueling the *Question Mark*, 4 January 1929
Courtesy US Air Force

The Consequences of the Airmail Act

Aerial refueling was important for the Army. But other, everyday things brought aviation into the mainstream for most Americans. Two of the most important were airmail service and the birth of commercial airlines.

The Post Office Department started the first airmail service on 15 May 1918. It used a few planes borrowed from the Army. Regular airmail service started 1 July 1924.

Airmail not only sped up mail delivery—it contributed a great deal to the development of the airlines. The Airmail Act of 1925—also known as the Kelly Act—allowed private companies to carry mail under contract with the US government. This was a big boost for the aviation industry. Government contracts ensured a steady flow of money to the new airlines. In fact, the money from carrying the mail was so good for the airlines that their planes often had hardly any room for people. Most mail planes carried only two or three passengers.

Lighting the Way for the Mail

THE FIRST AIRMAIL PILOTS in the 1920s had a tough job. They flew in rebuilt warplanes with open cockpits. They flew through rain, fog, and high winds. They had no radios, weather stations, instruments, or beacons.

A rotating light beacon
Julie DeGuia/Shutterstock

One of the most important early airmail routes went between New York and Chicago. These planes flew over the Allegheny Mountains. The route was so dangerous that pilots called it "the graveyard run."

What's more, the airmail service wasn't holding its own against the railroads. The trains, after all, rolled on day and night. To meet the competition, postal authorities introduced night flights.

At first, Post Office staff, farmers, and other people built bonfires to light the pilots' way at night. Then came electric beacons. These were powerful rotating lights mounted on 50-foot towers. Towers were built every 10 to 15 miles along a cross-country route. Emergency landing fields were built about every 30 miles. Lights for landing and navigation were soon added to planes as another safety feature.

The government launched regular airmail service on 1 July 1924. At that time, the United States had the world's first regular night service on a lighted airway. The route ran between New York City and the West Coast. From this "trunk" airway, branch lines grew all over the country. This was another major advance in aviation.

That changed with the passage of the Air Commerce Act on 20 May 1926. The act provided for the first federal safety regulation of aviation for pilots and aircraft. It also sparked the growth of commercial airlines.

In 1930 Postmaster General Arthur F. Brown got Congress to pass the McNary-Watres Act. This act was an amendment—*a revision or change*—to the Air Mail Act of 1925. The McNary-Watres Act led to United Airline's contract to build the Boeing B-247 and other aircraft. Such contracts played an important role in air service across the seas as well. The seaplanes Pan Am needed to fly the mail over water led to regular passenger service across the Atlantic and Pacific oceans. The act also encouraged airlines to fly bigger planes that held more passengers.

The Introduction of Passenger Service in Aviation

It took a while before the advantages of air travel would overcome the disadvantages of passenger discomfort, bad weather, and cost. The first scheduled airline flight in the United States took place in 1914 between Tampa and St. Petersburg, Florida. In Europe, passenger service began in Germany in 1919 and was soon followed by French flights between Paris and London.

In the 1920s, an air traveler might find himself (or less often herself) one of five passengers in an enclosed, unheated cabin. The noise of the engines was deafening. The ride was bumpy as the plane flew through turbulence, and sometimes pilots had to fly at treetop level to get under a cloud or avoid getting lost.

By the end of the decade, however, Charles Lindbergh's vision of civil aviation was taking form in the United States. Within a year of his 1927 flight, the number of licensed pilots in the country grew from 1,500 to 11,000. The number of licensed planes also rose sharply. Building and flying airplanes became the country's most profitable business. By 1929 there were 44 scheduled airlines. These are *airlines that have flights that depart and arrive at set times*. The number of airline passengers grew from 6,000 in 1926 to 173,000 three years later.

Competing for passengers, who worried about comfort and safety, the airlines worked with aircraft companies to build them better and better planes. But these planes couldn't fly higher than 10,000 feet, because there was not enough oxygen at higher altitudes. At that level, aircraft also encountered more storms and turbulence. This would be a problem until 1940, when Boeing introduced the 307 Stratoliner, which had the first pressurized cabin and could fly at 20,000 feet.

In 1926, the first male stewards appeared on flights between Detroit and Chicago to attend to passengers and to load luggage. Then on 15 May 1930, Boeing Air Transport introduced the first female flight attendants—then called *stewardesses*. Nurse Ellen Church convinced Boeing that nurses were best able to care for passengers. So at first these women were nurses—they even wore nurses' uniforms in flight. A stewardess had to be shorter than 5 feet, 4 inches tall, and single. She couldn't weigh more than 118 pounds and had to be between the ages of 20 and 26.

Government regulation of aviation developed along with the new industry. Until 1938, several government agencies were involved in making the rules for aviation. In that year, Congress passed the Civil Aviation Act, which created the Civil Aeronautics Authority. The new agency had the power to decide on airline fares, airmail rates, airline routes, mergers, and cooperation between airlines. Congress created a separate agency, the Air Safety Board, to investigate air accidents. In 1940 the two boards were merged into the Civil Aeronautics Board.

This improved regulation and improvements in technology made the airline industry safer and more stable and ensured its financial success. The number of airline passengers grew from 474,000 in 1932 to 1,176,858 in 1938. But even this was only 7.6 percent of the number of passengers who traveled by long-distance train. It would be many years before more Americans traveled by air than by train.

The Contributions of Aircraft Manufacturers to Commercial Aviation

As you read in the previous lesson, many aircraft companies fell on hard times when the government canceled their contracts at the end of World War I. William Boeing owned one such company. Despite the setback, he saw a future in aviation. He kept his company going. As a result, Boeing was in a good position when the government began to support aviation again.

The opportunity came in the form of the new airmail service. When the government decided to let private firms carry the mail, new companies sprang up to do the job. To help these firms, the government offered subsidies. A subsidy is *government money paid to a person or company that serves the public.*

When the government began to support passenger service, too, new rules gave airlines an incentive—*a motivating reward*—to fly larger planes with more passenger space. The rules also encouraged the use of planes that could fly in all types of weather.

The Boeing 247

United Air Lines, National Air and Space Museum, Smithsonian Institution, NASM-14082

Soon Boeing Air Transport won a contract to build a two-engine aircraft for United Airlines. In 1933 Boeing rolled out the Boeing 247.

The Boeing 247 was the first all-metal airliner. Its wings were placed low on the plane's body. It had a stressed skin—*an outer covering that can stand up to the push-and-pull forces of flight.* Its landing gear was retractable—it *folded into the aircraft.* Each of its two engines had a cowling—*a covering to protect and streamline the engine.*

The B-247 could carry 10 passengers and 400 pounds of mail. It could cruise at 189 miles an hour (mph). "Same-day" service between New York and San Francisco was now possible. Modern airline service had begun.

Shortly after United introduced the B-247, a second airline got into the act. Transcontinental and Western Airlines (TWA) signed a contract with Douglas Aircraft of Santa Monica, California, to build an even bigger plane. The result was the Douglas Commercial-2, or DC-2. It came out in May 1934. It cruised at 192 mph. It could carry 14 passengers and several thousand pounds of mail up to 900 miles.

The C-47—the government ordered 10,000 of these planes during World War II.
Courtesy US Air Force

Meanwhile, a third airline—American Airways—was flying foreign-built aircraft. American was also losing money. It asked Douglas Aircraft to improve on the DC-2.

The result was the DC-3. The DC-3 could carry 24 passengers, or 5,000 pounds of cargo, a distance of 1,200 miles. American Airways rolled out the first DC-3 in June 1936. Douglas added soundproofing and upholstered seats to greatly reduce noise and vibration. The DC-3 became one of the most successful planes ever built. By 1939 it was carrying at least 75 percent of all commercial traffic.

Later, during World War II, Douglas developed a military version of the DC-3—the C-47. Douglas built some 10,000 of these planes for the Army Air Force. The C-47's official name was the Skytrain. But pilots called it the Gooney Bird. ("Gooney bird" is another name for albatross, a large sea bird. Albatrosses are superb fliers. They can fly long distances without tiring.) Some C-47s are still in use.

Another important advance was Pan American Airways' seaplane Clippers. The Clippers came to represent a way of traveling in style and luxury. But they also marked a major step forward in aircraft development.

Pan Am started out in 1927. It flew the first airmail route between Key West, Florida, and Havana, Cuba. In time the route extended down the Atlantic coast of South America.

Pan Am pilots soon found themselves flying over water more often than over land. And in remote areas, seaplane bases were easier to build than land airports for ordinary airplanes.

So Pan Am decided that the kind of "bigger and better" plane it needed was an advanced seaplane. The company hired Igor Sikorsky, who had designed *Le Grand*. (He later won fame for helicopter design.) Sikorsky designed a four-engine "flying boat"—the S-40. It could fly 125 mph and carry 40 passengers. Pan Am used the S-42, a successor to the S-40, for survey flights to find routes across the Pacific.

Other airplane makers got into the flying-boat business. In 1934 Pan Am received a larger boat, the Martin 130, built by the Glenn L. Martin Company. The airline called it the *China Clipper*. On 29 November 1935, the *China Clipper* completed the first airmail flight between San Francisco and Manila, in the Philippines. By 1937 the route went all the way to Hong Kong. By that time, Pan Am was flying a round trip across the Pacific every seven days.

Regular passenger and airmail service across the Atlantic began on 20 May 1939 with the Boeing 314. Many considered this the "ultimate flying boat."

There were only about two dozen seaplane Clippers. But they defined an era in air travel. They had an excellent safety record during their six and a half years in service. Pan Am used the name *Clipper* for other aircraft until the company went out of business in 1991. The name of its famous aircraft lives on because some other companies have adopted it.

The era of passenger-carrying seaplanes was short. During World War II, aircraft design made great strides. Four-engine land planes improved. New runways appeared around the world. As a result, seaplanes lost their competitive edge.

They gave way to new types of land-based aircraft.

Pan American Airways *China Clipper* over Oakland, California, in 1936
Everett Historical/Shutterstock

William E. Boeing

Unlike most other pioneers of flight, William E. Boeing came to aviation as a businessman. He was the son of a wealthy Detroit businessman.

He left Yale University in 1903 to start a timber business in the Pacific Northwest.

A few years later, Boeing saw a public exhibition of flying in Los Angeles. He became fascinated with aviation. He made his first flight in 1914. He decided he wanted to build his own planes. He thought he could build better planes than those in use at the time.

He hired his friend George Conrad Westervelt, an engineer, to design and build a twin-float seaplane. A twin-float is *an airplane with floats for landing on or taking off from a body of water.*

It was a success. Boeing launched the Boeing Airplane Company, later called Boeing Air Transport. In 1917 he sold the US Navy 50 of his Model C seaplanes for use in World War I.

Like other airplane builders, Boeing lost his government contracts at the end of the war. He kept his business going by making furniture, cabinets, and boats.

But Boeing didn't lose interest in aircraft. Soon he built the Boeing-1, or B-1, a commercial biplane. On 3 March 1919, he and his pilot, Eddie Hubbard, opened the first international airmail route. They flew between Seattle, Washington, and Vancouver, British Columbia. A one-way trip was 140 miles.

Soon Boeing won the contract for the San Francisco–Chicago airmail route. He served the route with a Boeing 40-A mail plane. Air, not water, kept the plane's engine cool. This made the plane hundreds of pounds lighter. Boeing 40-As, he said, were designed to carry mail and people, not radiators.

In 1934 Congress made it illegal for airmail carriers and aircraft builders to be part of the same company. Boeing had to break up his firm. But his reputation was assured. In that same year, he won the Guggenheim Medal for his contributions to aviation.

✔ CHECKPOINTS

Lesson 3 Review

Using complete sentences, answer the following questions on a sheet of paper.

1. Charles Lindbergh's transatlantic solo flight opened the door to what?

2. What was the name of Lindbergh's plane?

3. What milestone did Amelia Earhart achieve on the five-year anniversary of Lindbergh's record?

4. What happened to Amelia Earhart?

5. Who made the first successful blind flight?

6. What happened when a pilot lost sight of the horizon?

7. Besides speeding up mail delivery, what was the other contribution of airmail service?

8. What was the McNary-Watres Act?

9. Why couldn't early passenger planes fly higher than 10,000 feet?

10. In what year did Congress pass the Civil Aviation Act?

11. What was the Boeing 247?

12. How many Pan Am Clipper seaplanes were there?

APPLYING YOUR LEARNING

13. What were the roles of heroes such as Lindbergh and Earhart in developing aviation? What was the role of the US government?

Artist's rendering of P-51B Mustangs in aerial combat
Tomas Picka/Shutterstock

The Evolution of the Early Air Force

Chapter Outline

> " Allied Air power was decisive in the war in Western Europe.... In the air, its victory was complete. At sea, its contribution, combined with naval power, brought an end to the enemy's greatest naval threat—the U-boat; on land, it helped turn the tide overwhelmingly in favor of Allied ground forces. "
>
> The United States Strategic Bombing Survey, 1945

The Army Air Corps

Quick Write

_____

_____

The Army, Navy, and Congress were reluctant to create an equal branch of the military dedicated to airpower. After reading the story about Brigadier General Billy Mitchell, explain how he drew attention to airpower's potential.

Learn About

- the creation of the Army Air Service
- the creation of the Army Air Corps
- the growth of the Army Air Corps
- significant developments concerning the Army Air Corps
- the rationale of advocates for an independent Air Force
- the rationale of objectors to an independent Air Force
- the creation of a separate Air Corps Headquarters

AFTER WORLD WAR I Brigadier General William "Billy" Mitchell wanted to find a way to get military leaders and the US Congress to pay attention to his calls for an independent air service. He'd seen how airpower helped turn the war in the Allies' favor. This included the major role of aircraft in the Battle of Saint Mihiel in 1918.

Airpower was emerging as an offensive weapon and a powerful defensive tool. Mitchell thought the Army Air Service ought to be under its own command. But the Army, Navy, and Congress saw things differently. To them, airpower was auxiliary— *functioning as a branch of another military organization*—to the Army's ground forces. In their view, aircraft played secondary roles. For example, they thought the role of aircraft was to provide reconnaissance and ground-troop support, not to lead attacks.

In 1920 Mitchell proposed a test to challenge prevailing notions about the country's defense. He suggested that his Airmen sink ships. (At that time the Navy's battle fleet was America's first line of defense.) The test would show how planes could defend the country against an attack from the sea.

In 1921 the Navy reluctantly agreed to the test. It provided several German vessels captured during World War I. One of the ships was the "unsinkable" battleship *Ostfriesland*.

On 13 July Mitchell's pilots sank a destroyer off the coast of Virginia with light bombs. On 18 July they hit a cruiser. It went under, too. They tried to sink the *Ostfriesland*, but even 1,000-pound bombs couldn't do the job. So on 21 July the pilots dropped 2,000-pound bombs. The "unsinkable" battleship rolled over and sank in about 20 minutes. But the Army and Congress still weren't convinced. They didn't believe an independent air service could help the armed forces.

Navy admirals disagreed, however. They immediately ordered that aircraft carriers be built. The United States had its first aircraft carrier within eight months of the *Ostfriesland*'s sinking.

Vocabulary

- auxiliary
- grades
- ordnance
- incompetent
- treasonable
- insubordination
- bombsight
- overhaul
- corps
- pursuit aircraft
- annex
- logistics
- autonomy

Brigadier General Billy Mitchell's pilots bomb the captured German battleship *Ostfriesland*.
Courtesy US Air Force Enlisted Heritage Hall

The Creation of the Army Air Service

Most changes come in small steps. So airpower in the United States went through a number of makeovers. The major changes occurred between 1907 and 1947, a stormy period that saw the flowering of aviation and two world wars.

Even before the US government bought the *Wright Flyer* in 1909, it had set up the Aeronautical Division within the US Army Signal Corps. The Signal Corps started with balloons, and then added planes. The division existed from 1907 to 1914. Many consider its creation the birth of the US Air Force.

Next came the Aviation Section, US Army Signal Corps (1914 to 1918). It was up and running during World War I. The number of pilots grew to 10,000 by the end of the war. These pilots took on many roles. They went on reconnaissance missions after the United States joined the war in 1917. By 1918 they were taking part in dogfights and bombing runs.

One of the first major steps toward an independent air service took place around the time the Great War ended. President Woodrow Wilson used his executive powers to create the Army Air Service in May 1918. Under this order, the Air Service became a combat arm of the Army. The Army Air Service existed between 1918 and 1926. Although it was still part of the Army, it was a step closer to separate-but-equal footing with the Army and Navy.

President Woodrow Wilson
Everett Historical/Shutterstock

With the Army Reorganization Act of 1920, Congress wrote the change into law. The Army Air Service was no longer auxiliary to the ground forces. It was its own branch within the Army. This change gave the Air Service more control. But it still answered to the Army.

The National Defense Act, also passed in 1920, established the number of men and ranks in the Air Service. Today's Air Force still uses the grades— *ranks*— authorized under that act. The service could have 16,000 enlisted men. But Congress had cut back on defense spending after World War I. So the Air Service didn't have enough funds to enlist 16,000 men.

TABLE 3.1 The Different Stages of the US Air Arm From 1907 to Present

Air Arm	Date
Aeronautical Division, US Army Signal Corps	1 August 1907–18 July 1914
Aviation Section, US Army Signal Corps	18 July 1914–20 May 1918
Division of Military Aeronautics, Secretary of War	20 May 1918–24 May 1918
Army Air Service	24 May 1918–2 July 1926
Army Air Corps, General HQ Air Force	2 July 1926–17 September 1947 1 March 1935–1 March 1939
US Army Air Forces	20 June 1941–17 September 1947
US Air Force	18 September 1947–Present

The Creation of the Army Air Corps

With funds in short supply after the war, the Army was tightfisted in how much money it passed along to its air arm. This only increased the Air Service's desire for separate-but-equal footing with the Army and Navy.

Brigadier General Billy Mitchell believed that airpower would be crucial to winning any future wars or to defending American soil. He believed it would be easier to direct airpower if the Air Service were equal in stature to the Army and Navy. An independent service would also get a larger share of government money.

The US Department of War, which oversaw the Army, disagreed with Mitchell. It believed in a three-pronged national defense based on:

1. the Navy's battle fleet,

2. the Navy's coastal defenses, and

3. the Army's coastal defenses.

But based on what he'd seen in Europe during 1917 and 1918, Mitchell believed airpower was a necessary tool. First, casualties from trench warfare would decrease if bombers could cross enemy lines to hit supply routes and factories. Soldiers would no longer be stuck in one place. They would no longer die in waves of assaults.

M·I·L·E·S·T·O·N·E·S

Enlisted Men After the Great War

At the end of World War I, the Army Air Service had 195,000 enlisted men. Of these, 74,000 were overseas. What would these men do once the fighting stopped? The Army worked with the government to find jobs for some. In other cases, commanders wrote letters of recommendation for their enlistees. For instance, they would do this for their mechanics. They kept other Airmen in the service, even after discharge, until they could find work.

Second, as the Battle of Saint Mihiel showed, a mass of aircraft could overwhelm the enemy and bring the battle to him. Finally, planes could now carry heavier loads and fly greater distances. Before long, the Atlantic and Pacific oceans would no longer guarantee safety for the US coasts. Mitchell thought US airpower could thwart an enemy arriving by sea better than sea power could. So he launched a major public relations campaign for an air force independent of the Army and Navy.

Demonstrations to Support Independence

Mitchell's biggest, splashiest campaign maneuver was the sinking of the German battleship *Ostfriesland* in 1921. Although that event convinced the Navy to build aircraft carriers, not much else happened after that. So Mitchell tried new tactics. His goal was to draw the public's attention to the wonders of flight. If he got the public eye, he thought, people might ask their members of Congress to support airpower.

In 1922 Mitchell arranged for two pilots, 1st Lieutenant Oakley Kelly and 1st Lieutenant John Macready to fly nonstop across the United States. Their first two tries didn't succeed. They finally made it on the third try, in 1923. Kelly and Macready flew from New York to San Diego in 26 hours and 50 minutes. The flight was 2,520 miles long. Their Fokker T-2 aircraft had a 400-horsepower engine. They took advantage of a tailwind during the flight. Plus, they calculated that having little fuel left by the end of their voyage, and therefore less weight, would help them cross the Rocky Mountains.

The Douglas World Cruiser airplane *Chicago* at Hong Kong during its round-the-world trip

Edward Royden Carter, Sr., National Air and Space Museum, Smithsonian Institution, ID 2002-0053

In 1924 Mitchell tried an even bigger stunt—an around-the-world trip. He started out with four airplanes. Two of them—the *Chicago* and the *New Orleans*—finished the 26,345-mile journey. The trip took 175 days. The pilots visited cities around the globe, starting and finishing in Seattle, Washington. Also in 1924, Mitchell sent 1st Lieutenant Russell Maughan in a Curtiss PW-8 from New York to San Francisco. To people's astonishment, Maughan finished the trip in a single day. This showed that if the country were attacked, airplanes could fly in one day to defend the area under attack.

In 1923 Mitchell conducted a second series of bombing tests against ships. This time, the Navy let him use two World War I battleships, the USS *New Jersey* and the USS *Virginia*. Ten of Mitchell's 11 bombers missed the *New Jersey*. But one pilot, Sergeant Ulysses S. Nero, had two hits. Mitchell wouldn't let Nero continue, because the pilot hadn't followed instructions. But when the other pilots couldn't sink the ships, Mitchell gave him another chance.

The USS *New Jersey* after Sergeant Ulysses Nero's hit on 5 September 1923
Courtesy US Air Force Enlisted Heritage Hall

From 6,900 feet in the air at 85 miles per hour, Nero released his first ordnance through the New Jersey's smokestack. Ordnance is *military supply such as weapons, ammunition, combat vehicles, and equipment.* The ship sank. Next he dropped a bomb on the deck of the Virginia. It, too, sank to the bottom of North Carolina's coastal waters.

Mitchell pushed in other ways for an independent air force. He gave talks. He wrote articles. Meanwhile, the US House of Representatives and the Army General Staff formed committees to study possible directions for the Army Air Service.

In 1925 President Calvin Coolidge instructed a group of experts to find the "best means of developing and applying aircraft in national defense." This group, the Morrow Board, made three proposals:

1. Rename the Army Air Service the Army Air Corps.

2. Give the Army Air Corps a seat on the Army General Staff.

3. Appoint an assistant secretary of war for airpower.

Congress adopted these recommendations. The Air Corps Act became law on 2 July 1926.

President Calvin Coolidge
Everett Historical/Shutterstock

Brigadier General Billy Mitchell's Stamp on Airpower

Brigadier General William "Billy" Mitchell (1879–1936) was a controversial figure in US airpower. He played a vital role in the creation of the US Air Force. He believed the bomber should be a key weapon of warfare. He thought it could bring the battle to the enemy and shorten wars.

Brigadier General Billy Mitchell in 1922
Courtesy US Air Force Enlisted Heritage Hall

Mitchell got off to a great start in life. He was the son of a US senator from Wisconsin. In 1895 he entered George Washington University in Washington, D.C. He was only 16 and the youngest student at that time to enter that school. By age 18, he was a second lieutenant in the Wisconsin Volunteers. At 19, he was promoted to first lieutenant. By 23, he was a captain in the US Army.

Mitchell graduated from the Army Staff College in 1909. At age 32 he was assigned to the Army General Staff. The General Staff oversees the Army and makes any decisions on major policy changes. Mitchell was the youngest person ever posted to it.

During World War I Mitchell was chief of the Air Service for American forces in Europe. Experience in battle helped persuade him of airpower's great possibilities. The battles also convinced him that the air arm needed its independence.

After World War I Mitchell was named deputy chief of the Air Service. During those years, he conducted bombing tests such as the one against the *Ostfriesland*. He also spoke publicly and wrote about the need for a separate air force.

But in 1925 Mitchell got into trouble. He harshly criticized senior officers in the military. A Navy plane had recently disappeared during a flight to Hawaii. And a Navy dirigible had crashed, killing 13 crew members. Referring to these events, Mitchell said, "The high command of both the Army and the Navy are guilty of incompetency, criminal negligence, and almost treasonable administration of the national defense." Someone who is incompetent is *lacking the qualities needed for effective action*. A treasonable act is one that *involves a violation of allegiance towards one's country*.

Because he so openly criticized military officers, Mitchell was court-martialed for insubordination under the 96th Article of War. This article forbids "all conduct of a nature to bring discredit upon the military service." Insubordination is *a refusal to submit to authority*.

Mitchell was convicted. Rather than face a five-year suspension, he resigned from service in 1926. But he continued to speak for an independent air force. Unfortunately, Mitchell died in 1936. He never got to see the advent of powerful bombers such as the B-17 that played crucial roles in World War II.

In 1946, 10 years after Mitchell's death, Congress awarded him the Medal of Honor. The award recognized his insightful airpower theories.

Mitchell and Pearl Harbor

Some people are not only smart. They're also imaginative. They can put what they know in a new perspective. Brigadier General Mitchell was such a person. He predicted, as early as 1924, the Japanese attack on Pearl Harbor.

Mitchell visited Japan in 1924. He noticed the country seemed bent on expanding its territories. He wasn't sure when that would be. But he figured if Japan went to war to expand its influence in the Pacific, it would attack US bases in Hawaii and the Philippines from the air and sea. He wrote:

> Attack will be launched as follows: Bombardment, attack to be made on Ford Island [at Pearl Harbor in Hawaii] at 7:30 a.m.... Attack to be made on Clark Field [in the Philippines] at 10:40 a.m.

Seventeen years later, on 7 December 1941, the Japanese attacked Pearl Harbor in Hawaii. They struck Ford Island at 7:55 a.m. They hit Clark Field at 12:35 p.m.

Colonel Ulysses S. Nero:
Bombardier, Inventor, Engineer

Colonel Ulysses S. Nero (1898–1980) spent most of his career in the US military. He was an intelligent, confident, yet modest, man. His family sent him to work in a shipyard when he was 14. He completed high school at age 15 by taking night classes.

Nero enlisted in the US Army in 1917 as a private. He retired in 1952 as a colonel. In between, he served in World War I, World War II, and the Korean War. His contributions to the military were extraordinary. They included 12 patents for military equipment.

Nero's adventure in the military began in the Army's 13th Cavalry. His unit performed the US military's last horse-cavalry mission. It pushed Mexican bandit Pancho Villa back to his homeland. (In late 1917 artillery units replaced horse cavalry.)

Ulysses S. Nero in the 13th Cavalry, I Troop, Fort Riley, Kansas, in 1917

Courtesy US Air Force Enlisted Heritage Hall

Ulysses S. Nero as an officer (around 1942–1951)

Courtesy US Air Force Enlisted Heritage Hall

Nero then transferred to the US Army Signal Corps. He served in France in the Great War. He joined the Aviation Section of the Signal Corps in 1918, the same year it became the Army Air Service. In 1919, he returned to civilian life. But he felt he could do better in the military. So he reenlisted in 1921.

Nero became an expert bombardier. He made two important advances during his early years with the Air Service. In 1922 he invented a wireless means for pilots and ground crews to communicate. This brought him to the attention of Brigadier General Mitchell. Second, Nero invented a bombsight—*a device that helps determine when to drop a bomb*—that let bombardiers place their loads more accurately. He dropped nearly 10,000 bombs while running tests at the Aberdeen Proving Grounds in Maryland.

In 1923 Nero sank the USS *New Jersey* and the USS *Virginia* during tests arranged by Mitchell. This led Mitchell to promote him. The two men became good friends.

Over the next 30 years or so, Nero developed more inventions. For example, he designed bomb fuses. He entered World War II as a master sergeant and became well known, not only for his combat skills, but also for his ability to maintain aircraft. During the Korean War, he was the first to overhaul a jet engine. To overhaul is *to go over carefully and make needed repairs*.

Many people today call Nero the "father of US Air Force precision bombing."

The Growth of the Army Air Corps

Changing the name of the Army Air Service to Army Air Corps was significant. It boosted the idea that the air arm was no longer only in "service" to ground troops. The corps could conduct independent missions. A corps is *a branch or department of the armed forces having a specialized function.*

The Army Air Corps wouldn't gain full independence for another 21 years, however. It got off to a slow start for several reasons. First, many people felt that World War I was the "war to end all wars." They thought the world would never again fight such an all-out battle. As a result, Congress drastically reduced defense spending. Most Airmen returned to civilian life. Furthermore, when the Great Depression hit in 1929, many countries found it difficult to fund military projects.

But important changes would soon take place. By the late 1930s many people feared that war was about to break out in Europe. This helped lead to a growth spurt in the Air Corps. In addition, the years between World War I and World War II saw major advances in bombers and pursuit aircraft, or *fighter planes.*

The fear of war was well founded. The Nazi Party came to power in Germany in 1933. It began a campaign to build up Germany's armed forces. War shadows grew longer in Europe during 1938. Germany annexed Austria that year. To annex is *to incorporate territory into an existing political unit such as a country.* Austria didn't resist when German troops marched across its borders. Meanwhile, Germany's allies, known as the Axis Powers, were active, too. Italy waged war in Africa, and Japan had invaded China.

On 12 January 1939, President Franklin D. Roosevelt spoke to Congress about the need to rebuild the US military. US forces, he said, were "utterly inadequate." Three months later, Congress approved increasing the number of Army Air Corps pilot officers from 1,200 to 3,203.

Civilian Flight Schools

Meanwhile, the chief of the Air Corps, Major General Henry "Hap" Arnold, knew the corps didn't have the facilities to train more than 550 pilots a year. If a second world war broke out, the United States would need to train thousands of pilots a year—far more than the 3,203 pilots authorized by Congress.

Arnold had a great idea. Why not train military pilots in civilian schools? He asked Congress for the funding, but lawmakers turned down his request.

Arnold went ahead with his plan anyway. He approached eight World War I and civilian pilots. He asked them if they would train pilots for the Army. Although he offered no guarantee of pay, all eight agreed to do it. Congress finally authorized contracts for civilian flight schools in July 1939.

Under this plan, volunteers would check in with the Army for a physical and a psychological test. If they passed, they'd attend a civilian flight school close to home. Once a volunteer graduated, a military pilot would take him for a "check ride." If it went well, the volunteer would report for combat training at an Army base.

Arnold's idea eventually produced some 110,000 pilots per year. But more were needed.

Piper J-3 Cub
Richard Thornton/Shutterstock

Civilian Reserve Pilots

In 1939 the Air Corps tried another idea: the Civilian Pilot Training Program. Under this program, civilians could volunteer to train as civilian pilots. This reserve of civilian pilots would be available in case of a national emergency. Congress set aside $7 million a year for the program. The volunteers trained using Piper J-3 Cubs. In 1942 the program's name was changed to the Civil Aeronautics Authority War Training Service. About 300,000 reserve pilots earned their private-pilot certificates by the time the program ended in 1944.

African-American Pilots and the Military

At this time, black men were not permitted in the Army Air Corps or in the Civilian Pilot Training Program. But two African-American pilots—Dale Lawrence White and Chauncy Spencer—refused to accept this. They wanted to draw attention to the exclusion of black pilots from the military. So they made a 3,000-mile flight across the United States in May 1939 that brought them through Washington, D.C.

Chauncey Spencer (*left*) and Dale Lawrence White (*right*), African-American Aviation Pioneers
Courtesy US Air Force

While in D.C., they met Senator Harry Truman of Missouri. They told him about their mission. He was impressed and got Congress involved. On 22 March 1941 the all-black 99th Pursuit Squadron of Tuskegee, Alabama, was born. It was made part of the Civilian Pilot Training Program. The Tuskegee Airmen will be covered in more detail in the next lesson.

All three of these steps—civilian flight schools, civilian reserve pilots, and acceptance of black pilots—greatly increased the number of pilots available to the Army Air Corps and helped the United States prepare for war.

Significant Developments Concerning the Army Air Corps

In the 1930s Army Air Corps officers focused on aircraft development. They believed that if they could get the aviation industry to build a powerful, fast aircraft that could travel long distances, they could fulfill Billy Mitchell's dream of a long-range bomber.

Airplane manufacturers at that time were focusing on commercial aircraft—because that's where the money was. To get the manufacturers' attention, the Army Air Corps held a design competition for a multiengine bomber.

As you read in the previous lesson, Douglas Aircraft came out with two commercial aircraft, the DC-2 (1934) and the DC-3 (1936) about this same time. These aircraft put Boeing's commercial 247 out of date. Army officers gave Boeing a suggestion for its entry in the design competition. Instead of using a typical two-engine plane, they said, why not design a four-engine aircraft? Boeing did just that—building the Boeing 299.

Boeing's 299 flew to the contest site at Wright Field in Dayton, Ohio, in July 1935. It easily outclassed the competition. The aircraft had speed, range, and altitude. Although the Air Corps awarded the contract to another company, it ordered 13 299s. It renamed the plane the B-17. The corps could now finally fly long-range strategic bombing missions using one of the most important aircraft of this era.

Boeing 299
Courtesy US Air Force

B-17 Flying Fortress
Courtesy US Air Force

Curtiss P-36 Hawk
Courtesy National Museum of the US Air Force

The B-17 was faster than any pursuit aircraft in the United States at the time. This made the Army realize that it now needed better pursuit planes. It signed contracts for the Curtiss P-36 and the Seversky P-35. (The "P" stands for "pursuit.") These aircraft could guard American bombers and attack enemy bombers. The Air Corps developed other important pursuit aircraft, as well. When the United States entered World War II, it had Lockheed P-38s, Bell P-39s, and Curtiss P-40s in its pursuit arsenal.

One more important invention took place during these years. The Army borrowed the Norden Mark XV bombsight from the Navy to use in B-17s. This allowed the Air Corps to conduct precision daylight bombing by just a few aircraft in a tight formation instead of raids by a large number of planes saturating a wide area.

The Rationale of Advocates for an Independent Air Force

After Brigadier General Mitchell's resignation in 1926, others carried his ideas forward. The foundation of his airpower theory was the long-range bomber. Once Boeing built the B-17, long-range bombing missions could become a reality. Here, advocates believed, was a concrete reason for an independent air service. Airpower was an offensive weapon. It could strike at military bases and factories in enemy lands. It could do much more than protect ground troops. And it didn't need to be under the command of Army officers.

As long as airpower was a part of the Army, air advocates believed, it would remain underfunded and underdeveloped. History showed they were right—airpower had suffered as a subordinate service. As late as 1928, the Army placed greater emphasis on observation aircraft than on bombers.

Then in 1934, airpower faced another setback. As the result of a scandal involving civilian contractors, President Roosevelt turned over airmail delivery to the corps. Within short order, nine fatal crashes occurred. The crashes were not entirely the corps' fault. It didn't have enough money, for one thing. Its aircraft weren't outfitted with night instrument panels and other equipment. Pilots weren't well trained for night flight. These things made it clear to supporters of the Air Corps that airpower needed independence to grow as it should.

The Rationale of Objectors to an Independent Air Force

But not everyone agreed that airpower should be independent. The Army General Staff was the biggest proponent of keeping the Air Corps in the Army. The Army was, after all, steeped in history. Ground forces had been a part of war for thousands of years. Many in the Army saw airpower as no more than long-range artillery. For them, the main purpose of airpower was to support ground troops.

The Right Stuff

Major General Benjamin Foulois: From Army's First Pilot to Air Chief

Benjamin Foulois (pronounced "foo-loy"; 1879–1967) started his military career as an enlistee. He spent the last four years of his career as chief of the Air Corps—quite a leap. Like Brigadier General Billy Mitchell, he spoke out for an independent air force.

Foulois was only 5 feet, 6 inches, tall. But he loved adventure. And he loved to fly. Even when he was chief of the Air Corps, he spent more time in the air than many of his junior officers.

Major General Benjamin Foulois (*left*) was chief of the Air Corps from 1931 to 1935.

Courtesy US Air Force

Even in his early years of service, Foulois achieved several milestones. He became the Army Signal Corps' first pilot when he flew Dirigible No. 1 in 1908. He rode with Orville Wright in 1909. With the Wrights' help, he learned to pilot a plane while stationed at Fort Sam Houston, Texas.

Foulois served in World War I at home and abroad. After the war, he testified before the Senate Military Affairs Committee. He suggested that the committee sponsor a bill to create an air department.

Foulois held strong opinions, which helped and hurt him throughout his career. In oral and written statements, he criticized the Army and Navy for failing to support an independent air force. Nonetheless, he ended up as chief of the Air Corps from 1931 to 1935. He resigned in 1935 when he came under attack for the Air Corps' mishandling of the airmail mission.

They believed that while airpower was valuable both for defense and offense, it could not by itself affect the outcome of a war. They wanted the Army to keep total control of its air arm, just as the Navy controlled its own air arm.

In addition, the general attitude among the public and Congress favored defensive over offensive forces. But major advances in technology such as the B-17 would make the old ways more difficult to maintain.

The Creation of a Separate Air Corps Headquarters

When two sides can't agree, a compromise is often necessary. In 1933, Major General Hugh Drum headed an Army board that explored possible changes in the structure of the Air Corps. The board recommended that the War Department form a General Headquarters Air Force (GHQ). The GHQ would command the aerial combat arm. The Air Corps would retain training and logistical duties. Logistics is *the aspect of military operations that deals with the procurement, distribution, maintenance, and replacement of materiel and personnel*. Secretary of War George H. Dern endorsed the plan. But nothing happened for a few years.

In 1934, the War Department set up another board. Former Secretary of War Newton Baker chaired this group. It, too, proposed a combat group separate from training and logistical duties.

The recommendations of the Drum and Baker boards were implemented in March 1935, when the GHQ set up camp at Langley Field, Virginia. GHQ remained within the Air Corps and answered to the Army. Brigadier General Frank Andrews was senior officer of GHQ. In the past, Air Corps commanders had shared responsibility for tactical units. Now all combat aircraft would fall under Andrews's command. During peacetime, Andrews would answer to the Army chief of staff. In war, he'd report to a regional combat commander.

The nation's air arm continued to evolve as war approached. The Army Air Corps officially became the Army Air Forces on 20 June 1941. This brought the Air Corps and GHQ now under unified control. The new Air Force remained under Army command. But it could now oversee its own functions in combat, training, and maintenance.

Major General "Hap" Arnold took command of the Army Air Forces. Under him was Major General George Brett, who was chief of the Air Corps. Lieutenant General Delos C. Emmons headed the new Air Force Combat Command (formerly known as the GHQ).

This last change came not a moment too soon. By the end of the year, the United States would find itself fully engaged in war in both Europe and the Pacific. The experiences gained during that war, and the performance of the Army Air Forces, would finally lead to complete autonomy—*independence*—of the US Air Force with the passage of the National Security Act of 1947.

✔ CHECKPOINTS

Lesson 1 Review

Using complete sentences, answer the following questions on a sheet of paper.

1. Which American president established the Army Air Service in May 1918?

2. What did the Army Reorganization Act of 1920 mean for the Army Air Service?

3. What was the name of the captured German battleship Army pilots sank in 1921?

4. What three proposals did Congress adopt in 1926?

5. Why did the Army Air Corps get off to a slow start?

6. Why did President Roosevelt speak to Congress in 1939 about the need to rebuild the US military?

7. What did the Army Air Corps rename the Boeing 299?

8. What did the Norden Mark XV bombsight allow the Air Corps to do?

9. What did the board led by Army Major General Hugh Drum recommend in 1933?

10. What happened on 20 June 1941?

APPLYING YOUR LEARNING

11. Why do you think it took so many years to convince Congress that the Air Force should be independent, rather than a branch of the Army?

Quick Write

_____

_____

Many Soldiers and Airmen made great sacrifices to ensure US forces were victorious during World War II. One man was willing to sacrifice it all to save his crew. After reading the story about Staff Sergeant Henry Erwin, explain why he earned the Medal of Honor.

Learn About

- the strategic role airpower played in World War II
- the increased role of airpower in World War II
- the development of tactical and strategic air warfare
- the combat box formation and formation pattern bombing
- significant Allied air campaigns in the European theater
- significant Allied air campaigns in the Pacific theater

STAFF SERGEANT HENRY E. ("RED") ERWIN (1922–2002) was a radio operator on a B-29 bomber in the Pacific. On 12 April 1945 he and his crewmates were targeting a chemical plant in Koriyama, Japan. Erwin's other duty on board was to light and drop phosphorus smoke bombs.

One of the bombs he lit blew back up the bomb chute and struck him in the face. The bomb's flare was 1,100 degrees. It burned off his nose and one of his ears, and temporarily cost him his sight. In terrible pain, Erwin knew he had to get the fiery bomb canister out of the plane. For one thing, he was afraid the canister would burn through the metal floor into the bomb bay. For another, the smoke was making it impossible for the pilot to navigate. The aircraft was diving toward earth.

Then-Private Henry Erwin
US Air Force

Although gravely injured, blind, and on fire, Erwin carried the burning bomb canister to the front of the aircraft. He tossed it out of the copilot's window. The smoke cleared enough for the pilot to level out at 300 feet and make an emergency landing on Iwo Jima.

No one thought Erwin would live. Senior Army Air Force officers approved awarding him the Medal of Honor so they could give it to him while he was still alive. But he survived. Major General Curtis LeMay, then Commander of 21st Bomber Command, presented the medal. After going through 41 surgeries and 30 months of rehabilitation, Erwin regained his eyesight and use of one arm. He received a disability discharge as a master sergeant in 1947. He went on to work for 37 years for the Veterans Administration. He was the last enlisted man in the US Army Air Forces to receive the Medal of Honor. Erwin died in 2002 at age 80.

In 1997, the Air Force created the Henry E. Erwin Outstanding Enlisted Aircrew Member of the Year Award. It is given each year to an Airman, noncommissioned officer, and senior noncommissioned officer in the active-duty or reserve forces. It is only the second Air Force award named for an enlisted person.

Vocabulary

- sabotage
- casualties
- Allies
- Axis Powers
- Holocaust
- theater
- Luftwaffe
- occupation
- isolationist
- squadron
- flight
- blitzkrieg
- combined arms
- tactical
- interdiction
- materiel
- escort
- paratrooper
- embargo
- incendiary bombs

The Strategic Role Airpower Played in World War II

"To! To! To!" (Japanese code for "Charge! Charge! Charge!") With that order, Japanese pilots plunged from the skies over Pearl Harbor in Hawaii at 7:55 a.m. on 7 December 1941. Fifty fighters and 140 bombers strafed and bombed the US base. Less than an hour later, 40 more Japanese fighters and 130 more bombers dropped their deadly loads.

The Americans were caught off guard. They weren't prepared for an attack from the air. The Army and Navy thought any assault on Pearl Harbor would come by foot. Only a little more than a week before, they'd ordered all planes and ships grouped in clusters. They placed guards around the aircraft. The officers wanted to protect against sabotage—*the destruction of property by enemy agents in time of war*. This move proved disastrous for the American forces. For Japanese pilots, the clusters of planes must have looked like bull's-eyes.

In all, the Japanese destroyed 96 Army planes and 92 Navy aircraft. They crippled 159 more. They sank three US battleships— the *Arizona, California,* and *West Virginia.* They capsized the battleship *Oklahoma.* They also damaged four other battleships, three cruisers, three destroyers, and a seaplane. The casualties—*military persons lost through death, wounds, injury, imprisonment, or missing in action*—were high. The Navy and Marine Corps lost 2,117 members. Another 960 were missing and 876 wounded. The Army and Army Air Forces suffered losses, too: 226 killed and 396 wounded.

This captured Japanese photo shows the attack on Pearl Harbor under way. Torpedo wakes ripple the water, and smoke rises in the distance from the Army Air Corps' Hickam Field.

Courtesy National Archives and Records Administration, 520600

During the raid, the Army got just six fighters into the air. The Navy sent up 36 airplanes. But the Japanese lost only 28 planes and 64 men. The only real break for US forces was that the enemy did not touch a single aircraft carrier of the US Pacific fleet. All four ships were out on exercises.

The United States declared war on Japan on 8 December 1941. Three days later, on 11 December, the United States declared war on Japan's allies, Germany and Italy. England and its allies had already been fighting Germany and Italy for two years. The British joined America in declaring war on Japan.

The Japanese attack on Pearl Harbor is a fitting place to begin a discussion of America's entry into World War II. In many ways, this attack was symbolic of this major war. Another name for World War II is the *air war*. For Americans, the air war began with the Japanese air attack on Pearl Harbor. The war ended in 1945, when American aircraft dropped atomic bombs on the Japanese cities of Hiroshima and Nagasaki. The air war began for Britain and Europe in 1939, when Germany invaded Poland.

There were two sides during World War II. The Allies included *Britain, France, the United States, the Soviet Union, and China.* (The Soviet Union was the new name for Russia after the communist Russian Revolution overthrew the czar in 1917.) The Axis Powers included *Germany, Italy, and Japan.* Many other countries contributed to the Allies' effort, and a few others fought for the Axis Powers.

The War's Causes

World War II was the most horrific war in history. As the chart on the following page shows, more than 50 million people died.

The roots of the war lay in the end of World War I. After that war, Japan was the biggest power in the Far East. But it had few of the natural resources, such as oil, that a modern economy needs. So it was looking for ways to expand. Germany was also hurting. Britain and France had forced it to pay huge sums of money for war damage, which hurt Germany's economy.

By 1932 the Great Depression had caused millions of workers to lose their jobs around the world. It hit Germany especially hard. The people wanted change. So Adolf Hitler's National Socialist Party—the Nazis—won the 1933 elections. The Nazis preached a vicious brand of racism. They believed that other ethnic groups, such as Jews and Slavic peoples, were less human than Germans. They wanted to remove these groups—or even kill them—to make "living space" for a German master race. They wrongly blamed Jews for Europe's economic problems. They imprisoned or murdered anyone who disagreed with their teachings. The Nazis were responsible for the Holocaust, or *the mass murder of some six million Jews, mostly in death camps.*

Meanwhile, in Italy, dictator Benito Mussolini led his country into a series of wars. This included taking over Ethiopia, in Africa. Mussolini was a *Fascist.* The Fascists held dictatorial, nationalist, and racist views like those of the Nazis. In the Far East, Japan's military dictatorship was fighting in China and elsewhere for control of other people's countries and resources.

TABLE 3.2 Estimated Military and Civilians Killed in World War II, by Country

Country	Military and Civilians Killed
ALLIED POWERS	
Australia	30,000
Belgium	112,000
Britain	460,000
Canada	42,000
China	10,300,000
Denmark	3,000
France	270,000
Greece	490,000
India	36,000
Netherlands	264,000
New Zealand	10,000
Norway	16,000
Poland	2,630,000
South Africa	9,000
Soviet Union (Russia)	28,000,000
United States	300,000
Yugoslavia	305,000
AXIS POWERS	
Bulgaria	60,000
Finland	104,000
Germany	5,500,000
Hungary	320,000
Italy	400,000
Japan	2,100,000
Romania	900,000
TOTAL	**54,226,000**

Compiled by Professor Joseph V. O'Brien, Department of History, John Jay College of Criminal Justice, New York, NY

The final major player was Joseph Stalin, the dictator who headed the Communist Party in the Soviet Union. The Communists believed that the state should own all the means of production. They permitted no private ownership of land, factories, or businesses. They also persecuted religion, closing thousands of churches, mosques, and synagogues. Like the Nazis, they imprisoned or murdered those who disagreed with them.

Most Europeans and Americans rejected the Communists' views. The Nazis and Fascists particularly hated them. This didn't stop Hitler and Stalin from signing a treaty that allowed Germany to conquer most of Poland in 1939. The Soviet Union got the rest. It also took over the Baltic countries of Lithuania, Latvia, and Estonia, and launched a war against Finland.

But in 1941 Hitler double-crossed Stalin. He attacked the Soviet Union. Millions of Soviet civilians died in the fighting. In the siege of Leningrad (now St. Petersburg) alone, 900,000 people starved.

After the German invasion, the Soviet Union joined the Allies. With the United States and Britain, the Soviets helped defeat the Nazis.

The Right Stuff

General Carl A. Spaatz: First Chief of Staff, US Air Force

General Carl A. ("Tooey") Spaatz (1891–1974) flew in World War I. In 1929 he was the pilot of the *Question Mark* when it showed aerial refueling was possible. He remained in the military between the wars. During the Battle of Britain, he spent time in Britain, where he observed German tactics. He was also commander of air forces in several regions during World War II.

The West Point graduate served in every theater—*a large geographic area in which military operations are coordinated*— during World War II. He headed the Eighth Air Force in England. While the British conducted nighttime bombing raids over Germany, Spaatz had his pilots fly during the day. He was also responsible for the 12th Air Force in North Africa.

After the Allies defeated the Germans in Africa, Spaatz led the 12th and 15th Air Forces as well as the Royal Air Force in Italy. In 1944 he was put in charge of the US Strategic Air Forces in Europe. He oversaw airpower there until Germany's collapse. In July 1945 he was sent to the Pacific. His pilots delivered the atomic bombs on Japan. Although he did not agree with using atomic weapons, he carried out his orders.

After the war, Spaatz served for about a year as the first chief of staff of the new US Air Force. He retired in 1948. He earned many awards, including the Distinguished Service Cross. Spaatz was one of the foremost military leaders of World War II. He died in 1974 at age 83.

General Carl A. Spaatz (*right*) with the first Secretary of the Air Force, W. Stuart Symington, in 1947

Courtesy US Air Force

Germany's Opening Offensive

Germany began World War II using its Luftwaffe (pronounced looft-vahfeh)—
the German air force—in combination with ground troops. The Germans broke
through Poland's borders on 1 September 1939. In less than a month, they crushed
Poland's army, which was the fifth largest in Europe. Poland surrendered in just
20 days. Germany then rolled over a number of other countries in short order.
They included Norway, the Netherlands, Belgium, and France. All these countries
faced German occupation—*invasion, conquest, and control of a nation or territory
by foreign armed forces.*

But Germany's good luck changed when it struck Britain. Britain's airpower put
a stop to German airpower. This clash, which began in August 1940, was called
the *Battle of Britain.*

**A German Heinkel 111 bomber flies over London, England.
Below is the River Thames; photo taken 7 September 1940.**

Everett Historical/Shutterstock

Britain was in a fight for its life.
For a year, it stood alone against
the Axis onslaught. But it had a few
advantages over Germany. First, its
Royal Navy was superior to Germany's
navy. Second, it received important
supplies from the United States,
which was officially neutral. Third,
German aircraft weren't equipped to
fly the long distances needed to cross
the English Channel and conduct
missions in Britain. Even so, Germany
continued to strike Britain from the
air through much of the war. But
its strategy and airpower were never
able bring the British to their knees.
The British kept the Germans from
grabbing their island nation.

On 20 June 1941, Hitler invaded
the Soviet Union. Six months later,
Japan attacked the United States.
Now Britain had two powerful new
allies. Had Japan not attacked Pearl
Harbor, it's difficult to say how much
longer the United States would have
maintained its isolationist stance.
An isolationist country is *a nation
that does not enter alliances with
other countries.*

The Increased Role of Airpower in World War II

As is evident from the previous section, airpower had a much larger role in World War II than it did in World War I. During World War I, airpower was still a novel concept. This was especially true in that war's earliest years. All-metal planes were still new. Bombs were so light that pilots could carry them on their laps and drop them by hand. The pilots' work was mainly to observe enemy locations and support ground troops.

But by the end of World War I, things were changing. All-metal planes were becoming the norm. Bombs weighed as much as 2,000 pounds. Pilots engaged in dogfights. Some 1,500 planes fought in the Battle of Saint Mihiel in France in 1918.

The Right Stuff

The Foresight of General Henry Arnold

General Henry ("Hap") Arnold (1886–1950) served in both world wars. He learned how to fly from Orville Wright. Arnold was a West Point graduate. He first served in the infantry. In 1911 he transferred to the Aeronautical Division of the US Army Signal Corps.

Arnold thought airpower was essential to the future of the military. When troubles began brewing in Europe in 1938, he asked Congress for more funding for the Army Air Corps. He was especially interested in developing aerospace technology to give the United States an edge in achieving air superiority. He fostered the development of jet aircraft, rockets, rocket-assisted takeoff, and supersonic flight.

During the war, Arnold had a couple of jobs. He was commanding general of the US Army Air Forces. He also was the air representative on the US Joint Chiefs of Staff. In 1944 the Army made Arnold a five-star general. He is the only air commander to achieve that rank.

General Henry "Hap" Arnold (*left*) with World War II ace and Medal of Honor recipient Major Richard Bong
Courtesy US Air Force

Even so, much of World War I took place in the trenches. Infantrymen died in huge numbers. No country wanted its soldiers to suffer such losses ever again. That's one reason the use of airpower morphed so quickly between 1914 and 1918. It's also why airpower was used so heavily in World War II. During this second war, fought between 1939 and 1945, long-range bombers saw lots of action. These aircraft could fly over trenches and enter enemy territory. Not only could fighters protect bombers and transports, they could also drop bombs.

The Allies and Axis Powers used their aircraft to destroy airfields, supply lines, and military posts. They also used aircraft to try to break the will of enemy civilians. In fact, during World War II, civilians were often targets. This strategy had been used throughout history. But in World War II it greatly widened the scope of destruction. German bombs killed more than 40,000 civilians in and around London, for instance. The United States firebombed Tokyo and dropped atomic weapons on Hiroshima and Nagasaki, Japan.

Victory in World War II relied on contributions from all forces—land, sea, and air. Each was indispensable. But for the first time in history, airpower was the key to victory.

The Development of Tactical and Strategic Air Warfare

Now that airpower was more reliable, military leaders began to think more seriously about its prospects. Even in Brigadier General Billy Mitchell's day, visionaries knew aircraft would some day serve in more than just a supporting role. With World War II, that day arrived. Both the Allies and the Axis Powers soon developed new strategies for waging war in the air.

When World War I ended, both sides signed a peace treaty. It was named the Treaty of Versailles. Among other points, this treaty stated that Germany could not build a military air force. It was free, however, to develop commercial aircraft.

Germany used the progress it made in commercial planes as a cover for the advances it was secretly making in military aircraft. It was also quietly training pilots in South America. By 1932 Germany's military air force had three bomber squadrons, four fighter squadrons, eight observation squadrons, 1,500 trained pilots, and 3,000 pilots in training. A squadron is *an air force unit consisting of two or more flights*. A flight is *a unit that has two or more elements*.

In 1933 Adolf Hitler became chancellor of Germany. In 1935 Germany unveiled its Luftwaffe. Germany and Italy gave important air support to the fascist-backed "Nationalist" forces that won the Spanish Civil War—a conflict that raged from 1936 to 1939. In 1939 the German Army and Luftwaffe invaded Poland. Germany was once again a power to be contended with.

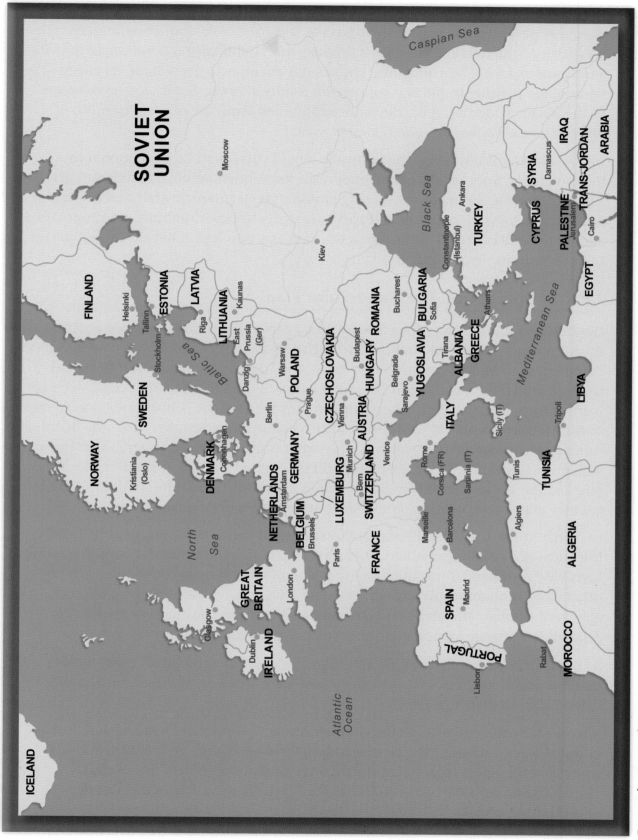

Europe between the wars

Wanting to avoid getting bogged down in trench warfare as it had in World War I, Germany perfected a new strategy to invade and control Poland. The Germans called it *Blitzkrieg*, which in English means *lightning war*. A blitzkrieg is *a war conducted with great speed and force*. In a blitzkrieg, the offense attempts to overwhelm its enemy. Because the fighting is quick, it supposedly results in fewer deaths and less damage to the invaded country. A blitzkrieg uses combined arms, *the coordinated efforts of different military branches, such as air and ground*.

In a World War II blitzkrieg, the Luftwaffe would strike first. Its pilots would fly behind enemy lines to take out an enemy air force, often before it could even get in the air. Then the German Army, using tanks to get its infantry safely across trench lines, would blow up railroads and strike at enemy troops. Combined arms were used a bit at the end of World War I, when the tank was developed. But they came into their own during World War II.

Tactical Operations: The Three-Point Plan

German and Italian forces were also in North Africa. From this base, they attacked British positions in the Mediterranean and along the Suez Canal in Egypt. The Axis Powers needed Middle Eastern oil. To get it, they had to gain control of the canal, through which oil was shipped. The fight between the Allies and the Axis Powers in North Africa began in 1941, when the Germans targeted the British on Malta, an island in the Mediterranean that was then a British colony. In November 1942, the British and Americans invaded French North Africa—what is now Morocco, Algeria, and Tunisia—which was controlled by the Germans and the Vichy French government. (*Vichy France* refers to the authoritarian French government that controlled the southern half of the country and several colonies after France surrendered to Germany in 1940.)

In North Africa, the United States and Britain used the same air policy at first. When the Luftwaffe attacked an Allied air base, only the aircraft at that base would respond. Each base commander was in charge of his planes. He did not coordinate with any other base commander. As a result, very few Allied planes were going up to meet attackers. German aircraft always outnumbered them. It became clear that if the Allies didn't change tactics, their huge losses would continue.

So Britain's Royal Air Force (RAF) and then the US Army brought all their planes under centralized control. This way, if a base were attacked, all Allied bases could defend it or retaliate together.

It worked. By the end of 1942 the German Afrika Korps under Field Marshal Erwin Rommel was crumbling. The Germans' supplies were cut off. By 1943 the Allies controlled the skies. That meant the infantry could now control the ground. The Allies had won the battle of Africa. The US Air Force still uses this strategy of centralized control.

A new plan for tactical operations also grew out of the Allies' experience in Africa. Something that is tactical *involves military operations that are smaller, closer to base, and of less long-term significance than strategic operations.* The theory had three points:

1. Air superiority. This was achieved by destroying opposing airfields, aircraft, oil and fuel tanks, and manufacturers of aircraft and spare parts.

2. Interdiction, or *the act of cutting or destroying an enemy's advance through firepower.* As part of interdiction, aircraft hit supply routes, railroads, bridges, highways, warehouses, troops, and means of communication.

3. Close ground support. Aircraft bombed and strafed within enemy territory and provided an aerial shield for Allied infantry.

The Right Stuff

Lieutenant General Pete Quesada: An Advocate of Close Air Support

Lieutenant General Elwood "Pete" Quesada (1904–1993) realized as early as the 1930s that "future war will require all sorts of arrangements between the air and the ground, and the two will have to work closer than a lot of people think or want." As commander of the First Air Defense Wing in North Africa, he put close air support into practice. He refined his idea as commander of the 12th Fighter Command, also in North Africa, in 1943.

Lieutenant General Elwood "Pete" Quesada
Courtesy US Air Force

Close air support has three major features:

1. Making ground and air commanders equal

2. Using centralized control

3. Establishing air superiority before committing ground troops

Another name for close air support is *tactical operations.*

Quesada later commanded the Ninth Fighter Command, which saw action on D-Day in 1944. It provided close air support to invading ground troops. Later, he was the first commander of Tactical Air Command. He retired from the Air Force in 1951. In 1958 President Dwight Eisenhower named him the first director of the Federal Aviation Agency.

Strategic Operations: Long-Range Bombing

One of the Allies' air-warfare strategies was long-range bombing. The Allies used this strategy a great deal, since they had more long-range bombers than Germany did. Germany's manufacturers produced mostly short- and medium-range bombers. This was because Hitler had figured most of his battles would be in continental Europe, and therefore close to Germany.

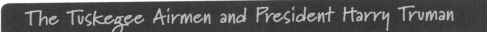

The Tuskegee Airmen and President Harry Truman

NEITHER THE ARMY AIR CORPS nor the Civilian Pilot Training Program (CPTP) accepted African-Americans at first. It was Senator Harry S. Truman, a Missouri Democrat and future US president, who got Congress to admit blacks into the CPTP. The Tuskegee Airmen were born. They flew fighters.

The men, all African-Americans, got basic flight training at the Tuskegee Institute in Alabama. Those who passed went on for combat flight training at Tuskegee Army Air Field. Tuskegee pilots formed the 99th Fighter Squadron, which saw action in North Africa. Pilots also joined the 332nd Fighter Group. The 332nd and the 99th fought side by side in Italy later in the war.

Creating a Legacy

Members of the 332nd and 99th were primarily assigned bomber escort duties. Of the 311 missions the two units flew, 179 were escorting bombers. From June 1944 to the end of the war, the Tuskegee Airmen performed with great skill and courage. On one occasion they shot down 13 German fighters. Often in their encounters with enemy fighters they were outnumbered. Colonel Benjamin Davis Jr., commander of the 332nd Fighter Group, once led 39 American fighters against 100 German fighters. The 332nd shot down five enemy fighters to one American lost.

Major James Ellison reviews the first class of Tuskegee cadets in 1941.

Courtesy US Air Force

Long-range bombing was an Allied air *strategy*; the approach used in North Africa involved Allied air *tactics*. Tactical operations apply to a specific fight. Strategic operations encompass the entire philosophy of a military's plan to win the war. The Allies relied heavily on long-range bombers to hit deep inside Germany and Japan and to destroy their ability to wage war.

Between the German blitzkrieg and Allied tactical and strategic plans, airpower was taking shape. Both sides fine-tuned operations throughout the war. And that fine-tuning continues today.

Tuskegee Airmen faced the best the Luftwaffe had, including the first jet fighters. On 24 March 1945, the 332nd became one of the first Italy-based fighter units to escort B-17s all the way to Berlin and back. Along the way, they met 25 German Me 262 jets. In the ensuing combat, the 332nd shot down three of the eight jets destroyed that day.

By the end of the war, the Tuskegee program produced 992 black pilots. Of those, 150 lost their lives in training or combat, and 32 became prisoners of war. Tuskegee Airmen had shot down 112 enemy aircraft and destroyed another 150 aircraft on the ground.

When Truman became president, he vowed to push for more rights for blacks in all branches of the military. His overall goal was to end racial segregation in the armed forces. In July 1948 he signed Executive Order 9981. It said: "It is hereby declared to be the policy of the President that there shall be equality of treatment and opportunity for all persons in the armed services without regard to race, color, religion, or national origin."

Red Tails of the 332nd Fighter Group take off to escort heavy bombers in 1944.
Courtesy National Museum of the US Air Force

The Tuskegee Airmen's service during World War II helped make this new order possible.

Then–Lieutenant Colonel Benjamin O. Davis Jr. (*left*)

Courtesy US Air Force

Then–1st Lieutenant Charles B. Hall scored the Tuskegee Airmen's first aerial victory in his P-40L Warhawk.

Courtesy National Museum of the US Air Force

General Benjamin O. Davis Jr.: All in the Family

The military was in Benjamin Davis Jr.'s blood. His father was an Army general. The younger Davis (1912–2002) would become the first African-American brigadier general in the US Air Force.

Davis trained in the Tuskegee program. In 1941 he led the all-black 99th Pursuit Squadron. He saw action in 1943 in North Africa. He also commanded the all-black 332nd Fighter Group. This group fought in 15,000 air battles in Europe during World War II.

Davis flew 60 combat missions and logged 224 combat hours. He earned the Distinguished Flying Cross, the Silver Star, the Croix de Guerre, the Star of Africa, and more. In 1998, Davis became a four-star general.

Charles Hall: A First for the 99th Fighter Squadron

1st Lieutenant Charles Hall was a fighter pilot with the all-black 99th Fighter Squadron. On 21 July 1943, he was flying a P-40 over Italy as part of the escort for a B-25 bomber. He saw two German Focke-Wulf 190s coming his way. He zipped this way and that, intent on stopping the enemy aircraft. Hall let off a spray of bullets. One of the German fighters went down. Hall thus became the first African-American pilot to score a kill during the war. He had two more by war's end. For his bravery, the US government awarded Hall the Distinguished Flying Cross.

The Combat Box Formation and Formation Pattern Bombing

In 1943, Brigadier General Curtis LeMay's bombers were coming under heavy fire over Germany. As a result, US losses were staggering. During the US Eighth Air Force's first flight into Germany in July, the enemy shot down 92 American bombers. A month later the Germans destroyed 60 more. In October antiaircraft fire and German fighters downed another 148 US bombers. Such losses could not continue.

Part of the problem was that the US bombers were flying into Germany unaccompanied. They had no Allied fighter planes to protect them. Normally fighters accompany bombers. But Allied fighters didn't yet have the range that Allied bombers had. By the end of the war, at least one fighter, the P-51 Mustang, would be developed to escort bombers all the way into Germany. In the meantime, the bombers' only defense was gunners all around the aircraft. But gunners weren't as effective a defense as a protective flank of fighters.

Furthermore, US pilots were conducting their precision-bombing missions during daylight hours. The RAF had lost many planes trying this. So the British switched to night bombing. Americans were responsible for daytime runs. They had the Norden bombsight, which helped them hit targets during the day.

General LeMay knew he had to do something to cut losses. He came up with two tactics: the *combat box formation* and *formation pattern bombing*.

M·I·L·E·S·T·O·N·E·S

Enlisted Pilots

Before World War II, the United States had more pilots than planes. But once the United States entered the war and the war-manufacturing industry heated up, there were more planes than pilots. This meant that more enlistees would get a chance to fly. Congress passed a bill on 3 June 1941 to encourage enlistee pilots.

There were 3,000 enlisted pilots from 1912 to 1942. Corporal Vernon Burge, whom you read about in a previous lesson, was the first. The main differences between noncommissioned and commissioned pilots were age and education. Enlisted pilots were between 18 and 22 years old. They had to graduate in the top half of their high school classes. They didn't have to attend college. Commissioned pilots were 20 to 27 years old. They had college degrees. Most enlistees who became pilots eventually did receive commissions.

Army command intended to use enlisted pilots for transport duties, not for combat. But the needs of war often meant that the enlistee pilots saw action. These pilots fought most of the air battles over North Africa, for instance. In the Mediterranean, officers who had started out in the military as enlisted men were in charge of all the troop carrier groups in the region. These troop carrier groups flew Soldiers in transport planes.

In all these ways, enlisted pilots contributed mightily to Allied victory.

LeMay instructed his bombers to fly close together. He called this the combat box formation. By sticking together, the gunners on the aircraft could more effectively protect their planes and others against enemy fighters. This tactic helped somewhat until long-range escort fighters became available later in the war.

Formation pattern bombing results when bombers fly in a combat box formation. Bombs dropped from aircraft flying close together will land closer together and can have a bigger impact in a small area.

The Right Stuff

General Curtis E. LeMay and His Bombers

General Curtis E. LeMay (1906–1990) rose from flying cadet to many leadership positions. He worked with fighter planes. He moved to bombers in 1937. He charted routes to Africa and England before World War II.

In 1942 LeMay was in charge of the 305th Bombardment Group in the European theater. These pilots flew B-17s. It was with this group that he developed the combat box formation and formation pattern bombing. Later, when placed in charge of B-29s in the Pacific, he adapted those bombing theories to the new theater.

General Curtis LeMay
Courtesy US Air Force

LeMay was a tough commander, but he was also tough on himself. He had a theory about war: "If you are going to use military force, then you ought to use overwhelming military force. Use too much and deliberately use too much…. You'll save lives, not only your own, but the enemy's, too." He applied this philosophy when his B-29s firebombed Tokyo in the most destructive air raid in history.

After the war, LeMay had a number of leadership roles. Among them was command of the US Air Force in Europe during the Berlin airlift, an operation in Germany that followed World War II. Back in the United States, he commanded the Strategic Air Command, which oversaw atomic-bomb operations.

In 1961 LeMay became the fifth chief of staff of the Air Force.

Significant Allied Air Campaigns in the European Theater

Germany resumed hostilities in Europe in 1938 to take lands it felt belonged to it: It occupied Austria and Czechoslovakia without firing a shot, and later invaded Poland. Most of Europe caved quickly before German aggression. Britain was an exception. This small island nation was about all that stood between Germany and total conquest.

Before the United States joined Britain in its campaign to free Europe, the military and civilian leaders of the two countries met many times. They talked strategy. The United States was already supplying Britain with ships, planes, and parts. The Allies considered the chance Japan would one day attack the United States. They asked themselves how this would affect the Allied strategy.

The United States and Britain came to some important conclusions. They decided that even if Japan struck the United States, the first objective of the Allies would still be to defeat Germany. Germany was in Britain's backyard. Its factories churned out excellent planes and tanks. It had been hammering Britain for two years. As of 1941 the combined forces of the US and England would have been hard pressed to fight all-out war on two fronts. But by 1944 that was no longer true. Helped greatly by the Soviets' battle with the Germans on the Eastern Front, they could take on Germany and Japan full force.

Once the United States entered the war, airpower had a big part in the European and Pacific theaters. It played both its old support role and its new offensive role of strategic bombing.

All Allied air actions in Europe had a single goal: to shut down the German offensive. The first great clash was the Battle of Britain.

The Battle of Britain

The Battle of Britain was one of the most important of the war. This was a defensive battle for the British, who were the first to stop the Nazi war machine.

The battle began in August 1940. The Germans did small-scale raids to test British strength. England relied on its fighters for defense. Both British resolve and poor German planning helped Britain hold out. As you read above, the Germans had only short- and medium-range bombers. They needed long-range bombers to hit Britain effectively.

Germany made another big mistake. It didn't count on British radar. Radar let the British spot German squadrons heading toward them across the English Channel. Because of radar, the RAF didn't have to waste fuel patrolling in the air. And it didn't have to waste manpower or put unnecessary wear and tear on its planes.

Having radar was a bit like being able to see into the future. It allowed the RAF to send its fighter pilots where and when they were needed.

Even so, German bombers did manage to get through to bomb London and the surrounding areas. They inflicted serious death and damage. But German efforts grew weak by 1941. The Luftwaffe had lost too many planes and crews to British fighters. The RAF had saved Britain. "Never in the field of human conflict was so much owed by so many to so few," said British Prime Minister Winston Churchill.

The Allies Versus the Axis Powers in Europe

When the United States declared war on Germany and Italy, a new phase of the air campaign began. Britain now had active allies in the United States and the Soviet Union, which had joined the war six months earlier. Before America's entry, Britain had been on the defensive. With America by its side, Britain mounted an offensive campaign.

Between 1942 and 1945, the Western Allies went hard after the German homeland. The US Eighth Air Force went on its first strategic bombing run over Germany on 17 August 1942. It used B-17 bombers with Norden bombsights for daytime precision strikes. Meanwhile, the RAF hit Germany at night. The Allies' strategy was threefold:

1. Protect Allied supply routes between the United States and Britain to stop the Germans from blowing up Allied ships carrying materiel—*the equipment and supplies of a military force*
2. Bomb the German war industry (factories, refineries, and warehouses)
3. Destroy German roads, bridges, and communication lines

B-17 Flying Fortresses on a bombing run over Neumunster, Germany, in 1945

Courtesy US Air Force

CHAPTER 3   The Evolution of the Early Air Force

The Right Stuff

Major Glenn Miller: Morale Booster

Glenn Miller was one of most successful American bandleaders ever. But at 38, he was too old to be drafted into the war. So he volunteered. He started as a captain in the Army Air Corps. Miller felt that his swing music could cheer up Allied troops overseas.

Miller put together the 418th Army Air Forces Band in 1943. Fifty Airmen—almost all enlisted—played for it. Many thought that this wartime band was even better than Miller's civilian band. The band played all over Europe. It made weekly radio broadcasts and often gave live shows every night. The musicians also did everyday military duties, such as playing Reveille and Taps.

On 15 December 1944 Major Miller took off from England for Paris. The aircraft never made it. No one ever found the wreckage. However, even without its leader, the 418th Army Air Forces Band continued to lift the troops' spirits throughout the remainder of the war. Miller's goal of helping his countrymen lived on. The band evolved into today's USAF premier jazz band, "The Airmen of Note."

Major Glenn Miller
Courtesy US Air Force

As noted earlier in this lesson, the Allied plan had one big hitch—the lack of fighter escorts. The Allies suffered huge losses, especially in 1943 over Germany. Not until March 1944 would bombers reach Berlin. Fighters eventually accompanied the bombers. From 1942 to 1943, the Allies also focused on German positions in France. The hop across the English Channel was just more than 20 miles.

In mid-1943 the US Army's Ninth and Twelfth Air Forces became free for duty in Europe. They'd been fighting in North Africa. Now they provided support to the Allies invasion of Italy. The Allies invaded the island of Sicily in July 1943 and Italy's mainland in September 1943. Upon Italy's surrender soon after, the Ninth and Twelfth turned their attention to support actions against Germany, including the D-Day invasion. (Fighting against German and Italian fascist troops in Italy continued until May 1945.)

Operation Tidal Wave

In 1943 the German war machine was going strong. Allied forces were trying to figure out how to slow it down. General Hap Arnold's advisory staff came up with a plan to cut off a vital Luftwaffe and German army resource—their fuel. This meant the destruction of the oil refineries at Ploesti (ploh-yesht), Romania. Although there were many raids on Ploesti during World War II, none was more effective or costly than the one conducted on 1 August 1943.

During the war, the Ploesti oil refineries produced approximately one-third of the fuel Germany used. By July 1943, five bomb groups began training for *Operation Tidal Wave* in North Africa. It was decided that all bombers were to be launched from Benghazi, Libya, to fly a low-level strategic strike mission against the refineries.

Operation Tidal Wave would be the largest bombing mission conducted by Allied Air Forces up to this point in the war. One hundred and seventy-seven B-24 Liberator bombers and 1,700 airmen would participate in this dangerous mission. There would be no fighter escorts available, and bombers were expected to drop their bombs at 300 feet above the target. Because the flight covered more than 2,000 miles, additional fuel tanks were added to the bomb bays to give the B-24s enough fuel to fly at low level and return to their base in Benghazi.

Consolidated B-24 Liberator over an oil refinery in Ploesti, Romania

Courtesy US Air Force

The Ploesti oil fields were heavily defended. The Germans had realized how important the oil fields were and placed 40 six-gun batteries that included antiaircraft guns, hundreds of heavy machine guns, and barrage balloons with heavy cables designed to cause aircraft to lose control if they hit the cable with their wings. The Luftwaffe also had placed approximately 400 fighter aircraft in the area to defend the oil fields.

Operation Tidal Wave did have some success. Almost 50 percent of oil production was lost after the bombing mission, but at a high cost to Allied aircraft and crews. Of the 177 B-24s taking part in the mission 62 were shot down or were so badly damaged that they could no longer fly. 310 airmen were killed in action, 108 were captured and held as prisoners of war, and 78 were held in neutral Turkey until the end of the war.

D-Day

The Western Allies delivered a backbreaking blow to Germany in 1944. They called it *Operation Overlord*. The purpose of this invasion, which would take place on "D-Day," was to retake Western Europe once and for all.

The D-Day invasion began on 6 June 1944 at Normandy, on the northern coast of France. But preparations had begun much earlier. For two months, bombers and fighters of the Army Air Forces and RAF had been striking at German positions in and around Normandy. They wanted to soften the German defenses. They hit airfields, railroads, and coastal barriers. They downed Luftwaffe planes. They wiped out as many military targets as they could within a 130-mile radius of the Normandy beaches where American, British, and Canadian Soldiers would land.

The night before the invasion, the Allies hit German forces extra hard. Hundreds of bombers, which normally flew at an altitude of 20,000 feet, raced through the air just 100 feet to 1,000 feet above ground. After dropping their bombs, the aircraft strafed targets on the ground.

On D-Day, fighters played a critical role. They, too, conducted bombing missions. The P-38 Lightning could carry two 1,000-pound bombs. One group of fighters flattened a German command center. In addition, fighters strafed German infantry. They protected ships crossing the English Channel en route to the Normandy shoreline. They were also used to escort, or *accompany*, bombers and air transports.

The first wave of transports that crossed the channel on D-Day was breathtaking. It was nine aircraft wide in a line extending for 230 miles. Many of the Soldiers arriving on the beach by air transport were paratroopers. A paratrooper is *an infantry Soldier who is trained to parachute, often behind enemy lines*. Transports also towed gliders carrying men and materiel. Most of these gliders were made of wood and fabric, just as the earliest planes were. The maneuver was huge. On the evening of 6 June one glider took off from England for France every 15 seconds.

A formation of Douglas A-20 bombers with specially painted stripes providing air support to the D-Day invasion
Everett Historical/Shutterstock

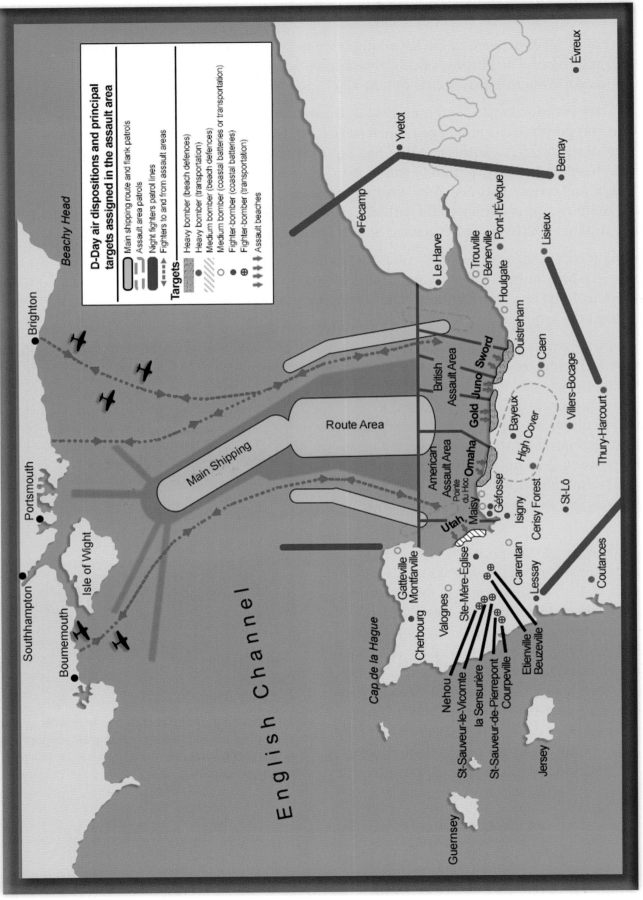

The D-Day Invasion

The D-Day invasion and the Battle of Normandy cost 57,000 Allied Soldiers and Airmen their lives. But it was a major turning point in the war. It gave the Allies a foothold in Europe. More than 1 million men landed along 60 miles of beaches within seven weeks of D-Day. But there was still more to be done to achieve final victory in Europe.

The Final Push

Despite these gains, the Allies had not yet won the war in Europe. From the beaches in Normandy, the Western Allies pushed through the rest of France, then Belgium, and Luxembourg. Meanwhile, on the Eastern Front, the Soviets pushed the Germans out of the Soviet Union and through Eastern Europe. In September the first US patrols entered Germany.

At the end of December 1944, the Germans made a desperate surprise counterattack in Belgium. They wanted to divide the Allied armies and force a negotiated peace. The epic battle in the Ardennes Forest is known as the *Battle of the Bulge.* Allied airpower provided crucial help to the brave ground troops in beating back this attack. Luftwaffe planes attempted to support German forces by attacking US troops on the ground. But in most cases Allied fighters stopped them short of their targets. Although poor weather limited flying on several days, Allied bombers seriously hampered German efforts. They bombed roads, railroads, and bridges behind the lines. This made it more difficult for the Germans to move up supplies and troops.

German defeat in the Battle of the Bulge not only sealed the Nazis' fate on the ground, it also destroyed German airpower. The commander of the Luftwaffe fighter arm, Lieutenant General Adolf Galland, wrote, "The Luftwaffe received its death blow at the Ardennes offensive."

The strategic bombing of Germany went on. The Allied bombers and escorts hit airplane factories, oil refineries, and roads. Allied manufacturers poured out thousands of airplanes and other supplies. The intensity of air battles grew. By 1945 most bombing runs over Germany involved between 1,000 and 1,500 bombers. The Eighth and Fifteenth Air Forces conducted these missions.

The Army Air Forces and RAF ran out of targets by 15 April 1945. They had unloaded 2.5 million tons of bombs on the Axis Powers in Europe. The United States and Britain lost 8,000 bombers and 7,000 fighters. But the Luftwaffe, despite its initial advantage, lost 33,000 airplanes. On 7 May 1945 the Germans surrendered. The European chapter of the war was closed.

Paul W. Airey: From POW to the First Chief Master Sergeant of the Air Force

In July 1944 Paul W. Airey was flying his 28th combat mission in the European theater. He was a technical sergeant and radio operator. He was flying on a B-24 over oil refineries around Vienna, Austria. Antiaircraft fire severely damaged the bomber. The pilot ordered everyone to jump. Airey parachuted from 18,000 feet into a field. Austrian farmers beat him and held him until German forces arrived. Airy became a prisoner of war (POW).

The Germans sent him to a POW camp called Stalag Luft IV. Later, when Allied forces approached the region, the Germans made all the prisoners march 400 miles to a camp deeper in Germany. British forces arrived in May 1945 and freed the POWs.

Despite his experience as a prisoner, Airey loved the Air Force. On 3 April 1967, he became the first Chief Master Sergeant of the Air Force (CMSAF). Now he was in the highest NCO position and the enlisted advisor to the secretary of the Air Force and Air Force Chief of Staff.

CMSAF Airey helped produce the Weighted Airman Promotion System (WAPS). This system included clear, weighted criteria for promotion, including test scores and time-in-grade, and is still in use today. He noted that "WAPS is the most equitable promotion system for enlisted personnel in any of the US armed services." Airey considered this his most important contribution as the CMSAF. He retired on 1 August 1970 and died in 2009.

Chief Master Sergeant Paul W. Airey
Courtesy US Air Force

The Women's Airforce Service Pilots

SHORTLY AFTER EUROPE WENT TO WAR IN 1939, two Americans tried to find a way for more women to get into the air. The result of their efforts was the Women's Airforce Service Pilots program (WASP).

This program didn't come about overnight. Jacqueline Cochran contacted First Lady Eleanor Roosevelt about setting up a training program for women pilots in September 1939, the month Germany invaded Poland. Nancy Harkness Love got in touch with Lieutenant Colonel Robert Olds about forming an all-women's ferrying squadron in 1940. These women's job would be to fly military aircraft from factories to bases.

It took a while to grant either request. First, America hadn't even entered the war as of 1939. Second, the country at that time had more pilots than planes.

But eventually the women got their wishes. Once the United States entered the war, the Army Air Forces needed to free men for combat duty. Cochran was in charge of training women through the Women's Flying Training Detachment (WFTD). Some 1,879 female pilots passed through her program. Love became director of the Women's Auxiliary Ferry Squadron (WAFS). In 1943 the Army Air Forces merged the two units into WASP. While Cochran was in charge of WASP, Love headed its ferrying-operations arm. WASP pilots were not members of the military but civil service employees. By the time WASP was broken up in December 1944, its female pilots had flown 60 million miles and ferried 77 kinds of aircraft.

Four women pilots from the WASPs trained to ferry the B-17 Flying Fortress
Credit: Courtesy US Air Force

Jacqueline Cochran: From Foster Care to the Air

Jacqueline Cochran (1906–1980) had grit. She was in foster care as a child. Cochran said she didn't get her first pair of shoes until she was 8 years old. She trained to be a beautician. She liked to make people happy through her work. But along the way, she caught the flying bug.

It started in 1932, when she met millionaire Floyd Bostwick Odlum in New York City. She told him she'd like to start a cosmetics company. Odlum said that in that case, she'd need to find a way to fly her goods to many markets. Cochran saved up money for flying lessons. Rather than cosmetics, flying became her career.

In 1938 Cochran broke a record with a nonstop flight from Los Angeles to Cleveland in eight hours, 10 minutes, 31 seconds in a P-35 fighter. This won the cross-country Bendix Race. Around this time, she reached an altitude of 33,000 feet—a new women's record. She performed other feats as well. Cochran liked to say: "I might have been born in a hovel, but I was determined to travel with the wind and the stars."

Jacqueline Cochran (*left*) with her adjutant officer and pilot trainees in Texas

Courtesy US Air Force

As early as 1939 she tried to get the US government to let her train women pilots to help with the war effort. The women couldn't take on roles in fighting, but they could fill support roles and allow more men to enter combat, she figured. The government turned her down.

But later President Franklin D. Roosevelt asked her to study ways to use female pilots in the Army Air Corps. Things went better this time. Cochran, with 25 other women, went to London and served in the British Air Transport Auxiliary in 1942. At Major General Hap Arnold's request, Cochran later established the Women's Flying Training Detachment within the Army Air Forces.

After the war, Cochran kept on flying. In 1953 she became the first woman to break the sound barrier.

Nancy Harkness Love's Early Love of Flight

Nancy Harkness (1914–1976) came from a wealthy Philadelphia family. She attended excellent schools: the Milton Academy in Massachusetts and Vassar College in New York. Early on, she fell in love with flying. She once buzzed her college campus and was suspended from her classes for two weeks.

As a young woman, Nancy fell in love with another pilot, Robert Love. He was an Air Corps Reserve officer. The two married in 1936. They founded an aviation business in Boston. Nancy Love got more flight time in other ways. Through the Bureau of Air Commerce, she was a test pilot for new landing gear with three wheels.

Nancy Love is best known for getting the Women's Auxiliary Ferrying Squadron set up. Major General Hap Arnold turned down her first proposal in 1940. Then in 1942 Robert Love talked to Colonel William Tunner, who was in charge of the stateside division of the Army Air Forces Ferry Command. Robert Love told Tunner about Nancy Love's piloting skills. Tunner desperately needed more pilots.

Nancy Love got her Women's Auxiliary Ferry Squadron. It had 25 female pilots. She was its director. After the war, she was awarded an Air Medal.

Nancy Harkness Love
Courtesy US Air Force

The Ninety-Nines

FEMALE PILOTS FACED ALL SORTS OF BARRIERS at the start of the 20th century. For example, they weren't allowed to compete in air races with men. Nor were they allowed to work as commercial pilots.

In 1929 there were only 117 licensed American female pilots. A few of them decided to form an all-women pilots' club. They sent letters to all the licensed women pilots. Ninety-nine of the women replied. So Amelia Earhart proposed the group be named The Ninety-Nines. Earhart was the first president.

At first, the women mostly discussed air races. But they gradually took on a more important role. They began to lobby for rights for women pilots. Before Word War II, they worked on the National Air Marking Program to create a navigation guide visible to the naked eye for pilots without instrument panels or radios. During the war, members joined the Women's Airforce Service Pilots. Those with nursing training became flight nurses and treated Soldiers wounded in battle.

The Ninety-Nines organization still exists. It has more than 5,500 members. And it continues the air-marking program to this day.

Significant Allied Air Campaigns in the Pacific Theater

Having defeated Germany, the Allies could turn their full attention to Japan. In 1931 Japan reached beyond its borders for more and more resources like oil. It invaded Manchuria and China. In 1940, after France fell to Germany, Japan snatched French Indochina. (French Indochina is today the three countries of Vietnam, Cambodia, and Laos.)

The United States and Britain wanted to put an end to these land grabs. They imposed a trade embargo on Japan. An embargo is *a legal ban on commerce.*

In response, Japan went after its biggest naval threat in the region: the US Pacific fleet at Pearl Harbor in Hawaii. If Japan could defeat this fleet, it could place bases on islands in the Pacific to protect its imports.

As it entered war with America, Japan knew it must maintain its navy. And even though the navy wasn't especially strong in the beginning, it was successful. It surprised the Americans at Pearl Harbor. It drove the Allies all the way to Australia by mid-1942.

The war in the Pacific was quite different from that in Europe. The European war was fought mostly on land. The war against Japan was fought mostly at sea and on a series of islands scattered across great distances. So airpower was used differently, too.

The US and Britain were up to their elbows with the war in Europe in 1942. Yet they began a Pacific offensive. It started with two important battles.

The Right Stuff

Major Arthur T. Chin: Early Ace of World War II

Chinese-American Major Arthur T. Chin (1913–1997) was born in Portland, Oregon. He took flying lessons as a teenager. Chin started the Portland Chinese Aero Club when still a teen with some of his friends. When Japan invaded China in 1931, they all wanted to go help China fight the Japanese.

When Japan again invaded China in 1937, Chin headed overseas to join the Chinese Air Force. The Chinese thought he was such a good pilot that they sent him to Germany for extra training. When Chin returned to the Chinese Air Force, he flew the Gloster Gladiator and the Curtiss P-40 Warhawk. He made five kills and got half credit for another. This made him an ace. He was one of the first American aces of World War II.

Major Arthur Chin
Courtesy of the American Airpower Heritage Museum

In 1939 Chin was shot down and badly burned. As he fell from his airplane, with his hands on fire, he managed to pull the ripcord to his parachute. Nearby Chinese peasants rescued him. He spent several years in recovery. In 1944 he flew again, now as a member of the US military. He delivered supplies over the Himalayan Mountains to Chinese troops. This was necessary because Japan had cut off land and sea routes to China. Chin remained in China until 1949, when the Communists took over the country. At that time he returned to Portland, where he died in 1997.

The Battle of the Coral Sea and the Battle of Midway

The Battle of the Coral Sea and the Battle of Midway put the brakes on the Japanese advance through the Pacific. These were air battles fought at sea. Airpower didn't play a supporting role; the US Navy's ships did. During these battles the aircraft carrier became the principal ship in the navy.

The Battle of the Coral Sea took place from 7 May to 8 May 1942. This was the first naval battle in history in which the opposing ships never saw each other.

It was fought entirely by aircraft. US and Japanese planes dive-bombed each other's aircraft carriers off the east coast of Australia. Japan lost two carriers, three heavy cruisers, one light cruiser, two destroyers, and 100 airplanes. The United States lost the aircraft carrier USS *Lexington*, one destroyer, one tanker, and 50 airplanes.

The two sides fought the Battle of Midway from 3 to 6 June 1942. Both sides launched planes from their carriers. The US knew where the Japanese ships were because it had broken the Japanese Navy's secret code. The Japanese suffered greater losses in this clash. They lost four aircraft carriers, one heavy cruiser, three destroyers, and 275 airplanes. In addition the Japanese Navy left the battle site with many damaged vessels, including three battleships, three heavy cruisers, one light cruiser, and a handful of destroyers. By contrast, the United States lost only one aircraft carrier (the USS *Yorktown*), one destroyer, and 150 airplanes.

With this battle, the tide of the Pacific war turned in favor of the United States. The Japanese never recovered from their losses at Midway.

Strategic Bombing in the Pacific

Less than a month before the Battle of the Coral Sea, America had delivered its first blow to Japan, with the famed Doolittle raid. Lieutenant Colonel Jimmy Doolittle led 16 B-25 bombers over Japan on 18 April 1942.

Until that day, Japan had promised its people their island nation was safe. Doolittle's raid proved otherwise. The bombers took off from the US Navy aircraft carrier USS *Hornet*. They hit Tokyo, Kobe, and other cities. Japan didn't shoot down a single B-25.

One of the Doolittle Raiders takes off from the USS *Hornet*.
Courtesy US Navy

There wasn't enough fuel to return to the *Hornet*, so most of the crews landed in China. One outcome of this raid was that Japan brought some of its air forces home for defense.

Two years later the United States made more strategic bombing attacks over Japan. On 15 June 1944 American B-29s took off from China. Later that year they took off from the Mariana Islands. Many Japanese civilians died in these raids. One reason was that the Japanese placed their factories in the middle of residential neighborhoods. Furthermore, in February 1945 the bombers switched from explosive bombs to incendiary bombs—*bombs designed to start fires*. The incendiary bombs created huge firestorms on the ground. Americans dropped such bombs on the cities of Tokyo and Kobe. An estimated 100,000 civilians died.

Many US bombers also met their end in these raids because they had to fly unescorted from the Marianas, some 1,500 miles away. To reduce their losses, the US forces fought long and hard for the island of Iwo Jima in 1945. Once they captured it, their new air base was only 750 miles from Japan.

The Atomic Bomb

By mid-1945 Germany had surrendered. A few weeks earlier, Harry S. Truman became president of the United States when Franklin D. Roosevelt died. The firebombing of Tokyo and Kobe was weakening Japanese resolve. But more was needed to break the Japanese military government's will. The Japanese had fought tenaciously to defend the islands of Iwo Jima and Okinawa. President Truman and US military leaders considered previous battles with Japanese soldiers, whose training had instilled in them not to surrender. The president and military leaders were convinced that trying to fight their way through the Japanese home islands would cost hundreds of thousands of US casualties—and the lives of millions of Japanese.

So Truman asked the military to use its newest weapon, the atomic bomb. The United States had two of them. In the first attack, Colonel Paul W. Tibbets Jr. piloted the *Enola Gay*, a B-29 bomber. It took off from Tinian Island in the Pacific with the first of the atomic bombs. The crew dropped it on the city of Hiroshima on 6 August 1945. Hiroshima was selected because it was a large manufacturing city and a major military headquarters supporting the Japanese war effort. After Japanese leaders gave no indication of surrendering, the US dropped the second bomb on Nagasaki, another major weapons-manufacturing city, on 9 August. Tens of thousands died in each blast. Tens of thousands more would die of radiation poisoning. Japan surrendered on 14 August 1945.

Colonel Paul Tibbets standing in front of the B-29 Superfortress *Enola Gay*

Courtesy US Air Force

World War II ended with the utter defeat of Germany, Italy, and Japan. But developments during the war set the stage for much of the next 40 years. The nuclear arms race, jet airplanes, and humanity's first steps in space all happened because of developments during the war. The war also ended in a new rivalry between the Western democracies and the Soviet Union.

At the same time, however, the US economy and the recovering economies of Europe would grow rapidly after the war. And advances in commercial aviation were at the forefront of that growth.

✔ CHECKPOINTS

Lesson 2 Review

Using complete sentences, answer the following questions on a sheet of paper.

1. What is the date of the Japanese attack on Pearl Harbor?

2. Who were the leaders of Italy and Germany?

3. What is one reason airpower morphed so quickly between World War I and World War II?

4. Besides airfields, supply lines, and military posts, what else was often a target in World War II?

5. To avoid getting bogged down in trench warfare, what new strategy did Germany perfect? What was its goal?

6. What were the three points of the Allies' new tactical operation plan that grew out of their experiences in North Africa?

7. What is the name of the general who thought up the combat box formation?

8. What is formation pattern bombing?

9. What was the name of the battle that first put a stop to the Nazi war machine?

10. What was the Allies' threefold bombing strategy against Germany?

11. Which two battles put the brakes on the Japanese advance through the Pacific?

12. What was the name of the US bomber that delivered the atomic bomb on Hiroshima?

APPLYING YOUR LEARNING

13. Based on the stellar record of the Tuskegee Airmen in World War II, describe one single accomplishment that helped solidify their legacy.

Significant Aircraft of World War II

Quick Write

_____

_____

Time and time again we read about heroic acts accomplished by military servicemen and women during wartime. After reading the story about Staff Sergeant Vosler, name three things he did to help his crew survive, which earned him the Medal of Honor.

Learn About

- the development of bombers during the war
- the development of fighters during the war
- the development of transports during the war

FORREST LEE "WOODY" VOSLER of Lyndonville, New York, was a radio operator and gunner during World War II. He was the second enlisted member of the Army Air Forces to receive the Medal of Honor.

Staff Sergeant Vosler was assigned to a bomb group based in England. On 20 December 1943, flying on his fourth combat mission over Bremen, Germany, Vosler's B-17 was hit by anti-aircraft fire, severely damaging it and forcing it out of formation.

Vosler was severely wounded in his legs and thighs by a mortar shell exploding in the radio compartment. With the tail end of the aircraft destroyed and the tail gunner wounded in critical condition, Vosler stepped up and manned the guns. Without a man on the rear guns, the aircraft would have been defenseless against German fighters attacking from that direction.

While providing cover fire from the tail gun, Vosler was struck in the chest and face. Metal shrapnel was lodged into both of his eyes, impairing his vision. Able only to see indistinct shapes and blurs, Vosler never left his post and continued to fire.

The heavily damaged aircraft struggled to stay airborne. Vosler volunteered to be thrown from the plane to lighten the load—this selfless request was denied.

He crawled back to his position at the radio and desperately tried to send out a distress signal. While the pilot was preparing to ditch the plane into the sea, Vosler, now completely blind and using only memory and sense of touch, managed to fix the radios and send the distress signal while rapidly fading in and out of consciousness.

As the aircraft began sinking into the sea, Vosler made his way onto the wing just in time to save the injured tail gunner from falling off into the frigid waters. He held him there with one hand, both men bleeding out and on the brink of death, until other crewmembers assisted them into the dinghy. A dinghy is *a small rubber raft that is used by people escaping from a sinking boat or aircraft.* Both men survived.

Vosler was awarded the Medal of Honor by President Franklin D. Roosevelt.

"The extraordinary courage, coolness and skill he displayed in the face of great odds, when handicapped by injuries that would have incapacitated the average crewmember, were outstanding," Vosler's Medal of Honor Citation. He was also promoted to technical sergeant.

Following his lengthy recovery period, Vosler was discharged from the military and went on to pursue his bachelor's degree. He served more than 30 years with the Veteran's Administration in Syracuse, New York. He counseled other veterans and performed community service. Vosler died in February 1992 at the age of 68.

Vocabulary

- dinghy
- Soviets
- bomb load
- flak
- bombardier
- kamikaze
- drop tanks
- flame out
- self-sealing
- transport

Technical Sergeant Forrest L. Vosler
Courtesy US Air Force

Broadly speaking, pilots flew three major kinds of aircraft in World War II: the bomber, the fighter, and the transport. Both the Allies and Germans also employed gliders to land troops behind enemy lines. This lesson will look at some of the most significant aircraft that participated in the conflict.

The Development of Bombers During the War

The US and Britain developed a full range of heavy, medium, and light bombers for both strategic and tactical operations. The Soviets, Germans, and Japanese, however, generally focused on smaller bombers to support ground or antinaval operations. (The Soviets were *the people and especially the political and military leaders of the Union of Soviet Socialist Republics—the official name of the Soviet Union*.) Germany's failure to develop a four-engine strategic bomber is often cited as an important reason it lost the Battle of Britain.

US Bombers

Boeing B-17 Flying Fortress

The Flying Fortress is one of the most famous airplanes ever built. It served in every combat zone. But it's best remembered as the workhorse of the American daylight bombing campaign against Nazi Germany. Although few B-17s were in service on 7 December 1941, production quickly sped up after the United States entered the war. Almost 12,800 of the bombers were built by the time production ended in May 1945.

A B-17 Formation bombing Dresden, Germany on 17 April 1945
Everett Historical/Shutterstock

The B-17 carried a crew of 10 and a bomb load of 6,000 lbs. A bomb load is *the total weight of bombs a plane can carry.* Its top speed was 302 mph, and it could fly more than 2,000 miles.

The B-17's crew did not fly in comfort. While the plane could fly higher than 30,000 feet, it was not pressurized. The men sat cramped for hours in terrible cold and often suffered from altitude sickness. While the aircraft bristled with 13 defensive machine guns, the Germans found its weakness was a front-on attack. But the plane was so well built that it could often make it back to base despite serious damage to wings, engines, the fuselage, or the tail.

Fortunately, American workers could produce two B-17s for every one that was shot down. By the end of the war, more B-17s were ready for action than ever.

Consolidated B-24 Liberator

The B-24 Liberator was in production by 1941. It had a 2,850-mile range and could fly 303 miles per hour (mph). It carried a crew of 12, had 10 machine guns, and could carry 8,000 lbs. of bombs. Some 18,000 were built during the war, more than any American aircraft in history.

An Army Air Forces (AAF) report from 1944 nicely expresses the reasons for designing the B-24:

> The Liberator was the result of the Army Air Forces' desire for a long-range running mate for the Flying Fortress. In football language, we sought a good ball carrier who was just as good at long end runs as he was at off-tackle smashes. We thought of the B-24 in terms of patrol and transport as well as bombardment, and it has performed all three functions splendidly.

The B-24 was employed in every combat theater during World War II. Because of its great range, it was well suited for such missions as the raid from North Africa against the oil industry at Ploesti, Romania, on 1 August 1943. This also made the airplane suitable for long over-water missions in the Pacific. The B-24's drawbacks were that it was physically difficult to fly and much more vulnerable to enemy flak than the B-17. Flak is *fire from anti-aircraft artillery.*

B-24s in flight over Italy during World War II
Everett Historical/Shutterstock

North American B-25 Mitchell

The B-25 medium bomber was the type used by Lieutenant Colonel Jimmy Doolittle in the 1942 raid on Tokyo. First flown in 1940, the B-25 had a range of 1,200 miles and could fly as fast as 275 mph. It carried a crew of six, 13 machines guns, and a bomb load of 4,000 lbs. By the end of the war, North American Aviation had built a total of 9,816 B-25s.

B-25s saw duty in every combat area. American, Dutch, British, Chinese, Soviet, and Australian pilots all flew the Mitchell. Beside its use for level bombing from medium altitudes, it was often used in the Pacific for bombing Japanese airfields and beach emplacements from treetop level. It was also effective at strafing and bombing enemy shipping.

B-25 Mitchell bomber
Everett Historical/Shutterstock

During its long career, the B-25 was modified several times. The first major change occurred with the G model, which included a 75-millimeter cannon and two fixed machine guns in the nose. In the J version, the most numerous type, the aircraft returned to its initial arrangement as a level bomber, with a transparent nose that included one flexible and two fixed .50-cal. guns.

Driven by requirements in the Pacific, J model was changed further to feature a solid nose that housed eight fixed machine guns for low-level attack. This allowed the B-25 to devastate vehicles and shipping with up to 14 forward-firing guns.

Martin B-26 Marauder

The B-26 Marauder, another medium bomber, flew mostly in Europe and the Mediterranean. It was particularly effective before D-Day in attacking bridges and transportation targets. It could fly 1,100 miles at a top speed of 285 mph. It carried five crewmembers and up to 3,000 lbs. of bombs. The original version of the bomber had four machine guns, but some later models had as many as 12. More than 5,260 B-26s were built.

The B-26 was tricky to fly and required an experienced pilot. It was also vulnerable to enemy flak. Even so, a smaller percentage of this bomber was shot down than of any Allied aircraft—less than one-half of one percent.

Although riddled with bullets in the left engine and wing, a B-26 bomber returns successfully to its base after a 1943 bombing raid in Tunisia.
Everett Historical/Shutterstock

B-26s bombed from medium altitudes of 10,000 to 15,000 feet. Because German fighters were concentrating on the heavier B-17s and B-24s, the medium bombers often met little opposition. American, British, Free French, Australian, South African, and Canadian aircrews all flew the B-26 in combat. It was the first AAF aircraft to operate at night in Europe.

Boeing B-29 Superfortress

The B-29 Superfortress was the long-range bomber of the Pacific theater. It was bigger and faster than the B-17 and the B-24. It could also fly greater distances—5,830 miles, with a top speed of 365 mph. It could carry a crew of 10 to 14 and 20,000 lbs. of bombs, and had 10 machines guns and a 20-millimeter cannon in the tail turret. The plane's biggest weakness was its vulnerability to equipment failure and engine fires, rather than enemy action.

B-29 crews worked in conditions that crewmembers of earlier bombers could only dream about. The cabins were heated and pressurized, and the guns were remote controlled.

The B-29 first flew in September 1942. AAF leaders decided to use the plane in the Pacific Theater, where its range enabled it to fly long missions against Japan over water from bases in China. As the United States continued to take back Pacific islands from the Japanese, the plane later flew from Saipan, Guam, and Tinian.

B-29s dropped the atomic bombs on Hiroshima and Nagasaki in August 1945. The planes in these missions were modified to remove all their armor and machine guns, except the tail turret. This saved weight so the aircraft could carry the heavy atomic bombs over longer distances. The B-29 returned to action in the Korean War.

A B-29 bomber in 1945 flies over the Nakajima Aircraft Co. Musashino Plant, Japan. Smoke on the ground shows the impacts of its bombs.
Everett Historical/Shutterstock

Douglas A-20 Havoc

The A-20 was a versatile light bomber flown by Allied pilots of many nations, including the Soviet Union. It went through many changes during the war. The model with the largest production, the A-20G, carried six forward-firing machine guns and a bomb load of 2,000 pounds. Its range was 950 miles and its top speed 317 mph. American factories built more than 7,000 of the planes, including 2,850 A-20Gs. The Soviets used the A-20 in a ground-attack role. In the Pacific, the A-20 was very effective at low-level strafing attacks against Japanese shipping and airfields.

An A-20G Havoc bomber with D-Day invasion stripes painted on the wings attacks a German machine-gun position on 8 June 1944.

Everett Historical/Shutterstock

Grumman TBF Avenger

The Avenger series aircraft will go down as one of the most potent carrier-based torpedo bombers of World War II. The Avenger was a needed replacement for the outdated Douglas TBD Devastator torpedo dive-bombers. The Avenger first saw service in 1942 and was assigned to the USS *Hornet* for combat in the Pacific Theater.

Restored Grumman Avenger

Philip Pilosian/Shutterstock

The crew of three consisted of a pilot in the forward position, the bombardier in the middle, and a rear-facing gunner. The bombardier is *the person in a military aircraft who controls when bombs are dropped.* The bombardier also had access to the lower fuselage, where he would manage the bombing functions of the torpedo to the front and a defensive machine gun in the rear. The Avenger could carry one torpedo or up to 2,000 pounds of bombs.

About 9,839 Avengers were built with 931 of these going to the British Royal Navy. Avengers were also built by General Motors and designated TBMs. These aircraft were also flown by New Zealand, and after World War II, by Brazil, France, the Netherlands, Uruguay, and Japan.

British Bombers

Avro Lancaster

The Lancaster was to the Royal Air Force (RAF) what the B-17 was to the US AAF. It first flew in 1941 and was one of the most effective heavy bombers of the war. The British used it as a night bomber, but it was versatile enough for other special assignments. It was equipped with groundbreaking radar and navigation devices. Like the B-17, it could take a good deal of punishment and still return home.

Restored Avro Lancaster bomber
IanC66/Shutterstock

The Lancaster carried eight defensive machine guns, and a bomb load of up to 22,000 lbs. Its range was more than 1,500 miles and its top speed 275 mph. It usually carried a crew of only seven, since the British didn't have enough trained airmen for more. The flight engineer doubled as the copilot, although he rarely had enough training to land the plane safely. If the pilot was killed, the crew usually bailed out.

About 7,400 Lancasters were built. Marshal of the Royal Air Force Sir Arthur Harris, who headed Britain's Bomber Command, thought so highly of the plane that he called it, "the greatest single factor in winning the war."

Handley Page Halifax

The Handley Page Halifax was the RAF's second four-engine bomber. It carried out its first raid in March 1941. It carried a crew of seven and a bomb load of 9,000 lbs. Its range was 1,260 miles and its top speed 312 mph. It was defended by nine light machine guns.

The Halifax's main drawback was this light defensive firepower. The plane suffered heavy losses in air raids. Beginning in 1942 early versions of the Halifax were taken off bomber duty and used to patrol the British coastline, carry paratroopers, and tow gliders.

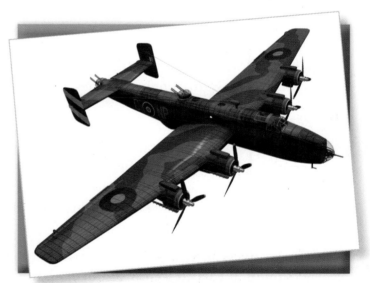

A 3-D drawing of a Halifax bomber
Plutonius 3d/Shutterstock

Artist's rendering of an Il-2 Sturmovik

master24/Shutterstock

Soviet Bombers

Ilyushin Il-2 Sturmovik

The Sturmovik was the Soviets' main ground-attack aircraft during the war. Some 37,000 were built, making it the most-produced plane during the conflict. Its role on the Eastern Front was crucial—Sturmoviks destroyed more German tanks than did any other aircraft. The Germans called it the *Black Death*, while Stalin was quoted as saying "The Red [Soviet] Army needs the Il-2 as it needs air and bread."

The Il-2 carried a two-person crew, two cannon, three machine guns, eight rockets, and a bomb load of 1,300 lbs. Its top speed was 251 mph, and its range was 373 miles. Its armor-plated fuselage protected the pilot, engine, and fuel. This allowed it to attack German tanks through a curtain of small-arms fire. Like any low-speed, low-altitude aircraft, however, the Il-2 was vulnerable to attack by German fighter planes.

Petlyakov Pe-2

The twin-engine Pe-2 started out as a dive-bomber to repel the German invasion of the Soviet Union in 1941. But it also served throughout the war as a reconnaissance aircraft, fighter-bomber, night-fighter, and light bomber as events required. The Pe-2 is often compared to the British Mosquito in its versatility.

The Pe-2 was faster than the Il-2, with a top speed of 336 mph and a range of 932 miles. It carried a crew of three, up to five machine guns, and a bomb load ranging from 2,600 lbs. to 3,500 lbs. The Soviets produced many variations of the aircraft, depending on its intended function. More than 11,000 were built.

Tupolev Tu-2

The Tu-2 bomber shares a distinction with the Pe-2—the designers of both planes were political prisoners in Stalin's prisons when they drew the original designs. Setting out in 1938 to produce a bomber better than the Luftwaffe's Ju 88, Andrey Tupolev did more than that—he created one of the most successful aircraft of the war. He also got himself freed from prison and awarded the Stalin Prize.

Tupolev Tu-2
Ivan Cholakov/Shutterstock

The Tu-2 carried two engines, four crewmembers, six machine guns, two wing cannon, and a bomb load of up to 3,300 lbs. It could fly as fast as 324 mph, as high as 29,000 feet, and had a range of 1,243 miles. It could take a significant amount of enemy fire and operate in harsh winter conditions.

Like the Pe-2, the Soviets expanded the Tu-2's function to many different uses—ground-attack aircraft, all-weather interceptor, reconnaissance aircraft, and even transport. It stayed in service until 1948, and 2,527 were built.

German Bombers

Junkers Ju 87 Stuka

In the first years of the war, the Stuka (pronounced SHTOO-kuh) spread terror across Europe as it swooped down on Polish, French, British, or Soviet troops with a telltale scream to drop its bombs. Although it played an important role in the success of Germany's Blitzkrieg, it proved less successful as time went on. It was slow at 255 mph and easily shot down by British and Soviet fighters. It had to be withdrawn from the Battle of Britain after the RAF destroyed whole formations. It again suffered heavy losses against the Soviets in the Battle of Stalingrad in 1942–43.

German Stuka dive-bombers over Poland in 1939
Everett Historical/Shutterstock

The two-person Stuka carried a twin machine gun, two wing cannon, and a bomb load of 4,000 lbs. Although 6,500 Ju-87s were built, by January 1945, fewer than 170 remained and manufacture stopped.

Heinkel He 111

The He 111 medium bomber was the pillar of German airpower, but it was already obsolete by the time World War II got under way. Deployed in the Spanish Civil War in the infamous raid on Guernica, it remained an effective weapon right until Germany surrendered.

The Germans developed the He 111 as an airliner that could secretly be converted to a bomber. Its top speed was 271 mph and its range 1,212 miles. It carried a crew of five and was armed with front and rear cannon and four machine guns. It could hold a bomb load of 4,400 lbs. About 7,300 He 111s were built.

Artist's rendering of a Heinkel He 111 German bomber

Kostyantyn Ivanyshen/Shutterstock

Although the He 111 was a powerful weapon, the Battle of Britain exposed it as vulnerable to fighter and anti-aircraft defenses. Even so, the aircraft continued in service, used against Allied shipping, in the invasion of the Soviet Union, and at the Battles of Stalingrad and Kursk, significant Soviet victories. It was also used to tow gliders and as a transport. The bomber made its last appearance as a launch platform for the German V-1 rocket—the first cruise missile—at the end of the war.

Junkers Ju 88

The Ju 88 was new when the war broke out on 31 August 1939, but it became Germany's main bomber of the war. Some 15,000 planes were produced, more than all other German bombers put together.

Like British, American, and Soviet twin-engine bombers, the Ju 88 proved versatile. Commanders could adapt it for minelaying, torpedo bombing, night-fighting, ground attack, and destroying tanks. It had a top speed of about 300 mph and range of 1,510 miles. It carried a crew of four, seven cannon, and a bomb load of about 4,000 lbs.

Junkers Ju88-D

Courtesy US Air Force

Ju 88s played a major role in the invasions of Norway and France. They took significant losses in the Battle of Britain, but saw widespread use in the invasion of the Soviet Union. They were very effective against Allied ground targets, but anti-aircraft fire and Allied fighters gradually reduced their numbers. As night-fighters, they had the range and electronic gear to intercept British bombers attacking Germany. At the end of the war the Germans used one model as a pilotless bomb delivered by fighter planes.

Japanese Bombers

Mitsubishi G4M

A land-based naval bomber, the G4M was an effective medium bomber that saw service throughout the war. The Japanese used it in China and against the Allies in the Pacific.

Mitsubishi G4M *Betty*
Courtesy National Naval Aviation Museum

Codenamed *Betty* by the Allies, the G4M is associated with two famous incidents. In the first, G4Ms along with Kate torpedo bombers attacked and sank the British battleship HMS *Prince of Wales* and the battle cruiser HMS *Repulse* off the Malaysian coast three days after Pearl Harbor. It was one of the worst days of the war for Britain's Royal Navy and showed the vulnerability of even heavily defended ships with no air cover. In the second incident, American P-38 fighters in April 1943 shot down two G4Ms in the Solomon Islands. Among those killed was the Japanese commander-in-chief, Admiral Isoroku Yamamoto.

The G4M had a long range of 3,765 miles and could travel at 272 mph. It carried a crew of seven, six defensive machine guns, and a bomb load of 2,205 lbs. It could reach an altitude of 29,000 feet. About 2,400 G4Ms were built.

The G4M's reliability and long range made it a feared aircraft. But it lacked sufficient armor for the crew and was prone to burn quickly if its fuel ignited—so much so that Americans called it the "flying cigarette lighter."

Mitsubishi Ki-21

First flown in 1937, the Ki-21 was the Japanese Army Air Force's standard medium bomber at the beginning of the war with the United States. Dubbed the *Sally* by the Allies, it had a top speed of about 300 mph and a range of 1,678 miles. It could reach altitudes of almost 33,000 feet. It carried six defensive machine guns, a crew of seven, and a bomb load of 1,654 lbs.

Mitsubishi Ki-21 *Sally* bombers
Official US Navy Photograph/Courtesy National Naval Aviation Museum

Like most Japanese aircraft, the Ki-21 suffered from weak defensive armament and inadequate armor protection for the crew. However, it proved to be a very effective weapon throughout the war, although it became obsolete well before 1945. It proved especially dangerous as a kamikaze aircraft at the end of the war. A kamikaze (kah-mih-kah-zeh) was *an airplane loaded with explosives to be flown in a suicide attack, especially against a ship.* Mitsubishi built 2,064 Ki-21s.

A restored Nakajima B5N torpedo bomber reenacting the Pearl Harbor attack

Kevin M. McCarthy/Shutterstock

Nakajima B5N

The B5N *Kate* was considered the best torpedo-bomber in the world at the time of Pearl Harbor. The Japanese used B5Ns both in China and the Pacific as land- and carrier-based attackers. Besides making up a large part of the Japanese force at Pearl Harbor, B5Ns were deployed effectively in battles at the Coral Sea and Midway. They received credit for sinking three American aircraft carriers—the USS *Hornet*, USS *Lexington*, and USS *Yorktown*—along with many other Allied ships.

As the war went one, however, the Allies' improved pilots and better fighters were able to counter the B5N, which was slow and heavy when fully loaded with torpedoes. The *Kate* had a top speed of 235 mph and a range of 1,237 miles. It carried a crew of three, three machine guns, and a bomb load of 1,760 lbs.

The Development of Fighters During the War

When the war began, both Germany and Japan produced fighter aircraft that were superior to most Allied aircraft. As the conflict progressed, however, the US, Britain, and the Soviet Union caught up to and surpassed the Axis powers with fighters that were more nimble and rugged, and that had a longer range. Just before the end of the war, however, both Germany and Japan introduced sophisticated advanced aircraft. Had these been introduced earlier, they could have changed the war's outcome.

US Fighters

Lockheed P-38 Lightning

The distinctive two-fuselage P-38 is one of the iconic images of World War II. This versatile long-range fighter saw service on all fronts. After first encountering it in North Africa, Luftwaffe pilots began calling it the *Der Gabelschwanz Teufel* ("the forked-tail devil"). It was subject to continuing improvement over its years of service.

The Lightning performed many different missions during the war, including dive-bombing, level bombing, strafing, photoreconnaissance, and long-range escort. When it began combat operations from England in September 1943, it was the first fighter with the range to escort bombers into Germany.

But it was in the Pacific that the Lighting gained real fame. Its long range enabled missions over vast ocean stretches, including the shootdown of Japanese Admiral Yamamoto in 1943. Seven of the top eight AAF aces in Pacific flew the P-38, which became the standard AAF fighter in the theater for most of the war.

The P-38 had a top speed of 414 mph and carried one pilot. Its heavy armament included a cannon and four machine guns. It could also carry 3,200 lbs. of bombs or 10 rockets. Some 10,000 P-38s were produced.

Four P-38s of the Fifteenth Air Force in formation over Yugoslavia in 1944
Everett Historical/Shutterstock

ONE OF THE MOST SIGNIFICANT combat missions of World War II was flown by P-38s and men of the 339th Fighter Squadron based at Guadalcanal. American code-breakers had intercepted a message detailing Admiral Yamamoto's planned visit to Bougainville Island, Papua New Guinea. Admiral Yamamoto was a Japanese marshall admiral and the commander-in-chief of Japanese naval forces. He oversaw the planning of the surprise attack on the US Pacific Fleet at Pearl Harbor, 7 December 1941.

Japanese Admiral Isoroku Yamamoto
Courtesy Naval History and Heritage Command, NH 63430

On 18 April 1943, 16 P-38 Lightning aircraft took off from Guadalcanal Air Field and flew northwest at just thirty feet above the water to prevent detection by Japanese military observers. The P-38 was chosen because it was the only fighter aircraft at the time that could fly the 1,000 miles necessary to intercept Yamamoto's airplane and return home. After almost four hours of flying, the American pilots spotted Yamamoto's aircraft flying in a formation with another Japanese bomber and six Japanese fighters as escort. Four P-38s attacked the bomber formation while the remaining 12 engaged the Japanese fighters. Within a few short minutes, both Japanese bombers were shot down, killing Admiral Yamamoto. This successful mission led to the elimination of Japan's naval commander and its most respected military strategist.

P-63E Kingcobra
Courtesy US Air Force

Bell P-39 Aircobra and P-63 Kingcobra

The P-39 was considered a failure as one of America's top pursuit fighters. But it revolutionized fighter aircraft design for that period. One of its distinguishing characteristics was the engine mounted behind the pilot. It didn't operate well above 17,000 feet, but it performed well for missions like ground strafing. A later redesign of the P-39 was renamed the P-63 Kingcobra. Although very similar in appearance, the Kingcobra was given a more powerful engine. In all, more than 3,300 Kingcobras were built, with more than 70 percent of them operated by the Soviet Air Force.

The Free French

The *Free French* were French forces that had escaped to Britain or were located in some overseas colonies. They rallied behind French General Charles de Gaulle in London to resist the Germans after the French government surrendered in 1940. Free French forces fought with the Allies in North Africa and throughout Europe. French Resistance agents operating inside occupied France were part of the Free French forces. The Free French became the official French government after they led the liberation of Paris in 1944.

Soviet pilots in particular appreciated its cannon, fired through the propeller hub, which was very useful in ground attack. Other P-39s were flown by the Free French forces.

Besides its cannon, the Aircobra carried two machine guns in the nose and four more under the wings. Its top speed was 376 mph, and it had a range of 650 miles.

Curtiss P-40 Warhawk

When Japanese fighters streaked out of the sky to attack Pearl Harbor in 1941, two P-40 Warhawks were able to take to the air and face them. The P-40 was the best American fighter available in numbers early in the war. It also flew in defense of the Philippines the same year, in China in 1942, and North Africa in 1943. The 99th Fighter Squadron, the first African-American US fighter unit, at one time flew P-40s. Three famous Soviet pilots became aces flying the Warhawk. It's perhaps best known as the fighter of the Flying Tigers in China, painted with shark's teeth on the nose.

Restored P-40 Warhawk painted with the shark-teeth insignia of the Flying Tigers
Joseph Sohm/Shutterstock

The P-40 was not the fastest fighter in the air, but it was reliable and extremely rugged in battle. It was particularly effective in close-air support of ground troops. It served throughout the war until more capable aircraft appeared. More than 14,000 P-40s were built. They served in the air forces of 28 nations.

The P-40 had a top speed of 362 mph and a range of 850 miles. It carried six machine guns in its wings and could carry a bomb load of 700 lbs.

The Flying Tigers

In 1937 then-Captain Claire Chennault resigned from the US Army Air Corps and accepted an offer to assist with reorganizing the air force of China, which was on the verge of war with Japan. By 1941 Chennault had started the 1st American Volunteer Group (AVG). He equipped the force by obtaining P-40B Warhawk aircraft that the British government was willing to give up in order to get an upgraded version of the P-40. But it took direct intervention from President Franklin Roosevelt to allow officers and enlisted personnel to resign from the US military in order to join the AVG in China. After the US entered World War II, the AVG was disbanded and reorganized under the US Army Air Corps. It became Fourteenth Air Force, now led by recommissioned Major General Chennault. Although the AVG was short-lived, its combat effectiveness was legendary, with an estimated 299 Japanese aircraft destroyed and another 153 aircraft probably destroyed.

Republic P-47 Thunderbolt

No US fighter was produced in greater numbers than the rugged, heavily armed P-47. Some 15,600 Thunderbolts were built and delivered to pilots in several countries, including the United States, Brazil, Free France, Great Britain, Mexico and the Soviet Union. When introduced in 1943, it was the heaviest and largest single-seat fighter ever built.

Restored P-47G Thunderbolt
IanC66/Shutterstock

Nicknamed the *Jug* by those who flew it, the P-47 was effective both as an escort for strategic bombers and as a ground-attack fighter. It was gradually replaced by the P-51 Mustang, which could escort bombers to targets beyond the P-47's range. But in support of the US Army in Western and Southern Europe during 1944–45, the Thunderbolt wreaked havoc among German armor, troops, and transport. P-47s also saw action against the Japanese in the Pacific and China. A longer-range version introduced late in the war allowed it to escort B-29s over Japan.

The P-47 had a maximum speed of 433 mph and a range of about 1,100 miles with drop tanks—*external fuel tanks that could be dropped from the plane when empty.* It carried eight machine guns and 2,500 lbs. of bombs or rockets.

North American P-51 Mustang

Perhaps the best-known and most effective US fighter, the game-changing P-51 operated in every combat zone of World War II. It was so versatile that it later saw service during most of the Korean War from 1950–53. Production of Mustangs reached 15,000.

The introduction of the long range P-51 with its British Rolls-Royce Merlin engine was a key moment in the bombing campaign against Germany. Equipped with drop tanks, the Mustang could make it to Berlin and back. In addition, when it arrived over Germany, the Mustang could also outperform almost all German fighters. Along with P-38 Lightnings, P-51s provided desperately needed protection for Allied heavy bombers, significantly cutting losses of aircraft and crews. By the end of the war, Mustangs had destroyed 4,950 enemy aircraft in the air, more than any other AAF fighter in Europe.

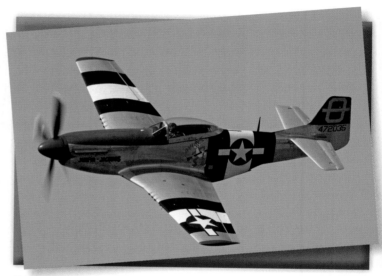

P-51D Mustang
Paul Drabot/Shutterstock

The P-51 could reach a top speed of 437 mph and had a range of 1,000 miles. It carried six machine guns and either 10 rockets or a bomb load of 2,000 lbs.

Grumman F6F Hellcat

The F6F was designed to replace the Grumman, F4F Wildcat. The Wildcat was the mainstay aircraft of the Pacific Fleet, but inferior to the Japanese Zero. The Hellcat used the same design formula as its predecessor, "but with more of everything." Its superiority and toughness significantly changed the war in the Pacific.

Entering service in 1943, the Hellcat's perhaps most famous service took place in June 1944 during the Battle of the Philippine Sea. In this engagement, known as the *Marianas Turkey Shoot,* Hellcats helped turn a Japanese attack into a disaster for the Japanese Navy. F6Fs destroyed almost 350 enemy planes with only 20 American aircraft lost. The battle devastated Japan's naval airpower, which never recovered. Serving in both the US Navy and the Royal Navy, Hellcats shot down 75 percent of all Japanese aircraft during the war.

An F6F Hellcat prepares to take off from the aircraft carrier USS *Yorktown* in November 1943.

Courtesy National Archives and Records Administration, ARC 520641

The F6F could fly up to 380 mph, with a range of 944 miles. It carried six machine guns in its wings, six rockets, and a bomb load of 2,000 lbs. More than 12,000 were built.

Navy F4U Corsairs in flight over South Pacific in 1943

Everett Historical/Shutterstock

Vought F4U Corsair

Called the *Whistling Death* by the Japanese for the sound it made in flight, the F4U Corsair may have been the finest carrier-borne fighter of the war. Vastly superior to the Japanese Zero, it established air superiority over the Pacific islands in the hands of US Navy and Royal Navy pilots. Flown from land bases by US Marines, it also showed its effectiveness in ground attack at Iwo Jima and Okinawa.

The Corsair was so effective that it continued in Navy service right through the Korean War, where it took on jet-powered North Korean MiG fighters. The French Air Force flew F4Us in several conflicts through 1962.

The Corsair was known for its "inverted gull" wing shape. It was fast, with a top speed of 470 mph, and had a range of about 1,000 miles. It carried six machine guns or four wing-mounted cannons and a bomb load of 2,000 lbs.

British Fighters

Supermarine Spitfire

One of the best and most famous of all World War II fighters, the Spitfire earned its reputation during the Battle of Britain when it helped beat back the Luftwaffe. Spitfires excelled in low-level dogfights, where their high maneuverability and skilled pilots neutralized the advantages German fighters—especially Messerschmitt Bf 109s—enjoyed at higher altitudes.

The sleek Spitfire could be immediately recognized by its narrow fuselage and pointed wings. Although it later went through many changes, in 1940 it carried eight machine guns or two cannon and four machine guns. As a fighter-bomber, it could carry 500 lbs. of bombs. Its top speed was 355 mph and range was 395 miles. Later versions had a longer range.

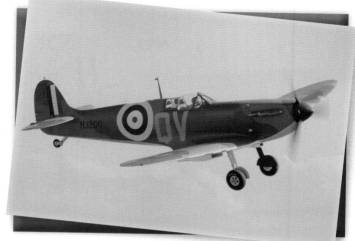

Supermarine Spitfire
Paul Wishart/Shutterstock

Spitfires also served as fighter-bombers and carrier-based fighters. More than 20,000 of the aircraft in several versions would be produced by the end of the war—the most of any Western Allied fighter. Spitfires served in every theater of the war.

Hawker Hurricane

While Spitfires did battle with the German fighters in the Battle of Britain, the Hawker Hurricane served as the bomber killer. The RAF's first monoplane fighter, it entered service in 1937. Nearly twice as many Hurricanes as Spitfires fought the Germans in 1940. The rugged Hurricanes shot down 80 percent of all German aircraft in the battle.

The Hurricane went through several changes during the war, but by 1941 its usefulness as an interceptor had ended. It went on, however, to serve as a fighter-bomber and "tank buster" in Europe, North Africa, and the Far East.

The Hurricane could reach speeds of 340 mph with a range of 700 miles. It carried 12 machine guns and a bomb load of 500 lbs. or eight rockets.

Hawker Hurricane
Courtesy US Air Force

De Haviland D.H. 98 Mosquito

The famous British Mosquito—nicknamed *Mossie*—was a versatile aircraft that saw heavy use during World War II. This fighter-bomber, reconnaissance, night fighter, patrol, and anti-ship aircraft was built mostly of plywood with a balsa wood core. The plane carried a two-person crew—a pilot and navigator who sat side by side.

De Haviland Mosquito

Kamira/Shutterstock

It was fast—the Mosquito could reach a top speed of 378 mph and carry a bomb load of 4,000 lbs. Its guns included four machine guns in the nose and four cannon under the cockpit floor. It could fly up to 1,855 miles and as high as 33,000 feet.

Almost 8,000 Mossies were built in Great Britain, Canada and Australia. Although best known for their service with the RAF, Mosquitoes also flew in several AAF units. Both air forces used Mossies as fighter-bombers, reconnaissance aircraft, and night fighters.

Gloster Meteor

The Meteor is notable as Britain's first jet fighter. Deployed about the same time as Germany's famous Messerschmitt Me 262 jet, it was soon in action destroying German V-1 buzz bombs in the air. Meteors never engaged in combat with piloted German aircraft, but they were used at the war's end in a ground attack role, destroying 46 enemy aircraft on the ground. Most combat losses of Meteors resulted from friendly fire, when the jets were mistaken for Me 262s.

Gloster Meteor

MAC1/Shutterstock

The early Meteor's top speed was 410 mph, and its range 500 miles. It was armed with four cannon; some types could carry 16 rockets under the wings.

Soviet Fighters

Mikoyan-Gurevich MiG-3

One of the few Soviet fighters available when the Germans invaded in 1941, the MiG was lightly armed and performed poorly at low altitudes. Even so, the second leading Soviet ace recorded most of his victories while flying it. It proved most effective as a bomber escort and close-support aircraft.

Mikoyan-Gurevich MiG-3
ID1974/Shutterstock

Early MiG-3s carried a machine gun over the engine and two over the nose. Later models featured an additional machine gun under each wing. Some models could also carry two small bombs or six rockets. The MiG-3 had a top speed of 398 mph and a range of 777 miles.

Yakovlev Yak-3

The Yak series of fighters appeared just as the German invasion of the Soviet Union began. Maneuverable and fast, the Yak could take on a German Messerschmitt or Focke-Wulf fighter or function as a ground attack aircraft. It functioned well even during the harsh Russian winter. Different versions of the plane had different weaponry and ranges.

The Yak-3 first appeared in 1944 with nearly 5,000 aircraft built. The Yak-3 had an impressive kill-to-loss ratio over Luftwaffe fighters thanks to high maneuverability, speed, and powerful machine guns. The Yak-3 had a powerful 1,700 horsepower engine added later that increased its top speed to 450 mph.

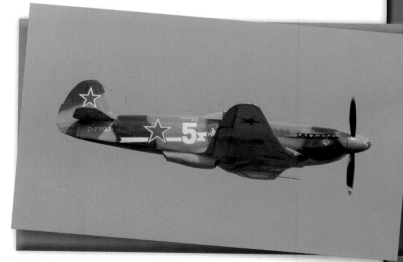

Yakovlev Yak-3
photokup/Shutterstock

The Yak-3 was superior to German fighters at low altitudes. Once a squadron of 18 Yak-3s met a force of 30 Luftwaffe fighters, and is claimed to have shot down 15 of them with the loss of only one Yak. The plane was the favorite of a Free French fighter group that operated with Soviet forces on the Eastern Front.

Yakovlev Yak-9

The Yak-9 was developed from an experimental version of the Yak-7. This fighter was designed about the same time as the Yak-3, but in the end would prove to be the most produced Russian fighter during WW II. It was lightly armed to keep its weight down and had a top speed of 404 mph.

The most common version, the Yak-9, was deployed after 1942 and played a vital role in turning back the Germans at the Battle of Stalingrad. Like most Yaks, it had a cannon in the propeller hub and one or two machine guns. The Yak-9 had a top speed of 372 mph and a range of 435 miles. Longer-range versions appeared later in the war.

Yakovlev Yak-9

John Steel/Shutterstock

Some 37,000 Yaks of different types were built, the largest number of any fighter during the war. There were more Yaks in the air than all other Soviet fighters put together. The final version was built after the war, and served with Communist forces in Korea.

Lavochkin La-5

The La-5, with its wooden fuselage and powerful engine, was one of the best fighters of the war—especially at low altitudes. Most Soviet aces in the war flew this aircraft. First deployed in numbers at the Battle of Stalingrad, it eventually played a leading role in giving the Soviets air superiority on the Eastern Front.

The La-5's top speed was 403 mph with a range of 475 miles. It carried two cannon mounted above the engine.

Lavochkin La-5 on display at Verkhnaya Pyshma, Ekaterinburg, Russia

Nikita Maykov/Shutterstock

German Fighters

Messerschmitt Bf 109/Me 109

The Bf 109, often called the Me 109, became the symbol of Luftwaffe airpower. First deployed during the Spanish Civil War in the mid-1930s, it had one of the most advanced aerodynamic designs of the time. Fast and maneuverable, it gave the RAF's Spitfires and Hurricanes all they could handle. It couldn't turn as tightly as a Spitfire, but it was faster in a climb or dive.

Messerschmitt Bf 109
Courtesy US Air Force

The Bf 109 excelled at high altitudes. But it in the Battle of Britain it was forced into escorting bombers at lower levels, where British fighters performed better. Another weakness was the Bf 109's short range. It couldn't accompany German bombers further than London. It wasn't unusual for Bf 109 pilots to run out of fuel on the return trip home. Then they had to bail out over the English Channel. This meant German bombers could not attack production and training targets in large parts of the British Isles—a major reason the Luftwaffe lost the battle. The Germans deployed longer-range models of the Bf 109 later in the war.

In the many pitched battles with the AAF over Europe, the Bf 109 often provided cover while the more heavily armed Focke-Wulf Fw 190s attacked the bomber formations. But as the war went on and the Allies on both fronts deployed superior fighters, the Bf 109 became unpopular with German pilots. Although the superior Fw 190 began to replace it, various models of the Me 109 remained in production to the end of the war. It remained the most numerous German fighter and is said to have shot down more enemy fighters than any other plane on either side.

The Bf 109's top speed was 354 mph; its range was 475 miles—later increased. Most models had two cannon and two machine guns. Versions of the Bf 109 continued to be produced after the war, until 1948 in Czechoslovakia and 1958 in Spain. About 33,000 Bf 109s were produced.

Focke-Wulf Fw 190

The Fw 190 first appeared in action in 1941 and was the best propeller-driven fighter Germany produced. At several points it was superior to existing Allied fighters, even at low altitudes. After Fw 190s shot down dozens of RAF planes during the 1942 British raid on Dieppe, France, the British had to rush to improve the Spitfire.

Fast, strong, and heavily armed, the Fw 190 could be adapted to many uses: fighter-bomber, ground attack, reconnaissance, and night fighting. It could take a lot of damage and still get home. Luftwaffe pilots generally regarded it as superior to the Bf 109, although the Messerschmitt performed better at high altitudes.

Focke-Wulf 190
Philip Pilosian/Shutterstock

The Fw 190 could fly at up to 408 mph, with a range of 519 miles. It could carry two cannon, four machine guns, and a 1,000-lb. bomb. Some 20,000 Fw 190s were produced.

Messerschmitt Me 262 Schwalbe

The Me 262 Schwalbe (SHVAL-buh, meaning *swallow*) was the world's first operational turbojet aircraft. First flown in 1942, it proved much faster than conventional airplanes. Fortunately for the Allies, development problems with its engines, Allied bombings, and cautious Luftwaffe leadership contributed to delays in producing large numbers of the aircraft.

Had German air defense been able to deploy the Me 262 in a timely manner, some observers believe the outcome of the war could have been different. But German dictator Adolf Hitler insisted instead that it be developed as a bomber. Even so, Luftwaffe leaders produced a small number of fighters for testing.

Messerschmitt Me 262
Courtesy US Air Force

There were many bugs to iron out. The jet was difficult to fly and dangerous to land. Tires often burst during landing, and engines were prone to flame out—*to fail for nonmechanical reasons.*

Even so, the jet was very effective against Allied bomber formation. AAF bombers responded by destroying hundreds of Me 262s on the ground. Allied fighter pilots found they could pick off the swift jets by hovering over their airfields and attacking them as they tried to land. Of the more than 1,400 Me 262s produced, however, fewer than 300 saw combat. Most Me 262s could not be deployed because of the destruction of Germany's transportation system. Many of those that were couldn't fly because they lacked fuel, spare parts, or trained pilots.

The Me 262 could travel at 540 mph with a range of 650 miles. It carried four cannon and 1,000 lbs. of bombs.

Japanese Fighters

Mitsubishi A6M Reisen

If the Messerschmitt Bf 109 symbolized German airpower in Europe, the A6M Reisen (pronounced ree-sin, meaning *zero fighter* in English) is the icon of Japanese airpower in the Pacific. Called simply *Zero* by the Allies, it was produced in greater numbers than any other Japanese aircraft.

The Zero was designed to be light and fast. Although that was a strength, it was also the plane's weakness. The designers omitted armor for the pilot, and the fuel tanks were not self-sealing—*able to seal a leak to prevent fuel from leaking or igniting.*

In the early part of the war, Allied aircraft like the P-40 were at a disadvantage in a dogfight to a Zero flown by a skilled pilot. But experience with the Flying Tigers in China and at the Battle of Midway taught US pilots important lessons. The key to fighting the Zero was to stay out of dogfights and instead use diving tactics and superior weaponry against the fragile Japanese fighter.

Mitsubishi A6M Reisen
Courtesy US Air Force

Later Allied aircraft were faster and had more firepower, ending the Zero's dominance. Japan responded by adding self-sealing fuel tanks and armor plate, but this made the plane heavier and less maneuverable. In addition, Japan was losing experienced pilots faster than it could replace them.

By the fall of 1944, the Japanese were using Zeros in kamikaze attacks. They used more Zeros than any other aircraft for such missions.

The A6M carried two cannon and two machine guns. It could travel at 346 mph and had a long range—1,930 miles. The Japanese built 10,815 Zeros.

Kawasaki Ki-61 Hien

Code-named *Tony* by the Allies, the Ki-61 Hien (swallow) was developed by Japanese designers working under a German engineer. It so resembled a Messerschmitt Bf 109 that American pilots often mistakenly reported they had fought Japanese flying the German fighter.

The Hien appeared in 1943 and pioneered Japan's use of self-sealing fuel tanks and armor for the pilot. This allowed it to score many victories against Allied aircraft. Its biggest drawback was its underpowered engine, which the Japanese were unable to correct before the war ended.

Kawasaki Ki-61 Hien
Official US Navy Photograph/Courtesy National Naval Aviation Museum

The Hien's top speed was 367 mph, with a range of 1,118 miles. It carried two nose cannon and two machine guns in the wings. About 3,100 Hiens were built.

Nakajima Ki-84 Hayate

The Ki-84 Hayate (hah-yah-tay, meaning *gale*) entered the war in the summer of 1944. Codenamed *Frank* by the Allies, it could climb faster and maneuver better than a Thunderbolt, Mustang, or Hellcat. Like the German Me 262, had the Ki-84 entered the war earlier, it could have caused the Allies serious difficulty.

Nakajima Ki-84 Hayate
Courtesy National Naval Aviation Museum

Unlike many previous Japanese fighters, the Ki-84 was not only fast—it was heavily armed and very rugged. It fought successfully in the Philippines and tenaciously at Okinawa. But it was beset by shoddy workmanship and problems with fuel lines and hydraulics. At the end of the war it was used to attack high-altitude B-29s, which did not play to its low-altitude excellence.

The Ki-84 could fly at 392 mph, with a range of 1,350 miles. It carried two cannon and two machine guns.

The Development of Transports and Gliders During the War

Transports were built to move people and cargo. But as military planes, they were less comfortable than commercial aircraft. In military terms, a transport is *a vehicle— aircraft, ship, or other—that carries people, supplies, tanks, and artillery.*

In World War II, transports were essential as never before for resupplying armies, medical evacuation, inserting paratroopers, and towing gliders.

Transports

Douglas C-47 Skytrain

The best-known Allied air transport was the C-47 Skytrain (called the *Dakota* in its British version). Dubbed the *Gooney Bird* by its uniformed fans, it was based on the Douglas Aircraft DC-3—a wildly successful civilian airliner introduced in 1935.

Beginning in 1942, the C-47 served in every combat theater of the war. It could operate even off primitive airstrips and was considered nearly indestructible. A C-47 could carry 28 passengers, or 18-to-22 fully equipped paratroopers, or about 6,000 lbs. of cargo or 18 stretchers and three medical personnel. It had a crew of three and could fly 1,513 miles. It could reach 232 mph but generally cruised at around 175 mph. Some 9,348 C-47s were built by the end of the war.

The C-47 proved its utility long after the war. It served in the Berlin Airlift, the Korean War, and even in the Vietnam War.

A C-47 painted with D-Day invasion stripes
johnbraid/Shutterstock

Douglas C-54 Skymaster

C-54 Skymaster
Courtesy US Air Force

The C-54 Skymaster was the AAF's first four-engine transport. It was the military version of the civilian DC-4E. Although the C-54 entered service in 1942, the civilian version didn't appear until after the war. With a range of 3,000 miles, the C-54 could fly nonstop to either the European or Pacific theaters.

During the war C-54s flew a million miles a month over the North Atlantic—some 20 round trips a day. A special C-54 became the first presidential aircraft, for President Franklin Roosevelt. The 2nd Ferrying Group, which used women pilots, flew C-54s.

The Skymaster had a crew of six—including two relief members—and a maximum load of 28,000 pounds of cargo or 49 passengers. About 1,120 C-54s were built.

Like the C-47, the C-54 served long after the war, including in the Berlin Airlift, the Korean War, and on into the 1970s. The Navy version was known as the R5D.

Curtis-Wright C-46 Commando

C-46 Commando
Courtesy US Air Force

The C-46 Commando was the primary transport of the Pacific Theater. The significant advantage of the C-46 is that it featured a pressurized cabin and could carry up to 36 combat-ready troops.

Although used in all theaters during World War II for carrying paratroopers and towing gliders, the C-46 gained fame by flying materials and supplies from India over the Himalayan Mountains or the "Hump" into China. This was a very dangerous flight, due to lack of navigational aids and the poor weather encountered over the "Hump."

With more than 3,000 aircraft built, the C-46 was a low-wing monoplane with retractable landing gear. It could obtain a top seed of 269 mph with an operational range of 1,200 miles. It was the largest and heaviest twin-engine transport of World War II.

Junkers Ju 52

Lovingly referred to by German soldiers as *Tante Ju* (Auntie Yu), the slow and noisy Ju 52 was the backbone German Army transport. It first flew in the early 1930s. Like the C-47, it was originally designed as a passenger airliner. And like its American counterpart, it was versatile, rugged, and reliable.

The three-engine Ju 52 would win no beauty contests, but it served the German Army everywhere in Europe, the Soviet Union, and North Africa. The Ju 52 flew rebel Nationalists in the Spanish Civil War. It dropped German paratroopers into Crete, a Greek island, in 1941. In 1942 it supported the Axis forces around Stalingrad in the Soviet Union.

Junkers Ju-52
IanC66/Shutterstock

Much smaller than the C-47, the Ju 52 carried a crew of three and 18 passengers. Its top speed was 165 mph and its range was about 540 miles. Ju 52s continued to serve in several countries after the war. The last one retired from commercial air service in New Guinea in the late 1960s.

Gliders

Gliders were used in World War II to land troops, weapons, and materiel behind enemy lines. The Germans had some early success with this at the Belgian fortress of Eben-Emael in 1940. Towed by Ju 52s, German gliders landed on top of the fortress and at nearby strongpoints. The silent nighttime attack took the Belgians by surprise, and they surrendered the next day.

The advantage of gliders was that large numbers of troops could be landed quickly without needing parachute training and without getting widely separated from each other. There were serious difficulties, however. Maneuvering a glider in the wake of the towing aircraft could be treacherous. Towing cables often broke early, leaving the glider to its fate miles from the target. And the gliders needed to land at 70 mph wherever they could find a strip of land. At less than 49 mph, a glider could stall and crash. Many accidents and deaths resulted.

Gliders figured in the Allied invasion of Sicily in 1943. In March 1944, American engineers and special forces led by British Major General Orde Wingate landed in gliders behind Japanese lines in Burma. *Operation Thursday* landed some 20,000 international soldiers from Britain, Burma, the United States, Hong Kong, and West Africa with the support of the RAF and AAF. Bringing bulldozers and other heavy equipment with them, they succeeded in building landing strips. That allowed more gliders to fly in during the following week, bringing more troops, weapons, and supplies—including pack mules.

Waco CG-4 glider
Courtesy US Air Force

Thousands of American, British, and Canadian troops used gliders to land behind German lines in France the night before D-Day on 6 June 1944, and again in the German-occupied Netherlands during the unsuccessful *Operation Market Garden* the following September.

Waco CG-4A Hadrian

The CG-4A was the US Army's most widely used glider. Almost 14,000 were built during the war. It could carry 4,060 lbs. of troops and cargo—15 fully equipped troops and two pilots. It could also carry a Jeep or a howitzer—a small cannon. Its maximum towing speed was 150 mph, although it was usually towed more slowly.

Airspeed Horsa

The British Airspeed Horsa was much larger than the CG-4A. Made mostly of wood, it could carry two pilots and about 25 troops. It could carry a Jeep or an antitank gun. It had a gliding speed of 100 mph. Some 3,655 Horsas were built.

DFS 230

The smaller German DFS 230 saw service throughout the war. It was an assault glider, meant to land on top of its target using a parachute for a brake. It could approach the target at a very steep angle and land within 60 feet. Armed with a machine gun, it carried nine soldiers and a pilot. Its gliding speed was 100 mph.

The DFS 230 was used in several offensive operations and to resupply surrounded German forces on the Eastern Front. It also participated in the successful German mission to rescue Italian dictator Benito Mussolini from prison after his overthrow. More than 1,500 DFS 230s were built.

✔ CHECKPOINTS

Lesson 3 Review

Using complete sentences, answer the following questions on a sheet of paper.

1. What were two drawbacks of flying the B-24 Liberator bomber?

2. Why was a smaller percentage of B-26 Marauder bombers shot down than of other Allied bombers?

3. Describe two pieces of equipment used on the Avro Lancaster that made it such a good nighttime bomber.

4. What was the most important factor in selecting the P-38 Lightning for the attack on Admiral Yamamoto's aircraft in 1943?

5. What was the most significant air battle of the F6F Hellcat—one that became a disaster for the Japanese Navy?

6. Which fighter became the world's first turbojet aircraft?

7. Why were transport aircraft so important in World War II?

8. What was the nickname given to the best-known Allied transport in World War II?

9. Which Allied transport was used to fly supplies and materials across the Himalayan Mountains?

APPLYING YOUR LEARNING

10. Both Allied and Axis countries built thousands of aircraft to conduct combat, reconnaissance, transport, and bombing missions in the hope of gaining a strategic advantage over their enemy. Which aircraft do you think played the most significant roles during World War II and why?

CHAPTER 4

An FAA air traffic controller at Midway Airport in Chicago
Courtesy National Air Traffic Controllers Association

Commercial and General Aviation Take Off

Chapter Outline

"Flying has torn apart the relationship of space and time; it uses our old clock but with new yardsticks."

Charles Lindbergh

Quick Write

_____

_____

Imagine you were a member of Congress reading about the Grand Canyon crash in the newspaper during the summer of 1956. After reading the following story, what new laws would you want passed to make it safer to fly?

Learn About

• What created the need for regulating aviation
• The organizations that provide oversight of aviation activities
• The impact regulation had on aviation
• The impact deregulation has had on commercial aviation

ON 30 JUNE 1956, two airliners left Los Angeles, one right after the other, a little after 9 a.m. One was a Trans World Airlines plane heading for Kansas City. The other was a United Airlines plane on its way to Chicago.

They flew through "controlled airspace" for a certain distance away from the airport. After that, they were on their own. In those days, there was no radar network to tell air traffic controllers where planes were located in real time. Pilots were supposed to pass specific geographic checkpoints. They would radio positions to their company dispatchers, who would in turn phone them in to the regional air traffic controller. Other than this radio contact, pilots had significant discretion over their routes.

The two planes were flying on visual rules, through uncongested space. It was a beautiful day, but there were some thunderstorms. Both pilots would need to take care to avoid them.

Some 90 minutes after takeoff, though, the two planes collided over the Grand Canyon. A garbled message came from the United flight: "Salt Lake, United 718…ah… we're going in." And then there was nothing. All radio contact from both flights was lost. Airline dispatchers and air traffic controllers tried in vain for several hours to reestablish contact. All 128 people aboard the two aircraft perished. A private pilot found the wreckage of both planes in the canyon. At the time, it was the worst commercial aviation accident in US history.

Investigators later determined the "probable cause" of the crash was that the two pilots simply didn't see each other until it was too late. Perhaps the thunderstorms got in the way. It was suggested that one or both of the pilots might have been trying to give passengers a better view of the Grand Canyon.

There was no radar tracking of the flights and no flight data recorders to guide investigators. (These are the "black boxes" you hear about in news reports whenever a plane crashes.) They had to piece the story together by examining the wreckage and listening to recordings of radio messages. Their findings led to a complete overhaul of the commercial aviation system in the United States.

Vocabulary

- air traffic control
- airways
- complacency
- decertify
- free market
- antitrust laws
- network industry
- flows
- grids

The severed tail of TWA Flight 2, photographed by National Park Service rangers during the accident investigation

National Park Service/Wikimedia Commons

The crash site in the Grand Canyon was designated a National Historic Landmark in 2014.

Courtesy National Park Service

What Created the Need for Regulating Aviation

The collision over the Grand Canyon was the first commercial airline crash to cause more than 100 deaths. But it wasn't the only major aviation tragedy to rattle public confidence in aviation during the 1950s. For instance, the historic city of Elizabeth, New Jersey, in the shadow of the Newark airport, suffered three plane crashes in a period of less than two months.

US air traffic had more than doubled since the end of World War II. Yet very little had been done to cut the risk of midair collisions. The Grand Canyon collision "really did underscore for the general public, for the first time, that much of the airspace in America was uncontrolled at that time," an aviation safety official said many years later. "Once you got up to 20,000 feet and beyond the terminal radars, it was see and be seen."

And yet this troubling string of accidents occurred just as people were beginning to get used to the idea of air travel. Business travelers had taken to criss-crossing the country by air when they wanted to seal a deal in person. And even ordinary vacation travelers were beginning to consider flying rather than traveling by rail.

It was just half a century after the Wright brothers made that first flight at Kitty Hawk— all of 12 seconds long. Yet aviation was already a booming new industry in the American economic landscape. It was clearly going to be a key part of the nation's transportation system in the years to come.

The federal government had begun to regulate the new commercial airlines in the 1920s and 1930s. But it was clear to President Dwight Eisenhower and to Congress that new approaches were needed.

Development of Federal Regulation of Commercial Flight

As you read in Chapter 2, Lesson 3, the Air Commerce Act of 1926 was the first regulation of aviation in the United States. In 1938, under President Franklin Roosevelt, a new federal agency took charge of civil aviation. It was called the Civil Aeronautics Authority. It set airfares. It also set airlines' routes.

In 1940 the president split this agency in two. Both new agencies were part of the Department of Commerce.

Roosevelt put one of them, the Civil Aeronautics Administration (CAA), in charge of air traffic control—*the ground-based system for keeping aircraft safely separated from one another.* The CAA also licensed pilots and planes. It enforced safety rules. It also developed airways, *the routes that planes must follow through the sky.*

Eventually CAA air traffic controllers would take over responsibility for takeoffs and landings at airports. After the war, radar helped these controllers keep up with the airline boom. In 1946 Congress gave the CAA the task of promoting development of the nation's civilian airports.

The second agency, the Civil Aeronautics Board (CAB), made safety rules. When an accident occurred, the CAB tried to find out what happened. (This was the agency that investigated the Grand Canyon crash.) The CAB also regulated airlines as businesses.

New Approaches to Aviation Safety

But after the horrifying crashes of the 1950s, Congress enacted new laws covering air safety. In 1957, President Eisenhower signed the Airways Modernization Act. Among other things, it required airliners to have flight data recorders.

The following year came the Federal Aviation Act of 1958. It meant to address issues raised by the new jet airliners just coming into service around that time.

The act transferred the duties of the Civil Aeronautics Administration (CAA) to a new body, the Federal Aviation Agency (FAA). The FAA had broader authority on safety matters than the CAA. The FAA also took over responsibility from the Civil Aviation Board (CAB) for making rules covering air safety. The CAB continued to regulate the airlines as businesses. It set fares and routes.

Retired Air Force Lieutenant General Elwood "Pete" Quesada was the first chief of the FAA. As you read in Chapter 3, Lesson 2, he had been a master tactician during World War II. After the war, he became President Eisenhower's special adviser on aviation. He was the president's pick to head the new agency. But Congress demanded a civilian chief. And so Quesada—still in uniform as an Air Force general—resigned his commission to take the new job.

He became known as a crusader for the flying public's safety: "The public acts in faith, faith in the system, and we'll see to backing up that faith," he said. "I'm here to represent the public, and dammit, the public will be protected."

He found out that pilots sometimes strolled through the passenger cabin when they should have been at the controls. He thundered, "This practice must cease forthwith."

On his watch the FAA improved radar and air traffic control systems. It also instituted other technical improvements that made flying safer.

The Civil Aeronautics Administration becomes the Federal Aviation Agency.

Courtesy Federal Aviation Administration

The Organizations That Provide Oversight of Aviation Activities

Since those changes of the late 1950s, the roles of the organizations that oversee aviation have evolved as the industry has evolved. Here is an overview of the principal federal agencies currently involved in aviation.

The US Department of Transportation

The FAA began life as an independent agency. At the time, the federal government had many different agencies focused on some form of transportation. But by the 1960s, President Lyndon Johnson had come to think it would be a good idea to bring all these agencies together in one place.

On 12 January 1966, in his State of the Union address, he first told the American people of his plan for a new executive department. He wanted Congress to authorize the US Department of Transportation (DOT).

The president believed a single department would help him pull transportation policies and programs together into one place. All modes—air, rail, highway, water, and even pipeline—would share a "home" within the government. Congress granted the president his wish later in 1966. On 1 April 1967, DOT began full operations. The FAA, renamed the Federal Aviation Administration, was folded into the new department.

The FAA has its headquarters in the Wilbur Wright and Orville Wright Buildings in Washington, D.C.

Mark Van Scyoc/Shutterstock

The Federal Aviation Administration

The mission statement of the FAA reads, "Our continuing mission is to provide the safest, most efficient aerospace system in the world."

Air traffic control remains a key responsibility for the FAA. Its Air Traffic Organization (ATO) consists of some 35,000 controllers, technicians, engineers and support. The ATO controls 30.2 million square miles of airspace. This is 17 percent of the airspace of the whole world. Besides all of the United States, this territory includes large portions of the Atlantic and Pacific oceans as well as the Gulf of Mexico.

Aviation safety is a top-level priority as well. As of this writing, the United States has been in a golden era of aviation safety. The United States hasn't seen a large airliner crash with major loss of life since 2001. The FAA ascribes much of that success to its "robust safety culture." The agency says it likes to look for risks before they can cause safety problem.

But some observers warn that one of the biggest safety threats may be complacency—*a feeling of satisfaction with the way things are, combined with a lack of alertness to danger.* And new technology can be a hazard. With too many automatic safety systems, these critics worry, pilots may forget how to do the actual work of flying an aircraft.

FAA air traffic controllers working in Grand Rapids, Michigan
Courtesy National Air Traffic Controllers Association

The Right Stuff

Chesley Sullenberger
s_bukley/Shutterstock

Captain Chesley Sullenberger: Hero of the Hudson River

One of the best-known cases of a damaged plane landing safely because the pilot had years of experience, and was not just relying on automated systems, occurred in New York in January 2009. But the story starts decades before at the US Air Force Academy, where Captain Chesley "Sully" Sullenberger flew glider aircraft as a student. Due to his exceptional flying abilities, he was appointed as a student instructor. After graduating in 1973, he flew F-4 Phantom II fighters until he left the US Air Force in 1980.

Captain Sullenberger flew commercial aircraft for the next 29 years. He was flying for US Airways and was taking off from New York's LaGuardia Airport when a flock of geese flew into his engines, knocking them out. He quickly realized he could not make it to any nearby airport and managed to land his Airbus 320 safely in the Hudson River. All 155 people aboard survived. The pilot still knew how to do things the old-fashioned way.

President Reagan and the Air Traffic Control Strike of 1981

Federal air traffic controllers unionized in 1968 as the Professional Air Traffic Controllers Organization (PATCO). In February 1981, the union began negotiations with the FAA for a new contract. Talks stalled. Then on 3 August, more than 12,000 PATCO members went out on strike. This defied a law prohibiting federal employees from striking. President Ronald Reagan called the strike a "peril to national safety." He ordered the controllers back to work within 48 hours, or they would be fired. On 5 August, he made good on his threat. He fired 11,000 controllers. Meanwhile, thousands of flights were canceled as the FAA scrambled to fill the gap left by the strikers.

In October 1981, the Federal Labor Relations Authority decided to decertify PATCO—*to revoke the union's authority to represent its members.* Within a couple of weeks, the FAA started accepting applications for new air traffic controllers. And soon after, those new controllers formed the National Air Traffic Controllers Association. In June 1987 the new union was certified as the sole bargaining unit for controllers working for the FAA.

Over the years, Congress has assigned the FAA additional duties. After a rash of airplane hijackings broke out in the 1960s, Congress gave the FAA a bigger role in security. This role has largely shifted to the Transportation Security Administration.

In 1968 Congress gave the head of the FAA power to set standards to limit aircraft noise. A 1970 law put the FAA in charge of a new airport development program. That law also gave the FAA responsibility for certifying airport safety.

The National Transportation Safety Board

Another part of the new DOT was the National Transportation Safety Board (NTSB). It was newly created in 1967. Its mission is to investigate accidents in all modes of transport. It also investigates accidents having to do with the transport of hazardous materials.

Until the DOT began operations, the Civil Aeronautics Board had responsibility for investigating air crashes. But once the DOT was launched, that investigative role was transferred to the new NTSB.

In 1974, Congress reestablished the NTSB as a completely separate body, outside the DOT. This was meant to give the board greater independence when it has to ask hard questions of the DOT and the agencies within it.

Congress gave the NTSB an additional responsibility in 1996: that of coordinating federal assistance to the families of aviation accident victims. Since 1996, this assistance program has been expanded to cover other kinds of transportation accidents, case by case.

In 2000, the agency established NTSB Academy. The purpose of the academy, now known as the NTSB Training Center, is to share technical skills and investigative expertise with NTSB staff and others in the transportation sector.

Since 1967, the NTSB has investigated more than 132,000 aviation accidents, as well as thousands of surface-transportation accidents. Besides its work in the United States, it also assists with other countries' accident investigations when asked. Its investigators are on call 24/7/365. The NTSB also maintains a Most Wanted List of Transportation Safety Improvements to keep the safety agenda in front of personnel at DOT and other agencies.

NTSB investigators remove the flight data recorders from the UPS 1354 crash in 2013.

Courtesy National Transportation Safety Board

The Transportation Security Administration

As you read earlier, the FAA was born out of tragedy. So it was with the Transportation Security Administration (TSA). On 11 September 2001, terrorists from the Al-Qaeda Islamist group hijacked four airliners in New York and Washington, D.C. They crashed two of them into New York's World Trade Center and one into the Pentagon in Washington. The passengers on the fourth flight resisted, and the terrorists crashed the plane into a field in Shanksville, Pennsylvania. In all, almost 3,000 people were killed.

Part of the response to these attacks was to strengthen aviation security. And so less than three months after the attacks, President George W. Bush signed the Aviation and Transportation Security Act. It created the TSA, a new agency to be responsible for aviation security. It took over this role from the FAA in February 2002.

Clouds of smoke rise from fires at the World Trade Center twin towers as a result of the terrorist attack on 11 September 2001.

Dan Howell/Shutterstock

A TSA officer scans a passenger at the Seattle-Tacoma International Airport.

Carolina K. Smith MD/Shutterstock

For its first few months, the TSA was part of DOT. But the Homeland Security Act of November 2002 created a new federal Department of Homeland Security. The TSA was moved into that new department on 1 March 2003.

The blue-shirted men and women who greet the flying public at airport security checkpoints are no doubt the most familiar part of the TSA. But the agency has other tasks as well.

It screens baggage, of course, and inspects cargo. The Federal Air Marshal Service, which began in 1962 as part of the FAA, now is part of the TSA. The TSA's Office of Intelligence and Analysis works to prevent terrorist attacks against the nation's transportation systems. And like the NTSB, the TSA has responsibilities for all modes of transport, not just aviation.

The Shoe Bomber and the Underwear Bomber

ON 22 DECEMBER 2001, Americans were still reeling from the 9/11 attacks when they got news of another attempted terrorist attack on an American aircraft. Richard Reid, a British citizen, boarded American Airlines Flight 63 from Paris to Miami intending to bring down the aircraft with bombs hidden in his high-top sneakers.

A flight attendant became suspicious when she smelled sulfur from the matches he was using to ignite the device. She and other crew and passengers overpowered Reid. Two doctors on board injected him with sedatives and the jet was diverted to Boston, escorted by F-15 fighters. No one was seriously hurt. Reid is serving life in prison.

Several years later, on Christmas Day in 2009, a Nigerian man, Umar Farouk Abdulmutallab, tried to blow up Northwest Airlines Flight 253 as it was preparing to land in Detroit. He had boarded the flight in Amsterdam, the Netherlands, with a bomb hidden in his underwear. Although he started a fire, there was no explosion. A Dutch passenger subdued him as flight attendants put out the fire.

Investigation revealed that Abdulmutallab was working with the terrorist organization Al-Qaeda in the Arabian Peninsula. He was tried, convicted, and sentenced to life in prison.

The Impact Regulation Had on Aviation

As the jet era began, the "big four" airlines—American, Eastern, TWA, and United—were still on the scene. They competed for passengers with several other smaller domestic carriers.

The Civil Aeronautics Board (CAB) controlled airline routes. It decided who could enter a market; that is, which carriers could offer service between specific points.

When an airline applied to serve a new market, the CAB gave carriers already flying in that area a chance to review the application. Not surprisingly, the established carriers often found a reason to turn down the applicant. They didn't want more competition. That made it hard for newcomers.

Between 1965 and 1978, for instance, the CAB approved fewer than 10 percent of airline applications for new routes. Continental had to wait eight years for approval to fly from San Diego to Denver.

The purpose of federal regulation was to ensure that the airlines operated efficiently and with the greatest good for the greatest number. But regulation sometimes had the opposite effect. It controlled airfares. The fares the CAB set guaranteed airlines a 12 percent return on flights that were 55 percent full. As a result, many people thought it cost more to fly than it should. They thought that regulation worked against free-market principles. A free market is *one that operates on the basis of competition and is not controlled by government.*

The Impact Deregulation Has Had on Aviation

When Jimmy Carter became US president in 1977, pressure for deregulation began to build. Congress passed the Airline Deregulation Act of 1978. This let airlines enter or leave markets and set fares as they saw fit.

Several things happened in response. First, airlines stopped serving many smaller cities where they weren't making money. The larger carriers shifted from "point-to-point" routing to a "hub-and-spoke" system. Passengers now flew from their local airports to a "hub" city, perhaps changed planes, and then continued on. Travelers flying from Boston to Chicago, for example, might have to stop in Pittsburgh.

Second, new airlines sprang up. Donald Burr founded People Express, for instance. It was a tight, "no frills" operation. His fares were almost as low as those on intercity buses. For a few years, his business boomed.

As a result, fares dropped dramatically. Airlines made a lot of money. More people flew. The number of air passengers reached 317 million in 1979.

Then some problems arose. Fuel costs skyrocketed. The US economy went into recession. The airlines expanded faster than they could manage. They began to lose money. The established carriers, with expensive union contracts, couldn't compete against newer carriers that paid their workers less. In 1981 US airlines had a net operating loss of $421 million. The number of passengers fell to 286 million.

A wave of airline bankruptcies followed. Two of the big four, Eastern and TWA, failed. So did Pan Am. Continental, United, and US Airways went bankrupt, too, but were able to reorganize and stay in business.

Analysts are still debating whether deregulation was a good idea. It certainly led to upheaval in the industry. Big airlines were hit worst. Passengers and small carriers benefited the most. Passenger travel more than doubled from the 1979 level, to 656 million people in 2006.

Some discount carriers, such as Southwest Airlines, made great strides. Founded in 1971 by Herb Kelleher and Rollin King, Southwest came onto the scene just a few years before deregulation. But it caught public attention, and market share, in the chaos of the new world of air travel. Southwest had a simple formula for success. It flew to less-expensive secondary airports. It flew point-to-point, rather than through hubs. It used only one model of aircraft. That meant maintenance could be standardized. It also meant any of its pilots could fly any of its aircraft. It turned flights around at the gate as fast as possible. It now has the biggest market share of any airline. It has never lost money for the year.

A Southwest Boeing 737 at the gate
robert cicchetti/Shutterstock

Alfred E. Kahn: Father of Airline Deregulation

When Alfred E. Kahn became the chairman of the Civil Aeronautics Board, in 1977, he didn't really know anything about airlines. He didn't even want the job. He had hoped President Carter would make him head of another federal agency.

But Kahn, an economist, ended up transforming aviation. Today people remember him as the "father of airline deregulation."

Once in the job, he quickly learned what he needed to about airline routes, costs, and prices. He pushed for a law to eliminate the old system of route maps and fare schedules under government control. And he had a knack for talking with people. He could convince them that he was right.

Kahn was a leader of a broad movement, beginning in the mid-1970s, for deregulation in many industries: rail, telephones, electricity, and even stock markets.

At the end of his career it was said of him, "His vision and actions resulted in a profound transformation of the US airline industry and strongly influenced international air transportation."

And the changes he pushed so hard for put him out of a job. He was the last chairman of the CAB. When the board shut its doors, it was the first total dismantling of a federal regulatory regime since the 1930s.

Another View of Deregulation

Most people believe that airline deregulation has been a huge success—but not absolutely everyone. Some skeptics say that if you look hard at the data, you get a different picture of the air travel scene than the consensus suggests.

Consider the air travel boom, for one thing. People who say deregulation was a good thing say that air travel tripled in the 30 years since airlines were cut free from the CAB. But critics make the case that air travel was already expanding before deregulation. It had risen 500 percent in the 20 years before deregulation.

Not everyone accepts that airline prices have fallen so far, either. One study, by a former official of both the CAB and the FAA, claims that "the grant of pricing freedom to the airline industry has generally resulted in average prices being higher than they would have been had regulation continued...."

The loss of airline service continues to be a problem in many places, including smaller cities in the heartland. After all, carriers are now free to pull out of markets they find unprofitable. Loss of service affects even cities like St. Louis, which was an important hub in the early days of transcontinental aviation.

Consolidation Within the Airline Industry

How do these critics explain all this? One of them has written, "Without constraints unfettered competition often becomes unfettered concentration."

The airlines continue to merge and consolidate. And government enforcers of antitrust laws—*laws meant to prevent monopolies*—have sometimes tended to look the other way.

People often note that the country's "legacy" airlines, with their high labor costs, have merged or gone bankrupt. But most of the new competitors that appeared on the scene in the early 1980s are gone, too. They have shut down or been bought out. More than 150 airlines have sought bankruptcy protection or gone out of business since 1978.

Before deregulation, 10 major airlines controlled 90 percent of the market, critics argue. Today, four control 70 percent of the market.

The Airlines as a Network Industry

It can be helpful to think of the airlines as an example of a network industry. Railroads, electricity grids, and telecommunications systems are other examples of network industries. Such industries are of huge importance to a modern economy.

A network industry is *an industry involving both flows and a grid*. The flows are *the mobile elements of a network industry*. These are the aircraft, the trains, the electricity, or the telephone calls. The grids are *the fixed structures of a network industry*. The airports, the tracks, and the power and telephone lines are all parts of grids.

One way to look at the way airlines have changed since 1978 is to say they have been *partially* deregulated. The flows have been deregulated, but not the grid. In theory, it's easy to start a new airline. In fact, it's hard for a startup to get landing slots and find space at the airport gate. This is even truer at airports where a single carrier dominates. And as more airlines have moved to hub-and-spoke routing, more airports have a single dominant carrier.

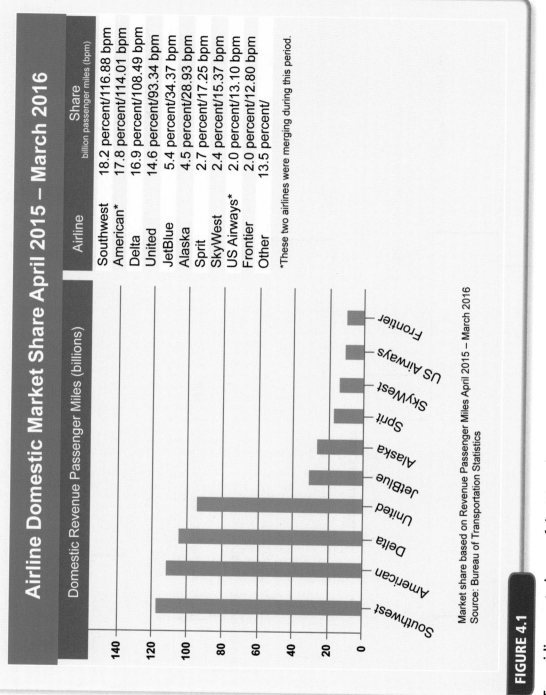

Airline Domestic Market Share April 2015 – March 2016

Airline	Share billion passenger miles (bpm)
Southwest	18.2 percent/116.88 bpm
American*	17.8 percent/114.01 bpm
Delta	16.9 percent/108.49 bpm
United	14.6 percent/93.34 bpm
JetBlue	5.4 percent/34.37 bpm
Alaska	4.5 percent/28.93 bpm
Sprit	2.7 percent/17.25 bpm
SkyWest	2.4 percent/15.37 bpm
US Airways*	2.0 percent/13.10 bpm
Frontier	2.0 percent/12.80 bpm
Other	13.5 percent/

*These two airlines were merging during this period.

Market share based on Revenue Passenger Miles April 2015 – March 2016
Source: Bureau of Transportation Statistics

FIGURE 4.1

Four airlines control most of the US market.

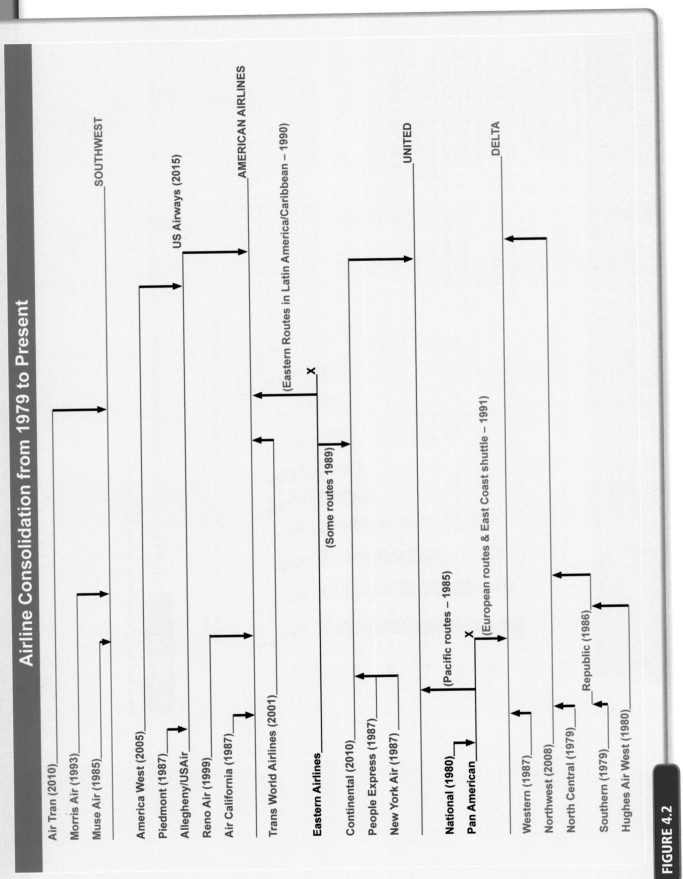

FIGURE 4.2

Since deregulation, airlines have merged and consolidated.

✔ CHECKPOINTS

Lesson 1 Review

Using complete sentences, answer the following questions on a sheet of paper.

1. Under which president did a new federal agency take charge of civil aviation in 1938?

2. Which law required flight data recorders ("black boxes")?

3. What did the Federal Aviation Act of 1958 do?

4. Who was the first chief of the Federal Aviation Administration (FAA)?

5. Under which president was the Department of Transportation created?

6. The FAA's Air Traffic Organization controls what percentage of the world's airspace?

7. How did the National Transportation Safety Board change in 1974?

8. Under which president was the Transportation Security Administration created?

9. The Transportation Security Administration is now part of which government department?

10. What effect did regulation of aviation have that was opposite to its purpose?

11. Who benefitted the most from airline deregulation?

12. Besides the airlines, what are three examples of network industries?

APPLYING YOUR LEARNING

13. Since the TSA was established after 11 September 2001, do you think airline security has improved? Provide examples of why or why not.

Quick Write

_____

_____

After reading the story about Howard Hughes, why do you think he turned to Lockheed when he needed a new plane for TWA?

Learn About

- the important commercial aircraft of the propeller era
- the major commercial airlines of the propeller era
- other developments in commercial airlines' operations

HOWARD R. HUGHES JR., son of a Texas oilman, was born in 1905. Young Hughes learned to fly at age 14. He quickly became a skilled pilot. When his father died, Howard Jr. inherited the family business, Hughes Toolco. He was a millionaire before he was out of his teens. He soon expanded Toolco to include a division called Hughes Aircraft.

He also gained fame as a pilot, setting many records for speed and distance.

In 1939 Hughes became the principal stockholder of Transcontinental and Western Air (TWA—later known as Trans World Airlines). A stockholder is _a person who owns shares of a public company_. This gave Hughes a voice in running the airline.

TWA had a fleet of state-of-the-art Boeings. They attracted attention—and passengers. They could fly coast to coast in 14 hours. That wasn't fast enough for Hughes, however. He wanted a new type of plane.

But TWA couldn't build it. New antitrust laws now kept TWA and other airlines from building their own planes. Hughes had to look elsewhere. He turned to Lockheed, a company he'd worked with before.

Hughes told the designers that he wanted a really fast passenger plane. So they chose a different type of engine, an 18-cylinder Wright R-3350. The plane's propellers were more than 15 feet in diameter. To enable the props to clear the ground, the plane needed very tall landing-gear struts, or braces. For better control, the plane needed a large tail surface. That led to a distinctive triple-fin tail design.

Hughes demanded that his new plane be built under strict secrecy. He got his wish until World War II. At that point, the government took over commercial planes for wartime service. The secret project was out in the open.

The new plane was the L-049 Constellation. Although designed for passengers, it was first used as a military plane (the Lockheed C-69 Constellation). The L-049 flew faster than the fighter planes of its day.

When the Constellation was ready for a test flight in 1944, Hughes was at the controls. The new plane, painted in TWA's distinctive red, flew nonstop across the country in less than seven hours. Hughes broke his own speed record with that flight.

TWA wasn't ready to offer regular nonstop cross-country service. But the Constellation cut about eight hours off the trip from coast to coast.

The Constellation and its counterparts from Douglas Aircraft, the DC-6 and DC-7, were the stars of air travel during the 1940s and 1950s. They were the fastest, safest, and most comfortable propeller-driven airliners ever built. Until the passenger jet came along in the late 1950s, they were the highpoint of air travel.

The Lockheed Constellation, with its triple-fin tail
Dan Simonsen/Shutterstock

Howard Hughes in 1938
Courtesy Federal Aviation Administration

Howard Hughes: Moviemaker and Aviator

Howard Hughes Jr. (1905–1976) learned to fly in his early teens. But before earning fame in aviation, he was a well-known movie director and producer. One of his movies was a World War I epic called *Hell's Angels*. He wrote and directed it himself. Filming began in 1928. He got 87 combat planes together and directed combat scenes in the skies over Mines Field. (The Los Angeles International Airport is there now.)

Years later, Hughes made another war movie, *Jet Pilot*, starring John Wayne. Hughes started filming in 1949 but didn't release the movie until 1957. He kept tinkering with the combat scenes to get them just right. This was long before the days of computer-generated special effects. He needed real planes for his action scenes.

The Air Force was grateful for Hughes's pioneering work in aviation. So it let him use military planes.

Hughes's movie included a scene with superstar pilot Chuck Yeager at the controls of a Sabre jet. It also showed Northrop's XF-89 Scorpion prototype, which appeared as a Russian fighter plane.

The H-4 Hercules (*Spruce Goose*) during its first and only flight

Courtesy Federal Aviation Administration

But Hughes is better known for another case of cooperation with the US armed forces. In 1942 German submarines were sinking US troop transports. Shipbuilder Henry Kaiser had an idea—why not build a fleet of flying boats? They would be made of wood because of a wartime shortage of metal.

When Kaiser got an $18 million government contract, Hughes signed on. The partnership didn't last long. Things didn't move fast enough for Kaiser. And so he pulled out.

Hughes renamed the aircraft the H-4 Hercules. But most people called it the *Spruce Goose* because of its wooden frame. Hughes hated the nickname. For one thing, the H-4 was made of birch, not spruce. He also thought the nickname belittled a good design and the workers who'd built it.

The H-4 was eventually the world's largest flying boat. Hughes flew it once for 60 seconds. It never flew again. It still holds the record for the largest wingspan in aviation history: 319 feet, 11 inches. Hughes maintained the plane until he died. Since 2001 it has been on display at a museum in McMinnville, Oregon.

As time passed, Hughes became more and more isolated and eccentric. Some people think he may have been mentally ill. The man who was once a public figure lived his final years in seclusion.

The Important Commercial Aircraft of the Propeller Era

As you read in Chapter 3, airpower helped the Allies win World War II. The war also exposed millions of Americans to aviation, often for the first time. More than 2 million Americans worked in the aircraft industry in the 1940s. More than 16 million served in uniform and saw airpower firsthand. Hundreds of thousands of them flew for the first time during the war.

After the war, interest in aviation was keen. People who wanted to start airlines could buy military-surplus planes at bargain prices. Many people wanted to work in the field. Many more now saw air travel as a great way to get across a vast country. Americans were ready to fly.

Waypoints

Pressurized Cabins

No matter how strong or large their planes, people who flew in the early days had one big problem: flying could literally make you sick. One reason was that there wasn't enough oxygen in the cabins.

The higher you go above sea level, the less oxygen is in the air. Mountain climbers deal with this problem all the time. If planes flew much higher than 10,000 feet in the early days, people on board got dizzy. Some even fainted.

One solution might be to fly low. But below 10,000 feet, planes often hit rough weather. That led to airsickness—motion sickness associated with flying. Airlines knew that if they could make passengers more comfortable, more people would want to fly.

The big breakthrough was the Boeing 307B Stratoliner. It made its first flight on 8 July 1940. It had a pressurized cabin. As the plane rose, air was pumped into the cabin. Even well above 10,000 feet, air pressure inside the cabin was the same as it is on the ground.

Boeing 307 Stratoliner
Dmitry Morgan/Shutterstock

The 33-seat Stratoliner could fly at an altitude of up to 20,000 feet. It reached speeds as great as 200 miles per hour.

The war did more for aviation than just make people aware of it. It also spurred many technical advances. New kinds of planes came into use. New airports appeared around the world. Weather forecasting got better. Navigational aids improved. These things made flying safer. Better fuel—100-octane aviation gas—gave aircraft engines more power. This meant planes could carry heavier loads and fly farther.

Radar, which helped the British keep an eye out for German bombers during the war, came into use in civil aviation, making air travel safer. And pressurized cabins—*cabins with normal air pressure even at high altitudes*—made air travel more comfortable.

The DC-3 (see Chapter 2, Lesson 3) was the most widely used aircraft right after the war. But before long, the airlines wanted to fly longer routes. They also wanted to carry heavier traffic. They turned to the civilian versions of two planes that first saw service in the war.

The C-54 Skymaster was the military version of the DC-4. The plane pictured here was the first presidential aircraft, ordered for President Franklin Roosevelt.

Courtesy US Air Force

The four-engine Douglas DC-4 was the civilian version of the C-54. And as you read earlier, the Lockheed Constellation started out as the C-69.

The Constellation had a pressurized cabin, so it could fly higher. It could also fly about 100 miles an hour faster than the DC-4. But the DC-4 won the first round of competition between the two. One reason is that DC-4s were easier to come by. More than 1,000 of them were built during the war.

Soon almost every airline was flying DC-4s. But when the supply of surplus DC-4s ran out, the Constellation became the top seller.

Meanwhile, Douglas and Lockheed kept developing bigger and better planes. Douglas had the DC-6, the DC-6B, DC-7, DC-7B, and DC-7C. The DC-7C was known as the "Seven Seas" because of its great range.

Douglas DC-6

Peter Gudella/Shutterstock

Not to be outdone, Lockheed developed the Super Constellation and the Starliner. These planes eventually had 100 seats. They flew at around 300 mph. They could cross the country nonstop in nine hours or less. They could also fly from New York to London.

By 1947 airlines flying shorter routes could choose between the Martin 2-0-2 and the Convair 240. These planes were faster than the DC-3. They were pressurized. They offered the same passenger comforts as the DC-6 and Constellation did.

Another development at this period was the rise of all-cargo airlines—*airlines that carried freight, not passengers.* Like early passenger planes, the first all-cargo planes were developed for the military. They included C-47s and C-69s.

Lockheed Super Constellation
IanC66/Shutterstock

Martin 2-0-2 interior seating
Lithium366/Shutterstock

Convair 240
Ivan Cholakov/Shutterstock

LESSON 2   The Propeller Era in Commercial Flight

Donald Wills Douglas Sr.: Aviation Pioneer

Donald Wills Douglas Sr. (1892–1981) was born in Brooklyn, New York. He entered the US Naval Academy at Annapolis, Maryland, at 17. He spent much of his time there working on model planes. His family and professors thought this interest would pass. But Douglas was hooked on planes. He left the academy before graduation to look for work as an aeronautical engineer.

Douglas enrolled in the Massachusetts Institute of Technology. He finished a four-year course in two years. The school offered him a job as assistant professor immediately.

After that, he lived in Connecticut, California, and Ohio. He served briefly as a civilian in the Army Signal Corps Aviation Section in Washington, D.C.

But Douglas's goal was to make it on his own in the aircraft business. In March 1920 he returned to Los Angeles, with $600 and a family to support. He hoed potatoes and washed cars to provide for his family.

And then he got his first aircraft order. It was from millionaire sportsman David R. Davis. They got together and formed the Davis-Douglas Co. The company built the Cloudster. It was the first aircraft to lift a useful load exceeding its own weight.

A Russian DC-3, designed in 1935, still flying in 2015
ID1974/Shutterstock

Davis soon lost interest in the company. He sold out to Douglas, who incorporated the Douglas Company in July 1921. Douglas landed his own Navy contract—to build torpedo bombers, starting with the DT-1. By 1928, the company was worth $25 million.

Douglas kept going through the Great Depression by building military aircraft. Soon after, he started building his famous airliners. By 1940 sales of DC-2 and DC-3 aircraft reached nearly $61 million.

Douglas remained president of his company until 1957.

Rigid Airships

BETWEEN THE WORLD WARS, another kind of aircraft had a moment of glory. This was the rigid airship, or zeppelin. (Airships were a type of lighter-than-air flying machine you read about in Chapter 1.)

The German maker Zeppelin was the most successful builder of airships. The Germans used them during World War I. At the end of the war, they had to surrender their airship fleet to the Allies. According to terms of the Treaty of Versailles, the Germans could no longer build military aircraft.

But by 1926 the Germans could once more build zeppelins. One of them, the *Graf Zeppelin*, flew more than a million miles, made 590 flights, and carried more than 13,000 passengers before it was retired.

But the most famous zeppelin was the *Hindenburg*. It was the largest and most luxurious airship ever built. It made 10 round trips between Germany and the United States. But on 6 May 1937, as it prepared to land in New Jersey, it exploded, crashed, and burned. Thirty-five passengers and crew members died. They were the first fatalities in scheduled airship operations.

The Crash of the *Hindenburg*
Everett Historical/Shutterstock

The US Navy also flew airships. In 1923 it built the *Shenandoah*. It was a flying public relations machine. It flew around the country visiting air shows and county fairs.

On 3 September 1925, however, the *Shenandoah* was caught in a storm over southern Ohio. It broke up. Part of the airship landed in a cornfield. Lieutenant Commander Charles E. Rosendahl brought the nose section to a safe landing. But 14 of the 43 crew members died.

Later, the Goodyear Tire and Rubber Company won a contract to build zeppelins in the United States. It built two airships for the Navy—the *Akron* and the *Macon*. Both met with disaster. The *Akron* crashed off the New Jersey coast in 1933, killing 73. The *Macon* plunged into the Pacific Ocean in 1935. Fortunately, Navy ships nearby saved all but two of the 83 on board.

After these accidents, the United States lost interest in airships. The *Hindenburg* disaster marked the end of efforts to use airships for commercial travel.

USS *Shenandoah* flying over the mouth of San Diego harbor in 1924
Courtesy Naval History and Heritage Command, NH 705

The Major Commercial Airlines of the Propeller Era

Many features of air travel today had their roots in these early years. Among them were flight attendants, frequent-flier discount programs, travel credit cards, and airline agents who could reissue tickets after a missed connection or a delayed flight. The airlines even offered a telephone reservation service.

Growth of Commercial Flight Use

The 1930s were a time of enormous growth in passenger air travel. The number of air passengers in the United States rose from 474,000 in 1932 to 1,176,858 in 1938. The number of air-passenger miles increased 600 percent between 1936 and 1941. The DC-3 was responsible for much of this growth. Still, long-distance travel was mostly by rail.

TWA began the first cross-country passenger air service between New York and Los Angeles on 25 October 1930. The first regular passenger and airmail service across the Atlantic began 20 May 1939. But as you read earlier, that was seaplane service—Pan American's "flying boats."

In October 1945 an American Airlines plane took off from New York and touched down at Hurn Airfield in England. This was the first commercial flight by a land-based plane from North America to Europe.

Aviation progressed during this period because leaders of the major airlines were competing with each other for passengers. Airline executives demanded more and more of aircraft. This led to intense competition among aircraft manufacturers.

American Airlines Douglas DC-3 US Mail Air Express aircraft, *Flagship Orange County* at the Lyon Air Museum, Santa Ana, California.

Denis Blofield/Shutterstock

Major Commercial Airlines

Four airlines dominated this period—American, Eastern, TWA, and United.

American Airlines

American Airlines grew from several companies launched in the 1920s to fly airmail. These companies joined to form the Aviation Corporation. AVCO, as it was called, quickly bought several small airlines.

In 1930, to streamline its operation, the company's board of directors voted to form a new company, American Airways. In 1934 the company's name became American Airlines.

The company's new president, Cyrus R. Smith, wanted a new plane to match his vision. American Airlines flew 18-passenger Curtiss Condors at that time. Smith wanted something bigger. He worked out a deal with Douglas Aircraft to build 20 DC-3s. The DC-3 became one of the most successful aircraft ever built. By 1939 American Airlines was flying more passenger miles than any other domestic airline.

Smith retired in 1968. He was a true pioneer of commercial flight.

Eastern Air Transport

Clement Keys, a former editor at The Wall Street Journal, promoted commercial aviation in the 1920s and 1930s. He eventually bought a small Philadelphia airline called Pitcairn Aviation.

Pitcairn became Eastern Air Transport on 17 January 1930. It served Boston, Atlanta, and Miami. It soon reached Richmond, Virginia. Eastern specialized in the East Coast. Its "Great Silver Fleet" connected the big cities of the Northeast with Florida vacation spots.

Eddie Rickenbacker, the World War I ace, was Eastern's general manager. Later he and some associates bought the airline from Keys and his investors.

Ford Trimotor
Todd Pettibone/Shutterstock

Transcontinental and Western Air Inc. (TWA)

TWA, like Eastern, had a connection with Clement Keys. Also like other major airlines, TWA started out carrying mail. Keys and other investors launched Transcontinental Air Transport (TAT) in 1928 as a mail carrier. But he thought the time was right for air-passenger travel. He offered a coast- to-coast service combining air and rail. Passengers rode in Pullman sleepers at night. By day, they flew in Ford Trimotors. But even with the support of Charles Lindbergh, the service lost money.

TAT merged with Western Air Express in July 1930 to form Transcontinental and Western Air, Inc. (TWA). TWA received its first mail contract immediately. It began coast-to-coast flights on 25 October 1930. The planes made overnight stops in Kansas City.

An early TWA aircraft on display at the National Air and Space Museum in Washington, D.C.

Jorg Hackemann/Shutterstock

Like many other airlines, TWA attracted strong and colorful personalities. Its first director of operations was William John Frye (1904–1959), a former Hollywood stunt flier.

One day when Frye was a teenager, three Army Curtis Jennies (See Chapter 3, Lesson 1) made emergency landings near a pond where he was ice skating. He forgot his skates to go help the fliers. By the end of the day he'd picked up pneumonia and a fascination with flight. He recovered from the first. The second stayed with him the rest of his life.

He became president of TWA at age 30. A licensed pilot, Frye kept TWA on the leading edge of technical advances. He helped set the specifications for the Douglas DC-1 and DC-2, as well as other planes.

When Frye wanted 33 Boeing Stratoliners built in 1938, he convinced a quirky millionaire named Howard Hughes to finance the deal. He later persuaded Hughes to buy a controlling interest in TWA. The airline was renamed *Trans World Airlines* in the late 1940s.

United Airlines

United Airlines began as part of the United Aircraft and Transport Corporation. This was a partnership between Boeing Airplane Company and Pratt and Whitney, the engine maker. United Airlines began as an operating division of the partnership on 1 July 1931. It advertised itself as the "world's largest air transport system."

New antitrust legislation soon required Boeing to sell the company off. But United remained important. On 30 March 1933 it introduced the Boeing 247 (See Chapter 3, Lesson 3). Many people call this the world's first modern passenger plane. Soon United was flying coast to coast in a little less than 20 hours.

Other Developments in Commercial Airlines' Operations

Transatlantic Service

From the time commercial aviation began, fliers dreamed of connecting North America and Europe.

It was a real challenge. North Atlantic skies are often stormy. Natural stopping places are few. Partly for that reason, some of the first transatlantic services crossed the South Atlantic. These routes connected West Africa and South America.

British Imperial Airways and Pan American Airways tried out transatlantic service in 1936. Before then, the British had hesitated to give Americans landing rights. Pan American first started service after winning a contract to carry US mail to Havana, Cuba, in 1927. By the 1930s, Pan Am's fleet had grown to bigger and faster flying boats. Expanding routes with home bases in Miami, Florida, and Brownsville, Texas, Pan Am was able to fly throughout Latin America.

By 1937, Pan American began seaplane service between the United States and Europe. The first passenger flight operation from the United States to Asia took place on 21 October 1936. In June 1945 the US Civil Aeronautics Board (CAB) allowed three carriers to operate regular air service across the Atlantic. They were American Export, Pan Am, and TWA.

That ended Pan Am's role as the sole US overseas carrier. It also led to a boom in air travel.

A Pan Am Clipper seaplane at the company's terminal in Dinner Key, Florida in 1935

Courtesy Federal Aviation Administration

Freight Airlines

In November 1910 a department store in Dayton, Ohio, shipped a bolt of silk by air to Columbus, Ohio—a distance of less than 100 miles. This was the first practical demonstration of freight shipping by air. Even for short routes, air express was already faster than the railroad.

But all-cargo airlines didn't emerge until after World War II. Companies found it hard to get into the cargo business. Passenger airlines tried to keep them out of airports. Passenger lines feared that freight carriers would upset the aviation industry with cheap rates and irregular service. Through the 1940s passenger airlines, freight carriers, and government regulators struggled for a solution. They needed to find a way to award contracts and set rates.

In August 1949 the CAB gave four all-freight airlines the go-ahead. They were Slick, Flying Tiger, U.S. Airlines, and Airnews. Only Slick and Flying Tiger lasted through the propeller era of aviation.

Freight airlines never grew as expected. They accounted for only a small share of air cargo. The big four passenger carriers and other passenger lines continued to carry freight. The passenger carriers had better facilities at airports and lower costs. Not until 1973, when Fred Smith launched Federal Express with a guarantee of overnight delivery, did an all-freight carrier come into its own.

A De Havilland Comet 4C, the world's first jet airliner, on display in East Fortune, Scotland

johnbraid/Shutterstock

Throughout the 1950s manufacturers worked on the jet aircraft that would eventually replace planes such as the Lockheed Constellation. On 2 May 1952 the world's first jet airliner, the British-made De Havilland Comet, made its first public demonstration flight in London. On 4 October 1958 a British Comet IV with 31 passengers made the first transatlantic commercial jet flight. On 10 December 1958 National Air Lines began the first jet passenger service in the United States. The aircraft was a Boeing 707. It flew between New York City and Miami, Florida.

The propeller era had ended. The jet age had begun.

✔ CHECKPOINTS

Lesson 2 Review

Using complete sentences, answer the following questions on a sheet of paper.

1. What was the *Spruce Goose*?

2. What did better fuel mean for airplanes?

3. Why did the DC-4 win the first round of competition against the Constellation?

4. What was the *Hindenburg*?

5. When was the first commercial flight by a land-based plane from North America to Europe?

6. Which four airlines dominated the postwar propeller era?

7. Why was it a challenge for commercial aviation to connect North America and Europe?

8. Why did freight airlines not grow as expected?

APPLYING YOUR LEARNING

9. How did World War II make Americans more aware of aviation? How might things have been different had there been no war?

General Aviation Takes Flight

After you've read about Clyde Cessna's background, explain in a few sentences how you think his experience might have been different had he been born 25 years later.

Learn About

- what created the interest for general aviation
- the different types of aircraft that make general aviation possible
- the different categories that make up general aviation

CLYDE CESSNA was born in Iowa in 1879 but grew up on a farm in Kansas. His mechanical talents first became apparent in that rural setting. It was a tough life growing up in a family of nine. He became a self-taught expert in repairing and then later developing and improving farm machinery.

He bought one of the first "horseless carriages" in his area and later became a mechanic and an auto salesman. For a time he ran a successful car dealership in Enid, Oklahoma.

But it was aviation that would capture his imagination. He was fascinated by Louis Blériot's flight across the English Channel in 1909. He bought his own monoplane and flew it. He visited air shows and met many of the famous daredevil pilots of the day. He traveled to New York to spend a month at an airplane factory, learning the fundamentals of flight and the art of plane building. Eventually he spent his life savings at the time to buy an exact copy of Blériot's monoplane. He flew this plane, and others of his own design, all around the Midwest, continually tweaking them for better design.

In 1927 he founded the Cessna Aircraft Company. Just a few years later, he abruptly withdrew from aviation after a close friend of his was killed in an air crash of a Cessna-built racing plane.

The company survived, though, through the Depression and World War II. Some of the most successful general aviation aircraft in the world bear the name Cessna.

Cessna is one of the most popular general aviation aircraft flying today.

mountainpix/Shutterstock

What Created the Interest for General Aviation

The United States has more than 5,000 airfields. Each of these has at least one paved runway. But only 500 of these fields offer scheduled passenger service—commercial airline service, in other words.

So what's going on at the more than 4,500 other fields? General aviation (GA). It may be easier to explain what general aviation is by saying what it's not: General aviation is *all aviation except scheduled commercial airline service and military aviation.*

That term came into use during the 1950s. *Private flying* and *business flying* are earlier terms that mean the same thing.

Whatever it's called, general aviation goes back to the earliest days of powered flight. It includes a range of aircraft, from small private planes to large business jets. Helicopters can be part of GA, too. So are aircraft specially modified for particular needs.

These planes, jets, and copters are put to a broad range of purposes. Of course they fly passengers. But GA aircraft also do crop dusting, firefighting, aerial photography and surveying work, medical emergency transportation, and law enforcement.

Charles Lindbergh's triumph in flying solo from New York to Paris captured the public imagination in the late 1920s. He gave a boost to all kinds of flight. He made people want to learn to fly. In particular, he encouraged people to explore the uses of aviation technology.

General aviation was just coming into its own during this period. The first use of airplanes to spray crops, for instance, was in the 1920s. Aerial surveying was another important early use of general aviation aircraft. And business executives were discovering that a private airplane was a good way to get to an important meeting.

Vocabulary

- general aviation
- bootlegger
- winged gospel
- avionics
- offshore
- liability insurance
- homebuilding
- bush flying
- crop dusting
- aerial firefighting
- air tanker
- aerobatics
- warbird

Cessna 750 Citation X jet
InsectWorld/Shutterstock

Earliest Pioneers—and Tinkerers

One of the advantages of going to work in a brand-new field is that it may matter less if you have no experience. After all, if the field is new enough, nobody else has much experience in it, either.

Eddie Stinson

That might have been what Eddie Stinson was thinking when he dropped out of school at 16 and headed for St. Louis. This was just a few years after the Wright Brothers' first flight in 1903. Eddie had a mission. He was determined to pilot an aircraft being made by a couple of novice builders in St. Louis. He pointed out to the builders that they had no real flight experience. Therefore, it made sense for them to hire him as their "test pilot." In fact, he didn't have any more flight experience than the builders. Indeed, he hadn't even seen an airplane before.

But he wasn't going to let that hold him back.

The plane was more of a kite than an aircraft. With a farmer's field as his runway, young Stinson got the plane off the ground—briefly. Then it crashed back to earth. It lost a wing on the way down.

The builders let Stinson keep what was left of the craft as payment for his work as a test pilot. And then they moved on to other work. For Stinson, though, the episode was the start of a lifelong career in aviation. His next stop: Dayton, Ohio, for flying lessons with the Wright Brothers.

Stinson Reliant SR 10 C in the hangar of the Musée Volant Salis in France

HUANG Zheng/Shutterstock

From there he went on to a career as a barnstormer, stunt pilot, and record-setting aviator. With his two sisters (Katherine and Marjorie, whom you read about in Chapter 1, Lesson 4), he also ran a flight school in Texas. They trained aviators for the US Army during World War I. And he founded the Stinson Aircraft Corporation in Detroit. It made aircraft for the US armed forces as well as business jets used to whisk oil company executives around the globe.

Like too many early aviators, Stinson died young—in a plane crash while on a sales trip on 26 January 1932. He was only 38, but he had already logged more than 16,000 hours of flight time—more than any other pilot at that time.

Benny Howard

The story of Benjamin "Benny" Odel Howard is similar to Stinson's. He, too, was a young man with a passion for flight. As a 19-year-old, he went to work in the Curtiss aircraft factory in Dallas. He soon bought a used biplane and a book on how to fly. What more did he need?

Once he took to the skies, though, he got into even more serious trouble than Stinson. On one of his early flights, he crashed his plane, killing his passenger and seriously injuring himself. After that, proper flying lessons seemed a good idea.

He got a commercial pilot's license and then stumbled into the field of aircraft design. A Houston bootlegger asked for his help in modifying an airplane. This was during the days of Prohibition—a period when the sale or production of alcoholic beverages was a crime. A bootlegger is *someone who makes or sells illegal liquor*. The bootlegger wanted a plane with a cargo hold that could fit 15 cases of booze.

Howard was able to do it, and the bootlegger was delighted. Soon Howard was flying a plane he had designed and built himself. He was still just 20 years old, and with a formal education that had ended after just a few months of high school.

As you read in Lesson 1, government oversight became more of a presence as aviation developed. Aviators had to pay attention to new regulations, at both the state and federal level. Pilots had to earn licenses. Aircraft had to be certified. The new regulations no doubt made flying safer. But they also made it harder for people to learn to fly. A teenager with a used biplane couldn't expect to learn to fly just from reading a book. (And that method didn't work out too well for Benny Howard in any case.)

What you might call a golden age of do-it-yourself general aviation was winding down.

The Howard DGA was a high performance airplane of the 1930s.
Richard Thornton/Shutterstock

Giuseppe Bellanca: Aviation Pioneer

Giuseppe Mario Bellanca was a young Sicilian who came to America in 1910 with a dream: He wanted to build aircraft in the New World. Three years later, in Brooklyn, he had built his first plane, the Parasol. He taught himself to fly it. The plane incorporated a revolutionary idea—the propellers at the front, and what we now call "the tail" at the back. That sounds obvious. But it's not how the Wright Brothers and other designers of the time had done it. Many pilots were afraid to try to fly the Parasol, with its unusual design. But those who dared to try it found it flew very well.

In 1914, Bellanca opened the Bellanca Aeroplane Company and Flying School. Among his notable students: Fiorello LaGuardia, who became a World War I flying ace. And later LaGuardia became famous as mayor of New York City. (New York City's major domestic airport is named for him.)

1920s Bellanca Pacemaker
Courtesy Federal Aviation Administration

Bellanca continued to design new aircraft for the rest of his life. But he is remembered above all as the man who put the propellers in front. His company is still in business: Today it is called the AviaBellanca Aircraft Corporation.

Government Efforts to Foster General Aviation

The federal government has tried at different times to encourage private flying, particularly during the 1930s. For instance, Eugene Vidal, an official in the Commerce Department, had an idea for a "poor man's plane." He pushed for a program that would encourage the design and manufacture of a safe, affordable aircraft. Ordinary families would be able own a plane just as they expected to own a car. These planes were meant to sell for $700—the equivalent of about $11,500 today in 2016.

The program did lead to some new designs. But overall, it was a failure. The companies that made the plane thought the price was just too low.

Another program to foster aviation was the Civilian Pilot Training Program, which you read about in Chapter 3, Lesson 1. As the name suggests, the idea was to increase the number of pilots in the US. This would create more potential buyers for the aircraft the country's manufacturers were turning out. And it would also mean that, in case of war, there would be more people who already knew the basics of flying. They could be quickly trained to fly military aircraft.

This program was another example of a government program that failed to live up to its initial promise. But it did train many civilian pilots.

And notably, these new pilots included women as well as men, and African-Americans as well as whites. The commercial airlines and even the US armed forces, on the other hand were not so inclusive at this time. It's a point worth making that in those early days, general aviation offered wider opportunities both to women and to people of color.

"The Winged Gospel"

Aviation has always been about more than just the laws of aerodynamics and getting heavier-than-air machines up into the sky. Aviation has been about dreams of freedom, and about new visions for the future.

The historian Joseph Corn has coined the term "the winged gospel" to refer to *the idealism surrounding flight, especially general aviation.*

One of the ideals of "the winged gospel" was that the airplane would be as common a form of transportation as the automobile. "An airplane in every garage" was the motto. It never quite happened, for a number of reasons. But "aviation for everybody" is an ideal that some cherish, even today.

Another idea was that aviation should be more open to people other than white males. Greater participation in aviation would lead, it was thought, to fuller participation in the larger society for both women and people of color. Again, this ideal has been only imperfectly realized. But to the extent it has been realized, it was realized first in general aviation.

A Major Challenge: Finding the Right Engine

One of the biggest challenges for those wanting to see "an airplane in every garage" was the aircraft engine. Into the 1930s, it was often the most expensive part of the aircraft. The engines that were relatively affordable, like the Curtiss OX-5, were so large and heavy they didn't fit well into smaller aircraft. The smaller, lighter engines on the market were very expensive and hard to get. Most of the best of them were produced in Europe.

Civil Air Patrol crews at Lantana Airport in Florida walking the line of Stinson Voyager aircraft in 1942–43

Courtesy Civil Air Patrol/Historical Society of Palm Beach County

Female members of the Civil Air Patrol practicing emergency medical procedures during a field exercise

Courtesy Civil Air Patrol

World War II and Its Effect on General Aviation

The coming of World War II is an example of the kind of "ups and downs" general aviation has seen through its history. An event happens that appears to be a setback. But then something else happens to create new opportunities. In the case of World War II, the setback was that the general aviation fleet was generally grounded during the war. (The same thing had happened during World War I.) But GA pilots and manufacturers found ways to take part in the war effort.

During World War II, GA pilots organized the Civil Air Patrol (CAP). This organization flew up and down the coasts throughout the war. They were looking for enemy submarines. They also flew over the nation's forests, keeping an eye out for fires. CAP pilots also flew emergency medical flights. In cases of natural disasters such as blizzards and floods, CAP pilots dropped emergency supplies. There was enough of this activity to help keep a number of GA airports open and active during the war.

The Civil Air Patrol eventually became an auxiliary of the Army Air Forces, and later the United States Air Force.

Waypoints

The Civil Air Patrol

The Civil Air Patrol still exists—it accepts young people between the ages of 12 and 19 into its yearlong cadet program in which cadets learn to fly, camp, get in shape, and push themselves to new limits. You can find out more at *www.gocivilairpatrol.com/index.cfm*.

GA aircraft makers found a role during World War II as well. They acted as subcontractors. The skilled workers in their factories turned out parts that would go into military planes.

They also found that some GA aircraft could take on specialized military roles. Army pilots flew small GA planes to spot targets for Army artillery. Other small planes were modified for use as training gliders for the Army's combat glider program.

A good example of a civilian aircraft that found new purpose—many new purposes, really—during the war was Stinson's Model 105 Voyage. It was a three-passenger plane with a strut-based wing mounted atop the fuselage. It could fly about 120 mph. Stinson sold about 530 Voyagers. But then came the war. The US Army "drafted" the Voyager and renamed it the L-5 Sentinel.

The Sentinel was one of the most used US aircraft in the war. It didn't need much room to land or take off, and it filled many roles. It could be used for reconnaissance, for delivering supplies, for getting wounded soldiers from the front lines and for rescuing personnel in tight spots. It could be used to lay wire. It could even be used to drop bombs. Stinson delivered over 3,500 Sentinels during the war.

Stinson L-5 Sentinel at the National Museum of the United States Air Force
Courtesy US Air Force

General Aviation After World War II

The end of World War II looked like a turning point for general aviation. Advocates thought the sector finally would really take off. But then it didn't quite do so.

Many people had learned to fly during the war. As the war ended, legions of new pilots returned to civilian life. Aircraft makers had high hopes that many of them would want to buy their own small planes for business or sporting use. Manufacturers thought the era of "a plane in every garage" might finally have come. But it didn't work out that way. The hoped-for boom in private aircraft purchases never took place.

Some sectors of general aviation did thrive, however. Business aviation was a very healthy sector. Companies bought planes to transport top executives and generally signal corporate prestige.

New technologies came to aviation during the postwar period, too. These benefited general aviation as well as commercial airlines and military aviation. Turbine engines, both jets and turboprops, came in during this period. These new jets wouldn't end up in anyone's garage. But they were in great demand as corporate aircraft.

The postwar period also saw major developments in avionics—*the radios and other electronic systems aboard an aircraft*. Pilots could rely on the new avionics to find their way. The new technology was a big step forward for general aviation pilots, who up until that point had had not much more than a compass in their planes.

Helicopters also came in during this period. Unlike small fixed-wing aircraft, helicopters had virtually no role in personal transportation. But they soon filled a number of other roles: in law enforcement, in medical evacuation, and live traffic reporting. Helicopters flew over jammed highways to give radio listeners tips for avoiding congestion. Helicopters have also been essential in certain industrial sectors: offshore oil and gas, for instance, or logging. Offshore in this case means *away from, or at some distance from, the shore*.

As helicopters advanced, many fixed-wing aircraft makers folded – even some that had done well during the war.

One problem that got worse over time was lawsuits against aircraft makers. The 1970s and '80s were especially bad from the manufacturers' perspective. Defending against these suits and paying for liability insurance pushed up the costs of aircraft. Liability insurance is *insurance that protects someone from claims arising from injuries or damage to other people or property*. Someone injured by an aircraft, for example, might sue the manufacturer for damages. The plaintiff might claim faulty design or workmanship.

Things might have been different if this upswing in lawsuits had occurred as exciting new engines and airframe designs were coming on the market. The new planes would have commanded higher prices. Aircraft makers would have had some "wiggle room." They could have padded their prices somewhat to cover the insurance costs.

But except for the avionics, the planes of this era were pretty much like the aircraft of the 1950s and '60s. It was hard to justify the higher prices to potential buyers. But the costs had to be passed along. As a result, many buyers were shut out of the market.

Congress has historically had an interest in aviation. It has tried to help over the years. But the liability problem still weighs heavily on the GA sector. The number of licensed pilots in the US peaked in 1980, and has been in decline since.

The Homebuilt Movement

One bright spot in general aviation since World War II is the "homebuilt" movement. The regulations that emerged in the late 1930s had made it impossible for individuals to build (whether from scratch or from a kit) and fly their own planes. As a 20-year-old, Benny Howard had been able to turn what he had learned from building a flying rumrunner for a Houston bootlegger into a career as an aircraft designer. But those days seemed to have come to an end.

A red, white, and blue patriotic Van's RV 7 airplane on display at the 2012 EAA AirVenture
Keith Bell/Shutterstock

In the early 1950s, though, the Experimental Aircraft Association (EAA) was formed. Its mission was to revive homebuilding. This is *the construction of aircraft by hand, typically in one's home or garage, rather than on a production line in a factory.*

The EAA has been quite successful. Factory production of aircraft slowed considerably over the years around the turn of the millennium. But homebuilding has thrived. By the late 1990s, hundreds of thousands of people were trekking to Oshkosh, Wisconsin, where the EAA is based, for its annual conference.

Year round, and across the country, the EAA also offers intensive weekend seminars. They're meant to teach people how to build their own planes. Additionally, one week each summer EAA members, aviation admirers, and more than 10,000 aircraft from all over the world attend EAA AirVenture in Oshkosh.

The main gate at the EAA 2012 AirVenture in Oskhosh, Wisconsin
Keith Bell/Shutterstock

The Different Types of Aircraft That Make General Aviation Possible

Small propeller planes seating just two or three people—private or personal planes—may be what most people think of when they hear the phrase *general aviation*. Those planes certainly are an important part of GA. But that term also covers business or corporate jets. This section will touch on some of the most significant aircraft, big and small.

Three Small Planes With a Big Presence

As you have read, the postwar period was hard for the makers of private planes. Even some manufacturers that had kept going during the difficult war years and contributed to the war effort went out of business during this period: Benny Howard's Darned Good Airplanes was one of these. (His company name came from the bootlegger's comment about the plane Howard had built for him.) So was the remarkable Eddie Stinson's. It survived his death in 1932. But it did not last as an independent entity much beyond the end of the war.

All this makes the survival of three manufacturers you are likely to have heard of all the more notable. They have been known as the Big Three of general aviation.

Piper Aircraft, Cessna Aircraft, (Clyde Cessna's company) and Beech Aircraft all worked hard to rebuild the personal aircraft market during the postwar years, through the 1970s. Among their successes: Each of them made the transition from fabric-covered to all-metal aircraft.

Piper Cub 75th anniversary airplane with snowskids for use in Alaska

Keith Bell/Shutterstock

The Piper Cub

The Taylor E-2 Cub made its first flight in September 1930. That plane only just barely took off. Its engine wasn't powerful enough to lift it more than five feet off the ground. But this bumpy start led to the famous Piper Cub.

The name change came after William Piper bought for $761 the business the Taylor brothers had founded a few years earlier. Piper has been called "the Henry Ford of aviation." He was one of those "airplane in every garage" people.

The Piper Cub debuted in 1938. It became one of the world's most popular general aviation planes. Piper later continued its Cub series with the PA-28 Super Cub.

The Cub series is one of the most popular and influential light aircraft ever manufactured. Of the more than 144,000 planes Piper has produced since 1927, some 90,000 are still flying.

Cessna

In 1946 Cessna Aircraft launched its C-120 and C-140. Both planes were all-metal high-wing monoplanes. Both were very successful.

The C-140 soon became the basis for another Cessna aircraft, the Cessna 170. That plane became the biggest-selling and most widely produced light aircraft in history. It was a stretched and enlarged version of the Model 140. The 170 originally had fabric-covered wings and v-shaped wings struts. Three fuel tanks gave it extra range.

Another Cessna plane captured public attention because it was the "star" of a TV series during the 1950s. *Sky King* was about the adventures of an Arizona rancher who liked to get around in a plane. The hero flew a Cessna 310. It has been described as one of the most attractive aircraft ever built. Cessna produced 310s for almost 30 years. They eventually became the company's most popular twin-engine model.

The Beechcraft Bonanza

The Beech Aircraft Corporation was the third of the "big three" aircraft manufacturers of the years after World War II. Beech seems to have been one firm that did experience a boom in private plane purchases after the war. The company had 7,000 combat aircraft during the war. Then Beech set itself up for peacetime by coming up with a revolutionary single-engine plane. It had a distinctive V-tail that saved on weight but didn't compromise control.

Vintage Cessna 140 preparing for takeoff
Barry Blackburn/Shutterstock

Cessna 310 on final approach to land
Brian McEntire/Shutterstock

Beechcraft Bonanza with its distinctive V-tail
Richard Thornton/Shutterstock

Beechcraft King Air C90B twin-engine airplane

Philip Arno Photography/Shutterstock

It was called the Bonanza. It was an all-metal low-wing craft with retractable landing gear. It could fly at 200 mph, at night, and in all kinds of weather. The Bonanza was as close as the public could get to a "fighter" plane. Beech had 1,400 advance orders before production even started. Production began in 1947 and hasn't stopped since. With 17,000 planes built, the Bonanza is one of the most successful aircraft in history.

Business Jets

It's tempting to say that business jets go back to before there were jet engines. And it would almost be true. Business flying goes back to the late 1920s. It was one of those sectors of general aviation that got a boost from Lindbergh's trans-Atlantic hop. Business executives began to see how travel by air, rather than by rail, or over (still primitive) highways could make them more productive.

The Staggerwing

In this new field, one of the aircraft that set the standard for high performance was another model from Beech Aircraft: Model 17, first flown in 1932.

Beechcraft Model 17 Staggerwing

Sergey Kohl/Shutterstock

It was known as the *Staggerwing*. It got that name because the top wing is set, or staggered, behind the bottom wing. It was unusual in its time in that it was specifically designed for business travel. It had powerful engines that made it faster than most military aircraft.

But it wasn't all about speed. Luxury figured in, too. Each Staggerwing was custom built by hand. Its cabin was trimmed in leather and mohair. The price was about $15,000—the equivalent of about $250,000 in 2016.

Learjets

Since the heyday of the Staggerwing, the standards for executive business travel have changed. Since the early 1960s, there's been one name that just about anyone who knows anything about business jets has heard: Learjet.

William P. Lear Sr. developed the Learjet. He wasn't interested in just another airplane for busy executives. He wanted to build a jet that could deliver the performance and amenities of a commercial airliner. He already had 150 aviation patents to his name when he came out of retirement to develop the new jet. And he started in with no market research to tell him whether there would be demand for the new machine. He just followed his own intuitions. But his new jet was a huge success.

Learjet 60XR on final approach to land
InsectWorld/Shutterstock

His first model, the Learjet 23, was the first small jet aircraft to enter mass production. And it was the first to be developed and financed by a single individual.

Gulfstream

Lear may be the name everyone knows—even those who can't afford one. The Learjet didn't come first, though. The Gulfstream I first flew in 1958. It soon became known as the "Rolls Royce" of business aviation. In fact, it had a couple of Rolls-Royce turboprop engines. It quickly gained a foothold in the business aircraft market. About the same time as the Learjet appeared, the Gulfstream II debuted in 1964. It had a range 50 percent greater than its predecessor. The Gulfstream III (1979) had a true intercontinental range. The 19-passenger Gulfstream IV, out in 1986, had a range of more than 7,000 miles.

In January 1988, Allen Paulson, Gulfstream chairman and a pilot, set a number of speed records for flying around the world in a Gulfstream IV. In fact, he circled the globe going eastbound in just under 37 hours. A Boeing 747-SP had set the previous record.

Paulson's feat illustrates that although business jets are part of general aviation (because they don't offer scheduled airline service), they are still serious jets.

Gulfstream IV
Gregory Kendall/Shutterstock

The Different Categories That Make Up General Aviation

Much of general aviation is simply a matter of moving people around. General aviation includes, for instance, a family of four flying a single engine plane from their house to their weekend home at the lake. A corporate executive preparing with aides for a difficult meeting as they fly across the country in a Learjet is also an example of general aviation. In some cases, the trip could be made on a commercial flight, or by some other mode of transportation. It just wouldn't be as convenient, although it may be cheaper.

Other areas of general aviation are more specialized. They've required specially adapted aircraft. Sometimes whole new designs have been needed, such as for crop dusting.

On the other hand, there's considerable overlap among aircraft. Some planes originally built as civilian planes found new uses in the military. And some military planes have been adapted for firefighting, bush flying, and crop dusting.

Personal Flying

Personal flying can be anything from someone who goes out to the local airfield for flying lessons occasionally to someone who flies a small plane to favorite fishing or camping spots. A few subdivisions in expensive neighborhoods have personal landing strips so that homeowners can fly in as well as drive.

Business Travel

The general aviation side of business travel involves everything from small planes like the ones used for personal flying to corporate jets like the ones Allen Paulson flew to set global aviation records. Like Arizona rancher Sky King of television fame, many ranchers find it easier to fly than drive over their holdings, and to get from place to place by air. Especially in the western parts of the country, distances are great, and weather is generally good. This makes air travel a good option.

Bush Flying

Bush flying is one of those rare places where the romance of the early days of aviation lives on. Bush flying is *aviation carried out in remote areas, typically not well served by roads or other modes of transport*. Alaska, Canada (especially its Arctic regions) and parts of Australia are places that rely heavily on bush pilots.

In a speech he gave in 1962, the veteran Canadian bush pilot C.H. "Punch" Dickins defined bush flying as "a pilot and mechanic, who are ready and willing to take any kind of a load to any destination, on or off the map, within the limits of their aircraft, and the financial resources of the customer."

Many early bush pilots were men who had learned to fly during World War I. They wanted to keep flying after the war. It wasn't hard for them to buy surplus military planes and set up as pilots.

Piper Bush airplane in the Wrangell St. Elias National Park and Preserve, Alaska

Joseph Sohm/Shutterstock

But by definition, the areas bush pilots serve are full of challenges. Landing strips are inadequate. Weather is changeable and often dangerous. Radio communications may be poor. Bush pilots' workloads are often uneven, "feast or famine." So is their cash flow. And it's not always easy to work with customers they've never seen, in places they've never visited.

All that said, for the communities they serve, bush pilots are indispensable links holding things together. They have the satisfaction of knowing that are doing essential work.

Opening the Canadian Arctic by Air

ONE DAY IN OCTOBER 1920, a fur buyer walked into the office of Canadian Aircraft, in Winnipeg, Manitoba. He needed to get home, to a place called The Pas. It was in Manitoba, but nearly 400 miles away. Canada is a vast country, and Manitoba is a big province. Even today, the journey would be several hours' drive. Back then, it would be an insurmountable distance. Canadian Aircraft accepted the challenge. Pilot and fur buyer flew hundreds of miles, over lakes and swamps and bogs. When they finally touched down, it was in a place never before visited by an aircraft with wheeled landing gear.

It was one of the earliest recorded commercial "bush flights." There are plenty of places farther north and even harder to get to than The Pas. But just as Lindbergh's trans-Atlantic flight was about to open people's eyes to new possibilities in aviation, so did this flight from Winnipeg. Even in those early days, people began to realize all the places their airplanes could take them. Within a year of that "first flight," oil companies were exploring within 100 miles of the Arctic Circle. Bush pilots checked for forest fires. They delivered mail. They surveyed timberlands and waterways. They transported sick or injured hunters and other workers from the bush. The brave bush pilots truly opened up northern Canada.

Crop Dusting

Crop dusting is *the application of fertilizers and pesticides to crops from the air*. It's an important element of general aviation. And it goes back to early days. In fact, it goes back to a specific date: 31 August 1921. That's when Lieutenant John A. Macready took off at the controls of a war surplus Curtiss Jenny from McCook Field in Dayton, Ohio. His mission: to wipe out the Catalpa sphinx moths that were chewing leaves off the trees in a nearby apple orchard.

He dumped a load of powered lead arsenate onto the trees and the caterpillars. A follow-up check showed that this "aerial application" of the pesticide had done the job. The caterpillars were gone. And a new use of aircraft had been found.

Crop dusting required a special set of piloting skills. Fliers needed to fly low to avoid getting chemical in the wrong areas. And the fields were full of hazards that were hard to see, such as fence posts and telephone or electrical wires.

Crop dusting became a big business, involving many different companies and types of aircraft. Before Delta Airlines became one of the largest passenger airlines in the world, it was Delta Dusters, a crop-dusting service.

A crop duster spraying a field of sunflowers
Steve Boyko/Shutterstock

The first crop dusters used retrofitted military surplus aircraft, like Lieutenant Macready's Curtiss Jenny. But eventually special planes were built for the task. The first of these appeared in 1950. Several different manufacturers got into the business of building planes for agricultural work, including Piper, Cessna, and Grumman.

Firefighting

Aerial firefighting—*using aircraft to dump water or chemicals onto wildfires*—got its start after World War II. Early efforts in this direction involved dumping water from wooden beer kegs aboard single-engine airplanes. These weren't especially effective.

But soon public safety officials in California worked with the US Forest Service to develop a practical air tanker to fight fires. An **air tanker** is *an aircraft used to deliver liquids from the air, typically water or fire retardant*. Eventually efforts shifted again. It seemed to make sense to retrofit large military aircraft to use as tankers. The planes were available and didn't cost too much. And they were certainly built to carry heavy loads under stressful conditions.

Many different aircraft have been modified for use as air tankers. But so far there has been only one aircraft specifically built for aerial firefighting—the Canadair (now Bombardier) CL-215. The first of these aircraft flew in October 1967. The plane continued in production until 1990. During those years, 125 planes were delivered to several countries in Europe as well as Thailand and Venezuela. Bombardier introduced the CL-415 in 1994.

A Bombardier CL-415 Super Scooper makes a water drop on a wildfire near Los Angeles, California.
Heather Lucia Snow/Shutterstock

Aerobatic Aviation

Aerobatics is the word for *the spectacular stunts, such as rolls and loops, performed in an airplane or glider, or by groups of airplanes flying together.* It's another part of general aviation. *Acrobatics in the air* is another way to put it. It's defined as "precise maneuvering in three-dimensional space." In aerobatic aviation, pilots think about maneuvering in terms of three things: position, velocity, and attitude.

Aerobatic aviators perform tricks such as plummeting in their planes earthward in an apparent loss of control, only to pull back up at the last minute and head skyward again—to cheers and applause from the audience.

Lincoln Beachey, whom you read about in Chapter 2, Lesson 2, is known as the father of aerobatic flying. But he had his critics at first. Orville Wright, for instance, called Beachey's feats "optical illusions." Beachey largely silenced his critics, however, after a 126-city barnstorming tour in 1914. He dazzled crowds. He won over luminaries like Thomas Edison, the inventor, and Carl Sandburg, the poet. He even made Orville Wright a fan. That may have been more significant. Wright retracted his earlier comment and called Beachey's exhibitions "poetry."

The field of aerobatic aviation has certainly expanded since Beachey's day. A couple of numbers make the case: A dictionary of aerobatic flight was published in 1961. It listed every aerobatic maneuver and position defined at that time. It was a catalogue of 3,000 items. Today the list has grown to 15,000.

Modern wingwalkers perform at an airshow.

Dmitry Birin/Shutterstock

Millions of people go to see aerobatic pilots perform at air shows every year. That makes aerobatics one of the country's top most popular spectator sports. Unfortunately, it's also one of the most dangerous. Each year, several aerobatic pilots are killed, due to equipment malfunction or pilot error.

A Blue & White Super Corsair warbird number 74 flown by Dick Becker on display at the 2012 EAA AirVenture

Keith Bell/Shutterstock

Warbirds

A warbird is a *vintage military aircraft*. Warbirds, along with the people who restore, maintain, and fly them, are yet another part of general aviation.

Earlier in this lesson, you read about the Experimental Aircraft Association (EAA), the organization that has helped foster a revival of homebuilt aircraft. The EAA also welcomes into its ranks those who work on warbirds. These enthusiasts are determined to keep the aircraft of the so-called golden age flying.

Types of Pilot Certificates

In aviation people might refer to the prized possession as a pilot certificate, but it's actually a license to learn. What follows are the different levels of pilot certificate. Descriptions for the different types of pilot certificates are provided below by the Aircraft Owners and Pilots Association (AOPA), a tax-exempt charitable, educational, and scientific organization. More information about AOPA can be found at the organization's website: *www.aopa.org*.

Student

All pilots start out as students. With the proper training, the student pilot certificate allows you to work toward the first big milestone in aviation: the solo. It will be one of the most exciting and memorable moments of your life. After additional training, you earn either your private, recreational, or sport pilot certificate, which allows you to take one or more passengers for rides.

Private

Almost all pilots in the United States earn a traditional private pilot certificate. It's what most people think of when they say that someone has their *private*. It has the fewest limitations. If you take additional training, your private can be upgraded to include more advanced capabilities, such as flying in bad weather, flying an airplane with two or more engines, or flying professionally.

Recreational

The recreational pilot certificate is a more limited form of the private certificate. It's a great way to earn your wings if you'll be flying close to your home airport during the daytime with no more than one passenger. It requires less effort and money to earn than the private. However, most people who start down this path eventually go on to earn the private certificate, anyway. If you become a recreational pilot, additional training and experience will allow you to easily upgrade to a private pilot certificate.

Sport

The sport pilot certificate was introduced in 2004. It's perfect for people who want to get back to—or want to start with—the basics of flying. Sport pilots fly smaller, lighter, less-complex, one- or two-seat airplanes. Sport pilots can only fly a special type of aircraft known as *light sport aircraft* (LSA). LSAs are popular around the world and are now being manufactured and sold in the United States. Because they are new, not every flight school will have light sport aircraft available. Sport pilots are not required to have medical examinations. With additional training and a medical certificate, you can easily upgrade to a higher level of certificate.

Advanced

With extensive training, an instrument rating can be added to the private pilot certificate. This enables you to fly in clouds and bad weather using instruments. Beyond that is the commercial pilot certificate, if you want to fly for hire, and certificated flight instructor, which allows you to teach other people to fly. At the highest level is the airline transport pilot certificate. It's required for airline, corporate, and charter pilots.

Air Force JROTC Cadet Moriah Graham

In May 2015, Air Force JROTC Cadet Moriah Graham made history by becoming the first high school African-American student from Delaware to earn a private pilot license. Moriah's words say it best: "For five years, obtaining my private pilot license was a goal of mine and for four of those five years, it was something that was a sort of fantasy; until I started ground school my junior year while in AFJROTC. That forced reality to sink in. My goal was to get my private pilot license and I knew it would not be easy, but it would be worth it. Through many trials and tribulations, I was able to make it. There were many obstacles in my way and quite frankly, there were times when even I did not think that I would make it. However, I reminded myself that I have people who love and support me no matter if I stumble or even fall a few times."

"On 28 May 2015, I achieved this goal and in doing so it showed me that through hard work, dedication, tenacity, perseverance and the help of God, anything and everything is possible. I completed this flight program not just for my license but to show other little girls who look just like me that they should never let anyone deter them from their dreams, because dreams can always be made true if you try hard enough. That is what the flight program has done for me."

Moriah Graham is truly a great young American marked with determination and resiliency. She set a goal, finished a mission, and fulfilled a dream.

AFJROTC Cadet Moriah Graham
Courtesy US Air Force

Lesson 3 Review

Using complete sentences, answer the following questions on a sheet of paper.

1. What aviation pioneer stumbled into aircraft design when a bootlegger asked him to modify a plane to fly illegal liquor?

2. Why did Eugene Vidal's program for a "poor man's plane" fail?

3. What did the Civil Air Patrol do during World War II?

4. Which companies are the Big Three of general aviation?

5. Who was William P. Lear Sr.?

6. What record did Allen Paulson set?

7. What enemy did Lieutenant John A. Macready attack on 31 August 1920?

8. What was the CL-215?

9. What did Orville Wright think of Lincoln Beachey's aerobatics?

APPLYING YOUR LEARNING

10. What do you think could be done to increase the number of general aviation pilots in the United States?

The Jet Era in Commercial Flight

Quick Write

_____

_____

After reading the vignette, why do you think commercial airlines were slow to start using jet aircraft?

Learn About

- how a jet engine works
- developments in commercial jet aircraft
- the switch to air travel in the United States
- future commercial aircraft

THE JET ENGINE is the technology that shrank the world. Jet airplanes fly faster and higher than propeller planes. That cuts down travel time and brings distant places closer.

And 1958 was the year of the commercial jet. In that year US airlines introduced jet service on both overseas and domestic flights.

Jet engines developed through the 1930s and 1940s. World War II and the Korean War saw the deployment of military jets. But commercial airlines took their time in adopting the new technology.

The airlines hesitated because jet engines were very different from the engines in propeller aircraft. These differences made jets an expensive investment. Jet engines burned much hotter than the engines in propeller aircraft. So they had to be made of alloys. An alloy is *a combination of different metals—or of metal and nonmetal—fused for strength, resistance to corrosion, or other desired qualities*. Alloys cost more than single metals.

Jet engines also used more fuel. Planes with jet engines had higher takeoff speeds. So they needed longer runways.

In view of these differences, airlines understandably took a wait-and-see attitude toward the new technology.

But Juan Trippe, chief executive of Pan American Airways, didn't want to wait. He'd already pioneered transoceanic air service with the "flying boats" known as Pan Am Clippers.

Trippe wanted to see Pan Am fly nonstop across the oceans. Some people thought that Comet jets would achieve this goal. A British manufacturer, De Havilland, built the Comet. But after a couple of crashes, the Comet's promise faded.

Who would now take the lead? Trippe decided to play Douglas and Boeing off against each other. These companies were two of America's largest airplane manufacturers. They competed for Pan Am's business. Douglas offered the DC-8 and Boeing the 707.

In October 1955 Pan Am signed on to buy 20 of the 707 jets and 25 of the DC-8s. Two years later, Boeing rolled out its first 707. And on 26 October 1958 Pan American introduced jet service from New York to London, with a stop in Newfoundland.

The first flight had 111 passengers. That was more people than had ever boarded a single regularly scheduled flight.

The fare was about the same as for a propeller plane: $272. It sounds like a good deal, but in 2016 dollars, that ticket would cost about $2,265.

The new service was a huge success. Several other airlines quickly adopted the 707. Pan Am continued to forge ahead. Within a year, it was able to get rid of the Newfoundland layover. It introduced nonstop service on Boeing 707-320s. Pan Am set the standard for the industry.

The era of passenger jet travel had a slow start. But once it took off, it soared. Around the world, airlines moved quickly to replace propeller planes with jets.

Boeing 707
Ivan Cholakov/Shutterstock

JUAN TERRY TRIPPE (1899–1981) was the founder and longtime chief executive of Pan American Airways or Pan Am.

Trippe was born in Sea Bright, New Jersey. His ancestors were English seafarers who came to Maryland in the 17th century.

While in his 20s, Trippe used some inherited money to launch Long Island Airways in New York. That venture failed. He tried again. This time he invested in Colonial Air. It flew mail routes between New York City and Boston.

But Trippe had bigger things in mind. He wanted to develop air routes in the Caribbean and South America. In 1927 he launched Pan Am. Under his leadership, it became the largest and most successful international airline in the world.

Trippe understood that success in the airline business meant knowing both economics and politics. So he reached out to aircraft builders and politicians as well as the public.

Trippe greatly improved Pan Am's passenger service. He helped develop new aircraft, from the Boeing 707s and DC-8s to the Boeing 747. He was president of the airline until 1968.

How a Jet Engine Works

About 100 BC, Hero of Alexandria developed this simple engine called an *aeolipile*.

Morphart Creation/Shutterstock

A Greek named Hero of Alexandria invented a type of jet engine around 100 BC.

But the history of modern jet engines begins with Frank Whittle. An engineer, he was also an officer in the British Royal Air Force.

On 16 January 1930 Whittle got a patent for his design of a jet aircraft engine. Unfortunately, the British government wasn't interested in this new technology until World War II broke out. But the German government was very interested in developing a jet engine and used Whittle's engine design to build its own. The Luftwaffe flew the first operational jet aircraft in 1942. On 26 July 1944, a German Me-262 became the first jet airplane used in combat.

In September 1941, the US Army Air Forces decided to build their own version of a jet fighter. Design work began in late 1941 based on Whittle's engine. On 1 and 2 October 1942, Robert Stanley made the first test flights of the Bell XP 59-A Airacomet, at Muroc, California. Two General Electric J31 engines were later used to power the production version of the new jet aircraft.

General Electric J31 on display in the Research and Development Gallery at the National Museum of the United States Air Force
Courtesy US Air Force

On 2 May 1952 the British Overseas Airways Corporation started the first regular jet airline service. It flew De Havilland Comets between London and Johannesburg, South Africa.

The Comet transformed air travel. It flew at 500 mph. It soared at altitudes of up to 30,000 feet.

But in 1954 two Comets had fatal accidents. Structural failure was the cause. Aircraft flying at high speeds and high altitudes are subject to enormous stress and pressure. This can lead to metal fatigue—*a slow weakening of strength in metal caused by repeated deformation, vibration, or other stress.* It's like what happens when you bend a paper clip back and forth. Eventually it breaks.

A research version Comet jet aircraft. Note the round windows— the original Comets had square windows, which proved fatal in flight.
david muscroft/Shutterstock.com

That's what happened to the British jets. The square windows on the two Comets couldn't take the stress and pressure. The aircraft broke up in the air. The accidents were setbacks for British aviation. But manufacturers learned a lot from them. The result was much safer aircraft. It's why all jet aircraft today have rounded windows.

The Science Behind Jet Engines

The word turbine means *whirl* or *spinning top*. A turbine engine, or jet engine, is *an engine driven by a moving fluid, such as water, steam, or air, that pushes against blades or paddles attached to a central shaft.*

Hot flowing gases power the turbine engines in aircraft. Some turbine engines connect to propellers.

The materials and engineering that go into a jet engine are complex. But the operation of a jet engine is simple.

A jet engine takes in air and accelerates it to extremely high speeds through an exhaust nozzle. The fast-moving air pushes the plane forward. This is the thrust force generated by the engine.

Jet engines have rotating parts. These parts can spin at tens of thousands of revolutions per minute.

A jet's spinning motions make it different from a reciprocating engine—*an engine powered by pistons that go back and forth.* Most of the aircraft you've read about so far had reciprocating internal-combustion engines.

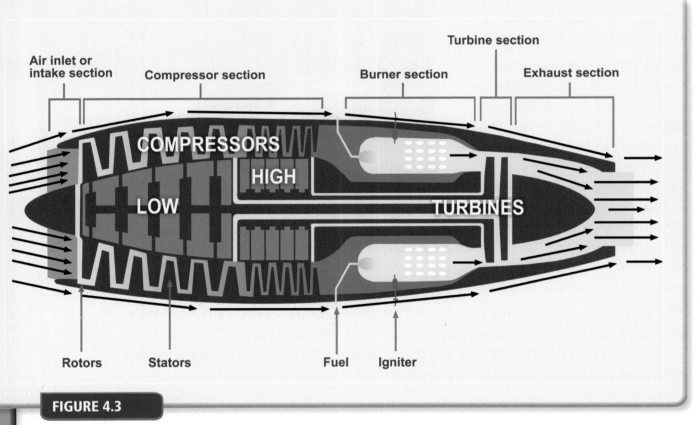

FIGURE 4.3

Sections and Parts of a Turbojet Simplified

Propulsion is *a driving or propelling force*. There are two basic types of jet propulsion: turboprop and pure jet. Both use a gas turbine engine. In a turboprop, the gas turbine is connected to a propeller. The jet exhaust provides some thrust, but the propeller provides most of it. In a pure jet, all the thrust comes from the jet exhaust.

All turbine engines have five basic parts: the *inlet*, the *compressor*, the *burner* (*combustor*), the *turbine*, and the *exhaust* (*nozzle*).

The Advantages of the Jet Engine

Turbine engines have many advantages over reciprocating engines. Turbine engines can fly higher and faster. They vibrate less because their parts spin, rather than slide back and forth. Cooling a turbine engine is easier because it takes in so much air.

But the biggest advantage of turbine engines is that they produce more thrust per pound of engine weight than reciprocating engines do. As a result, turbine engines can carry heavier loads.

Aeronautics has a special definition of weight. That definition relates to the basic forces of flight. Weight is *the force that directly opposes lift*.

Aviators always have to think about weight. It's possible to load an aircraft with so many passengers and so much baggage that it can't take off. The more weight an engine can lift, the better.

Developments in Commercial Jet Aircraft

By the mid-1950s Boeing had been building military jets for years. That experience helped Boeing build the 707. Once again, civil aviation benefited from lessons learned building military aircraft.

The 707—Pan Am's choice for its new transatlantic service in 1958— soon became the standard long-range jet. But airlines had other options: the Douglas DC-8 and the Convair 880 and 890.

Douglas DC-8. In the 1970s, Braniff Airlines had the artist Alexander Calder paint this plane to promote travel to South America.

Courtesy National Air and Space Museum, NASM-9A0276

Jets Get Smaller

Soon manufacturers started building smaller jets. These smaller jets worked well for short hauls. For example, in 1959 Air France put a new jet—the Caravelle I— into service. The French company Sud-Est Aviation built it. The Caravelle had an engine on each side of the rear fuselage. It was the first short-haul jet. It carried up to 90 passengers.

Caravelle I in Istanbul Airlines colors

EvrenKalinbacak/Shutterstock

Only one US carrier, United Airlines, flew the Caravelle. But the French aircraft had a big influence on American manufacturers. Soon they, too, started building smaller jets. They wanted to offer the benefits of jet speed, altitude, and comfort on shorter routes.

In February 1963 Boeing introduced the 727. It was versatile, but noisy. Boeing produced more than 1,700 of these tri-jet aircraft. A tri-jet is *an aircraft with three engines*. The 727 was good for smaller airports with shorter runways and fewer passengers.

Douglas introduced its short-haul jet, the DC-9, in 1965. The company merged with McDonnell Aircraft Corp. in 1967, forming McDonnell Douglas.

Douglas DC-9 operated by Hawaiian Air

Courtesy National Air and Space Museum/Ron Davies Photo Collection, 9A10179

Faced with competition from the DC-9 and British Aircraft Corporation's BAC 1-11, Boeing introduced the 737 in 1967. It incorporated several features from the 707 and 727, but featured six-abreast seating, made possible by engines mounted under the wings. The plane could operate even at small airports or unimproved fields. Its new technology meant there was no longer a need for a flight engineer—soon the two-person flight deck was the standard for all carriers.

Boeing 727
InsectWorld/Shutterstock

The 737 went through several generations and became the most popular plane in commercial history. In 2012 it became the first commercial jetliner to sell more than 10,000 planes. By 2014, Boeing was building 42 737s a month. The company planned to increase the total to 52 a month by 2018. The first model in 1967 carried 107 passengers; recent models can carry up to about 220.

Boeing 737 climbing into the sky after takeoff
Dejan Milinkovic/Shutterstock

Boeing 737-900 operated by United Airlines
Tupungato/Shutterstock

United Airlines Boeing 747

Vytautas Kielaitis/Shutterstock

Lockheed L-1011 operated by Euro Atlantic

InsectWorld/Shutterstock

McDonnell-Douglas DC-10 operated by Avient Aviation

InsectWorld/Shutterstock

Jumbo Jets

In April 1966 Boeing announced plans for the wide-body 747. It made its first flight in 1969. Airlines started flying it the next year.

The 747 can carry up to 600 passengers and crew. It dwarfed the 707. The aisle of the 747's economy-class section alone was longer than the Wright brothers' historic 1903 flight. The 747 was designed for long haul flights that would normally require other aircraft to make refueling stops. Boeing 747s can fly non-stop from New York City to Hong Kong, China. Some models even had an upstairs cocktail lounge for first class passengers.

Boeing is still building 747s, and airline companies around the world are still flying them. Even people who don't know much about aircraft can spot a 747. It has a distinctive bump on the top of its fuselage.

Lockheed and McDonnell Douglas were not far behind Boeing. They announced plans for jumbo jets in 1966. Both companies rolled out their new planes in 1970. The McDonnell Douglas DC-10 came out in August. The Lockheed L-1011 followed in November. Both aircraft can carry as many as 350 passengers. They can fly nonstop up to 4,000 miles.

Like the Boeing 747, the McDonnell Douglas DC-10 and the Lockheed L-1011 are still in use, although the last two are used mostly to carry cargo.

The Concorde

In 1976, the French company Aérospatiale and British Aircraft Corporation introduced the supersonic transport (SST) Concorde to passenger service. Supersonic means *faster than the speed of sound (about 770 mph)*. An engineering marvel, the Concorde could carry about 100 passengers and travel at 1,350 mph—more than twice the speed of sound. It flew at an altitude of 60,000 feet and could travel from London to New York in three-and-a-half hours. This meant a British businessperson could fly to New York for a meeting and return home the same evening.

The United States and Soviet Union both developed SSTs as well. But the Boeing 2707 program was cancelled in 1971. Then in 1973, the Soviet Tupolev Tu-144 crashed at the Paris Air Show during a demonstration flight. This greatly delayed its development. It finally entered passenger service in 1977, but flew for only a few months. It was withdrawn from service in 1978 for technical and safety reasons.

British Airways operated Concorde flights twice daily between London and New York, while Air France flew once a day between New York and Paris. Both airlines flew charter flights to other destinations.

Flying in a Concorde may have been exciting, but it wasn't always comfortable. Headroom was limited because of the narrow fuselage, and the windows were tiny. It was also expensive—by the 2000s, it could cost $7,000 for a one-way ticket and $10,000 for a round-trip fare.

An Air France Concorde on display in Paris
Senohrabek/Shutterstock

The plane was also very loud, which at first led to difficulties in obtaining permission to land in the United States. The Secretary of Transportation himself had to approve it. Many countries refused flyover rights because of the sonic boom the Concorde created. A sonic boom is *a pressure wave created when an aircraft flies faster than the speed of sound, heard on the ground as a crack or boom*. In addition, the SST was not very fuel efficient and cost a lot to maintain.

Even so, the Concorde flew commercially until 2003. Several factors ended the program. The price of fuel kept increasing. A fatal crash in Paris in 2000 led to expensive modifications. Finally, the number of air passengers decreased for several years following the terrorist attacks on 11 September 2001. Currently no SST is operating commercially, although manufacturers have plans on the drawing board for new ones.

A Global Industry

Until 1978 American manufacturers dominated the global aircraft industry. US manufacturers had 85 percent of the world market at that time.

But other countries soon started to catch up. US manufacturers felt heat from Airbus Industrie, a European consortium that was working on an aircraft called the A-310 advanced technology transport. A consortium is *an association of companies for some specific purpose.*

Boeing 757 operated by UTAir Aviation
Nordroden/Shutterstock

American manufacturers responded to this competitive threat. They came up with new products of their own. McDonnell-Douglas brought out its DC-9 Super 80. Boeing developed its 757 and 767.

Lockheed ended commercial aircraft production in 1984 because the L-1011 proved unprofitable. Lockheed and Martin Marietta then combined in 1995 to form the Lockheed Martin Corporation. Boeing and McDonnell Douglas merged in 1997. In 2001, Airbus became a single company.

Airbus A380 exhibition flight at ILA Berlin Air Show on 11 June 2010 in Berlin, Germany

Tom Klimmeck/Shutterstock

Today Boeing and Airbus are the world's major competitors in aircraft manufacturing. Among their latest aircraft are:

- the Boeing 777, which can take between 213 and 396 passengers,
- the Boeing 787 Dreamliner, which has carbon-fiber composite wings and can carry between 242 and 330 passengers, and
- the Airbus 380, the largest commercial aircraft ever built. It can transport from 544 to 853 passengers.

Boeing 787 Dreamliner operated by ANA airlines

Mike Fuchslocher/Shutterstock

LESSON 4   The Jet Era in Commercial Flight

Air safety is essential to keeping the public's trust in the air travel system. The National Transportation Safety Board (NTSB) investigates all air and other transportation accidents. It then makes recommendations to the FAA and the airlines on changes to make the system safer.

Take, for example, the crash of an Air Florida jet on a snowy day in Washington, D.C., in 1982. Safety experts and the industry learned lessons from that accident that have made flight safer for everyone.

Seconds after taking off from Washington National Airport on 13 January 1982, Air Florida Flight 90 slammed into the 14th Street Bridge over the Potomac River. The crash killed 78 passengers, crew members, and motorists.

Federal investigators from the NTSB found a big problem afterward: a copilot who couldn't persuade the pilot it wasn't safe to take off. They also found errors in the way the plane was de-iced. To de-ice an aircraft is *to remove ice from external surfaces of the airplane using specially formulated chemicals*.

The aircraft was covered with ice. Investigators believe that ice kept the plane's instruments from giving a true reading. The copilot noticed something wrong. He mentioned it to the pilot. But when the pilot ignored him, he didn't speak up again.

The silence was fatal.

One lesson: leaders need to make clear that it's OK to ask questions or point out problems. And followers need to know they have the right to speak up.

"This accident was pivotal because it helped draw attention to the fact that pilots need to communicate better," Robert L. Sumwalt III, vice chairman of the National Transportation Safety Board and a former airline pilot, told The Washington Post in 2007. "I don't know of any other accident that has had this amount of impact on aviation but also in other industries," he added.

The maritime and rail industries also learned a lot from the Air Florida crash. So have hospital executives concerned about medical errors.

At the Nebraska Medical Center in Omaha, for instance, surgical teams now use checklists similar to the ones pilots use. Medical center staff adapted these lists to cover the steps necessary for a safe surgical procedure. An operating team, like the team controlling a plane, has many members. Each team member has a vital role in safety.

The last item on the Nebraska team's checklist reflects a lesson straight from Flight 90: "If anybody sees any red flags, something they are uncomfortable with, bring it to [the surgeon's] attention."

The Switch to Air Travel in the United States

As air travel became cheaper, safer, and more accessible, bus and train service dwindled, except in densely populated areas.

In 1940 airlines of the United States carried around about 3 million passengers. In 1950 they carried 17 million.

In 1958, the year the first commercial jets were introduced, the number of passengers reached 30 million. In that year, for the first time, more transatlantic passengers arrived at their destinations by air than by sea.

By 1966 the scale had significantly tipped in the direction of air travel. An estimated 5,322,000 passengers crossed the North Atlantic that year. Of these, 89 percent traveled by air.

The Impact of the Jet Engine on the Commercial Flight Industry

Jet travel literally brought people around the world closer together. Friends on two continents could now keep in touch much more easily. Services such as the Eastern Air Shuttle (now the American Airlines Shuttle), which required no reservations, let business people fly on the spur of the moment. They could make day trips between Boston, New York, and Washington.

Jet travel let American students spend summers in Europe. Middle class families could cross the country over a long weekend to ski or surf or visit grandma.

Jet travel even brought a new term into the language: jet lag. Jet lag is *fatigue and sleep disturbance as a result of crossing time zones on a jet.*

The jet era brought changes to airports as well. They built longer, thicker runways. Chicago's O'Hare Airport introduced parallel runways. These let more than one aircraft land or take off at a time. Passengers boarded their aircraft through enclosed "jet bridges" instead of the old-fashioned passenger stairs.

When airlines switched to jets, they had to improve their maintenance standards. That meant better facilities on the ground and better-trained employees.

Pros and Cons of Commercial Flight Travel for Passengers

Today, the US economy—indeed, the economy of much of the world—depends greatly on the safety and efficiency of domestic and international air travel. The Wright brothers' short flight in 1903 has changed civilian life as much, if not more, than it did military history.

Still, some travelers weigh the pros and cons before they fly.

Pros

Jet airplanes offer passengers one big advantage: speed. And because flying is faster, a transcontinental flight is usually more comfortable than a cross-country bus or train ride. A flight across the ocean is far more comfortable than a weeklong voyage by ship. Passengers on business or vacation save precious time by flying.

Many parts of the world are accessible only by air. Jetliners can soar over miles of terrain that have no roads. They can fly over oceans to reach places once accessible only by ship.

The Heroes of United 93

MODERN AVIATION is a world of routines, procedures, and checklists.

But sometimes people have to act fast. They have to improvise. They have to find within themselves the ability to cope with situations they could never have imagined. The heroic actions of the passengers of United Flight 93 on 11 September 2001 are an example.

On that day terrorists hijacked four aircraft at almost the same time. They planned to turn the planes into guided missiles.

As you read in Lesson 1, the terrorists used two jetliners to bring down the twin towers of the World Trade Center in New York City. They slammed a third plane into the Pentagon, outside Washington, D.C. Nearly 3,000 people died in these attacks.

No one knows for sure what the hijackers intended to do with the fourth plane. That plane, United 93, was en route from Newark, New Jersey, to San Francisco. It had 37 passengers aboard, including four hijackers.

The hijackers took over the plane at 9:28 a.m. They reprogrammed the autopilot system for a new destination—Washington, D.C. At 9:32 a.m. one of the hijackers announced there was a bomb on the plane. This was a lie. The terrorists made the announcement to explain why the aircraft had changed its course abruptly in the air over northeastern Ohio.

Passengers and crew made phone calls from the plane. They learned about the attacks on the World Trade Center. They decided to rush the terrorists and try to retake the plane.

At 9:57 a.m., 29 minutes after the hijackers took over, the passengers made their move. As they tried to break through to the cockpit, the hijacker pilot rolled the plane from side to side. He pushed its nose up and down, trying to throw the counterattacking passengers and crew off balance.

The passengers continued their brave effort. They were seconds away from breaking through when the pilot turned the plane upside down and pushed the nose of the plane earthward.

Cons

Air travel has disadvantages, too. Some people still can't afford it. Airport security has added to travel times. That sometimes defeats the speed advantage of air travel. Weather delays can play havoc with the system. Especially in the northeastern United States, a train may get travelers to their destinations more quickly than a plane.

Flying has become much safer. But some people are still nervous about being confined in an aircraft. Some find the sensations of flying uncomfortable. Also, in an age of terrorism, planes have become a major target. Some people stay away from planes because they worry about hijackings. Some are put off by the security checks passengers must go through at airports to prevent terrorism.

Finally, travelers who want to see places, rather than just fly over them, prefer trains, buses, or cars.

The Memorial Plaza and Wall of Names at the Flight 93 National Memorial in Shanksville, Pennsylvania
Courtesy National Park Service

At 10:03 a.m., United 93 plowed into a field in Shanksville, Pennsylvania. It was all over in less than seven minutes.

The hijacker pilot's objective "was to crash his airliner into symbols of the American Republic," the 9/11 Commission report stated. "He was defeated by the unarmed, alerted passengers of United 93."

"We are sure that the nation owes a debt to the passengers of United 93." the report also said. "Their actions saved the lives of countless others, and may have saved either the US Capitol or the White House from destruction."

LESSON 4   The Jet Era in Commercial Flight

Future Commercial Aircraft

The commercial aircraft of the near future will look a lot like those currently in service—only updated and more efficient. In the longer term, however, some provocative ideas are on the drawing board, including a return to supersonic flight.

Airbus was scheduled to introduce its new A321neo (new engine option) by the end of 2016. At time of printing, the company holds a 70 percent share of the market for medium-size midrange jets. The A321neo carries 240 passengers.

Boeing is laying plans to respond with a new plane that would carry 270 passengers and serve the market between the largest 737 and the 787 Dreamliner. The company also plans to introduce a larger version of its 737 Max to carry 250 passengers. The new planes would take the place of the 757 and 767 in Boeing's lineup.

Boeing also plans to introduce a new long-range jet, the 777X, in 2020. A much larger aircraft, it would carry 350 to 400 passengers. It will feature carbon-fiber wings with folding tips, an advanced fuel-efficient engine, larger windows, and a wider cabin. Carbon fiber is *a very strong lightweight synthetic material made by heating acrylic fiber to very high temperatures.*

The aircraft of the future may include several new design features:

Some industry ideas designed for NASA of aircraft that burn less fuel, emit fewer harmful emissions, and make less noise

Courtesy NASA

- more-efficient wings in different configurations—*setups for different purposes*
- more-efficient tail sections, including perhaps no vertical tail at all
- higher-efficiency engines that burn less fuel and run more quietly— some may be integrated into the fuselage
- more use of lighter-weight composite materials, including more recyclable and environmentally friendly materials (composite materials are *materials made from two or more different materials that, when combined, have properties neither has by itself*)
- fuselages that have different shapes from the simple tube shape used today

Boeing's SUGAR Volt design for NASA

Courtesy NASA/The Boeing Company

In a NASA program, Boeing is working on a hybrid electric-plane concept engineers call "SUGAR Volt" (SUGAR stands for subsonic ultragreen aircraft research.) Much like a hybrid car, it would use jet fuel when high power is needed, as for takeoffs, then switch to battery power for the turbines when cruising. Engineers are also working to develop biofuels made from plant material to reduce the use of petroleum fuel and its greenhouse gases.

Meanwhile, in 2016 NASA announced that it would begin development with Lockheed Martin of a new SST that will break the sound barrier more quietly. Called Quiet SuperSonic Technology (QueSST), it aims to overcome the main barrier to supersonic flight today—the noise from sonic booms. NASA hopes to build on earlier experiments that used modified plane shapes to cut sonic-boom noise by about one-third. If Congress funds it, QueSST would be the biggest attempt yet at reducing this noise.

An artist's concept of a possible Low Boom Flight Demonstration Quiet Supersonic Transport (QueSST) X-plane design
Courtesy NASA/Lockheed Martin

Elsewhere, Virgin Group announced in March 2016 that it would partner with a company called Boom to develop an SST using existing technology. The plane would be more cost-efficient than the Concorde and allow people to fly round-trip from New York to London for $5,000.

Finally, several organizations are conducting research into hypersonic flight—*flight five times the speed of sound or faster*. A plane traveling that fast could fly from London to New York in less than an hour. Airbus has already obtained a patent for a hypersonic aircraft. While such planes are probably decades in the future, researchers believe they are possible. Certainly the technology used in their development will transform air travel as you know it today.

✔ CHECKPOINTS

Lesson 4 Review

Using complete sentences, answer the following questions on a sheet of paper.

1. Why do jet engines have to be made of alloys?

2. What caused the two Comet crashes of 1954?

3. What advantages do turbine engines have over reciprocating engines?

4. What is distinctive about the Boeing 747 that makes it easy to spot?

5. What factors ended the Concorde program?

6. What changes did the jet era bring to airports?

7. What one big advantage do jet planes offer passengers?

8. What are some design features aircraft of the future may include?

9. How long would it take to fly from New York to London in a hypersonic aircraft?

APPLYING YOUR LEARNING

10. How would widespread supersonic air travel change the world? What would be some good consequences, and what would be some bad ones?

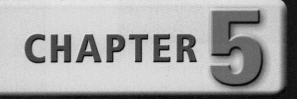

An F-4 Phantom, P-47 Thunderbolt, F-16 Fighting Falcon, and P-51 Mustang fly in a heritage-flight formation.

Courtesy US Air Force

The US Air Force Is Born

Chapter Outline

> *In the development of air power, one has to look ahead and not backward, and figure out what is going to happen, not too much what has happened.*
>
> Brigadier General William "Billy" Mitchell

The Army Air Forces Become the US Air Force

Quick Write

_____

_____

After reading the following vignette, write down three important facts about the Marshall Plan and what it did for Western Europe after World War II.

Learn About

• military developments after World War II

• the National Security Act of 1947 and the creation of an independent Air Force

• political developments after World War II

• the Cold War and how it affected US foreign policy and the US Air Force

• the Berlin Airlift and how the US Air Force helped break the Berlin Blockade

BY THE END OF WORLD WAR II, most of Europe was economically and politically devastated. American leaders feared that if Western Europe remained weak, it would fall under Communist control. The United States wanted to help Europe get back on its feet. So in 1948 Congress passed the European Recovery Program, also known as the Marshall Plan. The plan was *a strategy for rebuilding the countries of Europe and repelling communism after World War II*. The United States invited the counties under Soviet control to join, but the Soviets refused to allow them to participate.

The Marshall Plan was first suggested by then–Secretary of State George C. Marshall in 1947. Marshall had been a five-star general, chief of staff of the Army, and one of the president's senior military advisors during World War II. The Marshall Plan was a great success. It helped Western European industry get up and running again. It also boosted the US economy by opening up new markets for American goods.

The Marshall Plan was recognized as a great humanitarian effort. It earned Secretary of State Marshall the Nobel Peace Prize in 1953. He is the only general to receive this award.

Secretary of State George C. Marshall
Historical Office Public Affairs/Office of the Secretary of Defense

Military Developments After World War II

Vocabulary

- Marshall Plan
- democracy
- massive retaliation
- reserves
- National Guard
- integration
- superpower
- satellite government
- containment
- takeover
- aggression
- arms
- United Nations (UN)
- Strategic Triad
- missiles
- satellite
- nuclear deterrence
- Western Allies
- airlift

After World War II ended, the United States gave in to public pressure and began to reduce the military. It also began restructuring how the military was organized, based on lessons learned from World War II. This reorganization resulted in a new military establishment, later to be called the Department of Defense.

Force Reduction

The end of World War II began a new age for the US military. With Europe, Japan, and China in shambles from the war, the United States and the Soviet Union were the only two major powers remaining in the world. Taking an active role in world affairs was the best way to protect US national interests. This was especially true with the Soviet Union expanding its territories and influence. The United States and its allies saw this expansion as a threat to world peace and democracy. Democracy is *a form of government in which people choose their leaders by voting.* If the West didn't stop Soviet attempts to expand, Europe and perhaps the Middle East might fall under Soviet control.

At the same time, Americans wanted their military family members home from Europe and the Pacific, and to return to a peacetime economy. US leaders were certain that, with the invention of the atomic bomb, the United States had all the security it needed. No one would dare attack the United States or its allies for fear of massive retaliation—*returning an attack with a large-scale attack, including using the atomic bomb.* This led many people to believe that the United States no longer needed a large military force. The result was a period of confusion for US defense policy.

As a result, the United States rapidly reduced the size of its armed forces after World War II. Within a year after Japan surrendered, the Army shrank from 8 million Soldiers to less than 2 million. The Navy was reduced from 4 million Sailors to 1.6 million, and thousands of ships were retired. Both the Army and Navy created a reserve program in case of future wars. Reserves are *military forces not part of the regular military, but trained and organized for a quick call to action.* Another goal was to have a National Guard, *a military force recruited by each state, equipped by the federal government, and subject to either a state or federal government recall.*

By 1947, the Army Air Forces (AAF) had been cut from 2.3 million Airmen and 72,000 planes to about 300,000 Airmen and 10,000 planes. More than 90 percent of the AAF's mechanics left the service. By 1950, about 2 million personnel made up the entire military. This force's purpose was to meet the threat of communism.

Reorganization

As the US government was reducing the size of all military branches, it was rethinking how to fight wars. The atomic bomb had drastically changed warfare. Both civilian and military leaders saw the need to change US military organization based on the military experiences of World War II. They wanted to correct the intelligence failures and poor coordination between the Army and the Navy that helped lead to the disaster at Pearl Harbor. The law that changed the military organization was the National Security Act of 1947.

The National Security Act of 1947 and the Creation of an Independent Air Force

As you read in Chapter 3, airpower was vital to the Allies' victory in World War II. Between 1941 and 1945, the Army Air Forces developed new strategies and tactics. Engineers built more-powerful bombers and fighters. US planes delivered the atomic bombs on Japan that ended the war in 1945. US airpower grew up fast, and the atomic bomb made it mature even faster. By 1947, most people were convinced it was time for the Air Forces to gain independence from the Army.

The National Security Act of 1947

In July 1947 President Harry S. Truman signed into law the National Security Act of 1947. This act set the stage for military development in the years to come. It authorized the founding of the National Military Establishment (today's Department of Defense).

The law created the post of secretary of defense, who would answer to the president of the United States. It created the National Security Council and the Central Intelligence Agency. It established three branches within the National Military Establishment: the Department of the Navy, the Department of the Army, and the Department of the Air Force. This last change marked the creation of an independent United States Air Force (USAF). The first secretary of the Air Force, Stuart Symington, was appointed in September 1947.

Separate Air Force

As you have read in earlier lessons, the vision of a separate Air Force began with Brigadier General Billy Mitchell after World War I. But the proposal was not seriously considered until the Army Air Forces proved their military value in World War II. By the end of the war, the AAF had become the most powerful air arm in the world. It had long-range bombers that could deliver an atomic weapon. This made the AAF a powerful political tool and key to US plans for preventing another war.

Although the independent Air Force was created in July 1947, it did not receive full and formal independence until 18 September that year. On that day President Truman appointed Stuart Symington as the first secretary of the Air Force. It still took another two years for an orderly transfer of functions and personnel from the Army.

Waypoints

Integrating the Air Force

On 26 July 1948, President Truman issued Executive Order 9981. It called for equal treatment of all people in the military services, regardless of race, color, religion, or national origin. Of all the services, the Air Force was the most ready to answer President Truman's call. It was already studying ways to improve military efficiency. Integration means *including individuals from different groups in society or an organization as equals*. Secretary Symington met some Air Force leaders' objection to integration firmly. He told the generals he expected no one to get in the way. Those who didn't agree with the policy should resign. As early as 1947, Secretary Symington had said publicly that African-Americans should be able to enter the Air Force based on their merits and abilities rather than their race. Over the next few years, under his guidance the Air Force disbanded African-American units. It was the first service to be fully integrated.

The First Air Force Chief of Staff

General Carl Spaatz was the first US Air Force chief of staff. He had commanded many World War II operations in the European and Pacific theaters. As chief of staff, General Spaatz was in charge of military operations for the Air Force. Secretary Symington was in charge of administrative matters.

General Spaatz oversaw three major operating commands created in 1946: the Strategic Air Command (SAC), the Tactical Air Command (TAC), and the Air Defense Command (ADC). SAC was the atomic-weapons command. It was the best-funded command of the three. TAC was in charge of tactical, or smaller, air operations. ADC's role was to defend the country from air strikes.

President Truman signs the Presidential Proclamation designating 1 August 1946 as Air Force Day. With him are General Carl A. Spaatz, Commanding General of the Army Air Forces, and Lieutenant General Ira C. Eaker, Deputy Commander of the AAF.

Courtesy US Air Force

The Right Stuff

First Woman in the Air Force

Esther Blake enlisted on the first minute of the first hour of the first day that regular Air Force duty was authorized for women: 8 July 1948. Blake's active military career began in 1944. A widow, she joined her sons in the Army Air Forces. Blake joined the Women's Auxiliary Army Corps (WAAC) when she was told that her oldest son, a B-17 pilot, had been shot down over Belgium and was missing. Her younger son said she joined in hope of helping free a needed Soldier from clerical work to fight. She felt this would speed up the end of the war. Both of Blake's sons returned home from combat with only minor wounds and many decorations.

Blake remained in the Air Force until 1954, when she left due to disability. After leaving, she worked as a civil service employee at the Veterans Administration Regional Headquarters in Montgomery, Alabama, until her death in 1979.

Staff Sergeant Esther M. Blake
Courtesy US Air Force

Political Developments After World War II

With the defeat of Germany and Japan in World War II, the United States and the Soviet Union emerged as superpowers. A superpower is *a powerful, dominant country that has nuclear weapons.* So the world was left with two major political forces—Soviet communism and Western democracy.

The Soviets made it clear immediately after the war that they would not allow the nations they had occupied during the war to have their own forms of government. The Soviet Union began expanding the territories it controlled in Europe and other parts of the world. In 1939 the Soviet Union had occupied the Baltic states of Latvia, Lithuania, and Estonia; a small section of Finland; and a large portion of Poland. After the war, the Soviets set up Communist satellite governments in Bulgaria, Czechoslovakia, East Germany, Hungary, Poland, and Romania. A satellite government is *a government dominated politically and economically by another nation.* Communists also took power in Yugoslavia and Albania. Communism threatened Greece and Turkey, and large Communist parties were active in France and Italy.

The Soviets' greatest fear was another war with Germany. The Germans had invaded the Russian empire and the Soviet Union twice during the 20th century. During the 18th and 19th centuries as well, invasions of Russian territory had come from the west.

Communism was also spreading in East Asia. The Soviet Union put in power a Communist government in northern Korea, which it controlled after Japan surrendered. A decades-long civil war in China between Western-allied Nationalists and the Soviet-allied Communists turned in the Communists' favor. The Chinese Communists eventually won the war and took control of China.

In French Indochina, Communists were fighting a war against the French colonial army.

The Soviet Union was trying to increase its influence in the world. The United States was trying to decrease the Soviet Union's influence without going to war. The United States answered the spread of Communism with military aid under the Truman Doctrine and economic help under Marshall Plan. These efforts were known as containment—*the US Cold War policy to prevent the spread of communism in the world.*

In 1947, the United States sent military and economic aid to Greece and Turkey to enable them to resist a Communist takeover. A takeover is *the seizure of a country's military and political power.* In 1948, the Marshall Plan provided economic aid for the rebuilding of Europe after World War II. In 1949, the United States and other Western democracies organized the North Atlantic Treaty Organization (NATO). NATO was a treaty alliance to defend its members and preserve peace and security against aggression in Europe. Aggression is *hostile action against another country or government.* The increasingly tense standoff between the Soviets and the West developed into the Cold War.

Countries with Communist governments in the 1960s

CHAPTER 5   The US Air Force Is Born

The Cold War and How It Affected US Foreign Policy and the US Air Force

Most Americans expected a long period of peace after World War II. But that didn't happen. The country was about to enter a new kind of war. It wouldn't be another world war. It would be fought in smaller theaters. It would include a huge buildup of arms—*weapons*—including atomic weapons.

The United States would wage this war against a powerful country that had been one of its major allies in World War II: the Soviet Union.

What the Cold War Was

The *Cold War*, as it came to be called, lasted for more than four decades—roughly from 1948 until 1991. The primary players were the United States and the Soviet Union. The two countries disagreed on how the world should be run in the postwar years. The Cold War was their political, economic, and military rivalry. But both also had something in common. They wanted to avoid another worldwide war, a "hot" war or a direct military conflict between the two countries.

The Cold War got its name from Bernard Baruch, an American delegate to the United Nations. The United Nations (UN) is *a worldwide organization first formed in 1945 by the victorious Allies to maintain international peace*. In a 1947 speech, Baruch said, "Let us not be deceived—today we are in the midst of a cold war."

As you read earlier, the Soviets were putting Communist governments in place in the countries along their borders in Eastern Europe. They hoped a Communist Eastern Europe might buffer them from Germany. But they were afraid that America's powerful new atomic bomb would threaten their plan. The Soviets were still trying to develop the bomb.

M·I·L·E·S·T·O·N·E·S

Communism

The Communists believed that the state should own all means of production. They permitted no private ownership of factories or businesses. They also severely restricted or forbade private ownership of land. They supported dictatorship by a single party—the Communist Party—and did not permit free elections or respect human rights such as a free press, freedom of religion, freedom of speech, or freedom of association. Citizens of Communist countries could not emigrate to another country or live elsewhere, and very few were allowed to travel outside the Communist group of nations. Most Communist governments collapsed as the Cold War ended. By 2016, Cambodia, China, Cuba, Laos, North Korea, and Vietnam were the only surviving Communist governments. By then, their practice of Communist economic teachings varied widely.

B-36J Peacemaker
Courtesy US Air Force

The United States was confident it could keep the Soviets out of Western Europe because America alone had the atomic bomb. Eventually it developed a three-pronged method of delivering nuclear weapons called the Strategic Triad. (A triad is a group of three.) The Strategic Triad consisted of *land-based intercontinental ballistic missiles (ICBMs), submarine-launched ballistic missiles (SLBMs), and long-range bombers.* In other words, it consisted of land-, sea-, and air-based nuclear weapons.

The purpose of multiple methods for delivering nuclear weapons is to ensure that the United States can retaliate if it is attacked. If one type of weapon becomes vulnerable to an enemy (for example, because of an enemy's technological breakthrough), the other types would still be protected—and the United States would remain safe.

Then in 1949 the Soviets tested their first atomic weapon. Tensions between the two nations increased. Each side worried that the other might use its atomic bombs, with dreadful results. Yet it was this threat of total destruction that each side hoped would prevent the other from ever striking.

In a way, that fear had a preventive effect. But some serious face-offs did take place. The first was the Berlin Blockade (1948 to 1949), which you'll read about later in this lesson.

The Creation of the North Atlantic Treaty Organization (NATO)

Eleven Western European countries and the United States formed the North Atlantic Treaty Organization (NATO) in 1949. NATO nations promised to defend one another from Communist aggression. They agreed that "an armed attack against one or more of them shall be considered an attack against them all." The first NATO headquarters was in Paris.

Some people wondered why the United States joined NATO. After all, America tended to be an isolationist nation. So why did it join a military pact in a time of peace? The reason was simple: the United States was intent on keeping communism—with its pro-Soviet dictatorships and violations of human rights—from spreading around the globe. NATO seemed a good way to bond countries with a similar goal. As another indication of its support, the United States agreed to keep US troops in Western Europe in case any of its allies needed help.

In 1955 the Soviets responded to NATO's creation. They drew up the Warsaw Pact—named for the capital of Poland—with the East European Communist allies that they dominated. In this pact, or treaty, the Soviet leaders promised to safeguard any of their friends who came under attack.

How the USAF Was Organized to Fight the Cold War

SAC was the most crucial command in the Air Force at the time. In the early days of the Cold War, SAC had hundreds of B-50D Stratofortess aircraft, an improved version of the B-29. It also had B-36 Peacemaker, B-47 Stratojet, and B-58A Hustler bombers. KC-97L tankers refueled the bombers in mid-air.

SAC's role eventually expanded to running aerial reconnaissance. Spy planes, like the U-2, allowed SAC to spot Soviet missiles—*rocket-propelled vehicles that carry a weapon or warhead.*

Finally, as technology further improved, each side launched satellites into space. A satellite is *an object that orbits another object in space, such as a planet.* The satellites could check for an enemy nation's missiles on the ground. The US military built underground bunkers from which to keep track of its satellites. But SAC found that enemy atomic bombs could target its bunkers. So it created flying command centers called *Looking Glass.* These planes flew 24 hours a day, 7 days a week, for more than 29 years.

Convair B-58 Hustler
Courtesy US Air Force

Boeing KC-97L Stratotanker
Courtesy US Air Force

Lockheed U-2A
Courtesy US Air Force

How the Cold War Drove Developments in SAC

The invention and use of the atomic bomb during World War II finally led to the Air Force getting its independence from the Army. The Air Force could now perform a function that no other branch of the military could carry out.

Indeed, as the creation of SAC showed, the atomic bomb would shape the Air Force's mission. Today there are many means of delivering atomic bombs, including missiles and submarines. But in the years just after World War II, only airplanes could do this job.

Boeing B-52 Stratofortress
Courtesy US Air Force

Military and civilian leaders thought the atomic bomb would protect the United States from aggression. They called this protection nuclear deterrence, or *prevention of war by convincing an enemy that if he attacks, he will be destroyed by nuclear weapons*. The main duty of the Air Force at that time was to deliver the atomic bomb. SAC was the command within the Air Force that would fulfill the mission. Its bombers would drop the bombs if need be.

The US-Soviet rivalry and the atomic bomb drove decisions in aviation development. The Boeing B-52 Stratofortress bomber, with its 10,000-mile range, became SAC's main bomber. But it wasn't the first or last.

The Boeing B-47 Stratojet became the Air Force's first sweptback-wing multi–jet-engine bomber. The sweptback wing—a wing angled rearward from the point of attachment—was first designed by the Germans during World War II. This type of wing is more efficient at higher speeds than a straight wing. The wind can flow more easily over it. The Boeing B-47 first rolled off the assembly line in 1947 and entered service in 1951. But this plane could fly only 3,000 miles without refueling. That prompted the Air Force to ask for a longer-range bomber. Boeing won the contract to build its longer-range B-52, with the first one flying in 1954.

Boeing B-47 Stratojet
Courtesy US Air Force

Tactical Air Command (TAC) and Air Defense Command (ADC)

The Air Force had two other commands: TAC and ADC. TAC's mission was to be able to carry out tactical air operations anywhere in the world, without other US forces. ADC was responsible for stopping and destroying enemy air weapon systems fired at the United States. However, most Air Force dollars were still going to SAC.

From 1947 to mid-1950s, the size of TAC changed with the international situation and with funds made available to the command. By 1947 most of TAC's aircraft were from World War II and considered outdated. TAC did have three jet-powered aircraft, including the P-80 pursuit plane, later changed to F-80 Shooting Star. (The old "P" designation for pursuit aircraft was changed to the current "F" for fighter aircraft.) Along with this, TAC had the B-45 Tornado bomber and the F-84 Thunderjet fighter-bomber.

Mission-ready F-80C Shooting Star with two 1,000 pound bombs
Courtesy US Air Force

Republic F-84 Thunderjets fly in formation.
Courtesy US Air Force

Cutaway drawing of North American B-45 showing crew positions and aircraft systems
Courtesy US Air Force

LESSON 1 The Army Air Forces Become the US Air Force

Like TAC, the Air Defense Command was neglected in the early years of the newly independent Air Force. In the period following World War II, US leaders thought the country was relatively free from the threat of air attack. Even during the war, the need for air defense had not been brought to the attention of the American people.

In 1947, foreseeing the possibility of an air attack on the US, Air Force leaders approved a plan for building a large aircraft control-and-warning network. However, the Air Force was unable to get the funds to build this network until 1949. That was the year the Soviets exploded their first atomic bomb. This meant the threat of a nuclear attack on the United States was now real, and the country needed to plan for it.

The Air Force at this time was caught in conflicting currents. Although it was building its new organization in 1947, it was also trying to cut back to a size that the defense budget could support. From 1946 to 1947, the Air Force had gone from 218 to 52 fighter groups, only 11 of which were considered combat ready. Because of budget limitations, it was very difficult for the Air Force to maintain the 48 fighter groups that President Truman approved for 1950. The Air Force would have to wait until the Korean War to see any buildup of its fighter forces.

The Berlin Airlift and How the USAF Helped Break the Berlin Blockade

Before the end of World War II, the Allies were already talking about what to do with Germany when it surrendered. Based on the lessons they learned after World War I (see Chapter 3, Lesson 2), the United States, Britain, and France wanted Germany to prosper. That way it wouldn't drag Europe into yet another world war. But the Soviet Union had a different view. It wanted to dominate Germany so the Germans would never again invade Soviet borders.

The Allies' solution was to divide Germany in two parts. Each side could rule its part as it wished. The Soviets controlled East Germany, where they set up a Communist dictatorship. The Western Allies—*the United States, Britain, and France*—controlled West Germany, where they set up a democracy.

Germany's capital, Berlin, posed a problem. It was in East Germany. The four Allies split Berlin into four sectors, too. The Soviets got one sector—East Berlin. The Western Allies controlled the three sectors of West Berlin. But by June 1948 the Soviets decided they wanted all of Berlin. After all, it was in the Soviet-run part of Germany. The Soviets decreed that the Western Allies could no longer use roads, railroads, or canals to enter East Germany to deliver goods to Berlin. The first big clash of the Cold War and the first test of the new independent Air Force had begun.

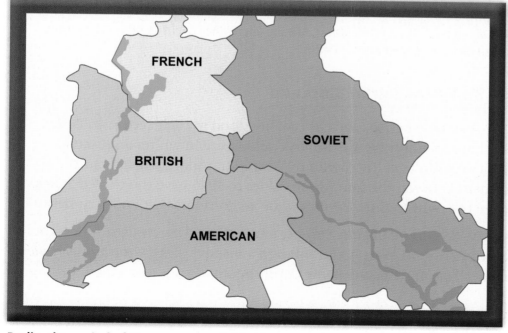

The Soviets controlled East Germany, while the United States, Britain, and France controlled West Germany.

Berlin, the capital of Germany, was divided between the Soviets, who would run East Berlin, and the Western Allies, who would manage West Berlin.

LESSON 1   The Army Air Forces Become the US Air Force

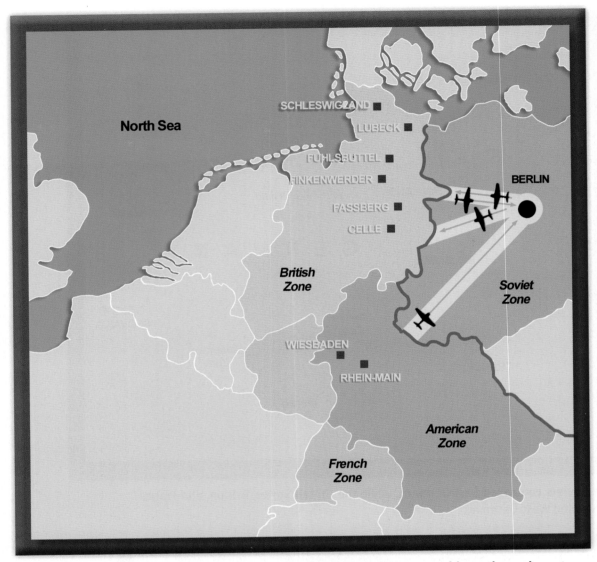

According to a 1945 agreement, the United States, Britain, and France could use three air routes over Soviet-controlled East Germany to enter Berlin.

How the USAF Broke the Berlin Blockade

The Western Allies had to get goods such as coal and food to their sectors in Berlin. Otherwise, more than 2 million West Berliners could freeze in winter and starve. If the Western Allies couldn't get into Berlin by ground transport, what about the air? A previous agreement between the four former Allies in 1945 gave the United States, Britain, and France the right to three 20-mile-wide air corridors that ended in Berlin.

General Lucius Clay, US commander in Europe, took action. The Western Allies would prevent the Soviet takeover of West Berlin through a massive airlift—*the transportation of personnel or material by air.* Thus the Berlin Airlift began. (It was also called *Operation Vittles.*)

While war usually calls for bombers and fighters, this was to be a bloodless battle conducted by cargo aircraft. Clay ordered Lieutenant General Curtis LeMay, then commander of US Air Forces in Europe, to make available as many cargo planes as possible. Clay asked Major General William Tunner, the transport expert from World War II, to command the airlift into West Berlin. The airlift began in June 1948, the same month in which the Soviets set up the blockade.

The Cargo Plane

Lieutenant General LeMay gathered more than 100 C-47 cargo planes for Major General Tunner. The *Gooney Birds*, as they were nicknamed, could each lug two to three tons of goods. But West Berliners needed 4,500 tons of food, coal, oil, and other supplies each day.

So LeMay got an even larger, faster transport plane into service—the C-54. It carried about 10 tons of cargo. By October 1948 200 C-54s were shuttling cargo to the city. USAF cargo planes were joined by transports from Britain's Royal Air Force. Some days, almost one cargo plane a minute landed in Berlin.

By May 1949 the Soviets caved. They realized that the US, Britain, and France would not give up their airlift, no matter the cost. By that time, the Allies had airlifted 1.75 million tons of goods into the blockaded city.

The last *Operation Vittles* Douglas C-54 prepares for takeoff from Rhein Main Air Base, Germany, on 30 September 1949.

Courtesy US Air Force

Lieutenant General William Tunner: Cargo Commander

Lieutenant General William Tunner (1906–1982) was a West Point graduate. He spent his career with the Army Air Corps and the Air Force.

Tunner's specialty was transport planes. During World War II he was chief of the Air Transport Command Ferrying Division. While in that post, he asked Nancy Love to form the Women's Auxiliary Ferry Squadron. Also during that war, he figured out how to safely transport supplies across the Himalayan Mountains to China. China was one of the Allies at that time.

Because of Tunner's success in China, General Lucius Clay tapped him to head the Berlin Airlift. Tunner was a very organized person. He knew that for any transport mission to succeed, it must run in an orderly manner. Tunner demanded strict schedules for flights, schedules for crews, and weather reports. As a result, the airlift had an excellent safety record. And the amount of cargo ferried to Berlin rocketed between 1948 and 1949.

Tunner recognized the importance of cargo planes to any Air Force operation. He also knew how undervalued they were. With the triumph of the Berlin Airlift, Tunner showed the world how to command transport missions.

Then–Brigadier General William Tunner in 1943
Courtesy US Air Force

Lessons the USAF Learned From the Berlin Airlift

The Berlin airlift helped convince American leaders of the need to build a stronger Air Force. The cargo plane came into its own during the airlift. It wasn't as flashy as bombers or fighters, but it saved a city from a Communist takeover. These workhorse transports formed the critical element in the American response to the Soviet blockade of Berlin.

The intensity of the airlift also taught cargo crews a lot about what they could achieve. They had daily chances to perfect air support. One year later, transports, bombers, and fighters would all be called on to fight the next stage of the Cold War: the Korean War.

Meanwhile, the blockade helped convince West Europeans of the threat the Soviet Union posed. It helped lead to the creation of NATO. And it contributed to the later creation of the democratic Federal Republic of Germany on the territory the Western Allies controlled.

The Berlin Airlift Memorial at the former Tempelhof Airport in Berlin. The three arcs symbolize the three air corridors through which the Americans and British flew supplies to West Berlin.

ArTono/Shutterstock

Then—1st Lieutenant Gail Halvorsen

Courtesy US Air Force

1st Lieutenant Gail Halvorsen: The Candy Bomber

1st Lieutenant Gail Halvorsen was one of the US pilots picked to fly C-54s during the Berlin Airlift. These pilots often had little to do while waiting for their cargo aircraft to be unloaded. One day, trying to pass the time, he talked with some German children who were peering through the airport fence. They asked if he had any candy. He told them that the next time he flew in, he'd wiggle the wings of his plane and then drop small packages of candy to them.

Halvorsen kept his promise. He rigged miniature parachutes with American candy bars and gum and then dropped them over Berlin for German children to retrieve. Many German children who didn't live near the airport wrote Halvorsen asking for candy to be dropped in their neighborhoods. They called him *Uncle Wiggly Wings*. He was also known as the *Candy Bomber*.

Soon many other pilots wanted to help. General Tunner learned about the candy drops and added his support, calling the effort *Operation Little Vittles*. People back in the United States joined the effort, too.

Halvorsen retired from the Air Force with the rank of colonel in 1974.

✔ CHECKPOINTS

Lesson 1 Review

Using complete sentences, answer the following questions on a sheet of paper.

1. What did the United States protect by taking an active role in world affairs?

2. What invention made US leaders certain the United States had all the security it needed?

3. What is the name of the law that created the independent United States Air Force?

4. Who was the first chief of staff of the USAF?

5. What was the Strategic Air Command?

6. Which two major political forces was the world left with at the end of World War II?

7. Who won the civil war between the Chinese Nationalists and Chinese Communists?

8. What was the Cold War?

9. Why did the United States join NATO?

10. What was the mission of Tactical Air Command?

11. When the Soviets Union decreed that the Western Allies couldn't deliver goods to Berlin using ground transport, how did the West get supplies to sectors of Berlin it controlled?

12. Which were the two main cargo aircraft of the Berlin Airlift, and how many tons could each carry?

13. What did the Berlin airlift convince American leaders of the need to do?

APPLYING YOUR LEARNING

Based on the lessons learned from World War II, how important do you think it is for the United States to maintain air superiority today? Provide a detailed explanation of why it is important or not.

Military Aircraft Development After World War II

Quick Write

_____

_____

After reading the vignette about Captain Joseph Kittinger, explain what qualities he must have had to be able to make his record-setting jump.

Learn About

- military aviation research after World War II
- significant contributions of test pilots in military aviation
- other significant military aircraft flown at Edwards AFB

AS AIRCRAFT FLEW HIGHER AND HIGHER, they began to reach the outer edges of the atmosphere. This created a need for new escape equipment for pilots. When bailing out at high speed, a pilot encountered extreme cold, lack of oxygen, and the tendency to enter a deadly fast spin during freefall.

To protect pilots, the Air Force developed a series of new parachutes that would open in stages—with small, medium, and then large parachutes deploying as the pilot fell. This allowed for a safe descent from extraordinary heights.

But someone needed to test the new parachutes. That someone was test pilot Captain Joseph Kittinger Jr. In 1959 and 1960, Captain Kittinger made several jumps from a balloon gondola to test the equipment.

In August 1960, Kittinger rode an Excelsior balloon gondola for an hour and a half to a height of 102,000 feet. That's more than 20 miles high and above more than 99 percent of Earth's atmosphere. A sign outside the gondola read, "This is the highest step in the world." At 40,000 feet, his pressure suit inflated, and he found that his right glove was not working. Not wanting to abort the flight, he decided not to tell mission control. His right hand swelled to twice its normal size, and he couldn't use it during the flight.

Stepping from the gondola, he freefell for 4 minutes and 37 seconds, reaching a speed of 614 mph. The parachutes worked perfectly, and Kittinger returned to the ground in a little more than 13 minutes. His jump showed that a person could be protected and escape at the edge of the atmosphere. Today every ejection seat in a fighter aircraft uses a small drone parachute to slow and stabilize the pilot before the main parachute unfolds.

Kittinger went on to serve three tours of duty in the Vietnam War. He was shot down in May 1972 and spent almost a year as a prisoner of war. He was promoted to colonel while a prisoner. After his release, he continued in the Air Force until retiring in 1978 with many honors.

Kittinger's freefall record stood until 2012. He participated as a capsule communicator for the jump that broke the record.

Vocabulary

- playa
- tumble
- Mach
- stealth aircraft
- prototype

Military Aviation Research After World War II

Today every aircraft flown by the US Air Force is first tested and flown at Edwards AFB, California. But Edwards AFB didn't start out this way. The base is located at the edge of Rogers Dry Lakebed in a playa that spreads out over 44 square miles. It's the largest dry lakebed in world. A playa is *a flat-floored bottom of an undrained desert basin that at times can become a shallow lake.* As water from winter rains is swept back and forth by desert winds, it smoothes the lakebed out to an almost glass-like flatness.

Early homesteaders thought of the dry lakebed as a wasteland, but in 1933 then–Lieutenant Colonel "Hap" Arnold saw it as a one-of-a-kind "natural aerodrome" or airfield. This led to him establishing the Muroc Bombing and Gunnery Range. It served Army Air Corps bombers and fighters for several years. By 1942, it was named Muroc Army Air Base.

Development of military aircraft normally took place at Wright Field in Ohio. However, due to the large volume of flight-test work needed during World War II, an alternative location was required. In 1942, a site was found along the north shore of Rogers Dry Lakebed, about six miles from Muroc Army Air Base. The first aircraft tested at Muroc was the Bell XP-59A Airacomet jet fighter, followed by the Lockheed XP-80 Shooting Star. (The *X* indicates the aircraft is experimental.)

In 1949 Muroc was renamed Edwards Air Base in honor of Captain Glen W. Edwards. He was a test pilot and native of California who died in 1948 flying another experimental airplane.

Every Air Force aircraft flown since the end of World War II had its beginning at Edwards AFB. The many decades following the war have seen a revolution in planes that could fly at speeds and to heights the Wright brothers could have hardly imagined.

A series of technology breakthroughs led to new aircraft that could perform as never before. These breakthroughs included powerful jet and rocket engines, swept wings, new fuselage shapes, and new electronics.

Aerial view of Edwards AFB, California. Note the runway markings painted on Rogers Dry Lake.

Courtesy US Air Force

Breaking the Sound Barrier

For a while, achieving faster speeds remained a challenge. The government, universities, and private industry all wanted to build faster fighter airplanes. But whenever such planes approached what came to be known as the *sound barrier*—the speed of sound, about 670 miles per hour—they shook badly. Sometimes they fell apart.

In 1945, the Army Air Forces and the National Advisory Committee for Aeronautics (NACA) began testing experimental aircraft for high-speed flight. (The NACA later became NASA.) These aircraft became known as the *X planes*.

The first of these was the Bell X-1. Its fuselage was shaped like a .50-caliber bullet, because experts knew an aircraft that shape would fly straight—it would not tumble, or *roll end over end*, at supersonic speed.

The X-1 had straight, very thin wings. It was powered by a rocket engine and dropped from a B-29 bomber. It also had a new system that allowed the pilot to raise or lower the entire tail a few degrees to allow the plane to fly level at high speed. The success of this design gave American fighter planes a technological advantage over other countries for several years.

The breakthrough occurred on 14 October 1947. Then-Captain Charles "Chuck" Yeager broke the sound barrier with the X-1. He reached 670 mph at 42,000 feet. Supersonic flight was born.

Yeager's feat brought a new word into the aviation dictionary—*Mach*. Mach (pronounced "mock") is *the speed of sound*. (Mach is named after 19th century Austrian physicist Ernst Mach.)

After this breakthrough, aircraft got faster and faster. The X-1A first flew in July 1951. It and the X-1B soon set new records, reaching Mach 2.44 (1,650 mph) and an altitude of 90,440 feet. The Bell X-1E didn't fly as fast, but proved that a very thin wing could be used on a supersonic aircraft. This led to the Lockheed F-104 Starfighter.

The X-1 with its mother ship, a B-29
Courtesy NASA

Reaching Mach 3

The Bell X-2 had a lot of problems in its early development. An explosion while the plane was still aboard the mother ship killed Bell test pilot Jean Ziegler and an observer.

The plane made its first flight in June 1952. It had a more-pointed nose and more powerful rocket engine than the X-1 series. It was designed to reach Mach 3 (2,094 mph). At this speed, friction from the air would heat the plane's skin to high temperatures. So the X-2 had to be made from a heat-resistant steel alloy. This research led to the SR-71 "Blackbird" reconnaissance plane.

On 23 July 1956 test pilot Captain Frank Everest flew the X-2 at 1,900 mph, or Mach 2.87. On 7 September, Captain Iven Kincheloe flew the X-2 up to 126,000 feet. He became the first human to fly higher than 100,000 feet. Twenty days later, Captain Milburn Apt took the X-2 aloft. He reached Mach 3.196, but sadly, the aircraft spun out of control and Captain Apt was killed.

The Douglas X-3 Stiletto was introduced in 1952. While the X-1 and X-2 were rocket-driven, the X-3 was jet-powered. And while the X-1 and X-2 had to be launched like a glider in mid-air, the X-3 took off from the ground.

Engineers built the X-3 to be the first jet aircraft to break Mach 3. But in 20 tries, it failed to do so. So the designers went back to the drawing board. Several more X planes followed.

An X-15 is dropped by a B-52 mother ship for a high-speed flight.

Courtesy US Air Force

North American X-15

The most successful X plane was the legendary North American X-15. Only three X-15s were ever built. But the aircraft played an important role in modern aviation and spaceflight history. Like the previous X planes, the X-15 tested two kinds of limits: speed and altitude.

The rocket-propelled X-15 was carried into the air by a B-52 for release. Soon after its initial flight, it was breaking records. The X-15 flew at speeds that exceeded 4,000 miles an hour, more than five times the speed of sound. It soared more than 50 miles into the sky to the edge of space, earning its pilots astronaut wings. In 1967, a slightly modified X-15 reached Mach 6.7.

Pilots tested the X-15 in 199 flights from 1959 until 1968. After the rocket plane was dropped from the mother ship, the pilot ignited the X-15 rocket and soared to the upper atmosphere. The plane would then glide without power to land on a dry lakebed. A typical X-15 flight lasted about 10 minutes.

Significant Contributions of Test Pilots in Military Aviation

As technologically advanced as they were at the time, these experimental aircraft would not have achieved anything without the pilots who dared to fly them. One writer has called these flyers "the most competent professional test pilots in history."

Being a test pilot was dangerous work. Many lost their lives. But this small group paved the way for both today's high-speed, high-performance aircraft and the US space program. This section takes a look at just a few of these courageous aviators.

Brigadier General Charles Yeager

Brigadier General Charles "Chuck" Yeager is best known for breaking the sound barrier in 1947. But he already had a long record of service by that time.

He was born in West Virginia in 1923. When he was 18 in 1941, Yeager enlisted as a private in the Army Air Forces. He worked as an aircraft mechanic and pilot. He was accepted for pilot training in 1942 under the "flying sergeant" program. He got his wings and flying officer appointment the following year.

Yeager became an ace in World War II. Between 1943 and 1945, he shot down 13 enemy aircraft, including five in one mission. He even shot down one of the new German Me-262 jets.

Then-Captain Chuck Yeager standing next to the Bell X-1 aircraft in which he broke the sound barrier in 1947
Courtesy US Air Force

After the war he became a test pilot. His work led to his selection as pilot of the first experimental rocket aircraft, the X-1. Yeager beat out 125 other pilots to get the job. He broke the sound barrier in October 1941. On 12 December 1953, he became the first pilot to exceed Mach 2 in level flight.

Later, Yeager served in the Vietnam War. He was a wing commander in 1966 and flew more than 120 combat missions. He received many Air Force honors, including the Distinguished Service Medal. He also won several major civilian trophies. He retired from the US Air Force in 1973.

Brigadier General Frank Everest

Frank Everest was born in 1920 and joined the Army Air Forces in November 1941. He shot down two German aircraft in North Africa in 1942 and four Japanese aircraft over China in 1945. His plane was shot down by ground fire in May 1945 and he became a prisoner of war until the war ended in August.

Then–Lieutenant Colonel Frank Everest sitting in the rocket-powered Bell X-2 research aircraft

Courtesy US Air Force

In 1946 Everest was assigned to the Air Force Flight Test Center at Wright-Patterson AFB, Ohio. During this time, he took part in testing the X-1, setting a new altitude record of 73,000 feet. He was transferred to Edwards AFB in 1951, where he tested several of the X planes and many new fighters and bombers. In 1953 he set a new world speed record of 755 mph in a YF-100.

Then-Captain Everest flew the X-1B to Mach 2.3 in December 1954, making him at the time the second-fastest man in the world. He became the "fastest man alive" when he flew the X-2 to Mach 2.87 in 1956.

General Everest retired from the Air Force in 1973. He died in 2004.

Colonel Jackie "Jack" Ridley

Jackie "Jack" Ridley was born in 1915. After graduating from high school in Sulphur, Oklahoma, he entered the University of Oklahoma and joined the ROTC program. He graduated in 1939 with a degree in mechanical engineering. Lieutenant Ridley was sent to Flying Training School at Kelly Army Air Base in Texas and earned his pilot's wings in 1942.

The Army Air Corps needed engineer-trained pilots, so instead of sending him to a combat unit, the Army ordered Ridley to the B-24 Liberator plant in Fort Worth, Texas, to conduct acceptance tests on the bomber. After two years, he was sent off to further his education, graduating from the Army Air Forces School of Engineering and later the California Institute of Technology, earning a Master of Science degree in Aeronautical Engineering.

Captain Ridley was later named as the project engineer for the Bell X-1 rocket powered airplane, joining test pilots Captain Chuck Yeager and Lieutenant Bob Hoover. Ridley's task was to analyze all of the technical data generated during the X-1 flights as the plane proceeded toward the unexplored region of supersonic flight. It was Ridley's adjustable horizontal stabilizer that allowed the X-1 to maintain control at supersonic speeds, allowing Captain Yeager to be the first man to break the sound barrier.

Colonel Ridley went on to work on many other aircraft test programs from the X-1 through X-5, B-47, F-86, and B-52. He was later promoted to chief, Flight Test Engineering Laboratory.

Captains Charles "Chuck" Yeager (*left*) and Jackie "Jack" Ridley (*right*) stand next to the cockpit of the Bell X-1 and B-29 mother ship.

Courtesy US Air Force

Colonel Ridley is credited with creating the Flight Test Center's basic philosophy still in use today. He died in 1957 flying as a co-pilot on a C-47 when the transport crashed into Mount Shirouma, northwest of Tokyo, Japan.

Captain Milburn Apt

A Kansas native, Milburn "Mel" Apt was born in 1924. He joined the Army Air Forces in 1942 and graduated from pilot training in 1944. He graduated from Experimental Flight Test Pilot School at Edwards AFB in 1954 and became a test pilot for new fighters and in the X plane program.

Captain Apt was flying the X-2 for the first time on 27 September 1956 when he became the first person to fly at Mach 3. Up to that point, his flight had gone perfectly. But as he turned back toward Edwards, the plane began to roll out of control to the left. Although Apt tried right the aircraft, it continued to roll and tumble out of control.

The X-2 was the first aircraft equipped with an escape capsule. Thrown around the cockpit, briefly knocked unconscious, and unable to regain control, Apt blasted the escape capsule away from the plane. But he was unable to get out of the capsule and deploy his parachute before the capsule crashed to earth, killing him. The Air Force awarded him the Distinguished Flying Cross after his death.

A. Scott Crossfield

Scott Crossfield was born in 1921 in Berkeley, California. He served in both the Army Air Forces and the Navy during World War II. Following the war, as a member of the Navy Reserve, he piloted FG-1D Corsairs for a Navy acrobatic team.

Crossfield joined NACA at its High Speed Flight Research Station at Edwards AFB in 1950. During the next five years he flew several X planes and new fighters, logging 100 rocket-powered flights. This made him the single most experienced rocket pilot. He became the first pilot to fly at Mach 2 on 20 November 1953 in the D-558-II Skyrocket at 62,000 feet.

Scott Crossfield (*center*) stands with two NACA officials in front of the D-558-II after the first Mach 2 flight.

Courtesy NASA

Crossfield left NACA in 1955 to join North American Aviation, where he worked on the X-15 program. He was responsible for many of the operational and safety features of the aircraft. He flew its first free flight in 1959 and qualified the first two planes before North American turned them over to NACA and the Air Force.

Crossfield won many aviation awards. He served in a number of civilian aviation jobs until he retired in 1993, including many years as a consultant to the House of Representatives Committee on Science and Technology in Washington. He was a strong supporter of the Civil Air Patrol. Upon his retirement, NASA awarded him the NASA Distinguished Public Service Medal. He died in 2006 when his private plane crashed after entering a thunderstorm over Georgia.

Neil Armstrong

Born in Ohio in 1930, Neil Armstrong served as a Navy pilot from 1949 to 1952. In 1955 he joined NACA. He served that agency and NASA for the next 17 years as an engineer, test pilot, astronaut, and administrator.

As a research pilot at Edwards AFB, he flew the X-15. He transferred to astronaut status in 1962. He was command pilot for the *Gemini 8* space mission, performing the first successful docking of two vehicles in space. As spacecraft commander for the *Apollo 11* mission in 1969, he became the first person to land on the moon and walk on its surface.

Neil Armstrong next to the X-15
Courtesy NASA

After returning from the moon, Armstrong held a variety of government and private-sector jobs, including a post as NASA's Deputy Associate Administrator for Aeronautics. He was awarded the Presidential Medal of Freedom, the Congressional Gold Medal, the Congressional Space Medal of Honor, and many other honors. He passed away in 2012 and was buried at sea in a Navy ceremony. In 2015, NASA renamed its flight research center at Edwards AFB the Neil A. Armstrong Flight Research center.

Other Significant Military Aircraft Flown at Edwards AFB

The test pilots who flew the X planes and other experimental aircraft also flew the test versions of the Air Force's new fighters, bombers, and transports. Many of these aircraft went on to play significant parts in the Cold War during the 1960s. Among them were the F-100 Super Sabre, the F-104 Starfighter, the SR-71 Blackbird reconnaissance plane, and the C-130 Hercules.

North American F-100 Super Sabre

The F-100 entered Air Force service in 1954. Extensive testing and experience with early versions of the aircraft led to many improvements in the F-100D model. The plane had a high accident rate, however, so a two-seat trainer model, the F-100F, was produced to give pilots better training. Many of these were later converted for the *Wild Weasel* program in Vietnam—discovering and attacking enemy radar and anti-aircraft sites.

The F-100 carried two cannon and air-to-air or air-to-surface missiles. It could also carry up to 5,000 lbs. of bombs. Some 2,294 F-100s were built, with production ending in 1959. Besides the Air Force, many NATO countries and other friendly nations flew the aircraft.

Lockheed F-104 Starfighter

The first experimental F-104 took to the air in 1952. It featured technology developed from the X-1E. The aircraft was produced in two major versions: a tactical fighter with a six-barrel cannon, and a day-night interceptor with Sidewinder heat-seeking missiles. An F-104 set a world speed record of 1,404 mph in 1958 and a world altitude record of 103,395 feet in 1959.

The F-104 was known for its straight, stubby wings. Its normal top speed was 1,320 mph, with a range of 1,250 miles. Its rate of climb was an incredible 48,000 feet per minute. The plane took a lot of skill to fly, however, and its accident rate was quite high.

The Air Force bought 300 of the planes, with another 1,700 serving in the air forces of several NATO allies and other friendly countries. Several foreign companies manufactured Starfighters as well. F-104s were in service somewhere in the world until 2004.

An F-100F Super Sabre performs at an air show in Ypsilanti, Michigan, in 2010.

Darren Brode/Shutterstock

The experimental XF-104 on its first flight in 1954

Courtesy US Air Force

Lockheed SR-71

The SR-71 was first developed as the YF-12 in the 1960s. It was to be a high-altitude, Mach 3 interceptor to defend against supersonic bombers. Based on the A-12 reconnaissance aircraft, the YF-12A became the forerunner of the highly sophisticated SR-71 strategic reconnaissance aircraft.

The SR-71 was the fastest (2,193 mph) and could reach the highest altitudes (85,068 feet) of all reconnaissance planes. Known unofficially as the Blackbird, it first flew in December 1964. From an altitude of 80,000 feet, it could take pictures of 100,000 square miles of the earth's surface every hour. The SR-71 had a range of 2,900 miles.

Lockheed developed the SR-71 after a U-2 spy plane piloted by Francis Gary Powers was shot down by the Soviets in 1960. President Dwight Eisenhower asked the company for a plane that enemy aircraft and missiles couldn't reach. Lockheed engineers had to develop a plane that could fly continuously at top speed, which would generate great heat. At the same time, the air temperature around the plane would be −60 degrees F. Lessons learned from the X planes helped here. Part of the solution was to build the plane from titanium. Another part was to paint it black, because black paint both absorbs and emits heat.

The Blackbird was an early attempt to build a stealth aircraft—*an aircraft that can't be detected by radar.* The builders succeeded in reducing radar's ability to track the plane by 90 percent. Although SR-71s were fired on many times, none was ever hit—it merely outflew the missile.

The Air Force retired its fleet of SR-71s in 1990 as budgets were cut, but brought them back from 1995 to 1997. NASA flew two others until 1999.

SR-71 Blackbird
Technical Sergeant Michael Haggerty/Courtesy US Air Force

Lockheed C-130 Hercules

Lockheed designed the C-130 as an assault transport that could land and take off from unpaved airstrips. It first flew in 1954. Since then, the Air Force has used the versatile plane for a variety of additional missions: medical evacuation; midair refueling of helicopters; search, rescue, and recovery; reconnaissance; and as a gunship. If the landing strip is inadequate, the C-130 can deliver cargo by parachute or using a low-altitude ground cable.

A US Air Force HC-130P lands at Royal Air Force Base Mildenhall in Great Britain. This long-range version of the C-130 is used for search and rescue or helicopter refueling.

IanC66/Shutterstock

One special version of the plane, the AC-130 Spectre, operated as a gunship in Vietnam and later conflicts. Instead of cargo, it carried an array of machine guns, cannon, anti-tank missiles and other weapons along one side of the plane. (Some versions carried conventional or precision bombs.) This created a devastating ground-attack aircraft.

More than 2,300 C-130s in various versions have been built. The workhorse was still in use as this book was written, both with the Air Force and many foreign countries. It will certainly fly for many years to come.

The C-130 carries a crew of five. Its cargo area can hold six pallets or 74 litters, or 92 combat troops or 62 paratroops, or any combination up to 42,000 lbs. Its maximum speed is 380 mph, with a range of 2,500 miles.

Northrop YB-49 Flying Wing

The Northrop YB-49 was a jet-powered heavy bomber developed shortly after World War II. (The *Y* designation indicates aircraft was a prototype.) A prototype is *an original or first model that is used for what comes later.* The flying wing design was never put into production. It was passed over in favor of more conventional bomber designs.

The first flight of the YB-49 took place on 21 October 1947, when the aircraft was flown from Hawthorne, California, to Muroc Army Airfield. Only two YB-49s were delivered to the Air Force. The aircraft was intended to be a high altitude, long-range bomber with lower drag characteristics, allowing the aircraft to have a greater range than conventional bombers of the day. The first YB-49 crashed in 1948, killing all crew members on board, including Captain Glenn Edwards, for whom the base was named a year later.

The YB-49 was a very unstable aircraft to fly, requiring the pilot to work continuously to maintain controlled flight. When the first YB-49 crashed during a test, it was speculated that after the aircraft left controlled flight it broke apart when the crew tried to recover. The second YB-49 caught fire and was destroyed when the nose gear collapsed during a high-speed taxi test.

The YB-49 Flying Wing program was cancelled in 1950. Although the flying wing concept appeared to be a failure, it was brought back decades later and would lead to the development of the B-2 stealth bomber being flown today. You'll read more about the B-2 in a later lesson.

Northrop YB-49 Flying Wing bomber at the Northrop facility, Hawthorne, California, 23 December 1948

Courtesy US Air Force

North American XB-70 Valkyrie

The futuristic XB-70A was originally conceived in the 1950s as a high-altitude, nuclear strike bomber that could fly at three times the speed of sound—any potential enemy would have been unable to defend against such a bomber.

By the early 1960s, however, new surface-to-air missiles (SAMs) threatened the survivability of high-speed, high-altitude bombers. Less costly, nuclear-armed missiles were also entering service. As a result, in 1961 the expensive B-70 bomber program was canceled before any Valkyries had been completed or flown.

Even so, the Air Force bought two XB-70As to test aerodynamics, propulsion, and other characteristics of large supersonic aircraft.

The first XB-70A flew in September 1964, and it achieved Mach 3 flight in October 1965. The second Valkyrie first flew in July 1965, but in June 1966 it crashed after an accidental mid-air collision. The third Valkyrie was not completed.

The first XB-70A airplane continued to fly and generate valuable test data in the research program until 1969.

While aircraft testing was under way in the late 1940s and early 1950s, the Cold War continued. Although the Western Allies won a peaceful victory with the successful end of the Berlin Airlift, a shooting war was about to begin in Korea. That war would teach the newly independent Air Force and its civilian superiors some hard lessons.

North American XB-70 Valkyrie being towed to its display location at the National Museum of the US Air Force

Courtesy US Air Force

✔ CHECKPOINTS

Lesson 2 Review

Using complete sentences, answer the following questions on a sheet of paper.

1. Where did every US Air Force aircraft flown since World War II have its beginning?

2. Who broke the sound barrier, and in what plane?

3. How long did a typical X-15 flight last?

4. What did Captain Ridley develop that allowed Chuck Yeager to break the sound barrier?

5. Who was the first pilot to fly at Mach 3?

6. Which test pilot became the first person to walk on the moon?

7. Which records did the F-104 Starfighter set in 1958 and 1959?

8. The SR-71 Blackbird was an early attempt to do what?

9. For which types of missions has the Air Force used the C-130?

10. Which aircraft led to development of the B-2 bomber?

APPLYING YOUR LEARNING

11. Based on the backgrounds of the pilots discussed in this lesson, what was the most important quality you found in test pilots of the post–World War II decades?

The Role of Airpower from the Korean War to the Vietnam War

Quick Write

After reading the vignette, write down five important facts about the first jet ace in history.

Learn About

- how the United States used airpower in the Korean War
- how aircraft were used in the Cuban Missile Crisis
- the role of airpower in the Vietnam War
- how air-to-air and surface-to-air missile technology changed aerial combat

YOU'VE ALREADY READ ABOUT the aces of World Wars I and II—brave men such as Eddie Rickenbacker. The Korean War, which began in 1950, introduced a new kind of ace: the jet ace. The name changed for a simple reason: most fighter aircraft flown in Korea had jet engines. Jet aces, like the earlier aces, had to score five kills to earn the title.

Colonel James Jabara was the first jet ace in history. He earned that record in the Korean War. The Oklahoma-born pilot's parents were from Lebanon.

Lieutenant Colonel James Jabara, the world's first jet ace, prepares to exit an F-86 after a flight.
Courtesy US Air Force

By the time the Korean War began, he was an experienced fighter pilot. He'd flown a P-51 in Europe during World War II. He went on 108 combat missions. He shot down one enemy aircraft and shared credit for a second kill.

In Korea, Jabara piloted an F-86 Sabrejet. These fighters flew about 670 miles per hour (mph). In his first tour of duty, Jabara scored six kills. During his second tour, he shot down nine more enemy aircraft. All 15 kills were MiG-15s, which were very tough and quick Soviet-built planes. Only one pilot shot down more MiGs. Jabara earned many medals in Korea and World War II, including a Distinguished Service Cross and two Silver Stars.

Sadly, Jabara died in a car accident in 1966 as he was preparing for his first tour in Vietnam. He was buried in Arlington National Cemetery along with his daughter, who also died as a result of the crash. The Colonel James Jabara Airport outside Wichita, Kansas, is named for him.

Vocabulary

- colony
- 38th parallel
- latitude
- limited war
- strike fighter
- nuclear war
- arms race
- international waters
- guerrilla warfare
- POW
- solitary confinement
- neutral
- heat-seeking missiles
- infrared light

How the United States Used Airpower in the Korean War

Korea was a Japanese colony from 1910 until 1945, when Japan surrendered to the Allies. A colony is *a region under the political control of a distant country.* After Japan surrendered, the Soviets and Western Allies needed to decide what to do with the Japanese troops stationed in Korea. They agreed that all troops north of Korea's 38th parallel would give up their arms to the Soviets. The United States would handle all Japanese soldiers south of the 38th parallel. The 38th parallel is *a line marking the original boundary between North and South Korea.* It refers to the boundary's latitude—*a line north or south from Earth's equator and parallel to it.*

But things didn't go according to plan. The Soviets set up Korean Communist Kim Il-Sung as North Korea's new leader. They wanted to spread communism not only throughout Europe but also through their neighboring countries in Asia.

China had become a Communist country in 1949. If North Korea became a Communist country, the Soviets could protect their border along Asia much as they were doing along their border with the countries of Eastern Europe.

On 25 June 1950 North Korean military forces crossed the 38th parallel in a move to take over South Korea. Two days later, the United Nations agreed to go to South Korea's aid. (The Soviet Union was boycotting the UN Security Council and was not present to veto the action.) Here was a chance for the United Nations to prevent a third worldwide conflict. American General Douglas MacArthur was the first commander of UN troops in this effort.

The United States entered the Korean War for much the same reason it conducted the Berlin Airlift. It wanted to stop the spread of communism. The Soviets and Americans weren't fighting with each other directly. Korea was the scene of the action. But they were fighting. They were engaged in a limited war—*a war in which opposing sides try to avoid a worldwide war and the possible use of atomic bombs by fighting with each other outside their own lands and sometimes through troops who aren't their own.* The Korean War was the first major military action of the Cold War.

The Course of the War

Fighting between Soviet-supported Communist forces and UN forces moved back and forth across the 38th parallel during the first year of the Korean War. Airpower played a big part in these frequent swings. In the summer of 1950 the North Koreans drove the UN forces all the way to Pusan, a coastal city in the southeast corner of South Korea. US fighter planes, stationed in Japan and on aircraft carriers, managed to gain time for UN ground forces to dig in. A few months later, in September 1950, the UN landed troops at Inchon, a town on the west coast of South Korea. These new UN forces, along with those still in Pusan, drove the North Koreans almost back to the 38th parallel. UN aircraft supported the ground troops.

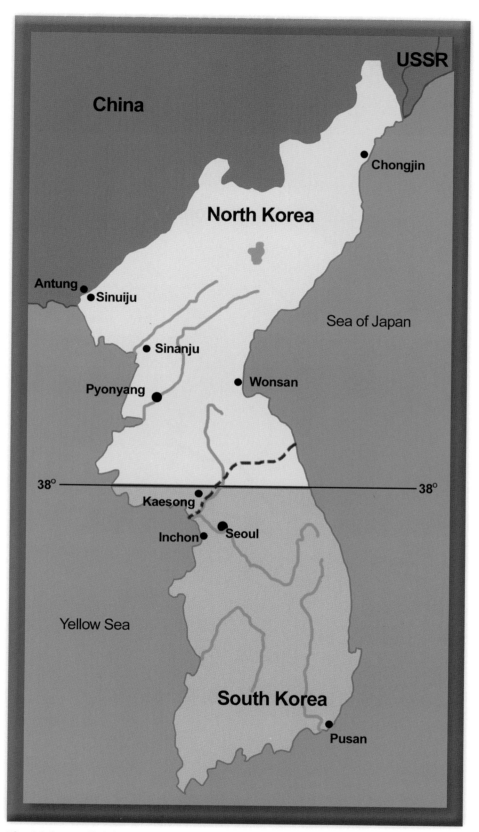

The 38th parallel divided Korea into North Korea and South Korea.

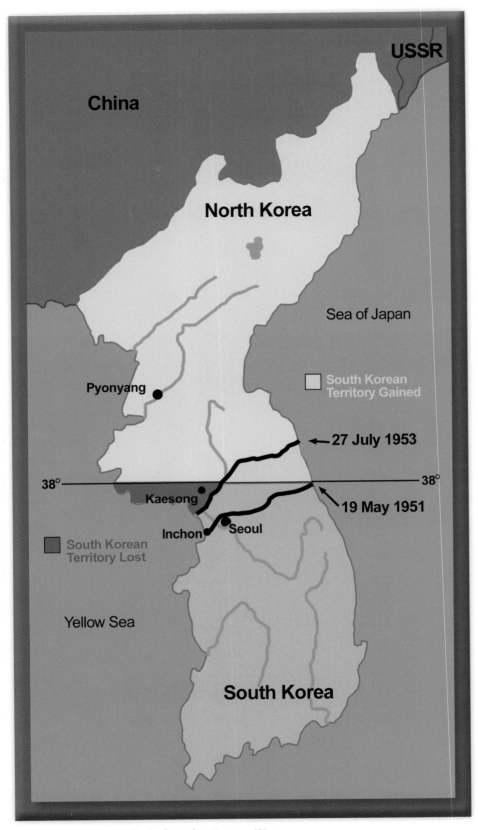

Korea as it was divided after the Korean War

Up to this point, the North Koreans hadn't offered much resistance from the air. Their air force was weak: it consisted of about 120 old Russian planes. But on 25 November 1950 things changed. General MacArthur led troops across the 38th parallel to the edge of China. The UN wanted to eliminate communism from all of Korea, not just from South Korea.

China didn't want the UN pushing along its borders. It entered the war on North Korea's side with 850,000 soldiers and 1,000 Soviet-made MiG-15 fighter jets. The MiG-15 was better than any plane the Americans had initially. In January 1951, with Chinese help, the North Koreans recrossed the 38th parallel and grabbed the South Korean capital, Seoul, a second time.

The United States and the UN wouldn't give up. Tough air battles took place. Although flying inferior fighters, US pilots received better training. By one estimate, they shot down nine MiG-15s for every one US fighter destroyed. Airpower proved once again it was a crucial part of modern war. The UN forces under General MacArthur took Seoul yet again in March 1951. They drove the North Koreans back across the 38th parallel.

At this point both sides realized they couldn't win. They began negotiating and finally signed a cease-fire agreement on 27 July 1953. The two Koreas remained divided.

Significant Aircraft of the Korean War

The most widely used US Air Force fighters in Korea were the F-51, F-80 Shooting Star, F-84 Thunderjet, and F-86 Sabrejet. At the same time, the Navy and Marine Corps flew missions from aircraft carriers. They piloted F-4U Corsairs, F9F Panthers, and AD/A-1 Skyraiders.

The F-51 was formerly the P-51 Mustang of World War II fame. The F-51 saw heavy use at the start of the Korean War because it had a longer range than the F-80 jet. This longer range was especially important early in the war, when US fighters had to take off from Japan.

In Korea, the F-80 flew as a day fighter, a fighter-bomber, and a photo reconnaissance plane. On 8 November 1950, in the first all-jet dogfight ever, 1st Lieutenant Russell Brown shot down a Soviet-built MiG-15—this despite the MiG's superiority as a fighter.

Originally used to escort B-29 bombers on long-range missions over North Korea, the F-84 Thunderjet performed best in close air support and as a daytime strike fighter—*an attack aircraft that can also function as a fighter.* F-84 pilots attacked enemy railroads, dams, bridges, supply depots, and troop concentrations.

While faster than the F-80, the F-84 was inferior to the speedier MiG-15 at high altitudes. If an F-84 pilot could get a MiG to engage at less than 20,000 feet, he stood a better chance of victory. While 18 F-84s were lost to MiGs, nine MiGs fell to fire from F-84s.

North American F-86 Sabre

The F-86 Sabre was the Air Force's first swept-wing fighter and the best American fighter jet of the time. It first flew in 1947, and in May 1948 set a new world speed record of 670.9 mph.

As a day fighter, the F-86 became the primary opponent of the Soviet-built MiG-15. Although the MiG was a technically superior plane, US pilots received far better training that showed in combat. Improvements in later versions of the Sabre helped close the gap. F-86 pilots shot down 792 MiGs, about eight times more wins than losses.

The F-86 carried six machine guns. It could fly up to 685 mph and had a range of 1,200 miles.

F-86 Sabres with their 51st Fighter Interceptor Wing "Checkertails" are readied for combat during the Korean War at Suwon Air Base, South Korea.

Courtesy US Air Force

Grumman F9F Panther

The F9F Panther was first delivered to the US Navy in May 1949 and saw its first combat in July 1950, when F9Fs flew strikes from the aircraft carrier USS *Valley Forge*. The F9F was used mostly for air strikes by Navy and Marine Corps pilots. Even so, F9Fs scored several victories against North Korean and Chinese MiGs. A photo reconnaissance version also saw extensive service.

Among the F9F pilots was Major John H. Glenn of the US Marine Corps. He also flew the Air Force F-86 and scored three kills. Glenn became an astronaut in 1959. He was the first American to orbit the earth.

The F9F was armed with four cannon. It could carry eight five-inch rockets or 3,000 lbs. of bombs.

An F9F Panther sits on the deck of the USS *Midway* while another flies overhead.

Courtesy National Archives and Records Administration, Catalog No. 80-G-434964

Douglas AD/A-1 Skyraider

The AD Skyraider, later renamed the A-1, could carry more bombs than a B-17. It excelled in attack and close air support. First flown in 1945, the A-1 became famous in the Korean War, attacking industrial targets; taking out bridges, railroads, and roads; and supporting ground troops. Like the B-17, the propeller-powered Skyraider could get its pilot back to base despite heavy damage from enemy fire.

The Skyraider also played an important role in the Southeast Asia war. Its ability to carry an immense amount of weapons and stay over the battlefield for extended periods made it a powerful weapon. This aircraft provided close air support to ground forces, attacked enemy supply lines, and protected helicopters rescuing airmen downed in enemy territory.

In a remarkable action, on 1 May 1951, eight A-1s from the USS *Princeton* attacked the Hwachon Dam with torpedoes. The destruction of the dam 50 miles northeast of Seoul, the South Korean capital, caused river water levels to rise, blocking a Communist troop advance.

The Skyraider's top speed was 343 mph and its range was 1,300 miles. It carried four cannon and 8,000 lbs. of bombs or rockets.

A-1 Skyraider in flight with its dive brakes deployed

Courtesy Naval History and Heritage Command, Catalog No. NH 94701

Mikoyan Gurevich MiG-15

The Soviets developed the MiG-15 following World War II, and the plane entered service in 1949. With a top speed of 670 mph, it was much faster than the American F-80 or F-84. Able to climb quickly and fly as high as 51,000 feet, it could escape from the early F-86 Sabres that were quickly sent over from the United States to take it on. The MiG-15 was so effective that the United States could fly B-29 bombing missions only at night.

The durable MiG-15 had a range of only 500 miles. In North Korea, however, it was able to operate close to its bases near the Yalu River in the north, safe across the Chinese border. American and other United Nations planes, on the other hand, had to fly all the way north to the area to engage MiGs. Thus the MiGs were frequently fully fueled, while the American planes had often only 20 minutes of fuel available for combat.

The MiG-15 carried three cannon and 2,000 lbs. of bombs. The Soviets produced 3,000 of the MiG-15 fighter version, with additional planes produced in other Communist countries.

A restored MiG-15 takes off from Nellis AFB, Nevada, during a 2009 air show.

Eugene Berman/Shutterstock

Lessons the USAF Learned From the Korean War

The US Air Force learned a number of important lessons from the Korean War. First, it realized it had been putting too much emphasis on the atomic bomb. The military had diverted too many funds from fighter development to bombers. The Korean experience made US planners understand that there were now two types of war: total war, like World War II, and limited war, like the Korean War.

In a limited war, atomic bombs aren't used. The purpose of a limited war is to prevent an all-out war in which atomic bombs might be used.

A second lesson was simply a reminder of one learned in World War II—the importance of air superiority. UN airpower took control of air space over Korea early in the war. This helped UN forces drive the North Koreans back across the 38th parallel. The MiG-15s may have been as good as any US planes, but the better-trained American pilots more than made up for that. US pilots controlled the air.

Third, all branches of the military learned the importance of flexibility. They had to be prepared for all-out war as well as limited war. Each war demands different strategies and tactics. Each war needs different kinds of equipment. Therefore, fighters, bombers, helicopters, and training must be maintained for all options in warfare.

As the Cold War continued, those lessons would be put to severe tests.

The Right Stuff

Captain Manuel Fernandez: Jet Ace

Captain Manuel "Pete" Fernandez (1925–1980) was the third jet ace of the Korean War. He took part in 124 combat missions. He shot down 14 MiG-15s and shared credit for a 15th kill. He was an F-86 Sabrejet pilot.

Fernandez didn't stop flying after the war. In 1956 he raced a new jet called the F-100C Super Sabre from California to Oklahoma. He averaged 666 mph. He set a record with this speed and won a Bendix Trophy. He also joined the Mach Riders of Nellis Air Force Base, Nevada. This group performed stunts as the barnstormers had done in the 1920s and 1930s. He retired in 1963.

Captain Manuel "Pete" Fernandez
Courtesy US Air Force

The Right Stuff

Lieutenant Colonel George A. Davis Jr.: Medal of Honor Recipient

Lieutenant Colonel George A. Davis Jr. (1920–1952) served in World War II and the Korean War. Because the two wars were so close together, many Airmen fought in both conflicts.

Davis had an extraordinary career. During World War II he flew 266 combat missions. He shot down seven enemy aircraft in the Pacific theater. He earned a Silver Star, a Distinguished Flying Cross, and an Air Medal.

On 10 February 1952, Davis led a group of four F-86 fighters on a mission over North Korea. Two of his planes had to head home because of damage. Davis knew he and the remaining plane must stick with their mission. They had to provide cover for a group of fighters bombing a North Korean railroad. Davis spotted 12 MiG-15s headed their way. He plunged his fighter toward the enemy formation,

Lieutenant Colonel George A. Davis Jr.
Courtesy US Air Force

despite being outnumbered. He managed to shoot down two of the MiGs before his own plane was hit. He died when his plane crashed into nearby mountains. For his brave act of self-sacrifice, Davis was one of only four Airmen who earned the Medal of Honor during the Korean War.

How Aircraft Were Used in the Cuban Missile Crisis

Many conflicts took place during the Cold War. There was the bloodless Berlin Airlift. There was the bloody Korean War. Then came the Cuban Missile Crisis in 1962. This event was the closest the United States and the Soviet Union got to nuclear war— *war involving the atomic bomb or the hydrogen bomb*. The hydrogen bomb, invented in 1953, was even more powerful than the atomic bomb.

Cuba had become a Communist country in 1960. In 1962 the Soviets sent bombers, fighters, and shiploads of equipment and men to build missile sites there. The Soviets wanted to intimidate the United States in its own backyard. Cuba is only 90 miles south of the southernmost point of Florida. Had the United States allowed the Soviet Union to keep these missiles in Cuba, the Soviets could have struck the US mainland with little warning.

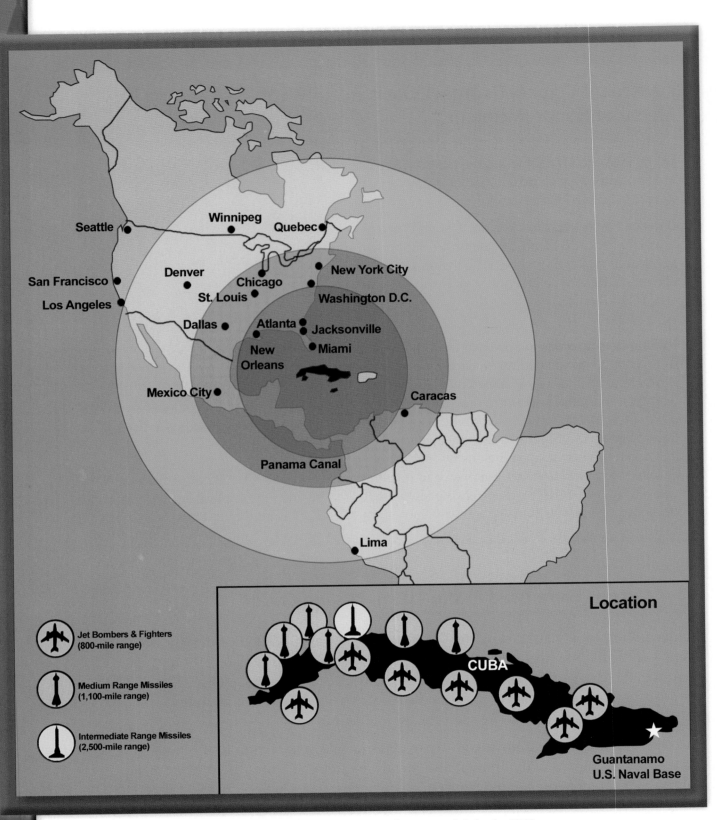

Seattle
Winnipeg
Quebec
Denver
New York City
San Francisco
Chicago
St. Louis
Washington D.C.
Los Angeles
Dallas
Atlanta
Jacksonville
New
Orleans
Miami
Mexico City
Caracas
Panama Canal
Lima

Jet Bombers & Fighters
(800-mile range)

Medium Range Missiles
(1,100-mile range)

Intermediate Range Missiles
(2,500-mile range)

Location

CUBA

Guantanamo
U.S. Naval Base

This map shows the location of Russian aircraft and missiles around Cuba in 1962.

The United States carefully watched developments in Cuba. US Air Force pilots went on aerial reconnaissance in the U-2. These pilots were from Strategic Air Command's (SAC) 4080th Strategic Reconnaissance Wing. They took photographs of Soviet missile bases in Cuba.

You read about the U-2 spy plane in Lesson 1 of this chapter. It was a single-engine, high-altitude aircraft. Its purpose was to gather information on enemy activities. It could fly at altitudes above 55,000 feet. Its glider-like wings worked well in the thin upper atmosphere. It was first tested in 1955.

Reconnaissance missions can be dangerous. Major Rudolf Anderson Jr. had already provided the US government with photos of missile sites. He went on another mission over Cuba on 27 October 1962. The Cubans shot him down with a surface-to-air missile (SAM). Anderson was the only American to die in the Cuban Missile Crisis.

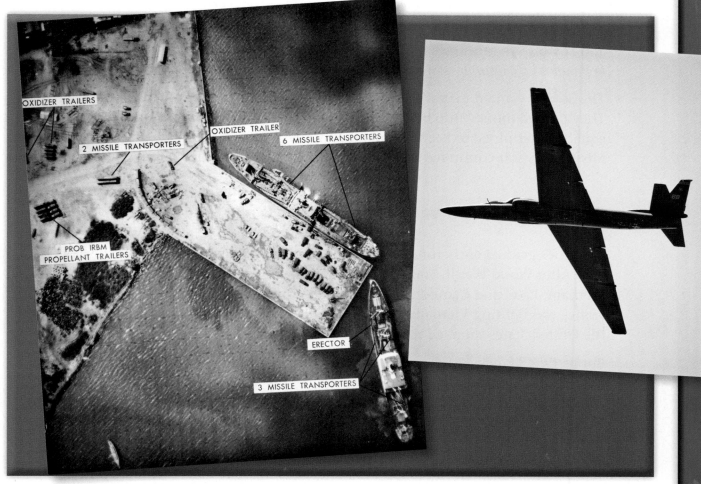

US reconnaissance photo of a Soviet missile site at Mariel, Cuba

Everett Historical/Shutterstock

U-2 Dragon Lady similar to the one used to take reconnaissance photos during the Cuban Missile Crisis

Eugene Berman/Shutterstock

President John F. Kennedy ordered a naval blockade of Cuba on 24 October. Soviet ships could no longer enter Cuban ports. At the same time, the Strategic Air Command prepared to deliver nuclear bombs. These two moves let the Soviets know how seriously the United States took the Soviet missiles.

Now a big question arose: would the Soviets try to break through the blockade and risk war?

The Outcome of the Cuban Missile Crisis

Twenty Soviet ships were sailing toward Cuba when Kennedy set up the blockade. About 500 miles from the United States, the Soviet ships turned away. One reason the Soviets backed down: they had fewer nuclear weapons than the Americans.

A few days later Soviet Premier Nikita Khrushchev ordered the missile sites dismantled. American U-2s flew over Cuba to make sure the Soviets kept their word.

The crisis had passed. But the standoff started an arms race between the Americans and Soviets. An arms race is *a competition for military supremacy in which each party tries to produce larger numbers of weapons and a better military force than the other.*

The Soviets wanted to make sure the United States could not force their hand again. They poured money into building their nuclear stockpile. The United States was equally determined to keep its superiority. The arms race accelerated after the Cuban Missile Crisis. It continued until after the Cold War ended in 1989.

The Role of Airpower in the Vietnam War

America's gradual entry into the Vietnam War marked another phase of the Cold War. After World War II, France tried to regain control of its colonies in Indochina—Vietnam, Laos, and Cambodia. Japan had occupied these colonies during the war. France was fighting Vietnamese forces led by Communist Ho Chi Minh. In July 1950 the United States supplied money to the French effort.

But in 1954 France withdrew from Vietnam after a serious military defeat. The Geneva Accords of 1954, an international agreement, split Vietnam in half along the 17th parallel. Soon the country fell into a civil war as the north tried to occupy the south. To the north were the Communists. Their allies were the Soviets and the Chinese. To the south were Vietnamese who opposed communism. The United States soon began providing military training and supplies to South Vietnam.

Not until 1961, however, did US forces see combat in Vietnam. About 11,000 troops, including Airmen, saw action in the early 1960s. They served mostly as advisers to South Vietnamese forces.

In 1964 things really heated up. North Vietnamese patrol boats attacked the USS *Maddox*. The American destroyer was off the North Vietnamese coast in international waters. International waters are *areas of the seas where ships from any nation have the right to travel*. The North Vietnamese thought the destroyer was involved in secret US raids along their coast.

Congress quickly passed the Tonkin Gulf Resolution. It allowed President Lyndon Johnson to order the military to strike back at North Vietnam. This was not a declaration of war. But it led to a huge land- and air-based campaign that lasted until 1973. At the war's peak, the United States had more than 500,000 troops in Vietnam. Military forces from other countries, notably Australia and South Korea, joined them.

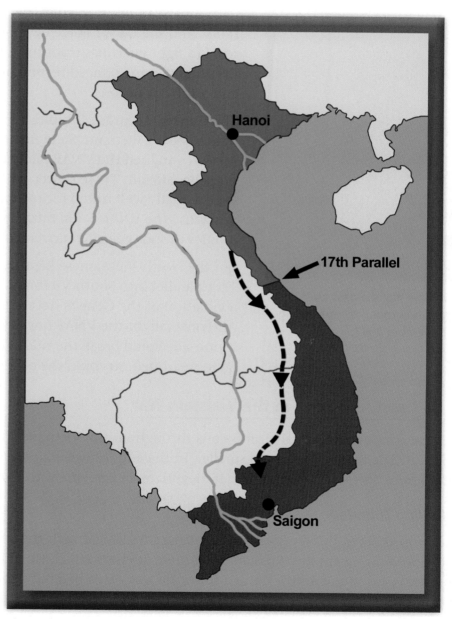

The 17th parallel divided Communist North Vietnam from Western-backed South Vietnam.

LESSON 3   The Role of Airpower from the Korean War to the Vietnam War

The US Air Force Trains the Vietnamese Air Force

Communist ground troops were the main threat to South Vietnam. For much of the war, these troops, called Viet Cong, conducted guerrilla warfare. That's *a type of fighting in which small bands of fighters hit more-powerful forces by surprise*. The Communists didn't have much airpower. Even so, the US Air Force trained members of South Vietnam's Vietnamese Air Force (VNAF). Given their experience in World War II and the Korean War, the US Air Force knew how to effectively bomb supply routes and hit enemy troops.

US Air Force A-1H Skyraiders make a pass over South Vietnamese tanks and ground troops during a training exercise in November 1963.

Courtesy US Air Force

The focus of the US Air Force was threefold. It gave the VNAF practice in tactical air operations. VNAF pilots flew as passengers with American pilots to study needed skills. And the US Air Force developed ways to fight guerrillas from the air. Eventually, it introduced reconnaissance and airlift operations.

The Geneva Accords prohibited the use of fighter jets in Vietnam. So at first the US Air Force trained the VNAF pilots to fly propeller aircraft. These slower-moving aircraft were actually well suited for reconnaissance missions. The VNAF could buzz low over the jungles to spot guerrilla movements.

But the North Vietnamese kept crossing the 17th parallel into South Vietnam. This was a violation of the Geneva Accords. So the Air Force taught the VNAF how to fly jets. If one side could break the rules, the United States reasoned, so could the other.

Ways the US Used Airpower in the Vietnam War

The US Air Force conducted tactical air missions throughout the Vietnam War. The theater was small. The targets were even smaller. In the end, however, it was strategic bombing that forced the North Vietnamese to negotiate an agreement to end the war.

Operation Rolling Thunder

President Johnson ordered the Air Force not to strike sites linked with the Soviets or Chinese. Johnson didn't want any Russian or Chinese advisers killed. He did not want to draw those two powerful countries into a full-scale war. (This had happened with Chinese troops during the Korean War.) The US conducted limited tactical air strikes on railroads, oil depots, and warehouses. Their purpose was to wear down the North Vietnamese without provoking the Soviets and Chinese.

These tactical strikes, called *Operation Rolling Thunder*, took place from 1965 to 1968. They weren't as successful as the United States hoped. Because they were limited, the strikes gave the north too much opportunity to rebuild and repair.

Several hundred US personnel were shot down and became POWs. These men were held for many years and most were severely mistreated. Meanwhile, regular North Vietnamese Army troops entered South Vietnam through neighboring Laos and Cambodia.

F-4C Phantoms refuel from a KC-135 tanker before making a strike against targets in North Vietnam.
Courtesy US Air Force

The Right Stuff

Airman 1st Class William Pitsenbarger: A First-Class Hero

Airman 1st Class William Pitsenbarger (1944–1966) was a crewman aboard an HH-43 helicopter that went on search-and-rescue missions. He was a pararescueman. His job was to care for the wounded and get them out of the jungle.

Pitsenbarger performed this role bravely on 11 April 1966 near Cam My, Republic of Vietnam. On that day, his job was to care for Soldiers who were under fire in South Vietnam. He treated the wounded in the middle of the action on the jungle floor. He placed the casualties in hoists to lift them 100 feet in the air to the chopper. When the enemy launched a major assault, he joined the firefight. Wounded three times, he continued fighting and helping others. He died in action that day.

The Air Force awarded Pitsenbarger the Air Force Cross. But Soldiers who were at the firefight that day asked that he receive a higher honor: the Medal of Honor. The secretary of the Air Force presented the medal to Pitsenbarger's father in 2000. Each year the Air Force Sergeant's Association gives the Pitsenbarger Award to an Air Force enlisted member for heroic acts that save a life or prevent serious injury.

Airman 1st Class William Pitsenbarger
Courtesy US Air Force

Captain Lance Sijan

One military historian has called Captain Lance Sijan the "model on how to behave as a POW." A POW is *a prisoner of war*. Sijan was a US Air Force pilot in the Vietnam War. He was only two years out of the Air Force Academy when the North Vietnamese shot him down on his 52nd mission. It was 9 November 1967.

Then–1st Lieutenant Lance Sijan boarding an F-4 Phantom for a combat mission.

Courtesy US Air Force

Sijan landed with a broken leg, a damaged hand, and a fractured skull. Yet when radioed by a search-and-rescue team, he refused help. He said he didn't want anyone placed in mortal danger on his account. He tried without success to grab a steel cable the rescue aircraft lowered to pull him out of the jungle. Antiaircraft fire forced the rescue aircraft to leave after 33 minutes. Sijan was stranded in enemy territory.

For more than six weeks, Sijan eluded the North Vietnamese in their jungles. He had to drag himself along the ground because of his broken leg. Finally, the North Vietnamese captured him. But Sijan escaped. When caught again, he was tortured. But he never gave his captors more than his name. They moved him to a POW camp in Hanoi, the North Vietnamese capital. Because of the mistreatment, his health gave out. He died 21 January 1968 as a POW.

The United States took a number of steps to honor Sijan. President Gerald Ford awarded him the Medal of Honor in 1976. The Air Force promoted Sijan to the rank of captain. The Air Force Academy named a cadet dormitory Sijan Hall. And the Air Force grants the Lance P. Sijan Award to those members who show similar bravery and professionalism.

The Tet Offensive

In January 1968 the North Vietnamese and Viet Cong surprised US and South Vietnamese forces with the Tet Offensive. The offensive got that name because it occurred over the Tet holiday, which is when the Vietnamese celebrate the lunar new year. Communist troops and guerrillas attacked 36 major cities in South Vietnam. The US Air Force airlifted troops to the front lines, attacked enemy soldiers, and bombed supply routes.

When the enemy surrounded 6,000 US Marines at their base in an area called Khe Sanh, airpower helped save the day. For two months, US cargo planes airlifted supplies. US aircraft also dropped 110,000 tons of bombs around Khe Sanh and blew up 3,000 enemy supply trucks. The Tet Offensive ended when US and South Vietnamese forces expelled the North Vietnamese from the south's major cities. Many North Vietnamese troops retreated north across the 17th parallel.

Operations Linebacker I and II

When President Richard Nixon took office in 1969, US tactics in Vietnam changed. Nixon wanted to get American troops out of Vietnam. He wanted to turn the effort over to South Vietnamese forces. He began dramatically cutting the number of US ground forces. But in 1972, the North Vietnamese tried another invasion similar to the Tet Offensive. Nixon told his military leaders to do whatever was needed to drive the North Vietnamese out of the south for good. The very short, but devastating strategic-bombing phase of the war began.

Air Force B-52s and Navy aircraft pounded North Vietnamese supply routes. The United States called this action *Operation Linebacker*. During this phase, US aircraft bombed many targets that were off limits during *Operation Rolling Thunder*. For a while, the North Vietnamese seemed willing to discuss a treaty. But they changed their minds.

Lockheed C-130 Hercules aircraft resupplied the besieged Marine garrison at Khe Sanh, South Vietnam, in 1968.
Courtesy US Air Force

B-52D Stratofortress releasing bombs over targets in Vietnam, 1967
Everett Historical/Shutterstock

In reply, Nixon ordered *Operation Linebacker II* in mid-December. B-52s flew over North Vietnam with 15,000 tons of bombs. The B-52s relentlessly bombed targets that had been off limits for years. Fifteen bombers were lost during the operation. In January 1973 the North Vietnamese signed a peace treaty with the United States. The final US troops withdrew.

Unfortunately, in 1975, the Communist North Vietnamese violated the treaty. They invaded the south, and took over South Vietnam anyway. This time the US did not help. Congress prohibited President Gerald R. Ford from spending money to do so.

The Right Stuff

Airman 1st Class William Robinson: From POW to 2nd Lieutenant

Airman 1st Class William Robinson was a member of a search-and-rescue team during the Vietnam War. He flew in an HH-43 helicopter.

On 20 September 1965 Robinson's group set out to rescue a downed pilot in North Vietnam. They flew 80 miles to the site with an armed escort. Enemy fire hit both US aircraft. Rules from headquarters forbade the escort to return fire. So it headed back to base. Enemy forces shot down Robinson's helicopter. It crashed into the jungle. The crew was taken prisoner.

Robinson spent eight years as a POW. The captors didn't treat the prisoners' wounds. They tortured the prisoners instead. They denied the POWs adequate food. They exposed them to all kinds of weather. All POWs spent time in solitary confinement. Solitary confinement is *when a prisoner is held in a cell alone and not allowed to talk to anyone*.

Robinson described this as "weeks, months, and years of boredom punctuated by moments, hours, and days of stark terror." But he survived. During his incarceration, he received "informal" Officer Candidate School training. When he returned to the United States, he was offered and accepted a direct presidential appointment to the rank of 2nd lieutenant. He received many awards, including the Air Force Cross, and retired with the rank of captain.

A North Vietnamese soldier guards Airman 1st Class William Robinson after his capture in September 1965.
Courtesy US Air Force

Significant Aircraft Used in the Vietnam War

In the early years of the war, US and (South) Vietnamese Air Force (VNAF) pilots flew World War II-era B-26 bombers. Another combat plane was the T-28, an aircraft originally built to train pilots. (The *T* stands for *trainer*.)

But in 1964 and 1965 Communist ground forces began to attack US bases. So the US Air Force brought over B-52 bombers and F-105 Thunderchief fighter jets. Air Force, Navy, and Marine F-4 Phantoms went into aerial combat with Soviet-built North Vietnamese MiGs. Meanwhile, *Wild Weasel* radar on the F-100F fighter could spot the location of enemy anti-aircraft radar and send a missile right at it.

North American T-28B Trojan/ T-28D Nomad

The T-28 was originally designed as a trainer and first flew in 1949. North American built 1,948 of the aircraft, ending production in 1957. In 1962, however, 200 T-28Bs were converted to T-28D Nomad tactical fighter-bombers. The Air Force and the VNAF used them for close air support of ground troops.

The T-28 could carry two machine guns along with 1,800 lbs. of bombs. It had a top speed of 346 mph and a range of 1,060 miles.

T-28B Trojan at the National Museum of the Air Force
Courtesy US Air Force

Mikoyan-Gurevich MiG-17

The Soviets developed the MiG-17 to replace the MiG-15 of the Korean War. Although it looks very similar to a MiG-15, it had a longer fuselage and more sharply swept wings. It first appeared in 1952, but few MiG-17s were built before the Korean War ended. More than 20 countries flew MiG-17s, including North Vietnam, whose air force flew them against US aircraft during the Vietnam War.

Restored MiG-17 at a 2015 air show in San Antonio, Texas
GizmoPhoto/Shutterstock

The MiG-17 was much slower than US F-105s and F-4s—its maximum speed was only 711 mph. But it had an advantage in maneuvering. So US pilots had to make sure to use their speed advantage when shooting MiGs down. From July 1965 to February 1968, F-105s and F-4s shot down 61 MiG-17s. Most US aircraft, by contrast, were lost to ground fire.

The MiG-17 had a range of 500 miles, although this could be extended with external fuel tanks to 1,160 miles. It carried three cannon, along with 16 under-wing rockets or 1,800 lbs. of bombs.

Republic F-105 Thunderchief

The F-105 joined the Air Force in 1958. Originally designed to carry nuclear weapons, it operated in Vietnam as a strike fighter and later against enemy anti-aircraft sites. During one four-year span, F-105s few 75 percent of all strikes against North Vietnamese targets. It played a key role in *Operation Rolling Thunder.*

F-105G Thunderchiefs refuel before a bombing mission in Vietnam, January 1966.

Courtesy US Air Force

Flying as fast as 1,386 mph with a range of 1,500 miles, the F-105 could hold its own against North Vietnam's Soviet-built MiG-17s and 21s. The standard production version, the F-105D, was armed with a cannon and could carry up to 12,000 lbs. of bombs—as much as an entire formation of World War II bombers. When fully loaded, however, the F-105 was far less maneuverable. MiG pilots learned this quickly and would engage the US fighters in hit-and-run attacks. These often forced the F-105s to drop their bomb load before reaching their targets so they could defend themselves.

About 600 F-105Ds were built. The F-105F version was a two-seater, and Republic built 143 of this model. About 55 of these were later converted to F-105Gs, which served as *Wild Weasel* aircraft. As the war went on, the F-105D was eventually phased out in favor of the McDonnell F-4 Phantom.

North American F-100 Super Sabre

When F-100 units deployed to Southeast Asia, they included a mix of one- and two-seat F-100s. Both types participated in traditional bombing missions in support of ground forces. As tactics developed, the two-seat F-100F became an important aircraft for two new missions—surface-to-air missile (SAM) suppression, known as *Iron Hand*, and high-speed forward air control (FAC), known as *Misty FAC*. As you read in the previous lesson, the F-100 also played a significant role in the *Wild Weasel* program.

McDonnell F-4 Phantom II

First developed for the US Navy, the F-4 Phantom began its Air Force career in late 1963. By the end of production in 1979, more than 5,000 F-4s had been built—more than 2,600 for the Air Force and 1,200 for the Navy and Marine Corps. The rest were sold to friendly foreign countries.

The Air Force sent its first F-4s to Vietnam in 1963. The F-4 fought in aerial combat against North Vietnamese MiGs as well as flying ground attack missions. It could carry twice as many bombs as two B-17 bombers. It typically carried eight air-to-air missiles and eight 750 lb. bombs. It had a maximum speed of 1,400 mph and a range of 1,750 miles. The lack of an internal gun was a problem for early F-4 pilots, because many of their air-to-air missiles misfired. The F-4E, which arrived in 1968, fixed this problem.

An Air Force F-100 Super Sabre fires a salvo of rockets at a jungle target, May 1967.
Courtesy US Air Force

F-4 Phantom II performing at Nellis AFB, Nevada, in 2009
Eugene Berman/Shutterstock

An A-6 Intruder attack aircraft is launched from the USS *Ranger* during flight operations conducted off the coast of North Vietnam in the Gulf of Tonkin, 14 December 1967.

Courtesy National Archives and Records Administration, Catalog No. K-42963

A-7 Corsair II
VanderWolf Images/Shutterstock

Grumman A-6 Intruder

The A-6, the world's first all-weather attack aircraft, joined the Navy in 1963. It served through the Vietnam War right up to *Operation Desert Storm* in Kuwait and Iraq, retiring in 1997. The A-6 could launch low-level attacks at long range in poor weather or darkness. One demonstration of its power was a nighttime attack on a North Vietnamese power plant. Two A-6s dropped 26 bombs, creating such damage that the enemy high command believed B-52s had carried out the attack.

The A-6 carried a crew of two and 18,000 lbs. of bombs or missiles. Its top speed was 644 mph, and its range 1,110 miles. The Navy and Marine Corps received 687 A-6s. Besides Vietnam, the plane saw action in Lebanon, Libya, and Iraq.

LTV Aerospace A-7 Corsair II

Serving both the Navy and Air Force, the A-7 first flew in 1965. It served from Vietnam through *Operation Just Cause* in Panama and *Operation Desert Storm* in Iraq. This attack aircraft was extremely accurate because of its electronic navigation and weapons-delivery system.

The A-7 had a top speed of 693 mph and a range of 980 miles. It carried a machine gun, Sidewinder missiles, and 10,000 lbs. of bombs. Besides its Navy and Air Force duty, it saw service in several Air National Guard units. About 1,569 A-7s were built, and some served in allied air forces until as late as 2014.

Mikoyan-Gurevich MiG-21

The MiG-21 was the most dangerous enemy plane in the air during the Vietnam War. It was as fast as the US fighters it faced and more maneuverable than the F-4 Phantom. North Vietnam had more than 200 MiG-21s. They shot down about 50 US aircraft. MiG pilots would attack using the sun or clouds as cover, make a quick pass, and then head for safety. The US Air Force destroyed 68 of the enemy planes in aerial combat.

The MiG-21 could reach a speed of 1,300 mph with a range of 870 miles. It carried two radar-guided or heat-seeking missiles. From 1955 to 1985 the Soviets built more than 10,000 of the fighters. The MiG-21 was a popular export for the Soviets—more than 50 countries, including friends of the United States, flew various versions of the plane.

MiG-21
ra3rn/Shutterstock

Sikorsky HH-3E Jolly Green Giant

The US Air Force developed the Sikorsky HH-3E helicopter, nicknamed the "Jolly Green Giant," to perform combat search and rescue (CSAR) during the Southeast Asia war. A highly modified version of Sikorsky's CH-3 transport helicopter, the HH-3E was used to rescue aircrew members in a combat area.

Fifty CH-3Es were converted to HH-3Es with the addition of armor, defensive armament, self-sealing fuel tanks, and a rescue hoist. With a watertight hull, the HH-3E could land on water, and its large rear door and ramp permitted easy loading and unloading.

The HH-3E Jolly Green Giant was equipped with a powerful external winch that allowed it to extract a downed pilot without landing.
Courtesy National Museum of the US Air Force

The first air-refuelable helicopter to be produced, the HH-3E's retractable fuel probe and external fuel tanks gave it a range limited only by the endurance of the aircrew. In 1967, two aerial-refueled HH-3Es set the long-distance record for helicopters by flying nonstop from New York to Paris, France. This long-range ability allowed HH-3Es to conduct CSAR operations anywhere in Southeast Asia.

The first Air Force HH-3Es arrived in Vietnam in 1967. They operated out of Udorn Air Base, Thailand, and Da Nang Air Base, South Vietnam. During the war, HH-3 crewmen were awarded one Medal of Honor, twenty-four Air Force Crosses, and more than 190 Silver Stars. The USAF retired its last HH-3Es in 1995.

Boeing KC-135A Stratotanker

Refueling in flight made long-distance flying operations possible in Southeast Asia. Heavily-laden aircraft like the F-105 Thunderchief, F-4 Phantom, and B-52 Stratofortress needed to refuel on the way to and from their targets. Getting gas from tankers allowed them to carry maximum bomb loads. Search-and-rescue helicopters increased their range with air refueling as well.

In-flight refueling depended on precise timing and navigation. Bombers, fighters and reconnaissance aircraft were carefully scheduled to meet tankers at given times and places.

When meeting B-52 bombers on long-distance missions, for example, three or four KC-135 Stratotankers would fly together, with the leader responsible for navigation and timing. The others stayed a mile behind and slightly above, and they spread out while refueling bombers to keep a safe distance between them.

A KC-135 refuels a B-52 over Southeast Asia in 1967.
Courtesy US Air Force

Waypoints

Better Pilot Training

While the US could claim air superiority over both North and South Vietnam, at one point the North Vietnamese were shooting down one US fighter for every two MiGs lost. US fighter commanders realized that Air Force, Navy, and Marine Corps fighter pilots needed better training. This led to creation of the Air Force Weapons School and the Navy's "TopGun" Fighter Weapons School of movie fame. The Navy estimates that the better training resulted in 12 MiGs shot down for every US fighter lost in dogfighting.

Refueling fighter and reconnaissance planes near combat zones was complicated. Several meeting areas over Thailand, Laos, South Vietnam and the Gulf of Tonkin, called "anchors," were set up so fighters could select the nearest airborne gas station on the way to and from their targets. Sometimes 50 or more aircraft met and circled over a wide area as fuel changed hands. Tankers often overflew hostile territory to meet and fuel planes that otherwise would not have made it home. Many pilots owed the success of their missions—and some owed their lives—to being refueled by tankers.

The Air Force based KC-135 tankers in Japan, the Philippines, Thailand and Guam. During the Southeast Asia War, tankers flew nearly 200,000 sorties, completing more than 800,000 refuelings. From 1964 through 1973, they pumped almost 1.4 billion gallons of fuel to other aircraft, enough to fill more than 2,120 Olympic-sized swimming pools.

Though tankers were not used for combat, missions could be dangerous. Twenty-five Air Force personnel died in tanker crashes, on takeoff or landing, in Southeast Asia.

Lessons the Air Force Learned From the Vietnam War

During the first few years of the war, the United States did not use airpower consistently. From time to time it halted the bombing raids. During these pauses, the United States tried to get the Communists to stop fighting. Instead, the North Vietnamese used the time to repair their supply routes and communication lines.

This experience taught the US Air Force that it must thoroughly defeat an enemy. It must not spare locations where Soviet and Chinese advisers might be stationed.

During *Operations Linebacker I* and *II*, B-52 bombers pounded supply routes and Communist positions until the North Vietnamese were compelled to talk.

The Top-Secret Mission of Chief Master Sergeant Richard Etchberger

Chief Master Sergeant Richard Etchberger (1933–1968) started out as a radar operator. He learned fast. During the Vietnam War, his superiors asked if he'd like to join a top-secret mission called *Project Heavy Green*.

The project was a joint mission of the US Air Force and the Central Intelligence Agency (CIA). The military needed a radar site close to the border of North Vietnam to better direct bombing runs. The site was in Laos, a country that was neutral, *not taking sides*. Because Laos was neutral, no US military member could be stationed there. So anyone wanting to take part in the mission had to resign from the military and go to work for a civilian contractor. Etchberger did just this.

From 1967 to 1968, Etchberger and 18 other Americans worked at the secret radar station in Laos. They directed 25 percent of all bombing missions over North Vietnam. But then the North Vietnamese forces learned of their site. They launched an air attack on 12 January 1968. That didn't succeed. So they launched a ground attack from 10 March to 11 March 1968.

Etchberger and his fellow workers fought as best they could. But many were injured or killed. Etchberger escaped enemy fire. He continued to fight until a helicopter came to pick up the survivors. He loaded his fallen friends one by one until it was his turn. He was fatally shot only after he boarded the copter.

Chief Master Sergeant Richard Etchberger in 1968

Courtesy US Air Force

After his death the Air Force awarded Etchberger the Air Force Cross. In a secret Pentagon ceremony in 1969, his wife Catherine accepted it. On 21 September 2010, President Barak Obama presented Etchberger the Medal of Honor. Etchberger's three sons accepted the award.

The Right Stuff

Airman 1st Class John Levitow Earns a Medal of Honor

Airman 1st Class John Levitow (1945–2000) was a gunship loadmaster in Vietnam. His duties included working with flares. On 24 February 1969 he displayed extraordinary courage on a night mission near Long Binh, South Vietnam.

The AC-47 gunship he was on came under heavy fire. (The crew later found out their ship had 3,500 punctures from enemy fire.) A mortar shell exploded on the ship's right wing. The explosion sent shrapnel through the body of the plane. It wounded many crewmen.

Forty pieces of shrapnel hit Levitow. Even so, he saved the life of one of his comrades who was about to fall through an open cargo door. When Levitow saw a loose flare headed toward the ammunition supply, he threw himself on top of it. He threw the flare out the cargo door barely a second before it exploded.

Then–Airman 1st Class John Levitow
Courtesy US Air Force

Levitow spent two months recuperating. Then he went on 20 more missions. For his brave act in 1969, he received the Medal of Honor in 1970. No other Airman of his rank or lower had ever received that award—the nation's highest military medal.

Major Robert Undorf and the Rescue of the *Mayaguez*

Major Robert Undorf was another Airman who served with honor during the Vietnam War. Undorf was an on-scene commander in 1975 for the rescue of the US merchant ship SS *Mayaguez* and its crew. Cambodian Communists grabbed the ship in May 1975. It was 60 miles off the Cambodian coast.

The Cambodian Communists took the *Mayaguez* to Koh Tang Island off the Cambodian coast. President Gerald R. Ford dispatched a force of roughly 200 Marines to retake the vessel and rescue the crew. The Marines expected light resistance on Koh Tang. But they soon found themselves in a tough firefight with up to 200 Cambodian troops. Three of their eight helicopters crashed and two others were disabled.

Meanwhile, a Marine boarding party seized the *Mayaguez* but found no crew members aboard. US aircraft carried out a bombing strike on the Cambodian mainland. After that, the Cambodians released the *Mayaguez*'s crew.

An Air Force pararescueman guides Marines to a rescue helicopter on Koh Tang.

Courtesy US Air Force

Getting the Marines off Koh Tang was another matter. While they fiercely defended their position, Major Undorf flew above the battle in an OV-10 forward-air-control aircraft. He directed supporting fire from USAF aircraft and helicopters on the scene. He then directed the rescue of the Marines from the island while continuing to bring in supporting fire. This was tricky, because at the end only three helicopters were available to pick up the Marines. More than once, Undorf himself made several strafing passes against Cambodian troops.

For his intelligent and brave execution of duties Undorf earned the Silver Star and the Mackay Trophy. The Air Force gives the trophy for the most outstanding flight by an Airman each year.

The Right Stuff

General Daniel James Jr.: The Military's First African-American Four-Star General

General Daniel "Chappie" James Jr. (1920–1978) was the first African-American to attain four-star general rank. He received a bachelor of science degree in 1942 from Tuskegee Institute and completed the Civilian Pilot Training Program.

During World War II James trained pilots, including the famous Tuskegee Airmen. He flew 101 combat missions in Korea. He went on 78 missions in Vietnam. He led one operation in Vietnam in which US Airmen shot down seven MiGs. This was a record during the Vietnam War.

James received his fourth star in 1975. At that time, he was commander in chief of the North American Air Defense Command and the Aerospace Defense Command. He directed all strategic aerospace defense forces in the United States and Canada.

He retired in 1978 as a special assistant to the Air Force chief of staff.

General Daniel "Chappie" James Jr.
Courtesy US Air Force

How Air-to-Air and Surface-to-Air Missile Technology Changed Aerial Combat

In the late 1950s, both the United States and the Soviet Union developed new anti-aircraft missiles. Air-to air missiles are launched from one plane against another. Surface-to-air missiles (SAMs) are launched from ground sites.

These were early versions of what are now called "smart" weapons." You can aim a bullet or shell, but you can't guide it to the target after you fire it. On the other hand, air-to-air missiles and SAMs can be guided to the target by radar or infrared homing. Missiles using infrared homing are called heat-seeking missiles—*missiles that track a target by seeking the infrared light it emits.* Infrared light is *heat radiation not generally visible to the naked eye.*

Air-to-Air Missiles

The Germans developed the first air-to-air missiles toward the end of World War II. These wire-guided missiles were meant to be fired from a fighter plane, whose pilot would then use a joystick to steer the missile. But like Germany's jet fighters, the missiles appeared too late in the war to affect the outcome. Allied bombers destroyed the factory where they were built.

The United States, Britain, and the Soviet Union all developed more-advanced air-to-air missiles in the 1950s. By the time of the Vietnam War, US planners believed all future air combat would be fought using missiles. As you read earlier, the F-4 originally carried only missiles and no guns.

This soon proved to be a mistake. Many missiles were duds. Also, a plane had no defense after firing all its missiles. So later models of the F-4 saw guns restored, and every US fighter since then has carried them. Meanwhile, missile technology has improved since Vietnam, and missiles have indeed become the most common air-to-air weapon.

Air-to-air missiles have many advantages over conventional aircraft guns. They can be fired miles away from the target. And the pilot doesn't have to maneuver to get in the right position to fire—a modern air-to-air missile can be fired from just about any angle to the target.

This has changed the nature of the dogfight. No longer do opposing planes have to maneuver against each other to get in the best position to fire. Now, when two opposing aircraft meet, the one who electronically spots the enemy first and gets off the first shot is the likely victor. This makes it important both to spot the enemy first and to make sure the enemy doesn't spot you first.

Surface-to-Air Missiles

In the same way as air-to-air missiles, SAMs can be a much more accurate defense against aircraft than conventional anti-aircraft fire. The Soviets showed the deadly accuracy of their radar-guided V-750 Dvina SAM when they shot down Francis Gary Powers's U-2 in 1960. The same missile, known by NATO as an SA-2, shot down Major Anderson over Cuba in 1962. The Soviet Union began exporting the SA-2 in 1960, and it's still used by many nations today.

In 1965 the Soviets began delivering the SA-2 to North Vietnam, where it posed a lethal threat to US aircraft. Some 110 Air Force planes were lost to the missiles. If US aircraft flew low to avoid, them, they exposed themselves to deadly anti-aircraft and small-arms fire.

As a result, Air Force and Navy aircraft were deployed to identify and destroy SA-2 sites. But SA-2 launchers could be packed up and moved in about four hours—before a strike could be organized. This led the United States to develop the *Wild Weasel* technology, which could electronically detect an SA-2 launcher and immediately attack it before the North Vietnamese could move it. These *Wild Weasel* missions were some of the most dangerous of the war.

The United States also deployed special Douglas EB-66 electronic warfare aircraft to jam North Vietnamese air defense radar. These were so successful that the North Vietnamese particularly targeted them. One was lost to MiG fighters and SAMs shot down five others.

Since the Vietnam War, advances in electronic guidance and detection systems have both made missiles more accurate, and defenses more effective. Likewise, stealth technology has made aircraft more difficult to detect. The balance between attacker and defender is constantly adjusting as the technology around aircraft, missiles, computers, and electronics progresses.

A North Vietnamese SAM crew in front of an SA-2 launcher
Courtesy US Air Force

Using complete sentences, answer the following questions on a sheet of paper.

1. Why was Korea divided after World War II?

2. What line did North Korean forces cross in a move to take over South Korea?

3. What did the Korean experience make US planners understand?

4. Why did the Soviet Union put missiles in Cuba?

5. Who was the only American to die in the Cuban Missile Crisis?

6. How did President John F. Kennedy react to the discovery of Soviet missiles in Cuba?

7. What did the Tonkin Gulf Resolution lead to?

8. How did the Tet Offensive get its name?

9. Why was North Vietnam able to take over South Vietnam?

10. How are air-to-air missiles guided to their target?

11. Why was arming the F-4 with missiles and no guns a mistake?

12. What could *Wild Weasel* technology do?

APPLYING YOUR LEARNING

13. Because North Vietnam eventually achieved its objective, many Americans conclude that the United States lost the Vietnam War. Do you agree? Why or why not?

This page not used

Other US Air Force Military Operations That Supported National Objectives

Learn About

- *Operation Eagle Claw* in Iran
- *Operation Urgent Fury* in Grenada
- *Operation El Dorado Canyon* in Libya
- *Operation Just Cause* in Panama
- Humanitarian Operations
- How the Cold War Ended

WHEN A MISSION INVOLVES flying aircraft into a location where there is no base, Air Force combat controllers must go in first to prepare the ground. Major John Carney was the lead combat controller for *Operation Eagle Claw*, the attempt to rescue the American hostages in Iran in 1980.

Major Carney secretly flew into Iran in a small CIA plane. He had one hour on the ground to survey and approve the site, install runway lights, and perform several other tasks. Using a nearby road as a starting point, he marched off a box for the landing strip, burying the runway lights at each corner. Then he buried a light 3,000 feet away from the box but centered on it. This would be the place for a landing aircraft to stop.

While he was working, four vehicles drove by on the road. All Carney could do to hide was to lie flat on the ground.

Carney returned to the site, called *Desert One*, 23 days later with the rescue force, including his team of combat controllers. He was worried about the runway lights. But when the switch was flipped, they turned on, allowing the C-130s to land safely in the Iranian desert. The controllers got all the planes landed and parked safely.

Unfortunately, disaster would strike later in the mission. When it did, Carney had to collect all the runway lights and navigation gear before the rescue force could depart.

Carney retired from the Air Force as a colonel. In retirement he served as president of the Special Operations Warrior Foundation, which gives scholarships to the children of special forces personnel killed in the line of duty.

As the years passed and the Cold War continued, the US Air Force's mission expanded. The US military has been involved in many operations supporting national objectives. These objectives are the desired results of national goals and interests. They may involve the safety of US citizens or efforts to stabilize a democratic government.

The US public's desire to avoid heavy casualties led to more reliance on airpower to support US goals. In addition, the Air Force's increasing ability to attack more precisely and with less risk of losing aircraft made airpower an attractive option.

Besides coordinating operations with its NATO allies in Europe, the United States conducted several operations of its own.

Vocabulary

- coup d'état
- Islamist
- extradite
- diplomat
- variable-geometry wings
- infiltrate
- tsunami

Operation Eagle Claw in Iran

The United States had supported the Shah, or king, of Iran for several decades following World War II. It saw Iran as an important barrier to Soviet Communist expansion in the Middle East. (Iran has a long border with lands that were then part of the Soviet Union.) The United States, Britain, and other allies also had important oil interests in Iran. At one point, in 1953, the United States and Britain backed a coup d'état—*the overthrow of a government*—to remove an Iranian prime minister. He wished to seize British oil assets and replace a British oil company with an Iranian state company.

The Shah's goal was to modernize Iran and make it an industrial power. But his government often treated opponents harshly, and corruption and mismanagement were widespread. Iran's conservative Shiite Muslim clergy deeply opposed modernization, with its introduction of Western ideas such as equality for women. Economic difficulties also contributed to rising discontent with the Shah's government throughout the 1970s.

After a year of civil unrest, the Shah fled Iran in February 1979. A senior Shiite cleric, Ayatollah Ruhollah Khomeini, returned from exile in France to form a new Islamist government. Islamist means *based on a fundamentalist interpretation of Islam that seeks to enforce Islamic values in all areas of life*. In October President Jimmy Carter allowed the Shah to enter the United States for surgery. This enraged the new Iranian government, which demanded that the United States extradite the Shah to face trial and an almost certain death sentence. Extradite means *to send a person who has been accused of a crime to another state or country for trial*. The Americans refused.

On 4 November 1979 Islamist "students" raided the US embassy in Iran. They took more than 60 US diplomats hostage. A diplomat is *a person who represents his or her country's government in a foreign country*. In return for the hostages' release, the Iranians demanded the US government return the Shah of Iran.

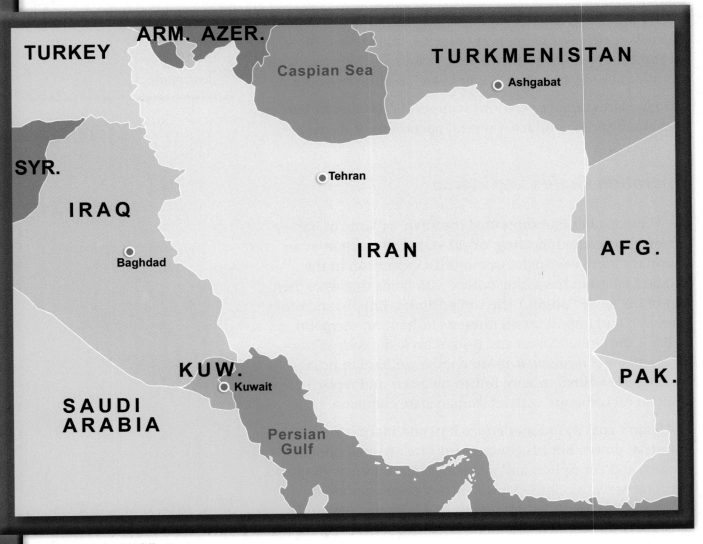

Iran and the Middle East

Islam

LIKE JUDAISM AND CHRISTIANITY, Islam claims its descent from the patriarch Abraham. The word *Islam* means *submission to the will of God.* The followers of Islam are called *Muslims.* Muslims believe in one God. They believe their religion was revealed more than 1,400 years ago in Mecca—today part of Saudi Arabia. They believe that Jesus, Moses, and Abraham were prophets of God, but that Muhammad was the final prophet.

The two main branches of Islam are *Sunni* and *Shia.* Both agree on the fundamentals of Islam, but they have serious differences on many religious questions. The Sunni branch is the larger of the two. Most of the major Arab countries are predominantly Sunni. The non-Arab Persians in Iran are overwhelmingly Shia. Iraq is an Arab country with a strong Shia majority, and large Shia majorities exist in Syria, Lebanon, Pakistan, and elsewhere. A good deal of the violence in the Middle East today can be traced to tensions between the two groups.

Negotiations to gain the hostages' release failed. So President Jimmy Carter ordered a military rescue. *Operation Eagle Claw* began—and ended—on 24 April 1980. Eight Navy helicopters took off from the aircraft carrier USS *Nimitz* in the Persian Gulf.

They headed for a patch of Iranian desert from which they planned to launch the rescue. But three of the helicopters had mechanical problems. Two turned back. The remaining six then ran into an unexpected dust storm, which delayed them an hour. When they arrived, the third helicopter with mechanical problems could not be repaired. This meant there were not enough helicopters to carry the assault team and the rescued hostages. The mission was canceled. As the remaining aircraft were preparing to depart, one of the helicopters and an Air Force MC-130 collided. Five Airmen and three Marines died.

Months later on 20 January 1981—the day President Ronald Reagan assumed office—the US and Iran reached an agreement to free the last 52 hostages. (Iran had released some earlier.)

The US military learned from the experience. It needed to better coordinate joint ventures between different branches of the military. In 1987 Congress passed a law that set up the US Joint Special Operations Command. Its purpose was to conduct special operations, which often involve more than one branch of the armed forces.

Operation Urgent Fury in Grenada

On 13 October 1983 Communists in the government of Grenada overthrew the prime minister and took over the island in the Caribbean. Many suspected Cuba and the Soviet Union were behind the plot.

The Communist takeover put at risk some 600 to 1,000 American students attending a medical college in Grenada. It also endangered hundreds of other Americans living on the island. President Ronald Reagan sent US troops into Grenada on 25 October to rid it of communism and to bring home the American citizens. The mission was dubbed *Operation Urgent Fury*.

Many US Air Force aircraft took part in the mission. One was the AC-130, a gunship that gave cover to troops securing an airfield in Grenada. The AC-130 took on enemy foot soldiers and attacked antiaircraft systems. Another aircraft was the EC-130, which can broadcast to enemy radio and TV receivers. In Grenada, the EC-130 crews relayed radio messages to local people so they'd know what was happening. A-10 attack aircraft supported Marines seizing a suspected enemy base. The C-141 Starlifter ferried home the students, and later, withdrawing US Soldiers.

Troops from the United States and several Caribbean nations ousted the would-be Communist government. By 15 December they had restored security. The US troops could go home.

The invasion of Grenada had consequences far beyond the Caribbean island. All branches of the armed forces learned some important lessons. The Air Force learned about the need for sufficient airfields and places to organize, or stage, troops and supplies. Navigation problems on C-130s during the invasion spotlighted the need for improved navigation equipment. Damage the C-130s suffered from ground fire led to better defenses against anti-aircraft fire.

Resistance by Grenadian and Cuban forces reinforced the lesson that air superiority is needed before airdropping troops. Also, the Air Force, Army, Navy, and Marines had difficulty communicating with each other—they couldn't talk to each other by radio, making it hard to coordinate their efforts.

Finally, the invasion revealed more flaws in the joint command between the services. This made it hard for the different branches of the military to work together as a team. As a result, Congress passed the Goldwater-Nichols Defense Department Reorganization Act of 1986. The led to increased joint command at the Pentagon, with one commander in charge of all the services participating in each operation. This is called a *Unified Combatant Command*.

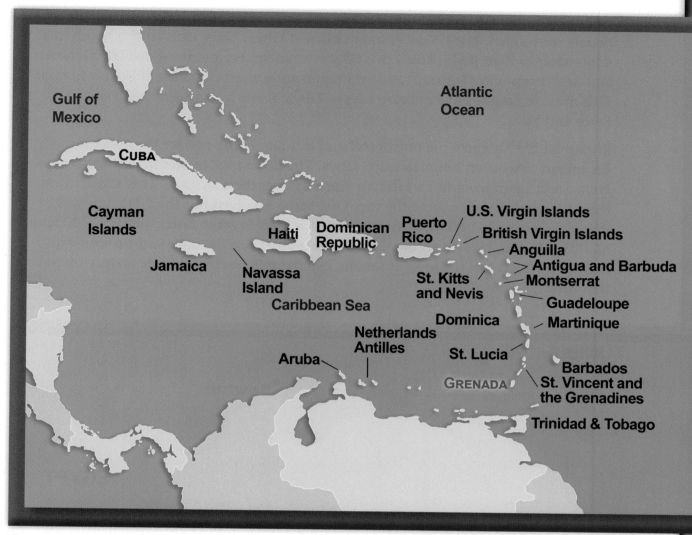

Grenada and the Caribbean Sea

Operation El Dorado Canyon in Libya

Terrorism against the United States and its allies was a problem long before the attacks on the World Trade Center and the Pentagon on 11 September 2001. In the 1980s, however, the terrorist groups launching the attacks were supported by national governments in countries like Libya and Iran. Sometimes agents of those countries' secret services were involved.

In December 1985, Libyan leader Colonel Mu'ammar al-Qadhafi expressed support for terrorists who attacked the Rome, Italy, and Vienna, Austria, airports. The terrorists killed 19 people and wounded more than 140. In January 1986, President Ronald Reagan's administration broke off diplomatic relations with Libya and closed the American Embassy in Tripoli. In March, the US Navy retaliated against Libyan naval vessels, aircraft, and missile sites that had attacked US ships. The Navy was sailing in international waters in the Gulf of Sidra that Qadhafi claimed for Libya.

In April, a bomb went off aboard TWA Flight 840 while flying over Greece. Four people were killed. The US government blamed Libya. Three days later, a bomb in a dance club in West Berlin killed two US service members and wounded 200 Germans and Americans. On 14 April President Reagan authorized *Operation El Dorado Canyon*. This mission targeted five military sites in Libya. It was a joint venture of the US Air Force and Navy.

Britain let the Air Force use one of its bases as a launching pad for the operation. US aircraft flew seven hours to reach Libya. The flight took longer than usual because France and Spain wouldn't let the Air Force fly over their airspace. This added more than 1,000 miles each way to the trip. One plane involved was the F-111 Aardvark, whose wings sweep back in flight to enable the craft to reach faster speeds. KC-10 and KC-135 refueling tankers accompanied these fighters on the 6,400-mile round-trip flight. The flight was the longest for any combat mission in Air Force history up to that time.

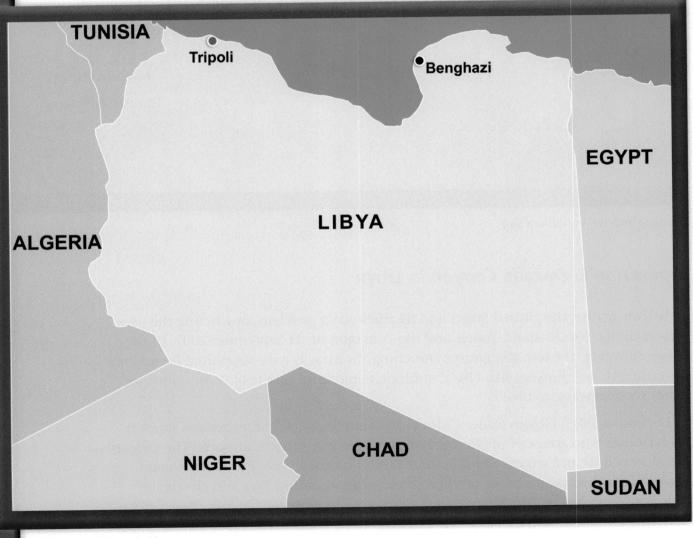

Libya and its neighbors

CHAPTER 5   The US Air Force Is Born

Other aircraft played a role as well. The EF-111 jammed Libyan radar. Navy aircraft such as the A-7, A-6, and F-14 joined the Air Force aircraft from carriers in the Mediterranean Sea. The Air Force F-111s struck a barracks and terrorist training camp in Tripoli. The Navy planes attacked an airfield and barracks in Benghazi, Libya's second-largest city.

The mission succeeded, although the Libyans shot down one F-111. But it was very controversial. Many countries criticized the American action. In the United States, the Navy believed it could have conducted the mission by itself. The Air Force wing commander thought the number of F-111s used was too large to maintain the element of surprise. And there were problems with the targeting systems on board the Air Force planes.

But the operation showed that the Air Force could strike targets thousands of miles away. And the technical problems with the F-111s were repaired, leading to that plane's great success five years later in *Operation Desert Storm*.

Operation Just Cause in Panama

Panamanian military leader (and dictator) General Manuel Noriega held power in his Central American country in the 1980s. At the time, the United States protected the Panama Canal under a long-standing treaty with Panama. The canal is a 50-mile route through which ships travel between the Atlantic Ocean to the Pacific Ocean. Some 40,000 Americans lived in Panama.

Noriega was also involved with smuggling illegal drugs and charged with murder and election fraud. Beginning in 1987, members of Noriega's Panama Defense Forces (PDF) began to regularly seize, beat, and harass US military personnel. Noriega was charged with drug trafficking by federal grand juries in the United States in February 1988. In early 1989 the PDF detained nine school buses filled with American children from nearby US bases.

Then in May Noriega's candidate lost the national elections. Noriega declared the election null and void. His supporters attacked and beat opposition candidates and killed one of their bodyguards. A US Navy sailor was kidnapped, robbed, and beaten. This led President George H. W. Bush to send another 1,900 US troops to guard US military installations in Panama. He also withdrew many family members of US service members so the PDF couldn't harass them.

Then a senior PDF commander tried a coup d'état against Noriega. It failed, and Noriega declared that "a state of war" existed between Panama and the United States. In December PDF guards at a roadblock killed a US Marine lieutenant in a car carrying four off-duty US military officers. They also beat a Navy lieutenant who witnessed the incident and assaulted his wife.

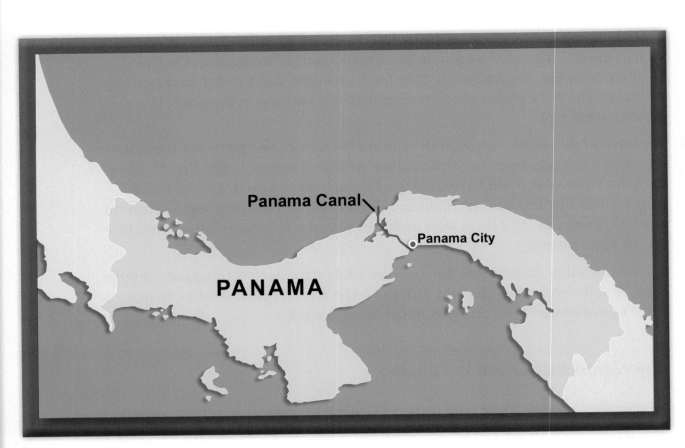

Panama

In response to all of this, the United States undertook *Operation Just Cause*. President Bush said the purpose was to "safeguard the lives of Americans, to defend democracy in Panama, to combat drug trafficking, and to protect the integrity of the Panama Canal treaty." He ordered Noriega's immediate arrest and extradition to the United States to face drug-smuggling charges.

Just Cause was a joint operation of the Air Force, Army, Navy, and Marines. The Air Force's new F-117 Nighthawk stealth fighter saw its first combat duty. Furthermore, the Air Force delivered 9,500 Army paratroopers in the largest airdrop since 1944. The mission ran from December 1989 until 12 January 1990. US forces arrested Noriega on 3 January 1990. He was convicted in a US court of drug trafficking and money laundering. Elsewhere, a French court convicted him of money laundering, and a Panamanian court convicted him of murder. His US sentence ended in 2007. In 2010, after several appeals, he was extradited to France. A French court released him in 2011 and he was returned to Panama, where he is currently serving his murder sentence.

Operation Just Cause was the first operation under the new joint command structure of the Goldwater-Nichols act. Although the operation was a short one, the system seemed to perform well. It was a sign of things to come—within a year, Iraqi forces invaded Kuwait, and US forces would be deployed to Saudi Arabia in *Operation Desert Shield*.

Significant Aircraft of the Late Cold War Period

General Dynamics F-111 Aardvark

The F-111's design reached back to the Bell X-5 experimental aircraft, which first flew in 1951. The X-5 had a jet engine. Its main experimental function was its wing design. It had wings that could sweep back up to 60 degrees during flight. The sweptback-wing design meant faster flight.

The F-111 fighter-bomber first flew in 1964 and entered Air Force service three years later. Like the X-5, it had variable-geometry wings— *wings that can be swept forward for takeoffs or slow flight, or swept backward for high-speed flight.* The plane could fly very low and hit targets even in bad weather.

F-111 Aardvark
Courtesy US Air Force

In 1972 the Aardvark was sent to Vietnam, where it was used for night strikes against North Vietnam. It was also used against Libya in 1986 during *Operation El Dorado Canyon.* Some 566 of the planes were built.

The F-111 carried two crew members and one cannon. It could carry up to 24 conventional bombs. Its top speed was 1,452 mph with a range of 3,632 miles. The Air Force retired the F-111 in 1996.

Lockheed F-117A Nighthawk

The Lockheed F-117A was developed in response to an Air Force request for an aircraft able to attack high-value targets without being detected by enemy radar. By the 1970s, new materials and techniques allowed engineers to design an aircraft with radar-evading or stealth qualities. The result was the F-117A, the world's first operational stealth aircraft.

F-117 Nighthawk
Courtesy US Air Force

The first F-117A flew on 18 June 1981, and the first F-117A unit, the 4450th Tactical Group (renamed the 37th Tactical Fighter Wing in October 1989), became operational in October 1983. The F-117 remained classified until November 1988. It first saw combat during *Operation Just Cause* on 19 December 1989, when two F-117As attacked military targets in Panama.

A total of 59 F-117As were built between 1981 and 1990. In 1989 the F-117A was awarded the Collier Trophy, one of the most prized aeronautical awards in the world.

Grumman F-14 Tomcat

The F-14 was made famous by the 1986 Tom Cruise movie *Top Gun*. It was developed to protect Navy ships from long-range Soviet bombers and patrol aircraft. With its long-range air-to-air missiles, the F-14 could take on enemy aircraft 90 miles away. Variable-geometry wings allowed it to operate at different speeds, depending on the mission.

Grumman delivered the first F-14s to the Navy in 1972. The aircraft fought its first combat in 1981, when F-14s downed two Soviet-built Libyan MiG-23s over the Gulf of Sidra. F-14s flew many missions in the Gulf War, Iraq, and Afghanistan.

An F-14 Tomcat from the aircraft carrier USS *Theodore Roosevelt* flies over Saudi Arabia in 1991.

Everett Historical/Shutterstock

Although the Navy retired the Tomcat in 2006, the plane still serves with the Iranian Air Force. The United States sold the planes to the Shah of Iran before he was overthrown in 1979 and his government replaced by the Islamic Republic of Iran. An Iranian pilot is the highest-scoring F-14 ace, having shot down 11 enemy planes during the Iran-Iraq War (1980 to 1988).

The Tomcat could fly up to 1,544 mph. It carried a crew of two, a cannon, and up to eight air-to-air missiles. Its range was 2,400 miles. Grumman produced 712 F-14s.

Mikoyan Gurevich MiG-23/27

The Soviets designed the MiG-23 to replace the MiG-21. The new plane was extremely successful—it was widely used by the Soviet Union, its Warsaw Pact allies, and many other countries for several decades. It had a more powerful engine and was the first Soviet aircraft with variable-geometry wings. The original MiG-23 was a fighter-interceptor aircraft. Its later sibling, the MiG-27, was developed as a strike fighter-bomber.

MiG-23 on display at an air base in Kubinka, Russia

ID1974/Shutterstock

The MiG-23 was first delivered to the Soviet Union and India in 1975. Russia retired the aircraft in 1994, but it served in India until 2009 and continued with several other air forces after that. It had a maximum speed of 1,553 mph and a range of 808 miles. The standard MiG-23 carried a twin-barrel cannon and 6,600 lbs. of missiles. About 5,050 MiG-23s were produced.

The MiG-27 was armed with a six-barreled machine gun and could carry up to 8,000 lbs. of bombs and missiles. Some 1,075 MiG-27s were built.

Lockheed MC-130E Combat Talon

The MC-130E Combat Talon provides the Air Force with an aircraft that can infiltrate and resupply special operations forces in hostile or enemy territory. To infiltrate is *to secretly enter or join something, such as a group or country, to gain information or do harm.*

MC-130s can fly well below radar coverage, avoiding detection in any type of weather condition. The MC-130 can also refuel other aircraft in flight. It first flew in 1966 and has seen service during the Vietnam War and every operation since.

An MC-130 Combat Talon like the one used for *Operation Eagle Claw* prepares to refuel aircraft near Japan.
Courtesy US Air Force

Lockheed C-141 Starlifter

The C-141 Starlifter was the Air Force's first major jet aircraft designed to meet military standards as a troop and cargo carrier. Lockheed (now Lockheed Martin) built a total of 285 C-141s. For more than 40 years, C-141s performed numerous airlift missions for the Air Force. With its great range and high speed, the Starlifter projected American military power and humanitarian efforts rapidly across the globe.

The Starlifter originated from a 1959 requirement for a fast, strategic transport aircraft that would serve as a workhorse for moving Army troops rapidly anywhere in the world. The C-141 made its maiden flight on 17 December 1963. The aircraft became operational in April 1965.

A C-141B Starlifter like the one used in *Operation Urgent Fury* flies over the Pacific Ocean with San Francisco in the background.
Ken Hackman/Courtesy US Air Force

Humanitarian Operations

Participating in humanitarian operations is a tradition older than the Air Force. It will continue as long as natural disasters and political crises create human suffering. People's need for emergency assistance can arise at any time. It can result from many causes, from earthquakes to civil war. America's military has stepped forward on countless occasions to provide medical assistance, food, and water at a moment's notice.

As early as 1919, air service airplanes dropped food to marooned flood victims along the Rio Grande River. During the 1920s, Army flyers bombed ice jams in Pennsylvania rivers to prevent flooding, restore safe navigation, and save bridges. In 1932 Army bombers dropped relief supplies to Navajo Indians in Arizona who were snowbound after severe blizzards. In the first 46 years since the US Air Force was established, it has conducted at least 490 relief airlift operations around the world.

The Berlin Airlift, *Operation Vittles*, is still the largest humanitarian airlift operation in history. In 15 months, US and allied planes flew 190,000 flights. They moved 1.75 million tons of coal, food, medicine, and other supplies into West Berlin. Air Force humanitarian efforts since then have continued in this time-honored tradition.

Operation Babylift and *Operation Frequent Wind*

Although all US combat troops departed South Vietnam in 1973, the war between North and South Vietnam was not over. In early 1975, the North Vietnamese Army launched a major attack that captured a number of provinces and cities in South Vietnam.

As the North Vietnamese army continued to move south, President Gerald Ford announced on 3 April 1975 that US aircraft would carry South Vietnamese orphans to the United States. This became known as *Operation Babylift*. The operation began tragically, however, when an Air Force C-5 Galaxy carrying more than 200 orphans and 37 Defense Department employees crashed shortly after takeoff, killing 155 of the 330 people on board. While the crash slowed the evacuation, *Operation Babylift* ultimately brought more than 2,600 orphans out of Vietnam to safety.

While *Operation Babylift* continued, C-141s were used to evacuate US citizens and dependents. By 19 April, US aircraft had flown out 6,000 people, including a number of Vietnamese-born US dependents—the spouses and children of US citizens. During the month of April 1975, the Air Force flew 201 C-141 and 174 C-130 missions to evacuate more than 45,000 people from South Vietnam. This included 5,600 US citizens.

Still, the US ambassador, his staff, and many more US citizens and refugees remained in South Vietnam. They would have to be evacuated by helicopter, in an operation known as *Frequent Wind*. US Marine helicopters were joined by 10 helicopters from the Air Force. Their flights marked the first significant deployment of Air Force helicopters from a US Navy aircraft carrier. In addition, Navy and Air Force fighters flew escort for the helicopters, while Air Force AC-130 gunships and KC-135 tankers provided additional support.

In dangerous circumstances, 71 US helicopters flew 660 missions between Saigon and the US Seventh Fleet. They evacuated more than 7,800 people from the US Embassy on 29 and 30 April. The operation ended on 30 April, and by noon that day, Communist flags flew over the Presidential Palace. On that final day, Air Force aircraft flew a total of 1,422 missions.

Operation Frequent Wind concluded more than two decades of US involvement in Vietnam. Although the evacuation of South Vietnam had ended, the Air Force still had to transport thousands of tons of cargo to refugee camps and move refugees from the Philippines to Guam. By the middle of May 1975, Guam harbored more than 50,000 Southeast Asian evacuees. The evacuation concluded with *Operation New Life* and *Operation New Arrivals*, which brought approximately 130,000 refugees to the United States. The aerial evacuation of South Vietnam was the largest such operation in history, with more than 50,000 evacuees transported mainly on Air Force aircraft.

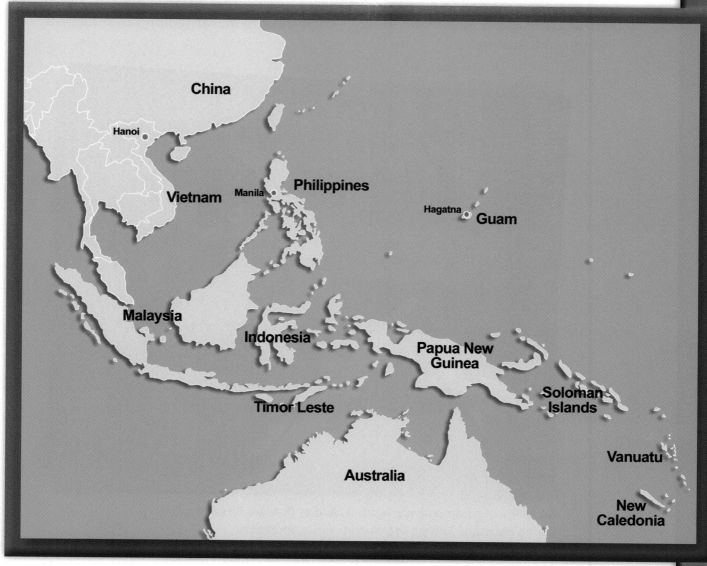

Vietnam, the Philippines, and Guam

Hurricane Katrina Relief Operations

Hurricane Katrina, with winds as high as 140 miles per hour, made landfall near Buras, Louisiana, on 29 August 2005. It devastated parts of Louisiana, Mississippi, and Alabama. The dense population of New Orleans was hardest hit. Floodwalls and levees failed, leaving about 80 percent of the city flooded for weeks. Nearly 100,000 residents struggled to survive as they awaited rescue.

Working with the Coast Guard and other agencies, Air Force helicopters played a key role during relief operations, particularly in New Orleans. They not only flew damage assessment teams into ravaged areas, but also performed extensive search-and-rescue operations. Using MH-53 Pave Low, HH-60 Pave Hawk, and UH-1 helicopters from bases across the country, the Air Force rescued 4,322 of the approximately 30,000 people saved. In one day, the members of the 347th Expeditionary Rescue Group rescued 791 people. In addition to rescuing survivors, the Air Force deployed Air National Guard Expeditionary Medical Support teams for the first time in a domestic crisis. These teams were set up in New Orleans, Gulfport, Mississippi, and Hancock County, Mississippi.

An Air Force pararescueman holds a child as they are lifted to safety during Hurricane Katrina search-and-rescue operations.

Courtesy US Air Force

The Air Force also flew hundreds of missions using C-130s, C-17s, C-5s, and KC-135s to airlift people, equipment, and supplies into and out of the region. Air Force aircraft transported 43,713 support personnel into the area. The Air Force sent personnel to New Orleans International Airport to establish a base of operations. It also evacuated 2,602 patients from areas affected by Katrina.

In addition, the Air Force transported 26,943 people to temporary homes in more than 35 states. In one of the largest such missions, 89 aircraft airlifted nearly 10,000 refugees to Lackland AFB, Texas, in one 55-hour period. The Air Force also performed other flying missions, including spraying insecticide to help prevent disease outbreaks. E-3 AWACS aircraft performed air traffic control for more than 1,000 helicopters. And U-2 reconnaissance aircraft overflew the area, providing aerial imagery of affected areas. In total, the Air Force flew 4,743 missions in support of Hurricane Katrina relief operations.

Operation Tomodachi

On 11 March 2011, a 9.0-magnitude earthquake occurred off the northern coast of Japan. It caused a massive tsunami that devastated parts of the country. A tsunami is *a very high, large wave in the ocean that is usually caused by an earthquake under the sea.* As many as 28,000 people were killed or missing. Millions of dollars worth of property was damaged.

It was one of the worst natural disasters in Japan's history. The US Geological Survey considered the earthquake to be the fourth largest in the world since 1900—and the largest in Japan for at least 130 years. While the Japanese government immediately responded, the US government stood ready to help.

As part of *Operation Tomodachi* (*friend* in Japanese), the Air Force sent HH-60 Pave Hawk helicopters to conduct search-and-rescue operations. Air Force C-17 Globemaster IIs ferried supplies, personnel, and equipment to Japan. KC-10 Extenders provided aerial refueling. In addition, C-130 Hercules transports delivered cargo and supplies, and conducted reconnaissance over devastated areas.

The status of the Fukushima Daiichi Nuclear Plant was of great concern during the recovery efforts. It had been damaged by the tsunami. Experts worried that a massive radiation leak could affect the already-devastated region. To determine the extent of the damage, the Air Force sent U-2 Dragon Lady and RQ-4 Global Hawk aircraft to conduct reconnaissance of the damaged plant.

In the first two weeks of *Operation Tomodachi*, the Air Force flew 225 missions. It transported 4.2 million lbs. of cargo and approximately 2,800 people. Although the loss of life and property was tragic, Air Force contributions to the relief effort built firmly on its own tradition of humanitarian-assistance missions that began with the Berlin Airlift.

Map of Japan showing the location of the 2011 earthquake and its closeness to the Fukushima Nuclear Power Plant

Augusto Cabral/Shutterstock

Humanitarian operations demonstrate that US military organizations have useful roles beyond the battlefield. Military operations can not only wage combat and destruction against enemies of the US and its allies—they can also save lives, repair, and rebuild. US military forces have a proud tradition of helping those who can't help themselves during and after disasters, a tradition that will continue.

How the Cold War Ended

In the decades of the Cold War, the United States and the Soviet Union never fought face to face. Neither side used nuclear weapons. They avoided total war.

But each side spent billions of dollars building up arms. This meant billions of dollars weren't going toward the everyday needs of civilians: better schools, better roads, and better power plants. This failure to pay attention to its people's needs severely weakened the Soviet Union.

The country's economy suffered. People had to wait in line to buy basic foods, such as bread. The people in the Communist countries of Europe also began to demand more respect for human rights. They wanted freedom of speech, freedom of religion, and the freedom to travel to other countries.

The Cold War came to a critical point in 1989. Soviet leader Mikhail Gorbachev had come to power in 1985. He tried to reform the Communist system by freeing the economy and improving human rights. But the effort came too late for Soviet communism. The Soviets' Eastern European allies saw their Communist governments fall one by one. In most cases, democracies took their place. East Germany and West Germany reunited into one democratic country. The Warsaw Pact dissolved.

The Soviet Union itself had been organized into 15 republics. The majority of the populations of the 14 republics outside the Russian republic were not ethnic Russians. By January 1991, the republics of Estonia, Georgia, Latvia, and Lithuania had declared their independence from the Soviet Union. In a March 1991 election, the residents of most of the other Soviet republics voted to make the Soviet Union a federation of independent republics with a common president, military, and foreign policy. Gorbachev negotiated a new union treaty and planned to sign it in August.

Before he could do so, however, several other Soviet officials attempted a coup d'état. They placed Gorbachev under arrest at his vacation house and tried to seize the government. But the citizens of Moscow, led by Russian republic President Boris Yeltsin, barricaded the "White House," the Russian republic's capitol building. The coup fell apart and Gorbachev returned to Moscow. The coup plotters were arrested.

Reaction to the coup from the other Soviet republics was swift. One by one they declared their independence. Gorbachev was unable to stop the disintegration of the Soviet Union. It broke apart into 15 independent countries, including Russia.

The Soviet Union ceased to exist on 26 December 1991. After four decades of tension, the contest of wills was over. The United States and its democratic allies in NATO had outlasted communism in Europe.

The Cold War's Aftermath

Some people thought the Cold War's end would bring a long period of peace. But instead, the ending of the Cold War ushered in a whole new era of regional conflicts. In a few countries of Africa and Central Asia, weak governments allowed terrorist groups to organize and train. Russia itself suffered economic and political difficulties and disputes with some of the former Soviet republics. In southern Europe, Yugoslavia—a mixture of ethnic groups divided into five republics—began to fall apart. These developments would challenge the United States and NATO in much different ways than the Cold War did.

✔ CHECKPOINTS

Lesson 4 Review

Using complete sentences, answer the following questions on a sheet of paper.

1. Why was the mission to rescue the American hostages in Iran canceled?

2. What did Congress do after the failed rescue mission?

3. Why did President Reagan send US troops to Grenada?

4. What flaws did *Operation Urgent Fury* reveal in US joint command? What did Congress do in response?

5. What caused President Reagan to authorize *Operation El Dorado Canyon*?

6. What did the operation show?

7. What did President George H. W. Bush say was the purpose of *Operation Just Cause*?

8. What happened to General Manuel Noriega?

9. By the final day, how many missions were flown for *Operations Babylift* and *Frequent Wind*?

10. What was the magnitude of the earthquake that hit northern Japan?

11. What factors led to the end of the Soviet Union?

12. When did the Soviet Union cease to exist?

APPLYING YOUR LEARNING

13. The Cold War lasted for four decades before the Soviet Union collapsed. What lessons might you learn from what caused this collapse?

Quick Write

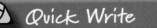

_____

_____

Why did Technical Sergeant Timothy Wilkinson receive the Air Force Cross?

Learn About

- how the United States used airpower in *Operations Desert Shield* and *Desert Storm*
- the role of airpower in *Operation Enduring Freedom*
- how airpower was applied in *Operation Iraqi Freedom*
- the role of US airpower in other military and humanitarian operations

IN 1993 FOLLOWERS OF AFRICAN WARLORD Mohammed Farah Aidid shot down two UH-60 Black Hawk helicopters in Mogadishu, Somalia. In the battle that followed, 19 US military personnel and one Malaysian soldier were killed, along with hundreds of Somalis. The US and other troops were in Somalia to support a United Nations peacekeeping mission.

Technical Sergeant Timothy Wilkinson was a member of the combat search-and-rescue team sent to the crash site. When his unit arrived, it got caught in the firefight with Aidid's followers. At the time, it was the longest firefight for US forces since the Vietnam War.

Wilkinson's duty was to treat the wounded. Again and again, he darted into the firefight to retrieve wounded crewmen as well as the bodies of Soldiers who had died.

During one dash, a bullet took a piece of skin off Wilkinson's face. "I learned then that life is a matter of millimeters and nanoseconds. If my head was turned a different way, I might be dead," Wilkinson said later. "Fortunately, all the bullets missed me, and my scars healed up nice."

Just as the rescue team's ammunition was starting to run out, help arrived. The crew was evacuated safely. Wilkinson was awarded an Air Force Cross for his courage that day. He was the first enlisted person to get this award since 1975.

Technical Sergeant Timothy Wilkinson
Courtesy US Air Force

How the United States Used Airpower in *Operations Desert Shield* and *Desert Storm*

The end of the Cold War did not bring the hoped-for peace. Instead, it created new tensions. Some alliances crumbled. The Soviet Union no longer had the might to spread communism. Only the United States remained a superpower.

Some saw opportunity in these changes. Saddam Hussein, the dictator of Iraq in the Middle East, who gained power by force, was one of them. He wanted to grab the oil fields of Kuwait, a tiny country south of Iraq. Hussein assumed no one would interfere with his plan, since Russia and the United States were no longer engaged in the Cold War. He thought the Russians and Americans wouldn't take sides in conflicts outside their borders as they had in the past. He was wrong.

On 2 August 1990 Iraqi forces marched into Kuwait. By 4 August, Iraq controlled its neighbor. Iraq had prepared well for the invasion. With 550,000 troops, it had the fourth-largest army in the world. It had 16,000 surface-to-air missiles (SAMs) and 750 aircraft. But Iraq would not get to keep Kuwait.

Why the United States Got Involved in the Gulf War

On 6 August 1990 Saudi Arabia—a US ally and a major oil supplier—asked its allies to protect it from neighboring Iraq. Saudi Arabia saw what had happened in Kuwait. It feared Iraq would try to take over nearby Saudi oil fields next.

The United Nations responded with Resolution 660, which ordered Iraq to leave Kuwait. The UN also passed Resolution 678, which permitted a coalition of UN troops to force Iraq out of Kuwait if it didn't withdraw by 15 January 1991. A coalition is *an alliance among nations*. The Allies, for example, were a coalition during World War II.

Vocabulary

- coalition
- sortie
- no-fly zone
- weapon of mass destruction
- insurgent
- genocide
- precision weapons
- strife
- secede

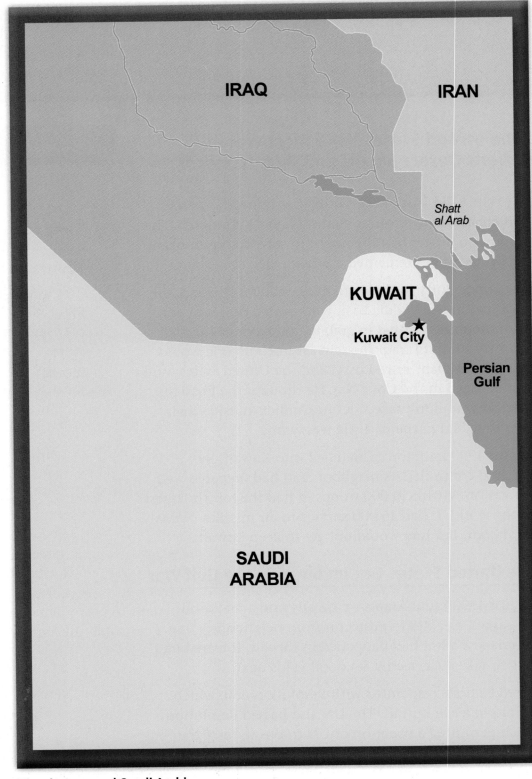

Kuwait, Iraq, and Saudi Arabia

On 8 August the United States sent forces to Saudi Arabia to deter an Iraqi invasion. The military dubbed the mission *Operation Desert Shield*. American and other UN troops "shielded" Saudi Arabia from aggression by placing troops and weapons on Saudi soil. The US Air Force arrived with Airmen, fighter planes, stealth fighters, bombers, gunships, tankers, reconnaissance planes, and transports.

At the same time, US military planners prepared for a second operation in case Iraq didn't meet the deadline to leave Kuwait. The United States called this action *Operation Desert Storm*. Many UN members, including Britain and France, contributed to it.

Iraq did not exit Kuwait as ordered. The stage was set for battle between Iraqi and UN forces.

US Airpower Shows Its Capabilities

The US Air Force, cooperating with the other services, worked out a plan to fight the air battle for *Operation Desert Storm*. Both military strategists and President George H. W. Bush wanted to avoid another Vietnam. They settled on three tactics:

1. Keep the air battle going. Do not pause. In Vietnam, such pauses gave the North Vietnamese time to rebuild and repair.

2. Conduct parallel air strikes. In other words, bomb many targets simultaneously. Don't focus on one target at a time.

3. Coordinate air-strike efforts of the US Air Force, US Navy, and other coalition air forces using one overall commander and one unified plan called an Air Tasking Order.

The Targets

The United States and United Nations decided that their air strikes would aim for four kinds of targets. They based their decisions on the theories of a 19th-century European named Carl von Clausewitz. He said that the best targets were at the "center of the enemy's gravity." This meant that US forces ought to begin by taking out the important targets, such as lines of communication. This would prevent Hussein from giving orders to his troops. The targets were Iraqi:

- communication sites,
- air defenses,
- supply lines and enemy troops, and
- threats to UN ground troops.

A formation of F-16s and F-15s flies over oil fields set on fire by the retreating Iraqi army during *Operation Desert Storm*.

Courtesy US Air Force

The Execution

On 17 January 1991 US air strikes on Iraq began. The first air strike was conducted by F-117A Nighthawk fighters. They flew through intense anti-aircraft and surface-to-air missile fire to bomb communications links, such as TV stations and telephone-relay stations in Baghdad, Iraq's capital. In only their second combat deployment and against a modern air defense system, F-117s were so successful that Iraq's command and control communication network never recovered.

The air armada, or large force of aircraft, that flew the first night of *Desert Storm* included every type of aircraft flown by coalition countries. They made parallel air strikes on Iraq's airfields and air-defense systems—such as SAMs and their radar support. They also hit supply lines and warehouses. With air superiority secured, UN ground troops were ready to move into Iraq.

On 29 January 1991 Iraq launched a counterattack against UN forces in Saudi Arabia. This attack failed. Then on 22 February 1991 a 100-hour battle began to drive the Iraqis out of Kuwait for good. US airpower took the skies over Kuwait. UN ground forces followed. Kuwait was at last free of Iraqi rule.

Lessons the Air Force Learned From the Gulf War

The United States had two goals in *Operations Desert Shield* and *Desert Storm*: to protect Saudi Arabia and to free Kuwait.

To achieve these aims, the US military drew up clear tactics and targets. The Air Force based many of these tactics and targets on lessons learned in other wars, such as Vietnam. One important lesson: don't give the enemy a chance to repair and rearm.

Grabbing air superiority early on gave the US and UN forces an edge as well. Once these forces had struck Iraqi air bases and destroyed communication lines, Iraqi pilots couldn't receive directions from commanders or get into the air.

Finally, US technology gave the UN effort the upper hand in the air. The F-117 stealth fighter, for instance, flew 1,271 sorties during *Operation Desert Storm*. A sortie is *a flight or an attack by a single combat aircraft*. The F-117 was the only aircraft to bomb central Baghdad. In addition, the KC-135 and KC-10 tankers made the long-distance war possible. They refueled more than 14,500 aircraft in midair.

The Right Stuff

Major General Paul T. Johnson: Exceptional Airmanship and Leadership

On 21 January 1991, then-Captain Paul T. Johnson was leading a formation of A-10s assigned to search-and-rescue operations in *Operation Desert Storm*. Captain Johnson was tasked to look for an F-14 crew that had been shot down the night before. During the next six hours he would lead his flight through three aerial refuelings, one attack on a possible missile site, and three hours of intensive searching deep inside enemy territory.

Risking his life, he flew his A-10 at 500 feet above the ground to pinpoint the survivor's location. When an enemy truck appeared to be heading toward his survivor, Johnson directed his flight to destroy it, securing the rescue. It was his superior airmanship and his masterful leadership that made this rescue happen—the first in the history of the A-10 weapons system.

For his extraordinary heroism, superb airmanship, and aggressiveness in the face of the enemy, Johnson received the Air Force Cross. As this book was written, he had advanced to the rank of major general.

Major General Paul T. Johnson
Courtesy US Air Force

Operation Provide Comfort

Following the 1991 Gulf War, the United States launched *Operation Provide Comfort*. Its purpose was to protect the Kurds, an ethnic minority in northern Iraq, and to provide food for Kurdish refugees fleeing into Turkey. Iraq's Saddam Hussein was fighting a rebellion the Kurds had launched against his government. He was also after Kurdish oil fields. Employing C-130s, the US Air Force delivered thousands of tons of relief supplies, including food, tents, and blankets to Kurdish camps. *Operation Provide Comfort* ended in 1996 and was replaced by *Operation Northern Watch*.

Operation Southern Watch

Starting in August 1992, the United States enforced a no-fly zone over Iraq. A no-fly zone is *airspace enemy aircraft aren't allowed to enter*. The operation divided Iraq into northern and southern zones. The Air Force E-3 Airborne Warning and Control System (AWACS) provided airborne radar to support coalition aircraft. The coalition flew combat air patrols over southern Iraq to protect the Shiite Muslim population and Kuwait. The effort was titled *Operation Southern Watch*.

Iraqi pilots regularly shot at US aircraft. Sometimes they entered no-fly airspace. This operation ended just before *Operation Iraqi Freedom* kicked off.

Operation Northern Watch

After US and UN troops subdued Iraqi forces operating against the Kurds, they still couldn't go home. They had to make sure Hussein didn't send his troops and aircraft into hostile action again. So the United Nations set up a second no-fly zone in the northern half of Iraq. This was done in part to protect the Kurds. The name of this mission was *Operation Northern Watch*.

Between 1997 and 2003, 1,400 US, British, and Turkish fliers supported the operation with 50 aircraft. The Iraqis shot at them daily, often using SAMs. The UN aircraft would occasionally strike back. The last US aircraft serving in the operation headed home on 17 March 2003. *Operation Iraqi Freedom* began two days later.

The Role of Airpower in *Operation Enduring Freedom*

Less than a month after the 11 September 2001 attacks on the World Trade Center and the Pentagon (see Chapter 4, Lessons 1 and 4), the US military unleashed *Operation Enduring Freedom* (OEF). The goal was to destroy the terrorists' organization and their bases in Afghanistan, a country in southwest Asia. The terrorists were from a group called Al-Qaeda. The Taliban regime, which ruled Afghanistan at that time, let Al-Qaeda forces train in its country. Therefore, OEF targeted members of the Taliban as well as of Al-Qaeda.

US Aircraft in Afghanistan

OEF began on 7 October 2001, when US Air Force bombers struck terrorist training camps and bases. At the same time, US Navy fighters made strikes from aircraft carriers, and US and British submarines launched missiles at targets in Afghanistan.

Within 18 months, coalition air forces flew more than 85,000 sorties. They conducted more than 48,000 airlifts of troops and cargo. They dropped more than 9,650 tons of bombs.

The main US Air Force combat aircraft involved were the B-1, B-2, B-52, F-15E, F-16, A-10, and AC-130. OEF began with an attack by eight B-1 Lancers. In the first six months of operations, B-1s accounted for 40 percent of the guided and unguided explosives dropped in Afghanistan.

The Longest Combat Mission in Air Force History

The B-2 stealth bomber flew the longest combat mission in US history supporting OEF on 7 October 2001. Flying from Whiteman Air Force Base, Missouri, two B-2s launched to bomb enemy targets in Afghanistan. The first part of the flight to Afghanistan required the bombers to fly west over the Pacific Ocean. Four air refuelings and 24 hours later the bombers reached their targets. After spending two hours dropping bombs on enemy locations, the B-2s headed south, only to have one redirected back to Afghanistan to bomb more targets.

Finally, after 90 additional minutes and all targets bombed, the bomber was able to head south to Diego Garcia, a small British-ruled island. This footprint-shaped island is located in the Indian Ocean and used by the US Navy and Air Force. The B-2 touched down at Diego Garcia after a little more than 44 hours of flying.

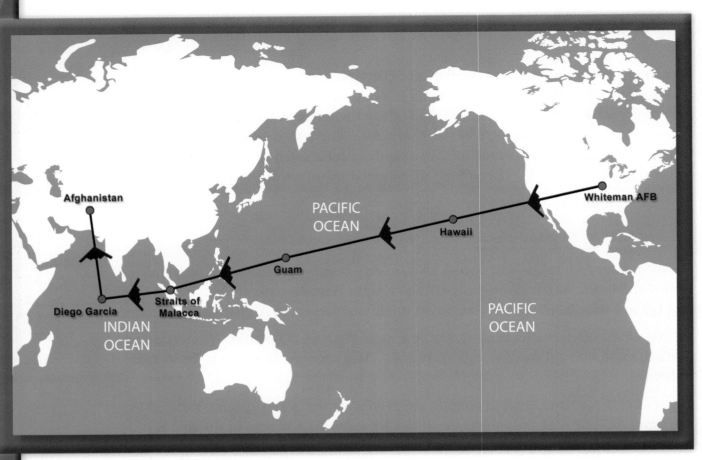

Approximate route of the B-2 bombers

The Hunt for Osama bin Laden

Al-Qaeda's leader, Osama bin Laden, took responsibility for the 11 September attacks. He fled his base in Afghanistan when the US invaded. For years afterward, American military and intelligence personnel worked to find him. Finally, in September 2010, the Central Intelligence Agency (CIA) learned that he was hiding in a large compound in Abbottabad, Pakistan. On 1 May 2011 a joint team of elite Navy Sea, Air, and Land Teams special operations force—commonly known as SEALs—and CIA agents raided the compound. They flew under cover of darkness in specially designed helicopters from Afghanistan. Bin Laden died in the firefight that followed.

Operation Freedom's Sentinel

While the war removed the Taliban regime and led to a new government in Afghanistan, attacks by pro-Taliban fighters have continued. *Operation Enduring Freedom* ended on 31 December 2014. But the United States—now joined by its NATO allies—continues to support the elected Afghan government through *Operation Freedom's Sentinel*. At the end of 2016, about 8,400 US and 6,000 other NATO troops remained in the country. US and NATO forces continued to provide close air support to Afghan soldiers.

The Right Stuff

Technical Sergeant John Chapman:
An Exceptional Brand of Courage

Technical Sergeant John Chapman was a combat controller during *Operation Anaconda* in Afghanistan. Air Force combat-control teams support special operations in the field.

It was in the early hours of 4 March 2002, in what became a 17-hour ordeal on top of Tukur Ghar Mountain in southeastern Afghanistan. *Operation Anaconda*—a coalition effort to destroy Taliban and Al-Qaeda units—was just starting.

Sergeant Chapman was attached to a Navy SEAL team. The team's MH-47 helicopter was hit by Al-Qaeda machine gun fire. A rocket-propelled grenade then hit the helicopter, causing a SEAL team member to fall from the aircraft into enemy-held territory.

The helicopter made an emergency landing more than four miles from the fallen SEAL. Chapman called in an AC-130 gunship to protect the stranded team.

Chapman called in another helicopter to evacuate his stranded team. Then he volunteered to rescue his missing team member from the enemy stronghold. He engaged and killed two of the enemy before advancing and engaging a second enemy position—a dug-in machine gun nest.

From close range with little cover, Chapman exchanged fire with the enemy. Finally he died after receiving multiple wounds. Because of his actions, his team was able to move to cover and break enemy contact.

The Navy SEAL leader credited Chapman with saving the lives of the entire team. In gratitude, the Navy named a cargo ship after him. For his bravery and courage, the Air Force awarded him the Air Force Cross. He became the service's highest-decorated combat controller.

Technical Sergeant John Chapman in Afghanistan
Courtesy US Air Force

Senior Airman Jason Cunningham:
A Display of Uncommon Valor

Senior Airman Jason Cunningham was in the Navy before he decided to switch to the Air Force. He wanted to be a pararescueman. The pararescuemen's motto is "That others may live."

Airman Cunningham was the primary Air Force Combat Search and Rescue medic assigned to a Quick Reaction Force. His team was sent to recover American servicemen in the battle in which Technical Sergeant John Chapman was killed. Shortly before landing, his MH-47E helicopter took rocket-propelled grenade and small-arms fire. This severely disabled the aircraft and caused it to crash land. The assault force formed a hasty defense. Three members were killed immediately; five others were critically wounded.

Despite enemy fire, and at great risk to his own life, Cunningham stayed in the burning fuselage of the aircraft to treat the wounded. As he moved his patients to a more secure location, mortar rounds began to hit within 50 feet of his position. Disregarding this extreme danger, he continued the movement and exposed himself to enemy fire on seven separate occasions.

After a time the second casualty collection point was also endangered. Cunningham braved an intense attack while moving the critically wounded to a third collection point. He was mortally wounded and quickly deteriorating, but he continued to direct his patients' movement and transferred care to another medic.

Cunningham had given medical treatment to the wounded while under fire for seven hours. He was killed saving the lives of 10 service members. The Air Force awarded him the Air Force Cross after his death.

Senior Airman Jason Cunningham (*center*) with two fellow Airmen in Afghanistan
Courtesy US Air Force

Medal of Honor

The Medal of Honor is the nation's highest US military decoration for valor or bravery in combat. It is awarded to members of the armed forces. It is given for conspicuous gallantry and courage at the risk of life, above and beyond the call of duty. The Medal of Honor is sometimes called the *Congressional Medal of Honor* because the president awards it on behalf of the Congress. It is awarded rarely, and then only to the bravest of the brave. The recipients' valor must be well documented.

Medal of Honor
Virginia Reyes/Courtesy US Air Force

Air Force Cross
Virginia Reyes/Courtesy US Air Force

Air Force Cross

The Air Force Cross is second only to the Medal of Honor as an award for valor. The other military services have a similar award. It is awarded to members of the Air Force for extraordinary heroism while engaged in military operations involving conflict with an opposing foreign force or while serving with friendly forces against an opposing enemy force.

Silver Star

The Silver Star Medal is the nation's third-highest award designed solely for valor in combat. It is awarded to members of the military for distinguished gallantry in action against an enemy of the United States or while serving with friendly forces against an opposing enemy force.

Silver Star
Virginia Reyes/Courtesy US Air Force

Bronze Star
Virginia Reyes/Courtesy US Air Force

Bronze Star

The Bronze Star Medal is awarded to any person in the military who distinguishes himself or herself by heroic or meritorious achievement or service. The service must not involve participation in aerial flight. It must occur while he or she is engaged in an action against an enemy of the United States.

How Airpower Was Applied in *Operation Iraqi Freedom*

The US military and its coalition partners launched *Operation Iraqi Freedom* (OIF) on 19 March 2003. It began with an air and ground campaign that quickly became known as *Shock and Awe*. Within 22 days, coalition forces reached Baghdad. The coalition met some resistance. But the coalition forces mostly overwhelmed the Iraqis with airpower, tanks, and troops.

The objectives of OIF were to remove Iraqi leader Saddam Hussein from power and to rid the country of weapons of mass destruction (WMD). A weapon of mass destruction is *a chemical, biological, or atomic weapon that can kill large numbers of people in one use.*

US forces captured Hussein on 13 December 2003. After a long trial, the new Iraqi government executed him on 30 December 2006. Despite their success in capturing Hussein, however, US and coalition forces found no WMDs in Iraq. This led many Americans to question the purpose of invading.

Throughout OIF, insurgents, including members of Al-Qaeda, poured into the country to fight US and allied forces. An insurgent is *a rebel or guerrilla fighter.* In January 2007 President George W. Bush greatly increased the number of US troops in Iraq to help the new Iraqi government fight the insurgency. This "surge" ended in July 2008.

The last US combat brigade left Iraq in August 2010. OIF was renamed *Operation New Dawn* to reflect the reduced American role there. By the end of 2011, all US troops had left Iraq.

The Rise of Islamic State

The remnants of Al-Qaeda in Iraq in 2006 organized a new terrorist organization called *Islamic State in Iraq.* It continued fighting withdrawing coalition troops and the new Iraqi government. Meanwhile, in 2011, a civil war broke out in Syria next door. Islamic State became involved in that fighting and renamed itself *Islamic State in Iraq and the Levant* (ISIL). (It is also referred to in the press as *Islamic State* or *ISIS.*)

ISIL managed to seize a wide swath of territory in Syria and Iraq, including the large Iraqi cities of Mosul and Fallujah. When ISIL attacked the home villages of a religious minority called the *Yazidis*, President Barak Obama ordered air strikes. He wanted to protect US forces sent back to aid the Iraqis and to prevent genocide. Genocide is *the attempt to wipe out all members of a racial, religious, or ethnic group.*

In September 2014, President Obama announced creation of an international coalition of countries to defeat ISIL. In October 2015, the Defense Department named actions by US and allied forces against ISIL in both Iraq and Syria *Operation Inherent Resolve*. By November 2016, US and coalition aircraft had carried out some 16,000 airstrikes. About 10,000 of these were in Iraq. Both Air Force and Navy aircraft participated.

The Right Stuff

Chief Master Sergeant Kevin Lynn: A Historic Impact on the Future of the Iraqi Army

Meritorious service can involve many types of action. For example, Chief Master Sergeant Kevin Lynn helped establish the first military police academy in Iraq.

He was deployed there from 28 February to 23 July 2004. Chief Lynn and fellow Air Force security forces members renovated a bombed-out former Republican Guard base in Taji, Iraq. They turned it into a new police academy. Lynn served as commandant of the school. Starting from scratch, they developed and taught a course for the academy in just nine days.

At the same time, Lynn was also a battle-tested veteran. He and his team continued to train forces during the "April Offensive." This consisted of 18 days of nonstop mortar and rocket attacks. Overall, Lynn survived 31 mortar and 34 rocket attacks that killed 10 soldiers and injured many others. He continually risked his personal safety to ensure mission success and guarantee his team's safety. He provided security on numerous convoy missions and patrolled East Gate on Taji Military Training Base.

Chief Master Sergeant Kevin Lynn and his team transformed a war-torn environment into a successful military police academy.
Courtesy of Chief Master Sergeant Kevin Lynn

In all, Lynn and his team graduated more than 500 military policemen and 40 military police instructors. For his work, Lynn received the Bronze Star Medal on 14 December 2004.

Airman 1st Class Elizabeth Jacobson: An Extraordinary Commitment to Her Country

Airman 1st Class Elizabeth Jacobson, 21, was providing convoy security on 28 September 2005 near Camp Bucca, Iraq, when a roadside bomb struck the vehicle she was riding in.

Airman 1st Class Elizabeth Jacobson
Courtesy US Air Force

The Riviera Beach, Fla., native was assigned to the 17th Security Forces Squadron at Goodfellow Air Force Base, Texas. Airman Jacobson had been in the Air Force for two years and had been in Iraq for more than three months. She was the first female Airman killed in the line of duty in support of *Operation Iraqi Freedom*.

"She was an outstanding Airman who embraced life and took on all the challenges and responsibilities with extraordinary commitment to her country, her comrades, and her family," said Colonel Scott Bethel, 17th Training Wing commander at Goodfellow.

"Her dedication to the US Air Force and serving her country was evident in all aspects of who this young lady was," he said.

US Aircraft in Iraq and Afghanistan

The US Air Force used many aircraft in Iraq and Afghanistan. These ranged from the stealth F-117 fighters flying into Baghdad to hit command and control targets to the giant C-5 Galaxy cargo planes carrying troops and supplies into these theaters of war. All Air Force aircraft have played a significant role in all operations of the longest running war in US history.

McDonnell Douglas F-15 Eagle

The twin-engine F-15 all-weather fighter entered Air Force service in 1974. It was designed to replace the F-4 Phantom. It was the first US fighter with more engine thrust than aircraft weight. This allowed it to gain speed while climbing.

The F-15 has been produced in both a single-seat and a Strike Eagle two-seat version. The two-seat version is an attack aircraft as well as a fighter. Israeli F-15s saw the first combat in 1979, shooting down several Syrian MiG-21s. American F-15s scored 32 of 36 air victories in *Operation Desert Storm* in 1991, and shot down three Serbian MiG-29s during *Operation Allied Force* in 1999.

An F-15 Eagle fires an AIM-7 air-to-air missile.
Master Sergeant Michael Ammons/Courtesy US Air Force

The F-15 is armed with a cannon and can carry eight air-to-air missiles and 15,000 lbs. of bombs. Its maximum speed is more than 1,875 mph and its range is 600 miles. Around 1,600 F-15s have been built. Israel, Japan, and Saudi Arabia also fly F-15s. An Air Force modernization program announced in September 2016 would keep the trusty F-15 flying for many years to come.

General Dynamics F-16 Fighting Falcon

In service since 1979, the F-16 has been produced in both one- and two-seat models. A versatile and highly maneuverable aircraft, it can fly more than 500 miles, deliver its weapons in all weather, and defend itself against enemy fighters. The aircraft can withstand up to nine times the force of gravity.

The F-16 flies as fast as 1,345 mph with a range of 1,407 miles. It carries a 20-millimeter (mm) cannon and up to 16,000 lbs. of air-to-air missiles, air-to-ground missiles, and bombs. Belgium, Denmark, Turkey, Egypt and Israel are among the 25 foreign nations that have purchased the F-16. General Dynamics, now part of Lockheed Martin, has built 4,500 of the planes.

The Air Force Thunderbirds flying F-16s at a 2012 air show at Andrews AFB, outside Washington, D.C.
Chris Parypa Photography/Shutterstock

Mikoyan Gurevich MiG-29

The Soviets developed the original MiG-29 to meet the challenge of the American F-15 and F-16. It serves as both an air-defense fighter and a ground attack aircraft. It began service in 1983 and features new radar and sensors that can identify aircraft flying below or targets 60 miles away.

Czech MiG-29 at a 2012 air show in the Czech Republic

JeP/Shutterstock

Once a MiG-29 pilot can see his target, the plane becomes very dangerous indeed. The pilot's helmet contains tracking sensors so that the pilot need only turn his head, and the helmet locks the missile sensors on the target.

The MiG-29 has a top speed of 1,519 mph and a range of 889 miles. It can climb an astounding 65,000 feet in one minute. Armed with a 30 mm cannon and six air-to-air missiles, it can carry almost 9,000 lbs. of bombs. Mikoyan Gurevich has built 1,625 MiG-29s in different versions. The plane continues to serve in the Russian and many other air forces today.

Fairchild Republic A-10 Thunderbolt II

The A-10 is the first Air Force aircraft designed specifically for close air support of ground forces. It is named for the famous P-47 Thunderbolt, a fighter often used in close air support during the latter part of World War II. The A-10 is very maneuverable at low speeds and low altitudes to ensure accurate weapons delivery. It carries the systems and armor needed to survive in this environment.

A-10 Thunderbolt II fires its 30 mm Gatling gun during a competition, 2 June 2016.

Senior Airman Christopher Drzazg/Courtesy US Air Force

The A-10 is intended for use against all ground targets, but specifically tanks and other armored vehicles. The Thunderbolt II's great endurance allows it to stay over the battlefield longer than most fighters. Its short takeoff and landing capability permits it to operate from airstrips close to the front lines. The A-10 is armed with a 30 mm seven-barrel Gatling gun that sticks out of the aircraft's nose. It's loaded with armor-piercing ammunition that can penetrate tanks and armored personnel carriers.

The first A-10A was delivered to Davis-Monthan AFB, Arizona, in October 1975.

Northrop Grumman B-2 Spirit

The B-2 merged the "flying wing" technology of the YB-49 (see Lesson 2) with stealth technology. This long-range bomber can deliver conventional or nuclear weapons while remaining virtually invisible to air defense radars.

A B-2 Spirit (*right*) flies in formation with a B-52 bomber.
Courtesy US Air Force

The B-2 first flew in 1989 and entered service in 1993. It flew missions in *Operation Allied Force* over Serbia, *Operation Enduring Freedom* over Afghanistan, and *Operation Iraqi Freedom* over Iraq. The aircraft has a crew of two people. It typically flies missions nonstop from Whiteman AFB, Missouri, to the target and back. The flights can take more than 30 hours and require several refuelings. The B-2 can deliver 40,000 lbs. of precision weapons. Precision weapons are *guided missiles and bombs*.

Boeing E-3 Sentry Airborne Warning and Control

The E-3 Sentry Airborne Warning and Control (AWACS) provides an accurate, real-time picture of the battlefield airspace. AWACS provides the following advantages:

- situational awareness of friendly, neutral, and hostile activity
- command and control of an area of responsibility
- battle management of theater forces
- all-altitude and all-weather surveillance
- early warning of enemy actions during joint, allied, and coalition operations

An E-3 Sentry AWACS lands at Tinker AFB, Oklahoma.
Courtesy US Air Force

The radar and computer systems on the E-3 Sentry can gather and present detailed battlefield information. This includes position and tracking information on enemy aircraft and ships, and the location and status of friendly aircraft and naval vessels. In time of crisis, data can also be forwarded to the president and secretary of defense.

E-8C JSTARS in flight
Staff Sergeant Shane Cuomo/Courtesy US Air Force

Boeing E-8C Joint Surveillance Target Attack Aircraft

The E-8C Joint Surveillance Target Attack Radar System (JSTARS) is an airborne battle-management, command and control, intelligence, surveillance, and reconnaissance platform. Its primary mission is to provide theater ground and air commanders with ground surveillance. This supports attack operations and targeting that contribute to the delay, disruption, and destruction of enemy forces.

The radar and computer systems on the E-8C can gather and display detailed battlefield information on ground forces. The information is relayed in near-real time to the Army and Marine Corps common ground stations and to other ground command, control, communications, computer, and intelligence centers.

KC-10A refueling F-16 and F-15 fighters
Courtesy US Air Force

Boeing KC-10A Extender

The KC-10 Extender is an advanced tanker and cargo aircraft designed to provide increased global mobility for US armed forces. The KC-10's primary mission is aerial refueling. But it can combine the tasks of a tanker and cargo aircraft by refueling fighters and simultaneously carrying the fighter support personnel and equipment on overseas deployments.

The KC-10 can refuel a wide variety of US and allied military aircraft within the same mission. The aircraft is equipped with lighting for night air-refueling operations.

Lockheed AC-130 Gunship

The AC-130 gunship has a combat history dating back to Vietnam. Gunships destroyed more than 10,000 trucks and were credited with many lifesaving close air support missions. During *Operation Urgent Fury* in Grenada in 1983, AC-130s suppressed enemy air defense systems and attacked ground forces. This enabled the successful assault of the Point Salines Airfield.

AC-130s also had a primary role during *Operation Just Cause* in Panama in 1989 when they destroyed Panamanian Defense Force Headquarters and many command and control facilities.

An AC-130 gunship jettisons flares during a training flight.
Courtesy US Air Force

During *Operation Desert Storm*, AC-130s provided close air support and force protection (air base defense) for ground forces. Gunships were also used in operations in Somalia, providing close air support for United Nations ground forces. Gunships also played a pivotal role in supporting the NATO mission in Bosnia-Herzegovina.

More recently, AC-130 gunships have supported *Operation Iraqi Freedom* and have been used in support of *Operation Enduring Freedom*. Finally, AC-130 gunships have played a pivotal role in the recent uprisings in the Middle East. Gunships provide armed reconnaissance and support of ground troops engaged against enemy forces.

Boeing C-17 Globemaster III

The C-17 Globemaster III is the newest, most flexible cargo aircraft to enter the airlift force. The C-17 can rapidly deliver troops and all types of cargo to main operating bases or directly to forward bases in the deployment area. The aircraft can perform tactical airlift and airdrop missions and can transport litters and patients during aeromedical evacuations when required. The flexibility and performance of the C-17 force help the total airlift system fulfill the worldwide air mobility requirements of the United States.

Paratroopers from the 82nd Airborne Division drop from a C-17 Globemaster III into a drop zone 28 April 2010.
Courtesy US Air Force

The Role of US Airpower in Other Military and Humanitarian Operations

In addition to the major military operations you've just read about, Airmen have flown and participated in many other missions since 1991. Some were combat missions. Others were humanitarian. Some were both.

Operation Provide Promise

Yugoslavia was formed from the southern Slav territories of Serbia, Bosnia and Herzegovina, Croatia, Macedonia, Montenegro, and Slovenia after World War I. The federation began to fracture in 1992. Ethnic strife, *an angry or violent disagreement between two or more people or groups*, and civil war had long been a part of this country's history.

The Bosnian Muslims (Bosniaks) and Bosnian Croats wanted to be independent of Yugoslavia. But the Bosnian Serbs and the Serbs in Serbia, under Yugoslav leader Slobodan Milosevic, didn't want them to secede, or *break away*. The Bosnian Serbs fought the Bosniaks and Bosnian Croats to keep Bosnia and Herzegovina in Yugoslavia. In 1992 the Serbs cut off food and other supplies to Sarajevo, Bosnia's capital.

In July 1992, the United States and 20 other countries launched a massive airlift, *Operation Provide Promise*. The United States and other nations flew in 160,000 tons of goods in 13,000 sorties. C-130s, C-141s, C-5s, and C-17s took part in this mission.

It was risky business. The Serbs shot at the cargo aircraft. They hit 10 US planes and shot down one Italian aircraft. The airlift lasted until January 1996. The Dayton Accords, signed 14 December 1995 at Wright-Patterson AFB in the Wright brothers' hometown, brought an end to the fighting.

Serbia

EACH OF THE FORMER YUGOSLAV REPUBLICS contains a mixture of ethnic groups. Serbs were the majority in Serbia, but made up significant minorities in Bosnia and Herzegovina, Croatia, and Montenegro. Likewise, large numbers of Croats live in Serbia and in Bosnia and Herzegovina. Serbia's province of Kosovo contained a large majority of ethnic Albanians. This ethnic mixture made the breakup of Yugoslavia more difficult, because the Serb minorities in the breakaway republics and Kosovo wanted to live under Serbian rule, not that of other ethnic groups. The dictator of Yugoslavia, Slobodan Milosevic, maintained his power partly by stirring up Serbs' fears of what would happen if Yugoslavia broke up.

A *Serb* is a member of the Serb ethnic group. A *Serbian* is a resident of Serbia.

Bosnia and Herzegovina, Croatia, Kosovo, Macedonia, Montenegro, Serbia, and Slovenia

Operations *Deny Flight* and *Deliberate Force*

Combined with the *Provide Promise* effort, NATO opened *Operation Deny Flight* over Bosnia. It ran from April 1993 to December 1995. NATO forces created no-fly zones for Serbian aircraft.

US pilots in fighters such as the F-16 shot down Serbian aircraft that violated the no-fly zone. In retaliation, Serbs grabbed UN peacekeepers. So NATO launched a mission called *Operation Deliberate Force*. NATO forces used precision-guided weapons and aircraft to hit the Serbians hard. UN forces also began protecting the peacekeepers. The Serbians gave in toward the end of 1995.

Operations Allied Force and Shining Hope

Despite the end of the Bosnian war, Yugoslavia continued to be a center of conflict. In 1999 Milosevic directed Serbian forces to attack ethnic Albanians in Kosovo. Kosovo was then a province in southern Serbia.

Milosevic didn't heed NATO's warnings to stop his attacks. So NATO launched an air campaign called *Operation Allied Force* in March 1999. NATO air forces flew more than 38,000 sorties. The air campaign succeeded in forcing Milosevic to withdraw his forces from Kosovo after 78 days. No ground forces were involved.

The US Air Force marked two "firsts" in this effort. The B-2 stealth bomber engaged in combat for the first time. And the United States used its 2,000-pound GBU-31 precision weapon for the first time. In fact, the B-2 bombers dropped the GBU-31s. They caused 33 percent of the damage inflicted on the Serbs in the first eight weeks of *Operation Allied Force*.

This operation also marked the only time a stealth aircraft has been shot down in combat. An F-117 was lost in combat to Serbian/Yugoslav forces. On 27 March 1999, a Serbian missile brigade downed the F-117A with a SAM.

The pilot, Lieutenant Colonel Dale Zelko, survived and was later rescued by NATO forces. However, the wreckage of the F-117 was not promptly bombed, and the Serbians are believed to have invited Russian personnel to inspect the remains. This would compromise the US stealth technology. Part of the plane is reportedly on display in a Belgrade museum.

Humanitarian airlifts were key to the success of this campaign. US airlifts, as part of *Operation Shining Hope*, kept Albanian refugees from starving while NATO crushed the Serbian attack on Kosovo.

Milosevic was indicted as a war criminal in 2000 and tried before a United Nations court. He was charged with crimes against humanity in Kosovo, violating the laws of war in Croatia and Bosnia, and genocide in Bosnia. He died in 2006 just before the end of his trial in the Netherlands.

Operations Provide Relief and Restore Hope

Somalia, an East African country, had a severe food shortage in 1992. Its people risked starvation. Beginning in August, the United States, in support of the United Nations, airlifted food through *Operation Provide Relief*. C-141s carried the goods to Kenya, another African nation. Smaller C-130s then flew the food into Somalia.

But there was a snag. Somali warlords often stole the food before it could reach the people. These warlords fired at US cargo planes. The United States shut down *Operation Provide Relief* in 1993. But it soon launched another mission, *Operation Restore Hope*.

Restore Hope had two goals. The first was to distribute food. The second was to go after the warlords and their gangs. *Restore Hope* ended in May 1993, when the United Nations took over the relief mission.

But in mid-1993 a warlord named Mohammed Farah Aidid directed his supporters to interfere with the aid mission. They ambushed and wiped out a Pakistani convoy. During the US effort to arrest some of his top lieutenants, the firefight in Mogadishu—which you read about at the beginning of this lesson—broke out.

In response, the United States started *Operation Restore Hope II*. It airlifted combat forces back into Mogadishu, and stationed AC-130s at bases in Kenya. But many Somalis supported Aidid. The United States abandoned the effort to arrest him and sought a political solution instead. US troops left Somalia in March 1994. Aidid died in 1996 as a result of wounds suffered in battle.

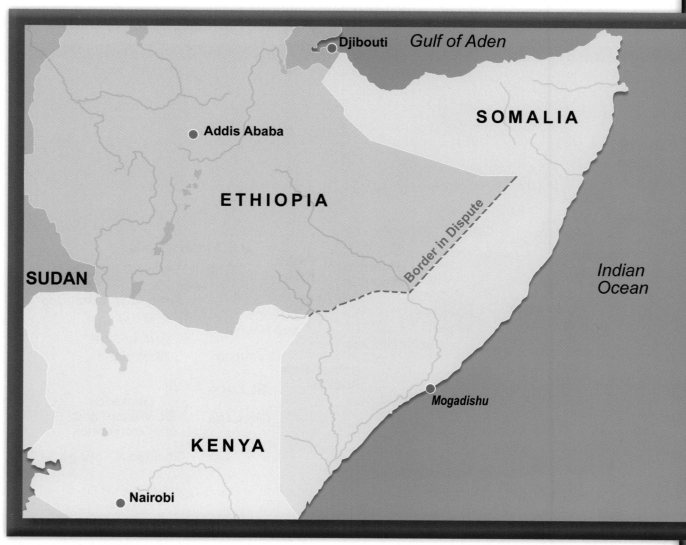

Somalia and neighboring countries in Africa

Operation Uphold Democracy

Haiti is a small country on a Caribbean island. In 1991 a military coup d'état removed its elected president, Jean-Bertrand Aristide, from office. The new leaders suppressed the Haitian people's rights. Many Haitians fled to the United States in boats or anything that would float. They tried to enter the country illegally.

Despite diplomatic efforts, by 1994 no solution was in sight. The Haitian economy was weak. More and more Haitians were trying to make the dangerous, 700-mile sea voyage to US shores. The United States drew up a plan to return Aristide to power. It was called *Operation Uphold Democracy*. In September 60 C-130s packed with US paratroopers headed toward Haiti. When the Haitian military leaders found out that US forces were headed their way, they gave up power. US troops entered Haiti peacefully.

In 1995 the United Nations took over the mission. It put a US commander in charge of UN operations in Haiti, which lasted until mid-1996.

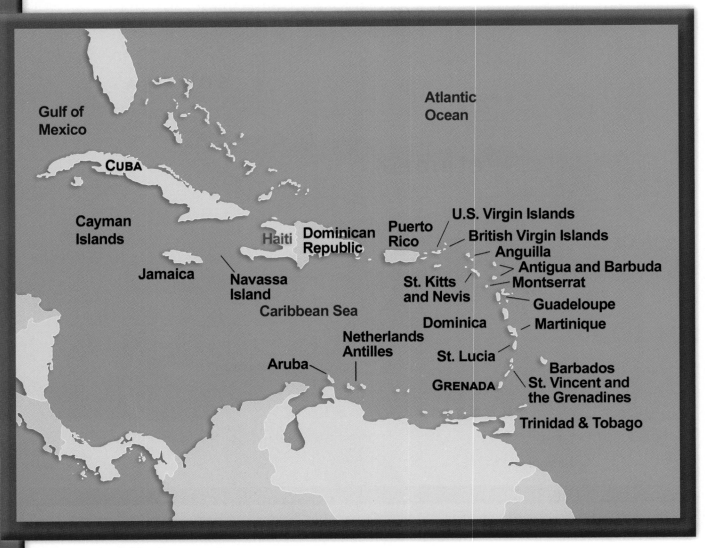

Haiti and neighboring countries

CHAPTER 5 The US Air Force Is Born

Operation Noble Eagle and NORAD

In addition to fighting terrorists overseas, Airmen have duties back home. Members of the Air National Guard, Air Force Reserve, and active Air Force serve in *Operation Noble Eagle* (ONE). Its goal is to safeguard American soil.

The North American Aerospace Defense Command (NORAD), a joint US-Canadian organization, runs ONE. As its name implies, NORAD has a big job: to defend the skies over the United States and Canada.

ONE began shortly after 11 September 2001. Within 16 months, US aircraft flew more than 27,000 sorties over American cities. They were on the lookout for suspicious aircraft, and they continue this job today. Fighters such as the F-15 Eagle or the F-16 Fighting Falcon shoot flares if they find an airplane flying in space where it is not supposed to be. For example, planes may not fly over the White House unless they have permission. If an airplane enters that airspace, Air Force fighters have the right to shoot it down if it does not respond to warnings and depart.

The tens of thousands of sorties flown under ONE include the following:

- round-the-clock combat air patrols over New York City and Washington, D.C.
- random patrols over urban areas, nuclear power plants, weapons storage facilities, and laboratories
- sorties in response to possible air threats in the United States
- air cover support for special security events such as the Winter Olympics in Utah, the World Series, the Super Bowl, space shuttle launches, United Nations general assemblies, presidential inaugurations, state funerals, and State of the Union addresses

A California Air National Guard F-16 prepares to refuel for an *Operation Noble Eagle* mission over San Francisco's Golden Gate.

Major Robert Couse-Baker/Courtesy US Air Force

Using complete sentences, answer the following questions on a sheet of paper.

1. What four kinds of targets did US forces want to aim for in *Operation Desert Storm*?

2. What were the two goals of the United States in *Operations Desert Shield* and *Desert Storm*?

3. What was the goal of *Operation Enduring Freedom* and which two groups were targeted?

4. What is the name of the operation by which the United States continues to support the elected government of Afghanistan?

5. What were the objectives of *Operation Iraqi Freedom*?

6. What is the name of the actions against Islamic State (ISIL) in Iraq and Syria?

7. What was *Operation Provide Promise*?

8. What were the goals of *Operation Restore Hope*?

APPLYING YOUR LEARNING

9. Reviewing the operations discussed in this lesson, do you think airpower alone can win a conflict? Or are ground troops always necessary as well?

This page not used

CHAPTER 6

An MQ-9 Reaper sits on a ramp in Afghanistan. The Reaper is remotely operated by pilots and sensor operators at Creech Air Force Base, Nevada.

Courtesy US Air Force

The Modern Air Force

"Despite the actions of our enemies, we must remain a moral force for good on the globe. Regardless of pressures that may come in terms of the nature of the campaign or what the enemy is doing, we can never back away from our values when we go into conflict."

General David Goldfein, Air Force Chief of Staff

The Development of Rotary-Wing Aircraft

Quick Write

After reading the vignette about Lieutenant Colonel Charles Kettles, why do you think it's important for members of a unit to know their fellow team members will support them? Is this true only for the military?

Learn About

- the development of early helicopters before World War I
- the further development of helicopters during the 1930s
- the use of helicopters in US military conflicts
- the helicopter's expanded role in military and civilian search-and-rescue operations

ON 15 MAY 1967, Soldiers from the 101st Airborne were battling hundreds of North Vietnamese in a rural riverbed near Duc Pho, South Vietnam. They were seriously outnumbered, and needed help fast. They needed helicopters to bring in reinforcements and to take the wounded to safety. Then-Major Charles Kettles volunteered his UH-1H "Hueys."

Around 9 a.m., the company of helicopters approached the landing zone. When the pilots and crew looked down, instead of a stand of green trees, they saw a wall of green enemy tracer bullets coming at them. Soldiers were killed before they could even leap off the choppers. But under withering fire, Major Kettles landed his helicopter and kept it there, exposed, so the wounded could get on and he could fly them to safety.

Kettles returned to the riverbed several times to evacuate his fellow Soldiers—all the time facing intense enemy fire and damage to his helicopter. The Army credits him with saving the lives of 44 Soldiers that day.

Kettles was originally awarded the Distinguished Service Cross for his heroism that day. He retired as a lieutenant colonel. Then on 18 July 2016, President Barak Obama upgraded the award to the Medal of Honor. On the same day, he tweeted out, "44 Americans came home because Chuck Kettles believed that we leave no man behind. That's America at our best."

Kettles dedicated his Medal of Honor to all the pilots and crew serving on his team that day. "I didn't do it by myself. There were some 74 pilots and crew members involved in this whole mission that day.... They did their job, above and beyond. So the Medal is not mine. It's theirs."

Vocabulary

- rotor
- rotary-wing aircraft
- torque
- boom
- outrigger
- medevac

Then-Major Charles Kettles standing next to a UH-1H helicopter during his second tour of duty in Vietnam in 1969

Courtesy US Army

The Development of Early Helicopters Before World War I

One of the last aircraft invented before World War I is one you can still see almost every day. You've seen these aircraft in action movies or caught a glimpse of them during the traffic report of your local television news station. They are helicopters.

Helicopters are different from the aircraft you've been studying in two important ways. First, they don't have fixed wings. Their wings rotate. Second, they take off and land vertically.

All aircraft need lift to remain in the air. Biplanes and monoplanes rely on their wings and forward motion to maintain lift. But what's to keep an aircraft in the air when it rises straight up the way a helicopter does?

Helicopters have rotors. A rotor is *a set of rotating horizontal airfoils (wings).* A rotor is very much like the propeller of a fixed-wing aircraft. Rotors are made up of blades, each of which acts as a wing. As the blades rotate, they lift the helicopter. That's why *another name for helicopters* is rotary-wing aircraft.

Rotary flight is different from fixed-wing flight. The early inventors didn't understand the forces facing the helicopter. And so it took them years to figure out how to design machines to address these forces.

The Wright brothers get most of the credit for developing the airplane. Developing the helicopter was another story. It involved several inventors in different countries and even over different centuries.

Leonardo da Vinci (1452–1519) designed a rotary flying machine (see Chapter 1, Lesson 1). In 1842 W. H. Phillips built a model of a steam-powered helicopter. But many improvements were needed to create a practical helicopter.

The first two manned attempts at helicopter flight were in 1907. Frenchman Louis Bréguet flew a helicopter that year. But he needed the help of four assistants to hold it steady. His countryman Paul Cornu also got a helicopter to lift off. Then in 1919 an American father-son pair, Emile and Henry Berliner, also built and piloted a helicopter.

The problem all these men faced can be stated in one word: torque. Torque is *a turning or twisting force.* It makes helicopters hard to balance. That's why Bréguet needed four assistants to steady his aircraft. Its rotating blades created torque. Torque means that while the blades were turning in one direction, the body of the aircraft spun in the other. Any truly successful helicopter design would have to take this into account and adjust for it somehow.

No one would find a solution for 30 years. But then aircraft designers came up with two answers. The first was to use two rotors and to make them spin in opposite directions. The second was to place a small rotor at the end of a long tail boom. A boom is *the section of the helicopter that connects the tail with the main body.* The tail rotor spins in a direction opposite that of the main rotor.

1932 Kellet K-2/K-3 Autogiro
Courtesy US Air Force

Some inventors who experimented with helicopters early in the 20th century gave up on them for a time. But 9 January 1923 marked another milestone flight. On that day, a Spanish Army pilot made the first successful flight in an autogiro. Juan de la Cierva of Spain built this aircraft. A front engine and propeller made the autogiro move forward.

But Cierva's machine had serious drawbacks. For example, it couldn't move in all directions. So during the 1930s, Cierva and other designers in Spain, France, and Germany continued to experiment.

The Frenchman Louis Bréguet was among this group. He'd turned away from helicopters, despite some early success. But by the early 1930s, he was thinking about them again. He established the Syndicate for Gyroplane Studies and hired a young engineer named René Dorand.

Bréguet didn't want to get people's hopes up too soon. He named his new aircraft the Gyroplane-Laboratoire. Using the French word for *laboratory*, he thought, would let people understand that the helicopter was experimental. His was another attempt to solve the problems of stability and control.

LESSON 1   The Development of Rotary-Wing Aircraft

The Further Development of Helicopters During the 1930s

It took years of experimenting, but by the late 1930s, aircraft designers had finally figured out how to control the helicopter in flight. They found answers to the problem of the rotor blade's torque.

The first helicopter a pilot could completely control was the Focke-Achgelis (FA-61). A German, Dr. Heinrich Focke, built it in 1937. This helicopter used the two-rotor approach to controlling torque. Its two rotors were mounted side by side on outriggers from the fuselage. An outrigger is *a frame extending laterally beyond the main structure of an aircraft*. It stabilizes the structure.

The world's first female helicopter pilot, Hanna Reitsch, demonstrated the FA-61 in 1938. She flew it inside a stadium in Berlin, Germany. She was able to hover and make 360-degree turns. She could fly backward, forward, and sideways.

The first practical helicopter, however, was Igor Sikorsky's VS-300. This design solved the problem of torque using a main rotor and a tail rotor. This is the basic design that most people picture when they hear the word *helicopter*. And as you continue through this lesson, you'll read about helicopters that have some form of this design.

The VS-300 made its first vertical takeoffs and landings in September 1939. The helicopter could carry a useful load and perform work. The pilot could control it well. The early experiments were tethered flight, or flights in which the aircraft was tied to the ground by cables. The helicopter's first free flight was 13 May 1940. Its top speed was 50 mph. It weighed 1,150 pounds.

Focke-Achgelis FA 61 in flight
Courtesy National Air and Space Museum, Smithsonian Institution, NASM 2002-19905

Even once the main problem with torque had been resolved, Sikorsky worked hard to overcome problems with vibration and control. At first, his helicopter flew "like a bucking bronco," according to an Army project officer.

Nevertheless, all later Sikorsky helicopters have been refinements of the VS-300. From this small aircraft, the helicopter has developed into the workhorse of the skies.

The first mass-production helicopter was the Sikorsky R-4. A prototype, the XR-4, made the first cross-country helicopter flight in history in 1942. It flew from Connecticut to Wright Field in Dayton, Ohio.

Igor Sikorsky and Orville Wright celebrate the first delivery of a Sikorsky XR-4 helicopter to the US government at Wright Field in Dayton, Ohio, in 1942.
Courtesy Federal Aviation Administration

The Right Stuff

Igor Sikorsky and the First Practical Helicopter

A Russian who moved to France before settling in the United States, Igor Sikorsky (1889–1972) is best known as the man who developed the first practical helicopter. But that wasn't Sikorsky's first claim to fame. He'd already made two other contributions to aviation.

A mosquito—yes, an insect—led to Sikorsky's first breakthrough. While a young flyer in the Russian Army, he produced a plane—the S-6A—that won the highest award in the Moscow air show. But on a later flight, a mosquito got caught in the fuel line, causing the engine to fail. Sikorsky had to make an emergency landing. That experience gave him the idea for an aircraft with more than one engine. This led him to build and fly the first successful four-engine aircraft, *Le Grand* (see Chapter 1, Lesson 4).

Sikorsky left his native country in 1918, after the Russian Revolution. In France, he won a contract to build a bomber for the Allies. But World War I ended soon after that. His bomber was not needed.

Sikorsky arrived in New York City in 1919. Unable to find a job in aviation, he lectured for a while. Then some friends and students who knew of his work in aviation pooled their funds to launch him in business. He formed the Sikorsky Aero Engineering Corporation.

Within a few years Sikorsky made his second major achievement. As you read in Chapter 2, Lesson 3, he designed a flying boat for mail service.

But Sikorsky still cherished a lifelong dream: to build a helicopter. When Igor was a child in Kiev, Ukraine (then part of Russia), his mother told him about Leonardo da Vinci's helicopter designs. He became fascinated by the idea of rotary-wing flight. People told him it was an impossible dream. Some of his own staff called it "Igor's nightmare."

In 1940 he achieved his dream. Today, the name Sikorsky stands for excellence in helicopters.

The Use of Helicopters in US Military Conflicts

The military first used helicopters in World War II. But the helicopter came into its own during the Korean and Vietnam wars. In both wars the US military used helicopters to carry the wounded and rescue downed pilots. They were well suited for the jungle warfare of Vietnam. There, the military used helicopters to place ground troops in battle areas and to outmaneuver enemy ground forces. Since that time, helicopters have been an important part of US military tactics.

The Helicopter in Korea

If you have one mental picture of the Korean War, it might be from the opening sequence of the long-running television series *M.A.S.H.* It featured shots of wounded Soldiers being airlifted from the front lines by helicopter. This is referred to as medevac—*medical evacuation*—service. The aircraft in that sequence were H-13 Sioux helicopters. They played an important supporting role in that series—and even more so in the war it was based on.

The H-13 was a military version of the Bell Helicopter Model 47. The Model 47 was one of the most successful helicopters of all time. Its prototype first flew on 8 December 1945, just months after the end of World War II. Production began soon after, and continued for nearly 30 years. The Model 47, in various military and civilian versions, was used for all sorts of purposes around the world.

The H-13 Sioux was the first rotary-wing craft to be delivered in the Korean peninsula. It was also the first US Army helicopter to be named after an American Indian tribe (Sioux). This practice continues today in the names of aircraft such as the Boeing AH-64 Apache and the Bell OH-58 Kiowa.

The H-13 had the classic early military helicopter design. It had a bubble canopy, providing good visibility for crew. It had the characteristic skeletal tail unit and skid undercarriage. It could seat two or three people. It had a Franklin or Lycoming engine, which drove its two-blade main rotor and two-blade tail rotor.

During the Korean War, patient litters were mounted on the exterior of the H-13 on skid racks.

Courtesy US Army

During World War II, helicopters had been used to scout or to search for submarines. But few helicopters—on either the Allied or Axis side—made it to the front lines.

That changed during the Korean War. H-13s, which had been serving as observation aircraft, were soon turned into flying ambulances.

The other primary rescue helicopter during the Korean War was the Sikorsky S-51. It could carry two crewmen plus a wounded Soldier. But there was so little room in the fuselage for the stretcher that the wounded man's legs would stick out the side of the aircraft from the knees down.

But helicopters were used in Korea for more than medevac service. The Sikorsky H-19 Chickasaw was an excellent multipurpose transport helicopter. It was used in later conflicts, as well. Versions of the H-19 have been adopted by armed forces around the world.

The H-19 had a distinctive stout appearance. Its flight deck sat on top of the passenger cabin. Sliding side doors made it easy for the troops aboard the copter to hit the ground. The cabin could carry 12 combat-ready troops or, in medevac mode, eight medical litters.

The US Air Force used the H-19 for search and rescue. The H-19 carried troops into combat but was unarmed itself. It didn't have quite the power needed to serve as an attack helicopter.

SH-19A Chickasaw air rescue helicopter
Courtesy US Air Force

The Helicopter in Vietnam

The Korean War had a relatively fixed battlefront. This meant that M.A.S.H. (Mobile Army Surgical Hospital) units could be fairly close to the action. There was a line behind which they could feel reasonably safe. Air ambulances didn't have to fly far or long to get the wounded to well-equipped field hospitals.

But Vietnam was a different kind of war. There were no clear front lines. Medevac helicopters often had to fly into battles to retrieve the wounded. Then they had to fly much greater distances than in Korea to bring the wounded to safety and medical help.

And so Vietnam would require a different kind of medevac aircraft. Fortunately, the Army had already identified one: the Bell Model 204, HU-1A (later UH-1A) "Huey."(This aircraft had an Indian nickname too: "Iroquois." But it was never much used.)

The Hueys soon became the primary medevac helicopters in Vietnam. They kicked up so much dirt as they took off with their wounded warriors that they were known by the radio call sign "Dustoff." Later versions of the Huey, such as the UH-1H, could carry three stretcher patients and a trained medic inside the cabin. Most American Hueys were in the service of the Army, but the other services also used them for medevac flights.

Air Force personnel on a combat assault mission over Southeast Asia in a UH-1 "Huey"

Sergeant Robert W. Ingianni/Courtesy US Air Force

The Right Stuff

1st Lieutenant James P. Fleming

On 26 November 1968, Lieutenant James P. Fleming and four other UH-1F helicopter pilots were returning to their base at Duc Co, South Vietnam, for refueling and rearming. Before they arrived, they received an emergency call for help from a Special Forces reconnaissance team.

The homebound force of two gunships and three transport helicopters immediately changed course and sped to the area without refueling. The six-man Special Forces team was pinned down by a large, hostile force not far from a river bank. As the gunships descended to attack the enemy positions, one was hit and downed. The remaining gunship made several passes, firing away with its miniguns, but the intense return fire from enemy machine guns continued. Low on fuel, the helicopters were being forced to leave and return to base.

Then-Captain James Fleming
Courtesy US Air Force

Lieutenant Fleming, piloting the only remaining transport helicopter, descended over the river to evacuate the team. Unable to land because of the dense foliage, he hovered just above the river with his landing skids braced against the bank. The lone gunship continued its strafing runs, but heavy enemy fire prevented the team from reaching the helicopter. The leader advised Fleming by radio to withdraw.

After pulling away, Fleming decided to make another rescue attempt before completely exhausting his fuel. He dropped down to the same spot and found that the team had managed to move closer to the river bank. The men dashed out and clambered aboard as bullets pierced the air, some smashing into the helicopter. The rescue craft and the gunship then returned safely to Duc Co, arriving with their fuel tanks nearly empty.

For this miraculous rescue, in which not a single life was lost, Fleming was awarded the Medal of Honor. He received this highest decoration for valor at the White House from President Richard M. Nixon 14 May 1970. Lieutenant Fleming remained in the Air Force, retiring in 1996 as a colonel.

The Huey did so much more than medevac, however. It became the symbol of the American involvement in Vietnam. And it's been called the most famous helicopter in the world. It's been in use in 1956, in the armed forces of the United States and many other countries. Since 1960, commercial versions of the Huey have been available too.

The UH-1 makes a distinctive loud "whomp whomp" noise. In forward flight, the tip of the advancing rotor blade moves fast enough to create a small sonic boom. For those who know aircraft, its twin-bladed rotor and rounded nose make it easy to spot.

The Huey was developed as manufacturers were shifting from piston to turbine engines. Turbine engines were lighter and more powerful, but also more expensive. The Huey was the US military's first turbine-engine helicopter.

Many variations of the Huey were produced. The Marines, worried about crashes over water, asked for and got a dual-engine Huey, for instance.

The Huey was such a success because it had the perfect combination of cabin room, speed, and ability to lift. The earlier piston engines just didn't give helicopters the power they needed for many military missions. But the Huey, with its turbine engine and other features, proved itself a rugged, reliable aircraft.

Another important helicopter in Vietnam was the Sikorsky HH-3E "Jolly Green Giant," which you read about in Lesson 3. Its long range made it invaluable in combat search-and-rescue missions.

Helicopters were the quiet stars of the Vietnam War. They found new roles to fill in the conflict. Units of helicopters transporting ground forces were referred to as *air cavalry*. This was a reminder of the fighting units on horseback from previous centuries.

The helicopter is a delicate aircraft, however, compared with fighters and bombers. It can be brought down by small arms fire. The military lost 5,000 helicopters in the war. Even so, they were very effective in the jungles of Vietnam. A helicopter could drop troops at the front lines so they wouldn't have to make long marches through thick undergrowth. It could hover while delivering supplies. In Vietnam's difficult terrain, its ability to land without a runway was more valuable than ever.

The Helicopter Since Vietnam

The Sikorsky S-70 helicopters (H-60 in military use) are the most popular family of helicopters after the Bell Hueys, which they are gradually replacing. There are a number of variants of this design. These are intended to meet the special needs of the Air Force, Army, Coast Guard, Marines, and Navy. US Customs and Border Protection and the Drug Enforcement Agency also use S-70s.

Sikorsky developed the S-70 in response to a request from the Army. Generals wanted an aircraft with better "crew survivability." This meant engines, rotors, and a transmission better able to withstand damage. It meant a crashworthy cabin "box," and an armor-plated cockpit, among other features.

The S-70 has two engines instead of just one. It has widely separated *redundant* electronic and hydraulic systems. That is, one system backs another if it fails. The S-70 has four main rotor blades. Its tail rotor is tilted at an angle that gives it some additional lift.

Sikorsky UH-60 Black Hawk

The Army's version, the UH-60 Black Hawk, first saw in combat when the United States invaded Grenada in 1983. The Army said its performance there showed the copter could still fly even after being seriously damaged. Eight years later, nearly half the Army's Black Hawks took part in the Gulf War. Only two were lost in combat. During the US mission to Somalia in 1993, though, several were lost. The Black Hawk proved vulnerable to rocket-propelled grenades fired from rooftops.

In the 1980s, the US Army started to replace the Huey with the Sikorsky UH-60 Black Hawk as a medevac aircraft. The Army wanted a helicopter that could carry more casualties at once. The Black Hawk had a larger fuselage and was faster than the Huey. These characteristics made it a valuable aircraft indeed during *Operation Desert Storm* in 1991.

US Army UH-60 Black Hawk helicopters operating in Iraq in 2010
Specialist Brandon D. Bolick/Courtesy US Army

The Black Hawk also fit in well as the Army changed its tactics for bringing the wounded to safety. Medevac helicopters no longer flew into firefights to retrieve the wounded, as they had done a generation before in Vietnam. Rather, the wounded would be brought out by the same aircraft that had delivered them to the front. Alternatively, dedicated search-and-rescue helicopters would pick up the wounded. In either case, casualties would be taken to a staging area. Some would be treated there, and from there, medevac helicopters would take the most seriously wounded to field hospitals.

The UH-60 has an unusual shape: long and low-set. It was designed to be able to fit inside a C-130 Hercules cargo plane with its rotors attached. Six can fit within a C-5 Galaxy.

Sikorsky HH-50 Pave Hawk

The HH-60 Pave Hawk is the Air Force version of the Army's UH-60 Black Hawk. It's been modified, however, for aircrew search and rescue in all weather situations. It was introduced in 1991. Its special missions are rescuing downed airmen and dropping special forces behind enemy lines. But it does more than that. It's been used in disaster rescue, notably in the US Gulf region after the hurricanes of 2005.

An Air Force HH-60 Pave Hawk takes off in a rescue exercise near Kotzebue, Alaska.

Staff Sergeant Edward Eagerton/Courtesy US Air National Guard

The Pave Hawk has a number of systems that make it distinctly an Air Force helicopter. These include night vision, forward-looking infrared, and automatic flight control. Its two engines drive two four-blade rotors. It can fly 184 mph and reach an altitude of 14,000 feet. It has room for two pilots, a flight engineer, and a gunner. Seating for passengers or room for medical litters is found in the cabin.

Boeing AH-64 Apache

Another important aircraft of the post-Vietnam period is the Boeing AH-64 Apache helicopter. The military doesn't use helicopters only for medevac or search-and-rescue missions. The Apache is designated as an attack helicopter. It officially began service in 1986. It has seen action in Panama and in the Persian Gulf region (*Operation Desert Storm*), when it took out Saddam Hussein's armored formations. More recently, the Apache has had a role in the Kosovo War as well as Iraq and Afghanistan.

But the Apache was developed in the waning years of the Cold War, to meet a perceived need in Europe. American military leaders wanted a "tank-killing" helicopter that would stand up to the rigors of ground combat in Europe, if Soviet and Warsaw Pact forces ever rolled through Germany's Fulda Gap to invade NATO territory.

That scenario never played out, fortunately. But today, despite the feats of high-altitude bombers and other fixed-wing aircraft, military planners still see helicopters like the Apache as essential to any plan for a ground battle.

AH-64 Apache helicopters
Courtesy US Army

Bronze Star for Pararescue Crew

On 3 June 2010, three American Soldiers were badly injured by the explosion of a roadside bomb in Afghanistan. A pararescue crew from the Air Force's 58th Rescue Squadron was sent to their aid.

Staff Sergeant Asher Woodhouse, Technical Sergeant Ryan Manjuck, and Technical Sergeant Jeffrey Hedglin all received the Bronze Star with valor for putting their lives at risk under enemy fire to rescue the wounded that day.

During his first deployment after recently training in pararescue, Sergeant Manjuck made an immediate impact. While under enemy fire, he provided hoist evacuations for wounded Soldiers and gave medical treatment to a critically injured patient.

Airmen congratulate Air Force Technical Sergeants Jeffery Hedglin and Ryan Manjuck, and Staff Sergeant Asher Woodhouse after they received the Bronze Star at Nellis AFB, Nevada, 13 April 2011.

Courtesy US Air Force

"I didn't really know what to expect with it being my first deployment," Sergeant Manjuck said. "I quickly realized that the training I received really helped. Every scenario we faced during our search-and-rescue missions had previously been addressed in the training I received over the last two years. Even though it was my first deployment, it really didn't feel that way."

Sergeant Hedglin acted as the Guardian Angel team leader during the incident. He organized and led the team into the high-threat combat area. Placing the lives of the wounded above his own, he managed to carry a wounded soldier more than 27 yards across open terrain while under fire to a helicopter for evacuation.

"During the incident, I was lucky to have the training that we do…," said Sergeant Hedglin. "That training helped me to know what to do and how to instinctively react in a high-stress combat situation."

Sergeant Woodhouse was able to spot and alert the aircrew of the HH-60 Pave Hawk, which was on the way to evacuate wounded personnel, of incoming surface-to-air missiles. Due to his situational awareness, the wounded individuals were safely evacuated from the hostile area.

"…we are constantly training," Sergeant Woodhouse said. "That training is what makes what we do become second nature and helps us to effectively accomplish the search-and-rescue mission."

Sergeant Woodhouse was also able to lead his element back into the hostile area to evacuate two injured Soldiers who were critically wounded by an improvised explosive device.

"Members of the rescue community and, more recently these three individuals, provide great comfort to families and military members in the fight knowing that there are such professionals willing to enter the hostile conditions to evacuate them if they are injured," said Navy Admiral Mike Mullen, chairman of the Joint Chiefs of Staff, in presenting the medals.

Even after receiving the Bronze Star, the recipients mostly gave credit to the individuals serving with them in Afghanistan.

"I'm accepting this award on behalf of the rescue community as a whole," Sergeant Hedglin said. "Without the whole rescue community working together so often, we wouldn't have the cohesiveness to be effective in our mission to save lives. It's humbling to be able to hear about my brethren in the rescue community and how they helped save people's lives."

Sikorsky MH-53 Pave Low

The MH-53 helicopters were originally HH-53 "Super Jolly Green Giants" used by the US Air Force in the Southeast Asia War. Over the years, however, they received many upgrades and improvements. After the 1960s, their skins were completely reworked. Their engines and rotors were also replaced. Along with these improvements came a new designation, MH-53 (*M* for Multi-mission and *H* for helicopter).

The most significant enhancement to the Super Jollies was the Pave Low program, which modified them for operating at night or during bad weather. Equipped with forward-looking infrared (FLIR) sensors, inertial global positioning systems (GPS), radar navigation systems, and terrain-following and terrain-avoidance radar, the MH-53 could fly clandestine or secret, low-level missions in any weather—day or night.

The MH-53M Pave Low IV has a system that greatly increased the aircraft's capabilities. This system gave the aircrew instant access to the total battlefield situation on a color, digital map screen that was compatible with night vision goggles.

In 2008 the Air Force Special Operations Command (AFSOC) retired the MH-53 from active service.

Sikorsky MH-53M Pave Low IV on display at the National Museum of the US Air Force

Courtesy US Air Force

Bell V-22 Osprey: Unlike Any Aircraft in the World

The V-22 Osprey is a joint-service combat aircraft that can fill many roles. It uses tiltrotor technology to combine the vertical abilities of a helicopter with the speed and range of a fixed-wing aircraft. With its rotors in vertical position, it can take off, land, and hover like a helicopter. Once airborne, it can convert to a turboprop airplane capable of high-speed, high-altitude flight. This combination results in global reach capabilities that allow the V-22 to fill an operational need unlike any other aircraft.

The Marines' MV-22 was the first to reach full operational capabilities in 2007.

The Air Force CV-22 was delivered to Air Force Special Operations Command's 1st Special Operations Wing at Hurlburt Field, Florida, becoming operational in 2008.

A CV-22 Osprey prepares to land as part of a training mission in northern New Mexico.

Courtesy US Air Force

A CV-22 Osprey over the canyons in northern New Mexico

Staff Sergeant Markus Maier/Courtesy US Air Force

A Life Net Medical Life Flight Evacuation Helicopter sits on the helipad at Lower Keys Medical Center in Key West, Florida.

Chuck Wagner/Shutterstock

The Helicopter's Expanded Role in Military and Civilian Search-and-Rescue Operations

Helicopters are used for medical transport, civilian police work, and to broadcast news and highway-traffic reports.

The National Park Service Branch of Aviation uses helicopters as well as fixed-wing aircraft in a broad range of programs within the parks. These include firefighting, law enforcement, resource management, and backcountry patrol.

Similarly, the US Forest Service relies on helicopters, particularly to fight fires. "The Forest Service uses tools in the air to manage fire on the ground," as the saying goes.

Helicopters also play important roles in other sectors, such as the construction, timber, and offshore oil industries.

But perhaps nowhere do helicopters play a more crucial role than in search-and-rescue work. The Coast Guard relies on them to save fishermen and sailors in distress at sea. In the floods after Hurricane Katrina that hit the Gulf Coast in 2005, the Coast Guard, Air Force, and other agencies used helicopters to rescue more than 30,000 people.

Helicopter crews flew damage assessment teams over flooded areas so that officials could see how bad things were as well.

In May 2006, President George W. Bush honored the Coast Guard for its response efforts. Citing the thousands of Coast Guard personnel who took part, Bush spoke of the operation as "one of the finest hours in the Coast Guard's 216-year history." The president added, "When Americans were at their most desperate, they looked to the skies for help, and they knew their prayers were answered when they saw the rescue choppers from the United States Coast Guard."

There would be a sequel to this story. And once again, the Coast Guard and its copters would play a strong supporting role.

In August 2016, Baton Rouge, Louisiana, was hit by some of the worst flooding in the city's history. More than 10 local rivers reached flood stage.

It was all the more poignant because so many people there had come to Baton Rouge as refugees from New Orleans after losing everything during Hurricane Katrina in 2005. These people had fled to what they thought was safer ground and rebuilt their lives. And now they had to start over again.

But as in the aftermath of Katrina, the Coast Guard was there. Teams in boats as well as helicopters rescued 245 people and 71 pets. Most of the rescues involved the elderly, or infants and young children. In some cases people were plucked off their rooftops. The Coast Guard also assisted more than 3,000 people in distress. Helicopters from the Louisiana National Guard and the Louisiana State Police flew food and water to motorists stranded along Interstate 12.

One grateful woman, who clearly felt she owed her life to the Coast Guard swimmer who whisked her into the helicopter that took her to safety, said later, "Because of him I get to celebrate weddings, births of grandchildren, great grandchildren...."

Coast Guard performing a rescue demonstration at Seafair on Lake Washington 5 August 2007

Philipe Ancheta/Shutterstock

Using complete sentences, answer the following questions on a sheet of paper.

1. What problem did all early helicopter designers face?

2. What are two solutions to the problem of torque?

3. Who was Juan de la Cierva and what did he accomplish?

4. What did Dr. Heinrich Focke accomplish?

5. Who was Hanna Reitsch and what did she do?

6. When did Igor Sikorsky's VS-300 make its first takeoffs and landings?

7. What was the first rotary-wing aircraft to be introduced into the Korean War?

8. Why did Vietnam require a different kind of medevac aircraft from Korea?

9. Why does the S-70 have an unusual shape?

10. What are five ways helicopters are used, besides military work?

11. After Hurricane Katrina, how many people were rescued using helicopters?

12. In which Louisiana city hard hit by flooding in August 2016 did helicopters rescue people?

APPLYING YOUR LEARNING

13. If you had to choose between learning to fly a helicopter and learning to fly a fixed-wing aircraft, which aircraft would you pick and why?

This page not used

The Significance of Stealth Aircraft

Quick Write

_____

_____

If you had been an American military planner in 1982, what lessons do you think would you have drawn from the Israeli experience with drones in the Bekaa Valley?

Learn About

- the development of stealth aircraft
- the development of precision weapons
- the development of unmanned aerial vehicles (UAVs)

FOR MUCH OF THE FIRST HUNDRED YEARS of aviation, the US military varied in its enthusiasm for unmanned flight. During both world wars, the US sought ways to deliver bombs without putting American crews at risk. Experiments with unmanned aircraft went on. But after both wars, interest waned.

This pattern continued through the 20th century. It held even after episodes like the shooting down of Francis Gary Powers's U-2 over the Soviet Union in 1962. This had made some military planners feel manned surveillance flights were too risky. But the United States continued largely to ignore the potential for unmanned flight.

The turning point came in 1982, however. Israel launched a volley of unmanned decoy aircraft in Lebanon's Bekaa Valley. The valley was protected by Syrian air defenses. The Syrians fell for the trick. They fired their surface-to-air missiles back at the Israelis. This let the Israelis know just where each launch site was. The Israelis then moved decisively to destroy the Syrian air defenses.

It was a stunning victory. It got American attention. US defense officials suddenly saw the potential of unmanned aircraft.

The Development of Stealth Aircraft

As you read in Chapter 5, Lesson 4, *stealth technology*—also called low-observable technology—goes back to the early 1970s. That's when an important study came out from DARPA—the Defense Advanced Research Projects Agency. DARPA is a government agency whose mission is "to make pivotal investments in breakthrough technologies for national security."

What the study showed was how much US military aircraft were at risk of detection and attack. Military planners had run war games modeling a possible Soviet invasion of Western Europe through the Fulda Gap in Germany. These war games suggested that if Soviet forces ever actually did invade, US and NATO forces would have trouble fighting them off.

The vulnerability the war games uncovered was partly the result of US adversaries getting better air defenses. They effectively combined the use of radar-guided surface-to-air missiles (SAMs) and air-launched radar-guided missiles, for instance.

But was it also partly the result of aircraft themselves having distinctive signatures, or *recognizable profiles and characteristics*. Their engines gave off heat signatures that adversaries could detect. The shapes of the planes were recognizable. And to a certain extent, their sophisticated electronic systems themselves made aircraft easier to track. (It's not unlike the way you can be tracked more easily if you're carrying your cellphone with you.)

After this study, it was clear that US defense planners needed some radical new ideas. The idea they decided to pursue was high-stealth aircraft.

Vocabulary

- low-observable technology
- signatures
- classified
- fifth generation
- reverse engineering
- drone
- unmanned aerial vehicles
- loiter time
- expeditionary teams

And so DARPA set out to develop some new strategies and technologies. They wanted to make US aircraft harder for enemy radar to "see." Low observable technology does this by reducing as much as possible the signatures of aircraft, vehicles, and other military assets. Researchers considered how these assets look to adversaries, how they sound, and how they show up on radar and sensor screens. They even considered the amount of heat that aircraft generated. This mattered because new infrared imaging displays let adversaries see that heat. The result of all this research was the modern stealth aircraft.

Every part of a stealth plane is designed to hide it from detection. Manufacturers use radar-absorbent materials, infrared shielding, exhaust cooling and shaping, and better ways to disperse heat. They seek to reduce visual signatures. They use special windshield coatings. The plane's paint can absorb and deflect radar pulses. Its shape cloaks the aircraft as well. Many details about stealth materials and design are classified—*withheld from public knowledge for reasons of national security.*

The stealth ability allows aircraft to undertake dangerous missions more safely. They can run reconnaissance without being caught. A stealth aircraft can bomb an enemy with little chance of being spotted, especially at night. Imagine if the Germans had been able to escape radar as they approached the British Isles in 1941. The Battle of Britain, and perhaps World War II, might have ended differently.

As you read in the last chapter, the first operational stealth aircraft was the F-117 Nighthawk. A few years later the B-2 bomber followed. The F-22 Raptor stealth fighter is the first air superiority fighter completely designed from stealth technology. The F-35 Lightning II stealth fighter, which you'll read about in the next lesson, will be next to join the Air Force fleet.

Lockheed Martin F-22 Raptor

The F-22 is both stealthy and maneuverable. It can fly long distances at supersonic speeds. It is effective against both other aircraft and ground targets. The aircraft is jointly produced: Lockheed Martin builds the forward fuselage and does final assembly. Boeing builds the wings and back fuselage. Pratt & Whitney supplies the engines.

An F-22 does a flyby in Dubai, United Arab Emirates, in 2009.
vaalaa/Shutterstock

The F-22 carries a 20-millimeter cannon and several Sidewinder air-to-air missiles. Its main internal weapons bays can hold up to six air-to-air missiles or two air-to-ground missiles and two 1,000-lb. bombs. It can fly at a top speed of Mach 2, and has a range of 1,850 miles. The F-22's sophisticated sensors allow it to identify and shoot down hostile aircraft before the enemy detects it.

The Air Force took delivery of the first F-22 in 2005. By the time production ended in 2012, 187 operational aircraft had been built. For a while, the aircraft experienced some operational problems related to pilots' oxygen supply. Lockheed Martin has since installed new equipment to fix the issue. The plane first saw combat in 2014 in Syria.

Russia's Sukhoi T-50/PAK FA Stealth Fighter

The Russian Sukhoi T-50 is meant to compete directly with the F-22 Raptor. Its manufacturer is Sukhoi OKB. This is a Russian aircraft maker that dates back to World War II.

When the T-50 is deployed, the United States will no longer have a monopoly on "fifth generation" stealth fighters. There is no precise definition of this term. But generally, fifth generation refers to *fighter aircraft using the latest technology as of 2016*. This means the latest aviation technology and radar-absorbing materials, as well as cutting-edge weaponry.

American experts see the PAK-FA as a worthy competitor to the Raptor. The PAK-FA will fly high and fast. That will give its missiles an extra boost at launch. And that, in turn, will give those missiles a much bigger range than otherwise.

The first T-50 prototype had its maiden flight in 2010. News reports suggest some slippage in the original timetable for serial production of the fighter. At this writing, production is expected sometime in 2017 or 2018.

India has worked with Russia on this aircraft and hopes to have its own version of the PAK-FA eventually.

A Sukhoi T-50 Russian stealth fighter does a fly-by at a 2011 air show in Zhukovsky, Russia.

Fasttailwind/Shutterstock

China's Chengdu J-20 Stealth Fighter

Beijing's answer to the F-22 Raptor made its public debut on 1 November 2016. That's when two of China's new J-20 stealth fighters made passes over Airshow China. This show takes place every other year. It was held in Zhuhai, China, 35 miles west of Hong Kong. It's often the place where China shows off new military hardware.

The J-20 is considered a big step forward in making the Chinese air force a Pacific power. As you read in Chapter 5, Lesson 5, Serbian/Yugoslav forces shot down an F-117 in 1999. The Chinese may have used reverse engineering of the F-117 to build their new J-20 fighter. Reverse engineering means *reproducing someone else's product after taking it apart and studying it carefully.* Wreckages of enemy aircraft shot down in battle can offer opportunities for reverse engineering.

Shenyang J-31 "Gyrfalcon" Stealth Fighter

Another fifth generation fighter being developed by China is the Shenyang J-31. Although not much is known about Chinese military weapons production, this fighter looks very similar to the US Air Force's F-22.

Some experts speculate that this fighter will be deployed as a naval fighter, based on the growing Chinese aircraft carrier fleet. China has stated that this aircraft is intended for export sales to other countries and not its own military. The aircraft is expected to reach operational status by 2018. Some countries have already expressed interest in buying it.

The J-31 stealth fighter is presented for the first time publicly at Airshow China 2014.
plavevski/Shutterstock

An MQ-1 Predator armed with Hellfire missiles flies a combat mission over southern Afghanistan.

Lieutenant Colonel Leslie Pratt/Courtesy US Air Force

The Development of Precision Weapons

Among the other modern weapons the Air Force has used in recent conflicts are precision weapons. Precision weapons are also known as *precision-guided weapons*, or PGMS. They are so accurate that they can be placed within feet of their targets.

Precision weapons are the wave of the future, because they can keep US forces far from combat. This helps keep US casualties down.

The air-to-surface Hellfire missile is one of the precision weapons used in Afghanistan. The MQ-1 Predator delivers the Hellfire. The Predator is a drone—*an unmanned aircraft*—that a pilot controls remotely. After the pilot has fired the missile, sensor operators guide the missiles to their targets.

Precision weapons have also played a large role in Iraq. About 70 percent of all weapons used in *Operation Iraqi Freedom* were of the precision type. These included the GBU-38 and GBU-39. GBU stands for *guided-bomb unit.*

The GBU-38 went into action for the first time in 2004, when it was used to bomb a terrorist meeting in central Iraq. F-16 fighters delivered those GBU-38s.

An Airman aligns a GBU-38 precision bomb at Bagram Air Base, Afghanistan.

Master Sergeant Demetrius Lester/Courtesy US Air Force

Weighing 500 pounds, they are smaller than some other bombs. But the GBU-38's size and accuracy let the military target a particular building without seriously damaging surrounding buildings. This precision approach puts nearby civilians at less risk. The US military tries to avoid civilian deaths when fighting in crowded areas such as Baghdad.

German "Fritz X" Guided Bomb on display at the National Museum of the US Air Force

Ken LaRock/Courtesy US Air Force

VB-1 Azon Guided Bomb on display at the National Museum of the US Air Force

Courtesy US Air Force

The US Air Force used the GBU-39 in combat for the first time on 5 October 2006 in support of ground troops in Iraq. At 250 pounds, it is the smallest guided bomb the Air Force has. F-15Es employ this weapon, which can strike within six feet of a target from 60 miles away.

A Brief History of Precision-Guided Munitions

Precision weapons have been around since World War II. Nazi Germany became the first country to use them. Its Fritz X PGM sank the Italian battleship *Roma* in 1943. The Italian fleet was on its way to surrender to the British, and the Germans wanted to prevent this.

The US experimented with many different types of PGMs. Most did not see combat. One that did, though, was the VB-1 Azon. The US successfully used it in Europe and in China, Burma, and India— mostly against bridges.

The Air Force used two guided bombs in Korea, also primarily against bridges: the VB-3 Razon and the VB-13 Tarzon. An aircraft would drop the bombs. Then the bombardier would use radio control to guide them by sight to their target.

Bombardiers could control the Razon and Tarzon bombs in two directions, or *axes*. They could control their *range* (up or down) and *azimuth* (left or right). Each bomb also carried a flare to make it easier to see after release.

The Air Force had mixed results with these two bombs in Korea. But they were the forerunners of more-widespread use of precision weapons in the future.

Real progress in the development of precision weapons came during the Vietnam War. In fact, despite their early problems, PGMs revolutionized the air war in Southeast Asia.

Early on, the Air Force used radio-guided AGM-12 Bullpup missiles. They had just a 250-pound warhead, however—too lightweight to do real damage to a target. The Air Force also had the GBU-8 and AGM-62 Walleye bombs. They had television guidance. But they had trouble distinguishing their targets. They were also too expensive or too small for targets like large bridges.

In 1968, however, the Air Force tested the BOLT-117 in combat. It was the world's first laser-guided bomb (LGB). It marked a major leap forward in technology.

The BOLT-117 had a hand-held or pod-mounted laser designator, or indicator. This lit up a target with a laser beam. A seeker head in the bomb then guided it to where the laser pointed. The BOLT-117's success led to the more powerful GBU-10 Paveway I, a conventional bomb with a laser-guidance kit attached.

BOLT-117 laser-guided bomb on display at the National Museum of the US Air Force

Courtesy US Air Force

Almost half of all LGBs dropped in Southeast Asia directly hit their targets. Most others hit within 25 feet. By the war's end, laser guidance kits turned standard bombs into *smart bombs*, 100 times as effective as free-fall, unguided bombs.

The Air Force continued to develop precision munitions through the 1970s and 1980s. Then during *Operation Desert Storm* in 1991, the public became aware of these weapons' abilities. Suddenly everyone knew what a smart bomb was.

Since then, PGMs have only become more effective. Weapons designers have found more ways to guide munitions to their targets. New types of targeting sensors can be found even in handheld ground systems.

Improved targeting means that weapons can be smaller but just as effective. And if bombs are smaller, more will fit onto a single aircraft, allowing it to strike more targets. Some new bombs even have pop-out wings that let them fly long distances independent of the aircraft delivering them. This lets the aircraft and its crew stay outside the range of enemy air defenses.

Air-Launched Cruise Missiles

In February 1974, the Air Force started development and flight-testing of the prototype AGM-86A air-launched cruise missile. The 86A model did not go into production. Instead, in January 1977, the Air Force began full-scale development of the AGM-86B, which greatly enhanced the capabilities of B-52s and B-1s while helping the United States maintain a strategic deterrent.

Although initially designed to carry only nuclear weapons, in June 1986 a limited number of AGM-86B missiles were converted to carry a high-explosive warhead and an internal global positioning system (GPS). These were redesignated as the AGM-86C. This modification also replaced the B model's terrain-following guidance system and combined a GPS capability with the existing inertial-navigation computer system.

Boeing AGM-86B (ALCM) being prepared for display at the National Museum of the US Air Force

Courtesy US Air Force

The small, winged AGM-86B/C/D missile is powered by a turbofan jet engine that propels it at sustained subsonic speeds. After launch, the missile's folded wings, tail surfaces and engine inlet deploy, allowing the missile to fly up to 1,500 miles to reach its target. The AGM-86 flies using an onboard GPS coupled with its inertial navigation system. This allows the missile to guide itself to the target with pinpoint accuracy.

The AGM-86C/D became operational in January 1991 at the onset of *Operation Desert Storm*. Seven B-52s from Barksdale AFB, Louisiana, launched 35 missiles at designated launch points to attack high-priority targets in Iraq. These "round-robin" missions marked the beginning of the air campaign for Kuwait's liberation. They were the longest known aircraft combat sorties up to that time (more than 14,000 miles and 35 hours of flight).

In 1987, the General Dynamics AGM129A advanced cruise missile (ACM) was introduced to provide the Air Force with a long range, highly survivable, strategic standoff weapon. The ACM uses laser sensor updates to give it high navigation accuracy.

Stealth technology gives it a low radar cross-section and increased chance to penetrate enemy defenses. The distinctive forward swept wing is an example of the application of stealth technology. A B52H bomber can carry up to 12 ACMs, allowing the bomber to attack multiple targets without having to enter enemy airspace.

General Dynamics AGM-129A being prepared for display at the National Museum of the US Air Force
Courtesy US Air Force

The US Navy also has developed cruise missiles that can be launched from ships and submarines. Tomahawk sea-launched cruise missiles are designed to fly at extremely low altitudes at high subsonic speeds. Their guidance systems are similar to those the Air Force uses. The Tomahawk's first operational use was in *Operation Desert Storm*, 1991, with immense success. The missile has since been used successfully in several other conflicts.

The Development of Unmanned Aerial Vehicles (UAVs)

General Henry H. "Hap" Arnold made a startling prediction at the end of World War II: "We have just won a war with a lot of heroes flying around in planes," he said. "The next war may be fought by airplanes with no men in them at all...."

His prediction didn't come true exactly as he stated it. Since World War II, the United States has fought in Korea, Vietnam, Iraq, and Afghanistan, among other places. And it has done so with plenty of heroes flying around in planes.

But events are certainly moving in the direction of Arnold's prophecy. The way wars are fought is changing. The conflicts in Iraq and Afghanistan sparked a revolution in unmanned aviation. But that revolution was made possible by a group of critical technical advancements. These include systems that automatically stabilize an aircraft, remote control, and the ability to connect to satellites. All this has led to a great demand for unmanned aircraft systems (UAS).

Unmanned aircraft, or unmanned aerial vehicles (UAVs), may be the wave of the future. But they go back to very early days of aviation. In fact, the revolution in unmanned aviation noted above was made possible by pioneering work done over the century before.

Charles Kettering, along with Orville Wright, built one of the first unmanned aerial vehicles in 1918. Nicknamed the Kettering Bug, it's generally regarded as the first practical example of an unmanned aircraft. It was a small biplane powered by a four-cylinder engine and guided by gyroscopes. It also had a barometer and a mechanical "computer."

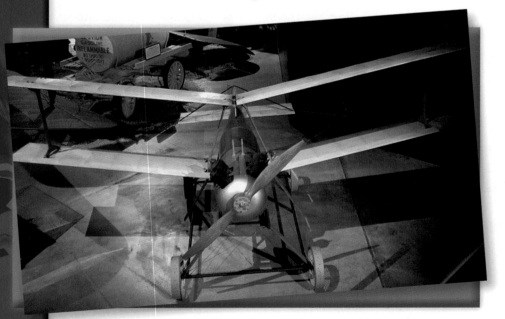

Kettering Aerial Torpedo "Bug" on display at the National Museum of the US Air Force

Courtesy US Air Force

This computer would count engine revolutions as a way to gauge distance. Then it would power down the engine and jettison the wings of the "bug" at a preset point. This was calculated before launch on the basis of wind speed and direction. Its wings gone, the fuselage would then crash into its intended target to deliver its payload. Built during the final months of World War I, the Kettering Bug was never used in actual combat, however.

After the war ended, US military interest in drones fell off sharply. Civilian hobbyists picked up the slack, though. Among these was British-born movie actor Reginald Denny. His career also included service as a World War I Royal Flying Corps observer and gunner, and later a stunt pilot. During the early 1930s, he grew interested in radio control. He built his own radio-controlled model airplane. He even opened up a shop on Hollywood Boulevard. On the eve of World War II, his Radioplane company won a sizable contract from the Army to produce drone aircraft.

During World War II, the United States tried to deliver bombs by means of unpiloted bombers. One such effort was *Operation Aphrodite*. It used specially modified B-17 Flying Fortresses and other planes. Pilots would fly the bombers partway to the target, arm the explosives, pass radio control to a "mother ship," and then bail out in parachutes. The personnel on the mother ship were supposed to guide the drone the rest of the way to the target. It never worked according to plan, however, and many crew died. Among those killed was Joseph Kennedy Jr., President John F. Kennedy's older brother.

Today's unmanned aerial vehicles and unmanned aerial systems were built on the foundation of these 20th-century pioneers. The following are some of the most important unmanned aircraft currently in use.

MQ-1B Predator

The MQ-1B Predator can be traced to that Israeli victory you read about at the beginning of this lesson. That episode reawakened US interest in acquiring unmanned aircraft systems. The Predator is an armed, multi-mission, medium-altitude, long-endurance, remotely piloted aircraft (RPA). It collects intelligence, and it also launches precision weapons.

The Predator has a long loiter time. Loiter time refers to a *combat aircraft's ability to stay aloft near its target while waiting to strike*. The Predator's missions include intelligence, surveillance, reconnaissance, close air support, combat search and rescue, and precision strike. The Predator is uniquely qualified for irregular warfare operations.

A Predator system consists of four sensor- and weapon-equipped aircraft, a ground control station, a Predator Primary Satellite Link, and spare equipment, along with operations and maintenance crews. The Predator can be taken apart and put into a freight container and shipped via C-130 Hercules transport aircraft.

An MQ-1 Predator armed with a Hellfire missile flies a training mission.
Courtesy US Air Force

MQ-9 Reaper

Like the Predator, the MQ-9 Reaper is an armed, multi-mission, medium-altitude long-endurance, remotely piloted aircraft. But the Reaper is larger and more heavily armed. And its priorities are different. The Reaper's primary mission is attacking targets. Intelligence collection comes second.

MQ-9 Reaper
Master Sergeant Dennis Henry/Courtesy US Air Force

A sensor operator and pilot fly an unmanned aerial vehicle from Creech AFB, Nevada.
Staff Sergeant N.B./Courtesy US Air Force

The Reaper has a particularly strong set of visual sensors. These help it with targeting. They include an infrared sensor, color/monochrome daylight TV camera, image-intensified TV camera, laser range finder/designator, and laser illuminator. Each of these sensors produces full-motion video that can be viewed as a separate stream or combined with the others.

The Reaper's laser range finder and designator precisely designates targets for laser-guided munitions. The Reaper can fire four laser-guided AGM-114 Hellfire missiles.

In its secondary mission of intelligence gathering, the MQ-9 helps support a range of operations. These include coastal and border surveillance, weapons tracking, enforcing embargoes, disaster assistance, and anti-drug operations.

Like the Predator, the Reaper can be taken apart and packed into a single shipping container for deployment anywhere worldwide on a C-130 Hercules.

The Reaper uses what is called a *remote split operations concept*. That is, some of its functions are controlled in the forward operating location—in Iraq, for instance. Take-off and landing of the unmanned system are typically handled from the forward location. Personnel based in the continental United States—at Creech AFB, Nevada—control the rest of the mission.

An RQ-4 Global Hawk lands at Misawa AFB, Japan.

Staff Sergeant Nathan Lipscomb/Courtesy US Air Force

RQ-4 Global Hawk

The RQ-4 Global Hawk is a high-altitude, long-endurance aircraft. A remote crew of three flies it. It provides global all-weather, day or night intelligence, surveillance, and reconnaissance (ISR). Global Hawk's mission is to support all US military forces anywhere around the world, in peace or war. Global Hawk offers imagery intelligence, signals intelligence, and moving target indicator (MTI) sensors.

The Global Hawk can fly at more than 60,000 feet, and for longer than 30 hours at a stretch. In 2014, a Global Hawk flew a 34.3-hour flight. This set the endurance record for the longest unrefueled flight by a US Air Force aircraft.

In 2016 the Air Force brought back "flying sergeants" for the first time since sergeants were trained to fly in World War II. These pilot-qualified noncommissioned officers (NCOs) were needed to help meet the shortage of trained officers to fly the Global Hawk.

RQ-11B Raven

The RQ-11B Raven is a "back-packable" system. It's of a type known as *man-portable UAVs*, meaning a person can carry it. The Raven provides target information for troops in the field and helps them know what is going on around them. This is called *situational awareness*. The Raven system includes two aircraft, each weighing less than five pounds and with a wingspan of 4.5 feet, plus a ground control unit with a remote video terminal and support equipment. The system includes an electro-optical camera and an infrared camera. It takes two specially trained Airmen to operate each Raven system. They can control it manually, or it can travel on its own along a preplanned route. The Raven is launched by hand. It flies 150 to 500 feet above the ground and can stay up for 80 minutes.

An Airman prepares to launch an RQ-11 Raven at Kirkuk Air Base, Iraq.

Senior Master Sergeant Don Senger/Courtesy US Air Force

The Raven has been in use since 2004 and is now used by all the service branches. The system has proven itself in combat in Iraq and Afghanistan, as well as other areas of conflict.

Scan Eagle

The Scan Eagle provides reconnaissance, surveillance, and target acquisition for Air Force security forces expeditionary teams—*teams sent for operations overseas*. It's classed as a small unmanned aircraft system: a Group 2 Small UAS. It includes four air vehicles plus a ground control station, remote video terminal, and a launch and recovery system. Two specially trained Airmen plus two maintenance personnel operate the Scan Eagle.

Scan Eagle aircraft are launched from a catapult and retrieved by the Skyhook system. This uses a hook on the edge of the wingtip to catch a rope hanging from a 30- to 50-foot pole. The Scan Eagle needs no runway for either launch or recovery.

A Scan Eagle launches from a catapult.

Courtesy US Air Force

Scan Eagle air vehicles have a wingspan of a little more than 10 feet. They weigh a bit less than 40 lbs. And their two-stroke engines have less horsepower than a typical walk-behind lawn mower. But they fly at an altitude of 16,000 feet and can remain aloft for more than 20 hours. Their day-night cameras and thermal imagers make them suited to operations around the clock.

Boeing originally developed the system at the request of the Marine Corps, as it sought ways to protect Marines deployed in Iraq.

Boeing X-45A J-UCAS

The Boeing X-45, had it gone into production, would have taken unmanned military aircraft even further than any of the aircraft you've just read about. The X-45 was part of the Boeing Joint Unmanned Combat Air System (J-UCAS). As that name suggests, it was meant to go into actual combat without a pilot or crew aboard.

The J-UCAS program began in 1998. It was a joint effort of DARPA, the Air Force, and the Navy. The program was meant to demonstrate that unmanned aircraft could knock out enemy air defenses, conduct surveillance, and execute precision strikes. The J-UCAS needed to be technically feasible, of course. But it also needed to prove its utility and value.

The X-45 was the first aircraft of its type. It was specifically designed for 21st-century combat operations within a networked system. The X-45 was a swept-wing stealthy jet. It landing gear retracted fully. Its skin was made of a fiber-reinforced epoxy composite. It had two internal weapons bays in its fuselage.

By 2005, the two X-45 demonstration vehicles (prototypes) had successfully concluded a series of flight tests. The next year 2006, they were packed up and shipped off to museums.

Boeing X-45A J-UCAS on display in the Research and Development Gallery at the National Museum of the US Air Force

Courtesy US Air Force

Northrop Grumman X-47 Pegasus

The X-47 was a Navy aircraft similar to the X-45. Northrop Grumman created the X-47 to help the Navy find out which fighter-sized tailless unmanned aircraft it could use on aircraft carriers. The idea was to launch unmanned fighters from carriers and send them off on attack missions.

Northrop Grumman X-47B aboard the aircraft carrier USS *Harry S. Truman*.

Courtesy US Navy

In August 2014 the X-47B made aviation history. It became the first-ever autonomous unmanned aircraft to be launched from and recovered on a carrier deck. Then in April 2015, the aircraft made history again. It successfully completed the first-ever autonomous aerial refueling of an unmanned aircraft.

By February 2016, though, the Navy seemed to have changed course. It canceled X-47 program.

Instead, the Navy will commit a relatively small sum to developing an unmanned aerial tanker. This new carrier-based aerial-refueling system will borrow from the technologies that made the X-47 successful in its test flights. CBARS is seen as a "combat multiplier." It would help extend the range of Navy fighters.

The X-47 still has advocates, though. They think the United States needs an unmanned fighter that can take off from an aircraft carrier. When Navy officials were ready to send their two prototypes off to a museum, as was done to the X-45s, congressional backlash forced them to reverse course.

Although both the X-45 and X-47 programs have ended for now, Air Force and Navy planners learned a great deal from both programs.

✔ CHECKPOINTS

Lesson 2 Review

Using complete sentences, answer the following questions on a sheet of paper.

1. What did a DARPA study in the early 1970s show about military aircraft?

2. Which aircraft became the first air superiority fighter completely designed from stealth technology?

3. What issue with the F-22 did Lockheed Martin have to fix by installing new equipment?

4. Which country was the first to use precision weapons, and in what year?

5. What was the BOLT-117?

6. By the end of the war in Southeast Asia, how much more effective were smart bombs than unguided bombs?

7. In which two countries have conflicts sparked a revolution in unmanned aviation?

8. What was the Kettering Bug?

9. Where are the personnel based who largely control MQ-9 Reaper missions?

APPLYING YOUR LEARNING

10. Do you agree with General Arnold that the United States will eventually win wars using planes without pilots? In a short paragraph explain why you would agree or disagree.

The Air Force of the Future

The F-35 Lightning II Joint Strike Fighter, KC-46 Pegasus Aerial Tanker, and B-21 Raider Global Strike Bomber

As technology evolves, the Air Force must update its fleet to make sure the United States has the best aircraft available. Given the time it takes to design, test, and build today's sophisticated planes, planners are always looking ahead to the next model. The following are some of the aircraft expected become operational soon or that are in the planning stage.

Lockheed Martin F-35A/B/C Lightning II

The F-35 Joint Strike Fighter is an unprecedented—and controversial—attempt to develop one aircraft to replace several different planes. The Air Force F-35A is intended to replace the F-16 and A-10 fighters. The Navy and Marine Corps F-35C variant is intended to replace the aging F-18 fighter.

F-35A Lightning IIs preparing to refuel
Staff Sergeant Madelyn Brown/Courtesy US Air Force

It can operate from any Navy aircraft carrier. The Marine Corps F-35B variant is a vertical takeoff and landing fighter that will replace the AV-8B Harrier. A fifth-generation aircraft, the F-35 aims to provide air superiority, defense, suppression of enemy air defenses, and close air support of ground forces.

In addition, several foreign countries, including Australia, Britain, Denmark, Israel, Italy, the Netherlands, Norway, Singapore, and Turkey are buying the F-35. Three different versions are being produced to meet the requirements of different services and nations.

The F-35 has the most advanced sensors yet on a fighter aircraft. Equipment includes a helmet-mounted display system that shows on the visor all the targeting and intelligence information a pilot needs to complete the mission. Besides Lockheed Martin, Northrup Grumman and British Aerospace are participating in production. Currently, the US military plans to buy up to 2,400 F-35s. Price and budget considerations may affect how many are actually purchased.

An F-35B Lightning II demonstrates vertical takeoff at the Royal International Air Tattoo at Royal Air Force Fairford, Gloucestershire, England.

SpaceKris/Shutterstock

A KC-46A (*right*) undergoes testing of its own refueling system. Here it receives fuel from a KC-10 extender, with a KC-135 off in the distance.

Christopher Okula/Courtesy US Air Force

Boeing KC-46 Pegasus

The KC-46A Pegasus aerial refueling aircraft is the first of a three-phase plan to replace the Air Force's aging air refueling fleet. It can carry more fuel, is more efficient, and has more room for cargo and medevac facilities than existing aircraft.

The KC-46A will be able to refuel any fixed-wing aircraft on any mission. A crewmember known as the *boom operator* controls refueling operations. This new tanker utilizes the same air refueling boom as the KC-10. It has center mounted drogue and wing aerial refueling pods. This allows it to refuel multiple types of receiver aircraft from the United States and allied air forces on the same mission. Besides carrying more than 212,000 lbs.—approximately 33,000 gallons—of fuel, it can carry up to 65,000 lbs. of cargo, 15 crew members, and from 58 to 114 passengers, depending on how the aircraft is loaded.

The KC-46A design is based on the Boeing 767 commercial airliner and was approved for production in August 2016. Boeing is scheduled to deliver 18 tankers by early 2018. The company is scheduled to build 179 KC-46 tankers by 2027.

B-21 Raider

In February 2016, Air Force Secretary Deborah James revealed the first drawings of the B-21 Long-Range Strike Bomber (LRBS). The future bomber was named the Raider in a contest among Airmen, honoring the Doolittle Raiders who took off from an aircraft carrier in B-25 bombers to attack Japan during World War II (see Chapter 3, Lesson 2). The B-21 is a key piece in the Air Force's future modernization plans.

The B-21 will give the Air Force the continued ability to launch air strikes anywhere in the world from the continental United States. It shares a resemblance to the B-2 bomber because it builds upon existing and developing technology. Current plans call for the plane to be manned, with an option for an unmanned version.

The first deployment is expected in the mid-2020s. The Air Force hopes eventually to have 100 B-21s.

An artist's conception of the B-21 Raider
Courtesy US Air Force

Current Issues in Cybertechnology

You have grown up in a world full of electronic devices—desktop computers, laptops, tablets, and smartphones. But it wasn't long before you were born that none of these existed.

Cyber is a prefix meaning *computer*. Advances in cybertechnology, or *computer technology*, have affected all the military services, especially the Air Force. Today's civilian and military aviation systems—ground control, air traffic control, and the actual flying of aircraft—wouldn't be possible without modern computers.

But cybertechnology has also introduced new threats and new ways for an enemy to attack the United States—its military, its civilian economy, and the workings of the government itself. To understand what these challenges are and how the United States is meeting them, a brief history is helpful.

An old mainframe computer

Everett Collection/Shutterstock

Evolution of the Modern Computer

The first electronic computers as we know them today were built in Germany, Britain, and the United States in the early 1940s. These were huge machines that used vacuum tubes. It took a whole room to hold less computing power than you can hold in your hand with today's mobile phones.

The first commercially available mainframe computer, the IBM/360, became available only in 1964. A mainframe is *a large, high-performance computer usually connected to several terminals and used by a large organization.*

A decade later, the first personal-computer kits became available. In 1977 Apple Corporation unveiled the groundbreaking Apple II desktop computer. IBM followed in 1981 with its release of the personal computer (PC).

In 1984 Apple released the Macintosh desktop. At this time it introduced the "Mac" operating system and the first computer mouse. In 1990, Microsoft released Windows 3.0, which soon overtook the Mac operating system (OS), since the number of PCs sold running Windows far outpaced the number of Macs sold. By early 1990s, some two-thirds of American office workers had a computer on their desk. Portable laptop computers soon followed.

An early BlackBerry phone

coronado/Shutterstock

This explosion was made possible by the evolution of computer memory and processing from large vacuum tubes to tiny microchips. As microchips became smaller and more powerful, computers did the same. Data storage moved from very large tape drives as tall as a door to smaller drives, then to 5 1/4-inch floppy disks, then to 3 1/2-inch disks, then to flash or thumb drives.

The introduction of wireless networking, or Wi-Fi, made it possible for computers to communicate with each other without wires and cable. Smaller and smaller chips led to the smartphone and tablet. In 1999 BlackBerry Limited introduced cellphones that could send and receive e-mail. Apple introduced the first smartphone, the iPhone, in 2007. A smartphone is *a cellphone with advanced computing ability.* Apple's iPad tablet followed in 2010.

Rise of the Internet

From the beginning, researchers wanted computers to be able to share data and computing power. When two computers were in the same building, this could be done by running cables between them. This created a computer network—*one or more computers linked together physically or wirelessly.*

As software developed and became more sophisticated, researchers at the Advanced Research Product Agency (ARPA) in the 1960s and 1970s developed a network of computers linked by telephone lines. (This government organization later became the Defense Advanced Research Product Agency, or DARPA.)

The resulting network was called ARPANET. As computers became smaller and more numerous, and networking technology more powerful, this network grew into the Internet—*a system of networks connecting computers around the world.*

Then in 1989, European researchers Tim Berners-Lee and Robert Cailliau developed hypertext—*digital text that contains electronic links to other texts.* They proposed using hypertext to create a World Wide Web of stored information. In 1990, Berners-Lee designed three important tools that made the World Wide Web (or just "the Web") possible:

- HTTP or Hypertext Transfer Protocol, a protocol, or *an electronic procedure*, used to send files and data over the Internet
- Hypertext Markup Language (HTML)—the code used to create text and documents and set up hyperlinks between them
- the first Web browser— *a program that accesses and displays files on the Internet or World Wide Web*

Web browsers and the Web itself have developed at breathtaking speed since that time. Computer scientists talk about its development to date as three phases—Web 1.0, 2.0, and 3.0.

HTML code lies behind each Web page.
Melody Smart/Shutterstock

Web 1.0 is sometimes called the *static Web*. That's because all a Web page did at first was display information. The user did not interact with it. You just read the information, which might not be updated all that often, except for early news sites.

Starting in about 2003, Web 2.0, or the *interactive Web*, appeared. Now the user could interact with the Web page to respond to content, create content, and use online software. This allowed the development of social networking—*interacting with other people through dedicated websites and applications (apps)*. Soon a whole host of social networking apps appeared—first MySpace, then Facebook, Twitter, LinkedIn, Instagram, Google+, and many others. User-generated information sites such as Wikipedia and blogs (from *Web logs*) also date from this time.

With all these people creating all this information, researchers believe the future is Web 3.0. According to Berners-Lee and others, this Web would function as a giant online database that would access, retain, organize, and categorize information. This would allow you to combine multiple searches into one. You could type or say a complex question or sentence, and the browser could pull all the information together for you.

Say you and your friends want to go see a movie and have a pizza afterward. You could type or say "I want to see an action movie and then get a pizza near the theater. What's available?" The browser would search the Web and organize the possible answers for you.

In the meantime, the *Internet of Things* is already becoming reality. Home appliances, automobiles, healthcare equipment and devices, and much more, can now be connected to the Internet. This allows a user to control or monitor them remotely.

Increasingly, people and organizations are storing their data on the cloud—*another name for the Internet*—instead of on their own computers and servers. This allows them to access their documents using any device—a laptop, tablet, or smartphone—anywhere in the world where there is an Internet connection. *Cloud services* mean that people can now also use software located on a remote server rather than download the software to their own computer.

Security and Privacy Issues

You know from your own experience that the combination of computers and the Internet has led to wonderful things. You have more information available to you at a moment's notice than people have ever had before. You can text with your friends while streaming the same TV program. You can play games or work on projects with people all over the world in real time.

But there is a dark side to this power. While it has opened up enormous possibilities for good things, it has also made it possible for people with harmful intentions to do bad things.

The Internet and computing ability have grown much faster than anyone could plan for. Early developers did not build security into computers, programs and apps, or the Internet. Many commands, e-mails, and messages are sent in the clear—anyone who can intercept them can read them. It did not occur to many people that bad actors would use these new abilities to do destructive things. But as soon as it became possible, it began to happen.

The problem is simple to describe but difficult to deal with. Without proper security, people without authorization can gain access to information stored in computers and on networks. They can steal, change, or destroy information and Web pages. They can gain control of remote devices and make them do their bidding. They can create armies of these machines to launch attacks on other computers and websites to prevent them from operating correctly.

Gaining access to a file, computer, or network that you're not authorized to see is called hacking. Some hackers do good work—companies and organizations ask them to test the security of their equipment and systems. These are sometimes called *white hat hackers*—from the days of old movie Westerns, when the good guys wore white hats. Hackers who have harmful or malicious goals are sometimes called *black hat hackers*—because the bad guys in those same movies wore black hats. But many people use the term *hackers* to mean hostile attackers.

Attackers have many ways to gain access to, or penetrate, a computer or network. First, they can get physical access to a machine. This can be prevented by controlling who can get near the equipment. Second, they can try to gain access to the machine over the Internet. If they know or can guess the password, they can log on. An essential defense here is using good passwords, keeping them secure, or avoiding them altogether. Scans of fingerprints, retinas, or faces offer better security. Encrypting data, e-mails, and messages—*converting data into secret code*—is another necessary defense. Anti-virus software and firewalls, or *programs and devices that monitor and restrict communication between computer systems and outside networks*, are also required.

A basic diagram of a firewall
scyther5/Shutterstock

Another way to penetrate a computer or network over the Internet is to find flaws or "holes" in the software that an attacker can manipulate to gain access. White hat hackers spend a great deal of time looking for these flaws to find them before attackers do. Responsible software companies issue corrections or *patches* to fix the flaws and plug the holes to prevent attacks. Microsoft, Apple, and other tech companies issue regular updates of their software containing these patches. That's why individuals and organizations should update their software regularly, and whenever these corrections are issued.

A third way to gain access is to persuade or fool an authorized user into giving the passwords to an attacker. Attackers also try to trick users into unknowingly loading harmful software onto a device or network that will allow the hackers to gain control of it.

Attackers have many scams to fool users. One is social engineering—*tricking people into giving out sensitive information such as passwords or credit card data*. Another is *shoulder surfing*, which is getting information off users' screens by looking over their shoulders or using a hidden camera to watch while they work. *Dumpster diving* is rummaging through wastebaskets and dumpsters to look for documents or old equipment that many contain sensitive information. *Pretexting* is pretending to be someone else—like a network administrator or a help desk—to trick the user into giving out information.

Another common method of attack is phishing—*tricking people into downloading harmful software or clicking on harmful links in e-mails or on websites*. For example, the attacker will send users an e-mail that claims to be from the users' bank or credit card company. If the users click on the link in the e-mail, they are taken to a website and asked to fill out forms with sensitive information such as their account numbers, dates of birth, mothers' maiden names, and so forth. The attacker can then use this information to gain access to users' genuine accounts and steal their money.

Malware is often introduced into computers on flash drives.

SK Herb/Shutterstock

The following scenario offers another version of this scam: You find a flash drive on the ground in the parking lot. You think one of your co-workers or an important visitor has lost it. You take the drive inside and insert it into your desktop computer to see what's on it and whom it might belong to. But unknown to you, the flash drive loads malware—*harmful software*—onto your computer and the network it's attached to, allowing an attacker to take control.

Methods such as these have allowed attackers to penetrate the networks of banks, large corporations, and government agencies, including the Pentagon. They have stolen people's personal and financial information, sensitive information about company products, classified government security information, and information about weapons systems.

The Inside Job

There's also a fourth way attackers can gain access to information. That's when an authorized user steals the information and sells or gives it to people who shouldn't have it.

There are two well-known cases of this happening to US government agencies. In the first, Army private Bradley Manning in 2010 stole some 750,000 documents stored online. He then gave them to the Wikileaks website. Most of these were classified, and many were sensitive State Department diplomatic messages. Manning, who has since changed her identity to Chelsea, was sentenced to 35 years imprisonment for espionage and stealing government property. President Barak Obama commuted her sentence in 2017 after she had served nearly seven years in prison.

In the second, a government contractor named Edward Snowden in 2013 downloaded sensitive classified information from the National Security Agency and leaked it without authorization to Wikileaks and journalists. Some of the information was widely published. Before the articles were published, Snowden fled to Hong Kong. He later went to Russia, where he has lived ever since. He has defended his actions, saying he was a whistle blower—*someone who uncovers and exposes wrongdoing in an organization*. The US government sees it differently: It has filed criminal charges against him.

Sometimes authorized users steal data.

Andrey Popov/Shutterstock

Who Are the Attackers?

When some people think of hackers, they might think of a young person trying to break into networks as a lark. But most hackers are serious, trained professionals. They may be working on their own. They may be working for organized crime. Or they may be working for a foreign government's intelligence service.

For example, the US government says that in several instances, Iranian government agents have launched attacks against American and European banks. They have overwhelmed the banks' websites with service requests so that the bank sites shut down.

The United States also says attackers working for the Chinese military have attacked the networks of many American companies and stolen their industrial secrets. They have also attacked the US government's own personnel records and stolen information about current and former government employees. In 2014 the United States filed criminal charges against five Chinese military hackers.

The US government has also accused attackers working for Russian intelligence services of attacking US government and commercial networks. During the 2016 US presidential elections, hackers working for Russian intelligence broke into the network of the Democratic National Committee and stole e-mails between officials of the Hillary Clinton campaign and other party leaders. They then gave the stolen e-mails to Wikileaks, who released them to the press. US intelligence officials accused Russia of trying to interfere in the elections by discrediting Mrs. Clinton and other Democratic Party officials.

The increasing number of such attacks in recent years has made it clear that American companies, the government, and the military services face a new type of warfare on a new front: cyberspace.

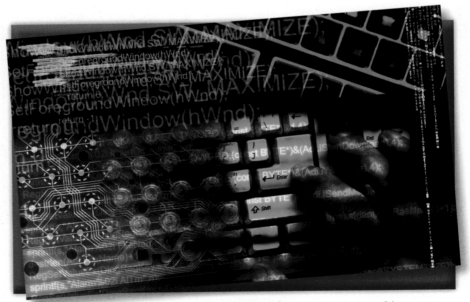

Hackers in cyberspace attacking computer systems are engaged in a new type of warfare.

Nomad_Soul/Shutterstock

Current Developments in Cyberwarfare

Cyberwarfare is *the use of cyberspace to interfere with an enemy's command and control, disrupt normal economic activity, steal intellectual property or government secrets, and prevent equipment from functioning properly.* As developments over the past few years have shown, this is not fantasy or science fiction: It is happening today. And the Air Force, Army, Navy, and Marine Corps must respond and be ready to fight in this new domain.

As noted earlier, cyberspace attackers can be foreign intelligence agents, terrorists, criminals, or just a lone individual with a grudge against the United States and its allies. Each can cause the same amount of damage. Each is equally a threat.

To counter such threats, the US Defense Department has developed a Cyber Strategy with three primary missions:

- to defend Defense Department networks, systems, and information
- to defend the US homeland and US national interests against cyberattacks of significant consequence
- to provide cyber support to military operational and contingency plans

To implement this strategy, the Secretary of Defense in 2009 directed the commander of the joint US Strategic Command to create a joint US Cyber Command. The new command has its headquarters at Fort Meade, Maryland, which is also the home of the National Security Agency (NSA). The NSA is the nation's signals and electronic intelligence agency. As this is written, the chief of the NSA is also the commander of Cyber Command. However, a debate is taking place in Washington over whether to divide the two.

The US Cyber Command seal
Adam Hartman/Courtesy US Cyber Command

Cyber Command's mission is both defensive and offensive. Each service has its own command to support the mission: Air Force Cyber Command, Army Cyber Command, Fleet Cyber Command (the Navy), and Marine Forces Cyber Command. Although the Coast Guard is part of the Department of Homeland Security, it also supports the mission through Coast Guard Cyber Command.

The Defense Department has also organized a Cyber Mission Force of 133 teams with different tasks. Cyber Protection Forces defend against the top threats to Defense Department networks and systems. Combat Mission Forces conduct cyberspace efforts in support of operations. These two types of teams will work with combatant commands in different parts of the world. National Mission Forces defend the United States and its interests against cyberattacks. They will operate directly under US Cyber Command.

Since defending the country in this way involves many departments and agencies of the US government, Cyber Command works closely, not only across the military services, but also with civilian officials as needed.

The Twenty-Fourth Air Force

Air Force Cyber Command is located with the Twenty-Fourth Air Force. Its origins date to 2006, when Secretary of the Air Force Michael Wynne and Air Force Chief of Staff General T. Michael Moseley decided to establish a cyberspace command in the Air Force. In 2008, new leaders Secretary Michael Donley and Chief of Staff General Norton Schwartz, announced the creation of a numbered air force to plan and conduct cyberspace operations. The Twenty-Fourth was placed under Air Force Space Command and headquartered at Lackland AFB, Texas—now part of Joint Base San Antonio.

One of the many units that make up the Twenty-Fourth Air Force is the 561st Network Operating Squadron at Peterson AFB, Colorado. Its crews of operators in a room full of computers keep a close watch on Air Force systems at 108 bases around the world. They work to help repel the more than 1 million attacks against Air Force networks each day.

Members of the 561st Network Operating Squadron work to defend and protect Air Force computers.

Airman 1st Class Dennis Hoffman/Courtesy US Air Force

Air Force JROTC cadets from Spokane, Washington, participate in the CyberPatriot IV competition at National Harbor, Maryland, in March 2012.

Airman 1st Class Alexander W. Riedel/Courtesy US Air Force

The CyberPatriot Program

In the end, protecting computer networks and systems is the responsibility of everyone who uses a computer. In 2009, seeing the need for more young people to be trained in cybersecurity, the Air Force Association (AFA) started the CyberPatriot program. The AFA is a nonprofit independent organization that unites current and former Airmen to promote understanding of airpower and its role in national security.

CyberPatriot conducts the National Youth Cyber Defense Competition. Teams of high school and middle school students compete to manage the network of a small company. They look for holes in cybersecurity and work to plug them while keeping services up and running. Regional winners go to Baltimore, Maryland, for the National Finals Competition.

Another activity of CyberPatriot is AFA CyberCamps, where students like you can learn the importance of cybersecurity and how to protect their personal devices and information from outside threats. Many Air Force JROTC cadets have participated in CyberPatriot events. You can learn more about the program at *www.uscyberpatriot.org*.

In this book, you're read about the history of aviation and the development of airpower. You read how the imaginative thinking of Leonardo da Vinci led people in following centuries to experiment with parachutes and gliders. You read about the Wright brothers' experiments that led to the first controlled, manned, heavier-than-air flight. You studied how aviation developed rapidly during World War I, how Charles Lindbergh captured imaginations with his trans-Atlantic solo flight, and how brave Allied flyers helped liberate Europe and the Pacific region in World War II. You read about the birth of the independent Air Force and the role airpower has played in US global interventions since then. Finally, you explored a bit the new world of cyberspace and the challenges it presents for defending the homeland.

Before you, as before no other generation in the history of mankind, the future of aviation and airpower lies bright with promise and possibilities. Will you be part of it?

✔ CHECKPOINTS

Lesson 3 Review

1. What is the F-35 an unprecedented attempt to do?

2. What kind of aircraft will the KC-46A be able to refuel?

3. Who developed the ARPANET?

4. What is a software patch?

5. Who can cyberspace attackers be? Which is the greatest threat?

6. Where is Air Force Cyber Command located?

APPLYING YOUR LEARNING

7. Explain some actions you can take to make the computers and devices you use more secure.

This page not used

CHAPTER 6   The Modern Air Force

References

CHAPTER 1 Exploring Flight

LESSON 1 Ancient Flight

Chisolm, D. E., Mitchell, N. L., & Roberson, P. Q. (Eds). (2002). *Aerospace Science: Frontiers of Aviation History* (Second ed.). Maxwell Air Force Base, AL: Air Force Officer Accessions and Training Schools.

Leonardo da Vinci. (n.d.). American Institute of Aeronautics and Astronautics. Retrieved from http://www.aiaa.org/content.cfm?pageid=425

Millspaugh, B. (2000). *Aerospace Dimensions: Module 1, Introduction to Flight.* Maxwell Air Force Base, AL: Civil Air Patrol National Headquarters.

Montgomery, J. (Ed.). (2000). *Aerospace: The Journey of Flight.* Maxwell Air Force Base, AL: Civil Air Patrol National Headquarters.

LESSON 2 The Early Days of Flight

Chisolm, D. E., Mitchell, N., & Roberson, P. Q. (Eds.). (2002). *Aerospace Science: Frontiers of Aviation History* (Second ed.). Maxwell Air Force Base, AL: Air Force Officer Accessions and Training Schools.

Chivalette, W. I. & Hayes, W. P., Jr. (n.d.). *Airmen Heritage Series: Balloons on High.* Suitland, MD: Airmen Memorial Museum.

Millspaugh, B. (2000). *Aerospace Dimensions: Module 1, Introduction to Flight.* Maxwell Air Force Base, AL: Civil Air Patrol National Headquarters.

Montgomery, J. (Ed.). (2000). *Aerospace: The Journey of Flight.* Maxwell Air Force Base, AL: Civil Air Patrol National Headquarters.

LESSON 3 The Wright Brothers Take Off

Bartlett, J. (2002). *Bartlett's Familiar Quotations* (17th ed.). Boston: Little, Brown & Company.

Chisolm, D. E., Mitchell, N. L., & Roberson, P. Q. (Eds.). (2002). *Aerospace Science: Frontiers of Aviation History* (Second ed.). Maxwell Air Force Base, AL: Air Force Officer Accessions and Training Schools.

Haulman, D. L. (2003). One Hundred Years of Flight: USAF Chronology of Significant Air and Space Events 1903–2002. Retrieved from http://afhra.maxwell.af.mil/chronologyofflight.pdf

Maj Gen Benjamin D. Foulois. (2006). National Museum of the US Air Force. Retrieved from http://www.nationalmuseum.af.mil/factsheets/ factsheet.asp?id=934

Millspaugh, B. (2000). Aerospace Dimensions, Introduction to Flight, Module 1. Maxwell AFB, AL: Civil Air Patrol National Headquarters.

Montgomery, J. (Ed.). (2000). *Aerospace: The Journey of Flight.* Maxwell Air Force Base, AL: Civil Air Patrol National Headquarters.

Nalty, B. C. (Ed.) (1997). *Winged Shield, Winged Sword: A History of the U.S. Air Force* (Vol.I). Washington, DC: United States Air Force.

The Wright Brothers: The Invention of the Aerial Age. (2006). National Air and Space Museum. Retrieved from http://www.nasm.si.edu/wrightbrothers/index.cfm

LESSON 4   Pioneers of Flight

Baker, R. F. (2003). Glenn H. Curtiss. US Centennial of Flight Commission. Retrieved from http://www.centennialofflight.net/essay/Explorers_Record_Setters_and _Daredevils/Curtiss/EX3.htm

Black Wings: African American Pioneer Aviators. (2002). National Air and Space Museum Retrieved from http://www.nasm.si.edu/blackwings/

Chisolm, D. E., Mitchell, N. L., & Roberson, P. Q. (Eds.). (2002). *Aerospace Science: Frontiers of Aviation History* (Second ed.). Maxwell Air Force Base, AL: Air Force Officer Accessions and Training Schools.

Chivalette, W. I. (2005). Enlisted History. In AFPAM36-2241V1, *Promotion Fitness Examination.* US Air Force.

Chivalette, W. I. (n.d.). Vernon L. Burge: First Enlisted Pilot. The Airmen Heritage Series. Suitland, MD: Airmen Memorial Museum.

Cochrane, D. and Ramirez, P. (n.d.) Women in Aviation and Space History: Bessica Raiche. Smithsonian National Air and Space Museum. Retrieved from https:// airandspace.si.edu/explore-and-learn/topics/women-in-aviation/Raiche.cfm.

Grant, R.G. (2007). *Flight: The Complete History.* New York: DK Publishing.

Haulman, D. L. (2003). One Hundred Years of Flight: USAF Chronology of Significant Air and Space Events 1903–2002. Retrieved from http://afhra.maxwell.af.mil/ chronologyofflight.pdf

Katherine Stinson. (2010). *Handbook of Texas Online.* Retrieved from https://tshaonline .org/handbook/online/articles/fst97

Marjorie Stinson. (n.d.) Togetherweserved.com Retrieved from http://airforce .togetherweserved.com/usaf/servlet/tws.webapp.WebApp?cmd=ShadowBoxProfile&type =Person&ID=109637

Montgomery, J. (Ed.). (2000). *Aerospace: The Journey of Flight.* Maxwell Air Force Base, AL: Civil Air Patrol National Headquarters.

Women in Aviation and Space History. (n.d.). National Air and Space Museum. Retrieved from http://www.nasm.si.edu/research/aero/women_aviators/womenavsp.htm

CHAPTER 2 Developing Flight

LESSON 1 Airpower in World War I

Feltus, P. (2003). Eddie Rickenbacker—America's "Ace of Aces". US Centennial of Flight Commission. Retrieved from www.centennialofflight.net/essay/Air_Power/rickenbacker/AP9.htm

Chisolm, D. E., Mitchell, N. L., & Roberson, P. Q. (Eds.). (2002). *Aerospace Science: Frontiers of Aviation History* (Second ed.). Maxwell Air Force Base, AL: Air Force Officer Accessions and Training Schools.

Chivalette, W. I. (2005). Corporal Eugene Jacques Bullard: First Black American Fighter Pilot. Retrieved from http://www.airpower.maxwell.af.mil/apjinternational/apj-s/2005/3tri05/chivaletteeng.html

Chivalette, W. I. (2005). Enlisted History. In AFPAM36-2241V1, *Promotion Fitness Examination*. US Air Force.

Frank Luke, Jr. (2011). National Aviation Hall of Fame. Retrieved from http://www.nationalaviation.org/luke-jr-frank/

The Great War and the Shaping of the 20th Century. (1996–2004). PBS and KCET. Retrieved from www.pbs.org/greatwar

Lauderbaugh, G. M. (n.d.). The Air Battle of St. Mihiel: Air Campaign Planning Process Background Paper. Retrieved from http://www.au.af.mil/au/awc/awcgate/ww1/stmihiel/stmihiel.htm

Manfred Richthofen. (1998). In *The New Encyclopedia Britannica* (Vol. 10, Macropaedia). Chicago: Encyclopaedia Britannica Inc.

Montgomery, J. (Ed.). (2000). *Aerospace: The Journey of Flight*. Maxwell Air Force Base, AL: Civil Air Patrol National Headquarters.

Royal Air Force. (2003). Royal Air Force History. Retrieved from http://www.raf.mod.uk/rafhome.html

World War I: Western Front: 1915–1917—Stalemate and Western Front: 1918—The Year of Decision. (1963). In *The Encyclopedia Americana* (Vol. 29). New York: Encyclopedia Americana Corporation.

LESSON 2 Expanding the Horizon from Barnstormers to the Mainstream

Air Markers. (1936). *Time*, 24 August 1936. Retrieved from http://www.time.com/time/magazine/article/0,9171,756537,00.html

Bessie Coleman. (n.d.). Women in History. Lakewood, OH: Lakewood Public Library. Retrieved from http://www.lkwdpl.org/wihohio/cole-bes.htm

Chant, C. (2002). *A Century of Triumph: The History of Aviation*. New York: The Free Press, a division of Simon and Schuster.

Chisolm, D. E., Mitchell, N. L., & Roberson, P. Q. (Eds.). (2002). *Aerospace Science: Frontiers of Aviation History* (Second. ed.). Maxwell Air Force Base, AL: Air Force Officer Accessions and Training Schools.

Floyd Bennett, Warrant Officer, United States Navy. (n.d.). Arlington National Cemetery. Retrieved from http://www.arlingtoncemetery.net/ bennettf.htm

Goerler, R., and Cullather, R. (n.d.). Admiral Richard E. Byrd, 1888–1957. The Byrd Polar Research Center at The Ohio State University. Retrieved from http://www-bprc .mps.ohio-state.edu/gpl/ AboutByrd/AboutByrd.html

Johnson, J. (2003). Heroes of the Sky. *Humanities*, September–October 2003, (Vol. 24, No. 5). Retrieved from http://www.neh.gov/news/ humanities/2003-09/heroes.html

Montgomery, J. (Ed.). (2000). *Aerospace: The Journey of Flight*. Maxwell Air Force Base, AL: Civil Air Patrol National Headquarters.

Onkst, D. H. (n.d.). Barnstormers. US Centennial of Flight Commission. Retrieved from http://www.centennialofflight.net/essay/ Explorers_Record_Setters_and_Daredevils/ barnstormers/EX12.htm

Rumerman, J. (n.d.). The Curtiss JN-4 "Jenny." US Centennial of Flight Commission. Retrieved from http://www.centennialofflight. gov/essay/Aerospace/Jenny/Aero3.htm

LESSON 3 Early Developments in Commercial Flight

Boeing History: Chronology. (n.d.). Boeing. Retrieved from http://www.boeing.com/ history/chronology/chron03.html

Boeing History: Model 40 Commercial Transport. (n.d.). Boeing. Retrieved from http://www.boeing.com/history/boeing/40a.html

Charnov, Bruce H. (2003). Amelia Earhart, John M. Miller and the First Transcontinental Autogiro Flight in 1931. Retrieved from http://www.aviation -history.com/airmen/earhart-Autogiro.htm

Chasing the Sun. (2005). PBS and KCET. Retrieved from http://www.pbs.org/ chasingthesun/innovators/wboeing.html

Chisolm, D. E., Mitchell, N. L., & Roberson, P. Q. (Eds.). (2002). *Aerospace Science: Frontiers of Aviation History* (Second ed.). Maxwell Air Force Base, AL: Air Force Officer Accessions and Training Schools.

Chivalette, W. J. (2005). *Sergeant William Charles Ocker: the Army's Third Enlisted Pilot*. Maxwell AFB, AL: Airmen Memorial Museum.

Douglas C-32. (n.d.). National Museum of the US Air Force. Retrieved from http://www.nationalmuseum.af.mil/factsheets/factsheet.asp?id=3292

Grant, R.G. (2007). *Flight: The Complete History*. New York: DK Publishing.

Haulman, D. L. (2003.). *One Hundred Years of Flight; USAF Chronology of Significant Air and Space Events, 1903–2002*. Maxwell Air Force Base, AL: Air University Press.

Lombardi, M. (n.d.). Century of Flight, 1911–1920: WWI and the Birth of Boeing. Retrieved from http://www.boeing.com/news/frontiers/archive/2003/march/ i_history.html

Milestones of Flight: Ryan NYP "Spirit of St. Louis." (n.d.). National Air and Space Museum. Retrieved from http://www.nasm.si.edu/exhibitions/ gal100/stlouis.html

Montgomery, J. (Ed.). (2000). *Aerospace: The Journey of Flight.* Maxwell Air Force Base, AL: Civil Air Patrol National Headquarters.

Nye, C. A. A. (2005). *Katherine Cheung, Aviatrix.* Retrieved from http://www.publicartinla .com/Downtown/Chinatown/cheung.html

Rumerman, J. (2003). Commercial Flight in the 1930s. US Centennial of Flight Commission. Retrieved from http://www.centennialofflight.net/essay/Commercial _Aviation/passenger_xperience/Tran2.htm

Rumerman, K. (2003). Amelia Earhart. US Centennial of Flight Commission. Retrieved from http://www.centennialofflight.net/essay/Explorers_Record_Setters_and _Daredevils/earhart/EX29.htm

When the Going Was Good: The Golden Age of Commercial Air Travel. (n.d.). National Air and Space Museum. Retrieved from http://www.nasm.si.edu/exhibition/ archives/clipper/clipper.htm

William Boeing, 1881–1956, American Inventor. (n.d.). HistoryCentral.com. Retrieved from http://www.historycentral.com/Bio/people/boeing.html

Yellowbridge.com. (n.d.). Famous Chinese-Americans in Aviation and Aerospace. Retrieved from http://www.yellowbridge.com/people/ aviation.html#cheung and http://www.yellowbridge.com/people/firsts.html

CHAPTER 3   The Evolution of the Early Air Force

LESSON 1   The Army Air Corps

Air Force History. (2001). In AFPAM 36-2241V1, *Promotion Fitness Examination.* US Air Force.

Brigadier General William "Billy" Mitchell. (n.d.). *Air Force Link.* Retrieved from http://www.af.mil/history/person.asp?dec=&pid=123006464

Boyne, W. J. (2003). Foulois. *Air Force Magazine,* February 2003. Retrieved from http://www.afa.org/magazine/feb2003/02foulois03.pdf

Chisolm, D. E., Mitchell, N. L., & Roberson, P. Q. (Eds.). (2002). *Aerospace Science: Frontiers of Aviation History.* (Second ed.). Maxwell Air Force Base, AL: Air Force Officer Accessions and Training Schools.

Chivalette, W. I. (2005). Enlisted History. In AFPAM 36-2241V1, *Promotion Fitness Examination.* US Air Force.

Chivalette, W. I. (n.d.). *Nero the Pioneer.* Suitland, MD: Airmen Memorial Museum.

Court Martial. (1925). *Time,* 2 November 1925. Retrieved from http://www.time.com/ time/magazine/article/0,9171,728580-2,00.html

Gen. Billy Mitchell. (n.d.). National Museum of the US Air Force. Retrieved from http://www.nationalmuseum.af.mil/factsheets/factsheet.asp?id=739

Haulman, D. L. (2003). *One Hundred Years of Flight: USAF Chronology of Significant Air and Space Events, 1903–2002.* Maxwell Air Force Base, AL: Air University Press.

Montgomery, J. (Ed.). (2000). *Aerospace: The Journey of Flight.* Maxwell Air Force Base, AL: Civil Air Patrol National Headquarters.

Nalty, B., (Ed.). (1997). *Winged Sword, Winged Shield: A History of the United States Air Force* (Vol. 1). Washington: US Air Force.

Thomas, W. C. (2004). The Cultural Identity of the United States Air Force. *Air Force Magazine,* 30 January 2004. Retrieved from http://www.airpower.au.af.mil/airchronicles/cc/thomas.html

LESSON 2 Airpower in World War II

The Afrocentric Experience. (n.d.). Blacks in Aviation. Retrieved from http://www.swagga.com/index.shtml

American Experience: Fly Girls. (1998). PBS Online. Retrieved from http://www.pbs.org/wgbh/amex/flygirls/index.html

American Experience: Race for the Superbomb. (1999). PBS Online. Retrieved from http://www.pbs.org/wgbh/amex/bomb/index.html

Assets and Liabilities. (1944). National Museum of the US Air Force. Retrieved from http://www.nationalmuseum.af.mil/factsheets/factsheet.asp?id=1688

Bednarek, J. (Ed.). (2004). *Generations of Cheverons.* Washington, DC: Air Force History and Museums Program, US Air Force.

Black Wings: African American Pioneer Aviators. (2002). National Air & Space Museum. Retrieved from http://www.nasm.si.edu/blackwings/ index.html

Boeing B-29 "Enola Gay." (n.d.). National Museum of the US Air Force. Retrieved from http://www.nationalmuseum.af.mil/factsheets/ factsheet.asp?id=2549

Chief Master Sergeant of the Air Force Paul W. Airey. (n.d.). *Air Force Link.* Retrieved from http://www.af.mil/history/person_print.asp? storyID=123006506

Chisolm, D. E., Mitchell, N. L., & Roberson, P. Q. (Eds.). (2002). *Aerospace Science: Frontiers of Aviation History* (Second ed.). Maxwell Air Force Base, AL: Air Force Officer Accessions and Training Schools.

Chivalette, W. I. (2005). Enlisted History. In AFPAM36-2241V1, *Promotion Fitness Examination.* 1 July 2005. US Air Force.

Cole, H. M. (1965). *The Ardennes: The Battle of the Bulge.* Washington, DC: Office of the Chief of Military History, Department of the Army. Retrieved from http://www.army.mil/cmh-pg/books/wwii/7-8/7-8_25.htm#p660

Desegregation of the Armed Forces. (n.d.). Truman Presidential Museum & Library. Retrieved from http://www.trumanlibrary.org/whistlestop/study_collections/desegregation/large/index.php?action=chronology

Doolittle Tokyo Raiders. (n.d.). National Museum of the US Air Force. Retrieved from http://www.nationalmuseum.af.mil/factsheets/factsheet.asp?id=1514

Escort Excellence. (2015). National Museum of the US Air Force. Retrieved from http://www.nationalmuseum.af.mil/Visit/MuseumExhibits/FactSheets/Display/tabid/509/Article/195963/escort-excellence.aspx

Feltus, P. (n.d.). The Ninety-Nines. Retrieved from http://www.centennialofflight.net/essay/Explorers_Record_Setters_and_Daredevil s/99s/EX21.htm

Gen Carl Spaatz. (n.d.). National Museum of the US Air Force. Retrieved from http://www.nationalmuseum.af.mil/factsheets/factsheet.asp?id=1131

Gen Curtis E. LeMay. (n.d.). National Museum of the US Air Force. Retrieved from http://www.nationalmuseum.af.mil/factsheets/factsheet.asp?id=1115

General Henry H. "Hap" Arnold. (2006). Retrieved from http://www.af. mil/history/person.asp?dec=&pid=123006476

Lieutenant General Pete Quesada. (n.d.). *Air Force Link*. Retrieved from http://www.af.mil/history/person.asp?dec=&pid=123006493

Major Arthur T. Chin, Chinese Air Force. (n.d.). Airpower Heritage Museum. Retrieved from http://www.airpowermuseum.org/exhibits/ acahof/assets/pdf/1997/chin.pdf

Master Sergeant Henry E. "Red" Erwin. (n.d.). *Air Force Link*. Retrieved from http://www.af.mil/history/person.asp?dec=&pid=123006484

Miskimins, S. M. (1986). *Operation "Tidal Wave"*. Airman Heritage Series. Suitland, MD: Airman Memorial Museum.

Montgomery, J. (Ed.). (2000). *Aerospace: The Journey of Flight*. Maxwell Air Force Base, AL: Civil Air Patrol National Headquarters.

The Ninety-Nines: Who Are the Ninety Nines? (2005). The Ninety-Nines Inc. Retrieved from http://www.ninety-nines.org/

O'Brien, J. V. (n.d.). World War II: Combatants and Casualties (1937–45). Retrieved from http://web.jjay.cuny.edu/~jobrien/index.html

Proctor, A. (n.d.). Enlisted Pilots: Soaring High From the Lower Ranks. Retrieved from http://www.af.mil/news/airman/1296/fly.htm

Shenkle, K. (n.d.). Major Glenn Miller. Arlington National Cemetery. Retrieved from http://www.arlingtoncemetery.mil/Explore/Notable-Graves/Other-Prominent-Figures/Glenn-Miller

Tuskegee Airmen. (n.d.). National Museum of the US Air Force. Retrieved from http://www.nationalmuseum.af.mil/factsheets/factsheet.asp?id=1356

USS *Arizona* Memorial. (n.d.). National Park Service, US Department of the Interior. Retrieved from http://www.nps.gov/archive/usar/ ExtendWeb1.html

Wells, M. K. (1988). The Human Element and Air Combat: Some Napoleonic Comparisons. *Airpower Journal*, Spring 1988. Retrieved from http://www.airpower.maxwell.af.mil/airchronicles/apj/apj88/wells.html

LESSON 3 Significant Aircraft of World War II

Airlift Mission—The Center of Gravity. (n.d.). National Museum of the US Air Force. Retrieved from http://www.nationalmuseum.af.mil/Portals/7/documents/education/airlift_mission_center_of_gravity.pdf

Airspeed AS.51 & 58 Horse Glider. (2016). De Havilland Aircraft Museum. Retrieved from http://www.dehavillandmuseum.co.uk/aircraft/airspeed-as-51-58-horsa-glider/

Alex, D. (2015). Douglas A-20 Havoc/Boston Light Bomber/Night Fighter. MilitaryFactory.com.com. Retrieved from http://www.militaryfactory.com/aircraft/detail.asp?aircraft_id=186

Avro Lancaster. (2015). WorldWar2Headquarters.com. Retrieved from http://worldwar2headquarters.com/HTML/aircraft/britishAircraft/landcaster.html

B-29 Superfortress. (n.d.). Retrieved from http://www.boeing.com/history/boeing/b29.html

Bell P-39Q Airacobra. (2015). National Museum of the US Air Force. Retrieved from http://www.nationalmuseum.af.mil/Visit/MuseumExhibits/FactSheets/Display/tabid/509/Article/196306/bell-p-39q-airacobra.aspx

Boeing B-17G Flying Fortress. (2015). National Museum of the US Air Force. Retrieved from http://www.nationalmuseum.af.mil/Visit/MuseumExhibits/FactSheets/Display/tabid/509/Article/196270/boeing-b-17g-flying-fortress.aspx

Boeing B-29 Superfortress. (2015). National Museum of the US Air Force. Retrieved from http://www.nationalmuseum.af.mil/Visit/MuseumExhibits/FactSheets/Display/tabid/509/Article/196252/boeing-b-29-superfortress.aspx

A Brief History of the Flying Tigers. (n.d.). Flying Tigers Association, American Volunteer Group. Retrieved from http://www.flyingtigersavg.com

Buske, George W., TSgt. (2011). Retrieved from https://airforce.togetherweserved.com/usaf/servlet/tws.webapp.WebApp?cmd=ShadowBoxProfile&type=Person&ID=134948

C-54 Skymaster Long Range Transport. (2015). WorldWar2Headquarters.com. Retrieved from http://worldwar2headquarters.com/HTML/aircraft/americanAircraft/skymaster.html

Consolidated B-24D Liberator. (2015). National Museum of the US Air Force. Retrieved from http://www.nationalmuseum.af.mil/Visit/MuseumExhibits/FactSheets/Display/tabid/509/Article/196286/consolidated-b-24d-liberator.aspx

Curtiss P-40E Warhawk. (2015). National Museum of the US Air Force. Retrieved from http://www.nationalmuseum.af.mil/Visit/MuseumExhibits/FactSheets/Display/tabid/509/Article/196309/curtiss-p-40e-warhawk.aspx

Curtiss P-40 Warhawk Fighter-Bomber/Fighter Aircraft (1941). (2016). MilitaryFactory.com. Retrieved from http://www.militaryfactory.com/aircraft/detail.asp?aircraft_id=75

DC-4/C-54 Skymaster Transport. (2016). Boeing. Retrieved from http://www.boeing.com/history/products/dc-4.page

De Havilland DH 98 Mosquito. (2015). National Museum of the US Air Force. Retrieved from http://www.nationalmuseum.af.mil/Visit/MuseumExhibits/FactSheets/Display/tabid/509/Article/196281/de-havilland-dh-98-mosquito.aspx

De Havilland DH98 Mosquito FB MK.VI. (2016). De Havilland Aircraft Museum. Retrieved from http://www.dehavillandmuseum.co.uk/aircraft/de-havilland-dh98-mosquito-fb-mk-vi/

DFS 230 Towed Transport Glider (1938). (2015). MilitaryFactory.com. Retrieved from http://www.militaryfactory.com/aircraft/detail.asp?aircraft_id=1190

Douglas A-20G Havoc. (2015). National Museum of the US Air Force. Retrieved from http://www.nationalmuseum.af.mil/Visit/MuseumExhibits/FactSheets/Display/tabid/509/Article/196256/douglas-a-20g-havoc.aspx

Douglas C-47D Skytrain. (2015). National Museum of the US Air Force. Retrieved from http://www.nationalmuseum.af.mil/Visit/MuseumExhibits/FactSheets/Display/tabid/509/Article/196271/douglas-c-47d-skytrain.aspx

Dwyer, L. (2014). Martin B-26 Marauder. The Aviation History Online Museum. Retrieved from http://www.aviation-history.com/martin/b26.html

Focke-Wulf Fw 190D-9. (2015). National Museum of the US Air Force. Retrieved from http://www.nationalmuseum.af.mil/Visit/MuseumExhibits/FactSheets/Display/tabid/509/Article/196261/focke-wulf-fw-190d-9.aspx

Gloster Meteor. (2015). WorldWar2Headquarters.com. Retrieved from http://worldwar2headquarters.com/HTML/aircraft/britishAircraft/meteor.html

Gloster (Armstrong Whitworth) Meteor Jet-Powered Fighter/Fighter-Bomber. (2016). MilitaryFactory.com. Retrieved from http://www.militaryfactory.com/aircraft/detail.asp?aircraft_id=123

Grant, R.G. (2007). *Flight: The Complete History.* New York: DK Publishing.

Grumman F6F Hellcat Carrier-Borne Fighter/Fighter-Bomber. (2016). MilitaryFactory.com. Retrieved from http://www.militaryfactory.com/aircraft/detail.asp?aircraft_id=146

Handley Page Halifax. (2015). WorldWar2Headquarters.com. Retrieved from http://worldwar2headquarters.com/HTML/aircraft/britishAircraft/halifax.html

Handley Page Halifax Heavy Bomber/Night Bomber Aircraft. (2016). MilitaryFactory.com. Retrieved from http://www.militaryfactory.com/aircraft/detail.asp?aircraft_id=233

Handley Page Halifax Mk III. (2016). The Allied Air Forces Memorial, The Yorkshire Air Museum. Retrieved from http://yorkshireairmuseum.org/exhibits/world-war-two-aircraft/handley-page-halifax-iii/

Hawker Hurricane. (n.d.). Aircraftaces.com. Retrieved from http://www.aircraftaces.com/hawker-hurricane.htm

Hawker Hurricane. (2016). Royal Air Force. Retrieved from http://www.raf.mod.uk/campaign/battle-of-britain-75th/aircraft/hawker-hurricane/

Heinkel He 111. (n.d.). Aircraftaces.com. Retrieved from http://www.aircraftaces.com/heinkel-111.htm

Heinkel He 111 Medium Bomber. (2016). MilitaryFactory.com. Retrieved from http://www.militaryfactory.com/aircraft/detail.asp?aircraft_id=99

Ilyushin Il-2 Sturmovik. (2015). WorldWar2Headquarters.com. Retrieved from http://worldwar2headquarters.com/HTML/aircraft/russianAircraft/Il-2sturmovik.html

Ilyushin Il-2/10 Sturmovik. (n.d.). Aircraftaces.com. Retrieved from http://www.aircraftaces.com/il-2-sturmovik.htm

Ilyushin Il-2 Sturmovik Ground Attack/Close Air Support Aircraft. (2016). MilitaryFactory.com. Retrieved from http://www.militaryfactory.com/aircraft/detail.asp?aircraft_id=134

Ilyushin Il-4 Russian Bomber, WWII. (2015). WorldWar2Headquarters.com. Retrieved from http://worldwar2headquarters.com/HTML/aircraft/russianAircraft/Il4.html

Junkers 87 Stuka Bomber. (2015). WorldWar2Headquarters.com. Retrieved from http://worldwar2headquarters.com/HTML/aircraft/germanAircraft/junkers87b.html

Junkers 88 Bomber. (2015). WorldWar2Headquarters.com. Retrieved from http://worldwar2headquarters.com/HTML/aircraft/germanAircraft/junkers88.html

Junkers Ju 88D-1/Trop. (2015). National Museum of the US Air Force. Retrieved from http://www.nationalmuseum.af.mil/Visit/MuseumExhibits/FactSheets/Display/tabid/509/Article/196268/junkers-ju-88d-1trop.aspx

Kawasaki Ki-61 Fighter (Tony). (2015). WorldWar2Headquarters.com. Retrieved from http://worldwar2headquarters.com/HTML/aircraft/japaneseAircraft/kawasakiKi-61.html

Kawasaki Ki-61 Hien Tony. (n.d.). Aircraftaces.com. Retrieved from http://www.aircraftaces.com/kawasaki-ki-61.htm

Kawasaki Ki-61 Hien (Tony) Fighter/Interceptor Aircraft. (2015). MilitaryFactory.com. Retrieved from http://www.militaryfactory.com/aircraft/detail.asp?aircraft_id=562

The Lancaster. (2016). Royal Air Force. Retrieved from http://www.raf.mod.uk/bbmf/theaircraft/lancasterhistory.cfm

Lavochkin 5/7. (n.d.). Aircraftaces.com. Retrieved from http://www.aircraftaces.com/lavochkin-5.htm

Lavochkin La-5. (2015). WorldWar2Headquarters.com. Retrieved from http://worldwar2headquarters.com/HTML/aircraft/russianAircraft/lavochkinLa5.html

Lavochkin La-5 Fighter. (2015). MilitaryFactory.com. Retrieved from http://www.militaryfactory.com/aircraft/detail.asp?aircraft_id=554

Lockheed P-38L Lightning. (2015). National Museum of the US Air Force. Retrieved from http://www.nationalmuseum.af.mil/Visit/MuseumExhibits/FactSheets/Display/tabid/509/Article/196280/lockheed-p-38l-lightning.aspx

Lockheed P-38 Lightning Heavy Fighter/Fighter-Bomber. (2016). MilitaryFactory.com. Retrieved from http://www.militaryfactory.com/aircraft/detail.asp?aircraft_id=74

Manning, R. (2012). Defining Courage: The Forrest L. Vosler Story. Malmstrom Air Force Base. Retrieved from http://www.malmstrom.af.mil/news/story.asp?id=123289509

Markowitz, M. (2015). The DFS 230 Assault Glider. Defense Media Network. Retrieved from http://www.defensemedianetwork.com/stories/classics-dfs-230-assault-glider/

Martin B-26G Marauder. (2015). National Museum of the US Air Force. Retrieved from http://www.nationalmuseum.af.mil/Visit/MuseumExhibits/FactSheets/Display/tabid/509/Article/196275/martin-b-26g-marauder.aspx

Medium Bombers. (2015). National Museum of the US Air Force. Retrieved from http://www.nationalmuseum.af.mil/Visit/MuseumExhibits/FactSheets/Display/tabid/509/Article/196171/medium-bombers.aspx

Messerschmitt Bf 109. (n.d.). Aircraftaces.com. Retrieved from http://www.aircraftaces.com/bf-109.htm

Messerschmitt Bf 109G-10. (2015). National Museum of the US Air Force. Retrieved from http://www.nationalmuseum.af.mil/Visit/MuseumExhibits/FactSheets/Display/tabid/509/Article/196264/messerschmitt-bf-109g-10.aspx

Messerschmitt Me 262A Schwalbe. (2015). National Museum of the US Air Force. Retrieved from http://www.nationalmuseum.af.mil/Visit/MuseumExhibits/FactSheets/Display/tabid/509/Article/196266/messerschmitt-me-262a-schwalbe.aspx

Mikoyan-Gurevich MiG-1/ MiG-3 Single-Seat Fighter Aircraft. (2016). MilitaryFactory.com. Retrieved from http://www.militaryfactory.com/aircraft/detail.asp?aircraft_id=512

Mikoyan-Gurevich MiG-3 Fighter. (n.d.) WorldWar2Headquarters.com. Retrieved from http://worldwar2headquarters.com/HTML/aircraft/russianAircraft/mig3.html

Mitsubishi A6M2 Zero. (2015). National Museum of the US Air Force. Retrieved from http://www.nationalmuseum.af.mil/Visit/MuseumExhibits/FactSheets/Display/tabid/509/Article/196313/mitsubishi-a6m2-zero.aspx

Mitsubishi G4M Betty. (n.d.). Aircraftaces.com. Retrieved from http://www.aircraftaces.com/mitsubishi-g4m-betty.htm

Mitsubishi G4M Long-range Bomber (Betty). (2015). WorldWar2Headquarters.com. Retrieved from http://worldwar2headquarters.com/HTML/aircraft/japaneseAircraft/mitsubishiG4M.html

Mitsubishi Ki-21 Long-range Bomber (Sally). (2015). WorldWar2Headquarters.com. Retrieved from http://worldwar2headquarters.com/HTML/aircraft/japaneseAircraft/mitsubishiKi-21.html

Mitsubishi Ki-21 (Sally) Medium Bomber Aircraft. (2016). MilitaryFactory.com. http://www.militaryfactory.com/aircraft/detail.asp?aircraft_id=558

Nakajima B5N (Kate) Carrier-Borne Torpedo Bomber. (2016). MilitaryFactory.com. Retrieved 29 June 2016. http://www.militaryfactory.com/aircraft/detail.asp?aircraft_id=374

Nakajima Ki-84 Frank. (n.d.). Aircraftaces.com. Retrieved from http://www.aircraftaces.com/nakajima-ki-84.htm

North American B-25B Mitchell. (2015). National Museum of the US Air Force. Retrieved from http://www.nationalmuseum.af.mil/Visit/MuseumExhibits/FactSheets/Display/tabid/509/Article/196310/north-american-b-25b-mitchell.aspx

North American P-51D Mustang. (2015). National Museum of the US Air Force. Retrieved from http://www.nationalmuseum.af.mil/Visit/MuseumExhibits/FactSheets/Display/tabid/509/Article/196263/north-american-p-51d-mustang.aspx

Petlyakov Pe-2 (Dawn) Dive Bomber/Light Bomber Aircraft. (2016). MilitaryFactory.com. Retrieved from http://www.militaryfactory.com/aircraft/detail.asp?aircraft_id=298

Republic P-47D (Bubble Canopy Version). (2015). National Museum of the US Air Force. Retrieved from http://www.nationalmuseum.af.mil/Visit/MuseumExhibits/FactSheets/Display/tabid/509/Article/196276/republic-p-47d-bubble-canopy-version.aspx

Sherman, S. (2012). Focke-Wulf Fw 190: Germany's Radial Engine Fighter of WWII. Acepilots.com. Retrieved from http://acepilots.com/german/fw190.html

Supermarine Spitfire. (n.d.). Aircraftaces.com. Retrieved from http://www.aircraftaces.com/spitfire.htm

Supermarine Spitfire. (2016). Royal Air Force. Retrieved from http://www.raf.mod.uk/campaign/battle-of-britain-75th/aircraft/supermarine-spitfire/

Supermarine Spitfire Mk IIA—Fighter Plane. (2015). WorldWar2Headquarters.com. Retrieved from http://worldwar2headquarters.com/HTML/aircraft/britishAircraft/spitfireIIA.html

Supermarine Spitfire Mk. Vc. (2016). National Museum of the US Air Force. Retrieved from http://www.nationalmuseum.af.mil/Visit/MuseumExhibits/FactSheets/Display/tabid/509/Article/196284/supermarine-spitfire-mk-vc.aspx

Trueman, C. N. (2015). Messerschmitt 109. The History Learning Site. Retrieved from http://www.historylearningsite.co.uk/world-war-two/world-war-two-in-western-europe/battle-of-britain/messerschmitt-109/

Tupolev Tu-2. (n.d.). Aircraftaces.com. Retrieved from http://www.aircraftaces.com/tupolev-2.htm

Tupolev Tu-2 (Bat) Fast Bomber/Multirole Aircraft. (2015). MilitaryFactory.com. Retrieved from http://www.militaryfactory.com/aircraft/detail.asp?aircraft_id=1010

Vought F4U Corsair. (n.d.). Aircraftaces.com. Retrieved from http://www.aircraftaces.com/f4u-corsair.htm

Vought F4U Corsair Carrier-Based Fighter/Fighter-Bomber/Night Fighter. (2015). MilitaryFactory.com. Retrieved from http://www.militaryfactory.com/aircraft/detail.asp?aircraft_id=87

Yakovlev Yak-1 (Krasavyets) Fighter Aircraft. (2015). MilitaryFactory.com. http://www.militaryfactory.com/aircraft/detail.asp?aircraft_id=555

Yakovlev 1/7. (n.d.). Aircraftaces.com. Retrieved from http://www.aircraftaces.com/yak-1.htm

Yakovlev Yak-3 Fighter Aircraft. (2015). MilitaryFactory.com. Retrieved from http://www.militaryfactory.com/aircraft/detail.asp?aircraft_id=635

Yakovlev 9. (n.d.). Aircraftaces.com. Retrieved from http://www.aircraftaces.com/yak9.htm

Yakovlev Yak-9. (2015). WorldWar2Headquarters.com. Retrieved from http://worldwar2headquarters.com/HTML/aircraft/russianAircraft/yak9.html

CHAPTER 4 **Commercial and General Aviation Take Off**

LESSON 1 The Development of Federal Regulations and Aviation

1956 Grand Canyon airplane crash a game-changer. (2014). *Associated Press,* 8 July 2014. Retrieved from http://www.cbsnews.com/news/1956-grand-canyon-airplane-crash-a-game-changer/

Airline Domestic Market Share April 2015–March 2016. (2016). US Department of Transportation, Office of the Assistant Secretary for Science and Technology, Bureau of Transportation Statistics. Retrieved from http://www.transtats.bts.gov

A Brief History of the FAA. (n.d.). Federal Aviation Administration. Retrieved from http://www.faa.gov/about/history/brief_history/

DOT created. (n.d.). US Department of Transportation. Retrieved from https://www.transportation.gov/50/collage#DOT__Created

Elwood "Pete" Quesada: The Right Man for the Right Job. (n.d.). Federal Aviation Administration. Retrieved from http://www.faa.gov/about/history/people/media/elwood_quesada.pdf

The Federal Aviation Act Of 1958. (n.d.). *Aviation Online Magazine.* Retrieved from http://avstop.com/history/needregulations/act1958.htm

Federal Aviation Administration. (n.d.). Air Traffic Organization. Retrieved from http://www.faa.gov/about/office_org/headquarters_offices/ato/

Hershey, R. D., Jr. (2010). Alfred E. Kahn Dies at 93; Prime Mover of Airline Deregulation. *The New York Times,* 28 December 2010. Retrieved from http://www.nytimes.com/2010/12/29/business/29kahn.html?_r=0

Hyman, V. (2015). How three planes crashed in three months in Elizabeth in '50s. *NJ.com,* 29 May 2015. Retrieved from http://www.nj.com/entertainment/arts/index.ssf/2015/05/how_three_planes_crashed_in_elizabeth_in_50s.html

Janson, B. (2016). 2016 one of the safest on record for airliners. *USA Today,* 15 February 2016. Retrieved from http://www.usatoday.com/story/news/2016/02/15/2015-another-safe-year-airliners/80398194/

Lang, S.S. (2010). Economist Alfred Kahn, 'father of airline deregulation' and former presidential adviser, dies at 93. *Cornell Chronicle,* 27 December 2010. Retrieved from http://news.cornell.edu/stories/2010/12/alfred-kahn-father-airline-deregulation-dies-93

Leadership and Organization. (n.d.). Transportation Security Administration. Retrieved from https://www.tsa.gov/about/tsa-leadership

Lessons Learned: Midair collision between a Trans World Airlines Lockheed 1049 and a United Airlines Douglas DC-7 over Grand Canyon, AZ. (n.d.). Federal Aviation Administration. Retrieved from http://lessonslearned.faa.gov/ll_main.cfm?TabID =3&LLID=50&LLTypeID=2#null

Morris, D. (2014). Airline Deregulation: A Triumph of Ideology Over Evidence. *The Huffington Post,* 12 February 2014. Retrieved from http://www.huffingtonpost .com/david-morris/airline-deregulation-ideology-over-evidence_b_4399150.html

National Transportation Safety Board. (n.d.). History of The National Transportation Safety Board. Retrieved from http://www.ntsb.gov/about/history/Pages/default.aspx

Saxon, W. (1993). Elwood R. Quesada, First F.A.A. Chief, Dies at 88. *The New York Times,* 10 February 1993. Retrieved from http://www.nytimes.com/1993/02/10/us/elwood -r-quesada-first-faa-chief-dies-at-88.html

Schalch, K. (2006). 1981 Strike Leaves Legacy for American Workers. *National Public Radio,* 3 August 2006. Retrieved from http://www.npr.org/templates/story/story .php?storyId=5604656

Smith, F. L., Jr. and Cox, B. (n.d.). Airline Deregulation. *Concise Encyclopedia of Economics.* Retrieved from http://www.econlib.org/library/Enc/AirlineDeregulation.html

Sumers, B. (2015). Southwest Is the Most Contrarian U.S. Airline and That's Why It Always Wins. *Skift.com.* Retrieved from https://skift.com/2015/07/31/whats-so -exceptional-about-the-southwest-exception/

Tolan, C., Patterson, T., and Johnson, A. (2014). Is 2014 the deadliest year for flights? Not even close. *Cable News Network,* 28 July 2014. Retrieved from http://www.cnn .com/interactive/2014/07/travel/aviation-data/

Transportation Security Timeline. (n.d.). Transportation Security Administration. Retrieved from https://www.tsa.gov/timeline

LESSON 2   The Propeller Era in Commercial Flight

A Brief History of Aviation. (n.d.). Air Transport Association. Retrieved from http://members.airlines.org/about/d.aspx?nid=7946

A Brief History of the Federal Aviation Administration. (n.d.). Federal Aviation Administration. Retrieved from http://www.faa.gov/about/history/brief_history/#3

Chasing the Sun: Constellation. (n.d.). PBS and KCET. Retrieved from http://www .pbs.org/kcet/chasingthesun/planes/constellation.html

Chasing the Sun: Howard Hughes. (n.d.). PBS and KCET. Retrieved from http://www .pbs.org/kcet/chasingthesun/innovators/hhughes.html

Chisolm, D. E., Mitchell, N. L., & Roberson, P. Q. (Eds). (2002). *Aerospace Science: Frontiers of Aviation History* (Second. ed.). Maxwell Air Force Base, AL: Air Force Officer Accessions and Training Schools.

Donald Wills Douglas Sr. (n.d.). Boeing Company. Retrieved from http://www.boeing .com/history/mdc/douglas.htm

Haulman, D. L. (2003). *One Hundred Years of Flight: USAF Chronology of Significant Air and Space Events, 1903–2002.* Maxwell Air Force Base, AL: Air University Press.

Montgomery, J (Ed.). (2000). *Aerospace: The Journey of Flight.* Maxwell Air Force Base, AL: Civil Air Patrol National Headquarters.

Rumerman, J. (n.d.). Commercial Flight in the 1930s. US Centennial of Flight Commission. Retrieved from http://www.centennialofflight.net/essay/Commercial _Aviation/passenger_xperience/Tran2.htm

Siddiqi, A. (n.d.). American Airlines. US Centennial of Flight Commission. Retrieved from http://www.centennialofflight.net/essay/Commercial_Aviation/American/ Tran15.htm

Siddiqi, A. (n.d.). The Beginnings of Commercial Transatlantic Services. US Centennial of Flight Commission. Retrieved from http://www.centennialofflight.net/essay/ Commercial_Aviation/atlantic_route/Tran4.htm

Siddiqi, A. (n.d.). Eastern Airlines. US Centennial of Flight Commission. Retrieved from http://www.centennialofflight.net/essay/Commercial_Aviation/EasternAirlines/ Tran13.htm

Siddiqi, A. (n.d.). A History of Commercial Air Freight. US Centennial of Flight Commission. Retrieved from http://www.centennialofflight.net/essay/Commercial _Aviation/AirFreight/Tran10.htm

Siddiqi, A. (n.d.). Trans World Airlines (TWA). US Centennial of Flight Commission. Retrieved from http://www.centennialofflight.net/essay/Commercial_Aviation/ TWA/Tran14.htm

Siddiqi, A. (n.d.). United Airlines. US Centennial of Flight Commission. Retrieved from http://www.centennialofflight.net/essay/Commercial_Aviation/UnitedAirlines/ Tran16.htm

Simonsen, E. (n. d.). Howard Hughes, Aviation Legend. Retrieved from http://www .boeing.com/news/frontiers/archive/2005/february/i_history.html.

William "Jack" Frye: Entrepreneur/Record Setter. (n. d.). National Aviation Hall of Fame. Retrieved from http://nationalaviation.blade6.donet.com/components/ content_manager_v02/view_nahf/htdocs/menu_ps.asp?NodeID=-915794956&group _ID=1134656385&Parent_ID=-1

LESSON 3 General Aviation Takes Flight

Become a Pilot: Types of Certificates. (2017). Aircraft Owners and Pilots Association. Retrieved from https://www.aopa.org/training-and-safety/learn-to-fly/become-a -pilot-types-of-certificates

Bednarek, J. (n.d.). General Aviation–An Overview. US Centennial of Flight Commission. Retrieved from http://www.centennialofflight.net/essay/GENERAL_AVIATION/ GA_OV.htm

Guillemette, R. (n.d.). Aerial Firefighting. US Centennial of Flight Commission. Retrieved from http://www.centennialofflight.net/essay/GENERAL_AVIATION/firefighting/GA17.htm

Guillemette, R. (n.d.). Aerobatic Flight. US Centennial of Flight Commission. Retrieved from http://www.centennialofflight.net/essay/GENERAL_AVIATION/aerobatic/GA19.htm

Guillemette, R. (n.d.). Beech Aircraft Corporation. US Centennial of Flight Commission. Retrieved from http://www.centennialofflight.net/essay/GENERAL_AVIATION/beech/GA9.htm

Guillemette, R. (n.d.). The Beechcraft Bonanza. US Centennial of Flight Commission. Retrieved from http://www.centennialofflight.net/essay/GENERAL_AVIATION/bonanza/GA10.htm

Guillemette, R. (n.d.). Bellanca Aircraft Corporation. US Centennial of Flight Commission. Retrieved from http://www.centennialofflight.net/essay/GENERAL _AVIATION/bellanca/GA1.htm

Guillemette, R. (n.d.). Benny Howard and His Darned Good Airplanes. US Centennial of Flight Commission. Retrieved from http://www.centennialofflight.net/essay/GENERAL_AVIATION/howard/GA5.htm

Guillemette, R. (n.d.). Bush Flying. US Centennial of Flight Commission. Retrieved from http://www.centennialofflight.net/essay/GENERAL_AVIATION/bush_flying/GA18.htm

Guillemette, R. (n.d.). Business Aircraft. US Centennial of Flight Commission. Retrieved from http://www.centennialofflight.net/essay/GENERAL_AVIATION/business/GA14.htm

Guillemette, R. (n.d.). Crop Dusters. US Centennial of Flight Commission. Retrieved from http://www.centennialofflight.net/essay/GENERAL_AVIATION/dusting/GA16.htm

LESSON 4   The Jet Era in Commercial Flight

737 Commercial Transport: Historical Snapshot. (2016). Boeing. Retrieved from http://www.boeing.com/history/products/737-classic.page

The 9/11 Commission Report. (2004). National Commission on Terrorist Attacks Upon the United States. Retrieved from http://www.9-11commission.gov/report/911Report.pdf

Airbus A380. (2016). Airbus. Retrieved from http://www.airbus.com/aircraftfamilies/passengeraircraft/a380family/

The Airbus Concept Plane. (2016). Airbus. Retrieved from http://www.airbus.com/innovation/future-by-airbus/the-concept-plane/the-airbus-concept-plane/

Biofuels: Renewable Jet Fuels. (2012). Boeing. Retrieved from http://www.boeing.com/innovation/#/environment/biofuels-renewable-jet-fuel

Boeing 777. (2016). Boeing. Retrieved from http://www.boeing.com/commercial/777/

Boeing 787. (2016). Boeing. Retrieved from http://www.boeing.com/commercial/787/

Bramson, D. (2015). Supersonic Airplanes and the Age of Irrational Technology. *The Atlantic.* 1 July 2015. Retrieved from http://www.theatlantic.com/technology/archive/2015/07/supersonic-airplanes-concorde/396698/

A Brief History of the Federal Aviation Administration. (n.d.). Federal Aviation Administration. Retrieved from http://www.faa.gov/about/history/brief_history/

British Airways. (n.d.). Celebrating Concorde. Retrieved from http://www.britishairways.com/en-gb/information/about-ba/history-and-heritage/celebrating-concorde

Concorde: Celebrating an Aviation Icon. (n.d.) Retrieved from http://www.concordesst.com/home.html

The Jet Engine and Sir Frank Whittle. (n.d.). Midland Air Museum: The Sir Frank Whittle Jet Heritage Centre. Retrieved from http://www.midlandairmuseum.co.uk/jet.php

Juan Trippe. (n.d.). US Centennial of Flight Commission. Retrieved from http://www.centennialofflight.net/essay/Dictionary/Trippe/DI128.htm

McDonnell Douglas DC-10 & Boeing MD-10. (n.d.). Airliners.net. Retrieved from http://www.airliners.net/aircraft-data/mcdonnell-douglas-dc-10-boeing-md-10/279

Montgomery, J. (Ed.). (2000). *Aerospace: The Journey of Flight.* Maxwell Air Force Base, AL: Civil Air Patrol National Headquarters.

Neate, R. (2016). Supersonic jet startup vows 'affordable' travel – if you have $5,000 to spare. *The Guardian,* 23 March 2016. Retrieved from https://www.theguardian.com/business/2016/mar/23/boom-supersonic-jet-travel-affordable-business-class

Ros, M. (2016). How real is the hypersonic aircraft revolution? *CNN.com.* Retrieved from http://www.cnn.com/2016/03/07/aviation/hypersonic-future-of-aviation/

Rosenberg, Z. (2016). NASA Aims to Build a Quiet SST. *Air and Space Magazine,* 2 March 2016. Retrieved from http://www.airspacemag.com/daily-planet/swiftly-silently-180958260/

Siddiqi, A. (n.d.). Deregulation and Its Consequences. US Centennial of Flight Commission. Retrieved from http://www.centennialofflight.net/essay/Commercial_Aviation/Dereg/Tran8.htm

Siddiqi, A. (n.d.). The Era of Commercial Jets. US Centennial of Flight Commission. Retrieved from http://centennialofflight.net/essay/Commercial_Aviation/Jet_Era/Tran7.htm

Siddiqi, A. (n.d.). The Opening of the Commercial Jet Era. (n.d.). US Centennial of Flight Commission. Retrieved from http://centennialofflight.net/essay/Commercial_Aviation/Opening_of_Jet_era/Tran6.htm

SUGAR Volt: Boeing's Hybrid Electric Aircraft. (2012). Boeing. Retrieved from http://www.boeing.com/innovation/#/environment/sugar-volt-boeing-s-hybrid-electric-aircraft

TransStats: The Intermodal Transportation Database. (n.d.). Bureau of Transportation Statistics. Retrieved from http://www.transtats.bts.gov/

We Weren't Just Airborne Yesterday. (2006). Southwest Airlines. Retrieved from http://www.southwest.com/about_swa/airborne.html

Wilber, D. Q. (2007). A Crash's Improbable Impact: '82 Air Florida Tragedy Led to Broad Safety Reforms. *The Washington Post,*12 January 2007, p A1.

Zhang, B. (2015). Airbus just patented a jet that could fly from London to New York in 1 hour. *BusinessInsider.com.* Retrieved from http://www.businessinsider.com/airbus-just-patented-a-jet-that-can-fly-from-london-to-new-york-in-1-hour-2015-7

CHAPTER 5 The US Air Force Is Born

LESSON 1   The Army Air Forces Become the US Air Force

Berlin "Candy Bomber." (n.d.). Hill Aerospace Museum, Hill AFB, Utah. Retrieved 29 January 2007 from http://www.hill.af.mil/museum/history/candy.htm

Chisolm, D. E., Mitchell, N. L., & Roberson, P. Q. (Eds.). (2002). *Aerospace Science: Frontiers of Aviation History* (Second ed.). Maxwell Air Force Base, AL: Air Force Officer Accessions and Training Schools.

Chivalette, W. I. (2005). Enlisted History. In AFPAM36-2241V1, *Promotion Fitness Examination.* 1 July 2005. US Air Force.

Historical Snapshot: B-47 Stratojet. (n.d.) Boeing. Retrieved from http://www.boeing.com/history/products/b-47-stratojet.page

Historical Snapshot: B-52 Stratofortress. (n.d.) Boeing. Retrieved from http://www.boeing.com/history/products/b-52-stratofortress.page

Integrating the Air Force. (2011). Air Force Historical Support Division. Retrieved from http://www.afhistory.af.mil/FAQs/FactSheets/tabid/3323/Article/458996/1948-integrating-the-air-force.aspx

Leuchtenburg, W. E., and the Editors of Time-Life Books. (1977). *The Life History of the United States: The Age of Change,* Vol. 12: From 1945. Alexandria, VA: Time-Life Books Inc.

Marshall Plan, 1948. (n.d.). US Department of State, Office of the Historian. Retrieved from https://history.state.gov/milestones/1945-1952/marshall-plan

Montgomery, J. (Ed.). (2000). *Aerospace: The Journey of Flight.* Maxwell Air Force Base, AL: Civil Air Patrol National Headquarters.

William T. Tunner. (n.d.). *Air and Space Power Journal of Air University.* Retrieved 26 January 2007 from http://www.airpower.maxwell.af.mil/airchronicles/cc/tunn.html

LESSON 2 Military Aircraft Development After World War II

B-2 Spirit. (June 2006). Air Combat Command: Office of Public Affairs. Retrieved from http://www.af.mil/factsheets/ factsheet.asp?fsID=82

Biography of Neil Armstrong. (2015). National Aeronautics and Space Administration, John Glenn Research Center. Retrieved from https://www.nasa.gov/centers/glenn/about/bios/neilabio.html

Blair Jr., C. (1957). The Last Flight of the X-2. *Air Force Magazine,* March 1957. Retrieved from http://www.airforcemag.com/MagazineArchive/Pages/1957/March%201957/0357last.aspx

Boyne, W. J. (1997). *Beyond the Wild Blue: A History of the U.S. Air Force.* New York: St. Martin's Press.

Brigadier General Charles E. "Chuck" Yeager. (1973). US Air Force. Retrieved from http://www.af.mil/AboutUs/Biographies/Display/tabid/225/Article/105165/brigadier-general-charles-e-chuck-yeager.aspx

Brigadier General Frank Kendall Everest Jr. (1972). US Air Force. Retrieved from http://www.af.mil/AboutUs/Biographies/Display/tabid/225/Article/107133/brigadier-general-frank-kendall-everest-jr.aspx

Creating the Blackbird. (n.d.). Lockheed Martin Corporation. Retrieved from http://www.lockheedmartin.com/us/100years/stories/blackbird.html

Day, D. A. (n.d.). Early X-Planes. US Centennial of Flight Commission. Retrieved from http://www.centennialofflight.net/essay/Evolution_of_Technology/early_X_planes/Tech27.htm

Day. D. A. (n.d.). The X-15 and Hypersonics. Retrieved from http://www.centennialofflight.net/essay/Evolution_of_Technology/X-15/Tech28.htm

Edwards' History. (2009). US Air Force, Edwards Air Force Base. Retrieved from http://www.edwards.af.mil/About/Fact-Sheets/Display/Article/393907/edwards-history

Excelsior Gondola. (2016). National Museum of the US Air Force. Retrieved from http://www.nationalmuseum.af.mil/Visit/MuseumExhibits/FactSheets/Display/tabid/509/Article/195681/excelsior-gondola.aspx

Garber, S. (1997). Charles E. (Chuck) Yeager. National Air and Space Administration History Office. Retrieved from http://www.hq.nasa.gov/office/pao/History/x1/chuck.html

Gibbs, Y. (Ed.). (2016). Former Pilots: A. Scott Crossfield. National Aeronautics and Space Administration. Retrieved from https://www.nasa.gov/centers/armstrong/news/Biographies/Pilots/bd-dfrc-p021.html

Iven Karl Kincheloe, Jr. (2013). Arlington National Cemetery Website. Retrieved from http://www.arlingtoncemetery.net/kinchel.htm

Lockheed AC-130A Hercules. (2015). National Museum of the US Air Force. Retrieved from http://www.nationalmuseum.af.mil/Visit/MuseumExhibits/FactSheets/Display/tabid/509/Article/197558/lockheed-ac-130a-hercules.aspx

Lockheed F-104C Starfighter. (2015). National Museum of the US Air Force. Retrieved from http://www.nationalmuseum.af.mil/Visit/MuseumExhibits/FactSheets/Display/tabid/509/Article/198067/lockheed-f-104c-starfighter.aspx

Lockheed F-104 Starfighter High-Speed Fighter/Interceptor Aircraft. (2016). MilitaryFactory.com. Retrieved from http://www.militaryfactory.com/aircraft/detail.asp?aircraft_id=113

Lockheed SR-71A. (2015). National Museum of the US Air Force. Retrieved from http://www.nationalmuseum.af.mil/Visit/MuseumExhibits/FactSheets/Display/tabid/509/Article/198054/lockheed-sr-71a.aspx

Merlin, P. (2011). Starbuster: 55 years ago Capt. Mel Apt conquered Mach 3, lost life on fated flight. US Air Force, Edwards Air Force Base. Retrieved from http://www.edwards.af.mil/News/Article-Display/Article/394758/starbuster-55-years-ago-capt-mel-apt-conquered-mach-3-lost-life-on-fated-flight

Milburn G. Apt. (2016). kansaspedia. Kansas Historical Society. Retrieved from https://www.kshs.org/kansapedia/milburn-g-apt/18258

North American F-100F Super Sabre. (2015). National Museum of the US Air Force. Retrieved from http://www.nationalmuseum.af.mil/Visit/MuseumExhibits/FactSheets/Display/tabid/509/Article/196002/north-american-f-100f-super-sabre.aspx

North American F-100 Super Sabre Fighter-Bomber/Air Superiority/Tactical Reconnaissance Aircraft. (2016). MilitaryFactory.com. Retrieved from http://www.militaryfactory.com/aircraft/detail.asp?aircraft_id=114

North American X-15A-2. (2016). National Museum of the US Air Force. Retrieved from http://www.nationalmuseum.af.mil/Visit/MuseumExhibits/FactSheets/Display/tabid/509/Article/195761/north-american-x-15a-2.aspx

Northrop YB-49. (2015). National Museum of the US Air Force. Retrieved from http://www.nationalmuseum.af.mil/Visit/MuseumExhibits/FactSheets/Display/tabid/509/Article/858861/northrop-yb-49.aspx

Ridley, Jack. (n.d.). Encyclopedia Astronautica. Retrieved from http://www.astronautix.com/r/ridley.html

Ridley, Jackie Lynwood. (2004). The National Aviation Hall of Fame. Retrieved from http://www.nationalaviation.org/our-enshrinees/ridley-jackie-lynwood/

US Air Force (2014). Stepping into the Unknown: Col (Ret) Joseph W. Kittenger, Jr [Video]. Retrieved from https://www.youtube.com/watch?v=YQerkyT4OWg&index=38&list=PLBV-tTF3X5uH_rvR6sZQPujDxnJcEQBsf

LESSON 3   The Role of Airpower from the Korean War to the Vietnam War

A-1H Skyraider. (n.d.). National Naval Aviation Museum. Retrieved from http://www
.navalaviationmuseum.org/attractions/aircraft-exhibits/item/?item=a-1h_skyraider

A-6E Intruder. (n.d.). National Naval Aviation Museum. Retrieved from http://www
.navalaviationmuseum.org/attractions/aircraft-exhibits/item/?item=a-6e_intruder

A-7E Corsair II. (n.d.). National Naval Aviation Museum. Retrieved from http://www
.navalaviationmuseum.org/attractions/aircraft-exhibits/item/?item=a-7e_corsairII

Andradé, D. J. & Conboy, K. (1999). The Secret Side of the Tonkin Gulf Incident.
Naval History, August 1999. Retrieved from http://www.usni.org/navalhistory/
Articles99/NHandrade.htm

Blinding the Enemy: EB-66 Electronic Warfare over North Vietnam. (2015). National
Museum of the US Air Force. Retrieved from http://www.nationalmuseum.af.mil/
Visit/MuseumExhibits/FactSheets/Display/tabid/509/Article/196013/blinding-the
-enemy-eb-66-electronic-warfare-over-north-vietnam.aspx

Boyne, W. (1997). *Beyond the Wild Blue: A History of the U.S. Air Force.* New York:
St. Martin's Press.

Capt Lance P. Sijan. (n.d.). *Air Force Print News Today.* Retrieved from http://www.af
.mil/mediacenter/transcripts/story_print.asp?storyID=123009132

Capt Manuel "Pete" Fernandez Jr. (n.d.). National Museum of the US Air Force. Retrieved
from http://www.nationalmuseum.af.mil/factsheets/ factsheet.asp?fsID=1082

Chisolm, D. E., Mitchell, N. L., & Roberson, P. Q. (Eds.). (2002). *Aerospace Science:
Frontiers of Aviation History* (Second ed.). Maxwell Air Force Base, AL: Air Force
Officer Accessions and Training Schools.

Chivalette, W. I. (2005). Enlisted History. In AFPAM36-2241V1, *Promotion Fitness
Examination.* US Air Force.

Col John H. Glenn Jr. (n.d.). National Museum of the US Air Force. Retrieved from
http://www.nationalmuseum.af.mil/factsheets/factsheet_print.asp? fsID=1099&page=1

Des Brisay, T. D. (1985). *Fourteen Hours at Koh Tang.* United States Air Force,
Office of Air Force History. Retrieved from http://books.google.com/books?id
=tE7C9PgPAO8C&pg=PA140&lpg=PA140&dq= robert+undorf&source=web&ots
=t-97OJwFet&sig=Dl7RODV8UFo9ZK6RYAZQ3 LnDkcc#PPP1,M1

F9F-2 Panther. (n.d.). National Naval Aviation Museum. Retrieved from http://www
.navalaviationmuseum.org/attractions/aircraft-exhibits/item/?item=f9f_panther

General Daniel "Chappie" James Jr. (n.d.). *Air Force Link.* Retrieved from http://www
.af.mil/history/person.asp?dec=&pid=123006480

James Jabara: Colonel, United States Air Force. (2006). Arlington National Cemetery
Website. Retrieved from http://www.arlingtoncemetery.net/jabara.htm

Joiner, S. (2013). The Jet That Shocked the West: How the MiG-15 grounded the U.S. Bomber Fleet in Korea. *Air & Space Magazine,* December 2013. Smithsonian Institution. Retrieved from http://www.airspacemag.com/military-aviation/the-jet-that-shocked-the-west-180947758/

Kapur, V. (2013). Evolution of Aerial Combat. Institute for Defence Studies and Analyses. Retrieved from http://www.idsa.in/issuebrief/EvolutionofAerialCombat_VivekKapur_080713

Leuchtenburg, W. E., and the Editors of Time-Life Books. (1977). *The Life History of the United States: The Age of Change,* Vol. 12: From 1945. Alexandria, VA: Time-Life Books Inc.

Lt Col George A. Davis Jr. (n.d.). National Museum of the US Air Force. Retrieved from http://www.nationalmuseum.af.mil/factsheets/ factsheet.asp?id=1073

Lockheed F-80C Shooting Star. (2015). National Museum of the US Air Force. Retrieved from http://www.nationalmuseum.af.mil/Visit/MuseumExhibits/FactSheets/Display/tabid/509/Article/196116/lockheed-f-80c-shooting-star.aspx

Lockheed U2-A. (n.d.). National Museum of the US Air Force. Retrieved from http://www.nationalmuseum.af.mil/factsheets/factsheet.asp?id=387

LTV A-7D Corsair II. (2015). National Museum of the US Air Force. http://www.nationalmuseum.af.mil/Visit/MuseumExhibits/FactSheets/Display/tabid/509/Article/196072/ltv-a-7d-corsair-ii.aspx

Maj Rudolf Anderson Jr. (n.d.). *Air Force Link.* Retrieved from http://www.af.mil/history/spotlight.asp?storyID=123009509

McDonnell Douglas F-4C Phantom II. (2015). National Museum of the US Air Force. Retrieved from http://www.nationalmuseum.af.mil/Visit/MuseumExhibits/FactSheets/Display/tabid/509/Article/196051/mcdonnell-douglas-f-4c-phantom-ii.aspx

Mikoyan-Gurevich MiG-15bis. (2015). National Museum of the US Air Force. Retrieved from http://www.nationalmuseum.af.mil/Visit/MuseumExhibits/FactSheets/Display/tabid/509/Article/196115/mikoyan-gurevich-mig-15bis.aspx

Mikoyan-Gurevich MiG-15 (Fagot) Single-Seat Jet-Powered Fighter Aircraft. (2016). MilitaryFactory.com. Retrieved from http://www.militaryfactory.com/aircraft/detail.asp?aircraft_id=124

Mikoyan-Gurevich MiG-17F. (2015). National Museum of the US Air Force. Retrieved from http://www.nationalmuseum.af.mil/Visit/MuseumExhibits/FactSheets/Display/tabid/509/Article/196057/mikoyan-gurevich-mig-17f.aspx

Mikoyan-Gurevich MiG-21PF "Fishbed-D". (2015). National Museum of the US Air Force. Retrieved from http://www.nationalmuseum.af.mil/Visit/MuseumExhibits/FactSheets/Display/tabid/509/Article/195970/mikoyan-gurevich-mig-21pf-fishbed-d.aspx

Miskimins, S. M., & Chivalette, W. I. (n.d.). CM Sgt Richard L. Etchberger: Top Secret Enlisted Air Force Cross Recipient. Suitland, Maryland: Airmen Memorial Museum. Retrieved from http://media.defense.gov/2015/Feb/02/2001329839/-1/-1/0/AFD-150202-036.pdf

Montgomery, J. (Ed.). (2000). *Aerospace: The Journey of Flight*. Maxwell Air Force Base, AL: Civil Air Patrol National Headquarters.

North American F-86A Sabre. (2015). National Museum of the US Air Force. Retrieved from http://www.nationalmuseum.af.mil/Visit/MuseumExhibits/FactSheets/Display/tabid/509/Article/196118/north-american-f-86a-sabre.aspx

North American P-51D Mustang. (n.d.). National Museum of the US Air Force. Retrieved from http://www.nationalmuseum.af.mil/factsheets/factsheet. asp?id=513

North American T-28B Trojan. (2015). National Museum of the US Air Force. Retrieved from http://www.nationalmuseum.af.mil/Visit/MuseumExhibits/FactSheets/Display/tabid/509/Article/196029/north-american-t-28b-trojan.aspx

North Vietnamese Air Force [NVAF] Operations. (2016). GlobalSecurity.org. Retrieved from http://www.globalsecurity.org/military/world/vietnam/nva-nvaf-ops.htm

Republic F-84E Thunderjet. (2015). National Museum of the US Air Force. Retrieved from http://www.nationalmuseum.af.mil/Visit/MuseumExhibits/FactSheets/Display/tabid/509/Article/196111/republic-f-84e-thunderjet.aspx

Republic F-105G Thunderchief. (2015). National Museum of the US Air Force. Retrieved from http://www.nationalmuseum.af.mil/Visit/MuseumExhibits/FactSheets/Display/tabid/509/Article/196044/republic-f-105g-thunderchief.aspx

Republic F-105 Thunderchief Fighter-Bomber/Reconnaissance/Wild Weasel. (2016). MilitaryFactory.com. Retrieved from http://www.militaryfactory.com/aircraft/detail.asp?aircraft_id=160

Ruhrstahl X-4 Air-to-Air Missile. (2015). National Museum of the US Air Force. Retrieved from http://www.nationalmuseum.af.mil/Visit/MuseumExhibits/FactSheets/Display/tabid/509/Article/196222/ruhrstahl-x-4-air-to-air-missile.aspx

SA-2 Surface-to-Air Missile. (2015). National Museum of the US Air Force. Retrieved from http://www.nationalmuseum.af.mil/Visit/MuseumExhibits/FactSheets/Display/tabid/509/Article/196037/sa-2-surface-to-air-missile.aspx

Sgt John L. Levitow. (n.d.). *Air Force Link*. Retrieved from http://www.af.mil/history/person_print.asp?storyID=123006519

Tankers at War: Air Refueling in Southeast Asia. (2015). National Museum of the US Air Force. Retrieved from http://www.nationalmuseum.af.mil/Visit/MuseumExhibits/FactSheets/Display/tabid/509/Article/196003/tankers-at-war-air-refueling-in-southeast-asia.aspx

Vietnam War: 1961. (n.d.). National Museum of the US Air Force. Retrieved from http://www.nationalmuseum.af.mil/factsheets/factsheet.asp?fsID=1256

Vought / LTV A-7 Corsair II Carrier-Borne Strike Aircraft. (2015). MilitaryFactory.com. Retrieved from http://www.militaryfactory.com/aircraft/detail.asp?aircraft_id=116

LESSON 4   Other US Air Force Military Operations
That Supported National Objectives

Alex, D. (2016). Mikoyan MiG-27 (Flogger) Ground Attack Aircraft. MilitaryFactory.com. Retrieved from http://www.militaryfactory.com/aircraft/detail.asp?aircraft_id=230

Ball, G. B. (2012). Operation Eagle Claw. Air Force Historical Support Division. Retrieved from http://www.afhistory.af.mil/FAQs/FactSheets/tabid/3323/Article/458949/operation-eagle-claw.aspx

Ball, G. B. (2012). Operation El Dorado Canyon. Air Force Historical Support Division. Retrieved from http://www.afhistory.af.mil/FAQs/FactSheets/tabid/3323/Article/458950/operation-el-dorado-canyon.aspx

Ball, G. B. (2012). Operation Urgent Fury. Air Force Historical Support Division. Retrieved from http://www.afhistory.af.mil/FAQs/FactSheets/tabid/3323/Article/458952/operation-urgent-fury.aspx

Boyne, W. J. (1999). El Dorado Canyon. Retrieved from http://www.afa.org/magazine/March1999/0399canyon.asp

Camps, C. T. (2006). Operation Eagle Claw: The Iran Hostage Rescue Mission. *Airpower,* 21 December 2006. Retrieved from http://www.airpower. maxwell.af.mil/apjinternational/apj-s/2006/3tri06/kampseng.html

Chisolm, D. E., Mitchell, N. L., & Roberson, P. Q. (Eds.). (2002). *Aerospace Science: Frontiers of Aviation History* (Second ed.). Maxwell Air Force Base, AL: Air Force Officer Accessions and Training Schools.

Chivalette, W. I. (2005). Enlisted History. In AFPAM36-2241V1, *Promotion Fitness Examination.*

Creen, M. J. (n.d.). A Sign of the Times: Operation Urgent Fury: Grenada. Retrieved from http://www.af.mil/news/airman/0197/grenada.htm

Cultural Studies: An Introduction to Global Awareness. (2010). Sudbury, MA: Jones & Bartlett Publishers.

F-111 Aardvark. (n.d.). *Air Force Link.* Retrieved from http://www.af.mil/news/story.asp?storyID=123006568

F-14A Tomcat. (n.d.). National Naval Aviation Museum. Retrieved from http://www.navalaviationmuseum.org/attractions/aircraft-exhibits/item/?item=f-14a_tomcat_flightline

Ferdinando, L. (2007). Panama's Noriega to be Released from US Prison in September. *Voice of America News,* 24 January 2007. Retrieved from http://www.voanews.com/english/2007-01-24-voa45.cfm

Garamone, Jim. (2005). America Remembers Desert One Heroes. *American Forces Press Service,* 26 April 2005. Retrieved from http://www.af.mil/news/ story.asp?storyID=123010370

General Dynamics F-111A Aardvark. (2015). National Museum of the US Air Force. Retrieved from http://www.nationalmuseum.af.mil/Visit/MuseumExhibits/FactSheets/Display/tabid/509/Article/196049/general-dynamics-f-111a-aardvark.aspx

Grumman F-14 D (R) Tomcat. (n.d.). Smithsonian National Air and Space Museum. Retrieved from https://airandspace.si.edu/collection-objects/grumman-f-14dr-tomcat

Grumman F-14 Tomcat Carrier-Borne Air Defence/Air Superiority Fighter. (2016). MilitaryFactory.com. Retrieved from http://www.militaryfactory.com/aircraft/detail.asp?aircraft_id=63

Haulman, D. L. (2003). *One Hundred Years of Flight: USAF Chronology of Significant Air and Space Events 1903–2002.* Retrieved from http://afhra. maxwell.af.mil/chronologyofflight.pdf

Hess, Michael. (2006). High Alert in 1986. *Air Force Link,* 27 April 2006. Retrieved from http://www.af.mil/news/story.asp?storyID=123018986

Marion, F. (2009). Air Force Combat Controllers at Desert One, April 24-25, 1980. *Air Power History,* Spring 2009. Retrieved from http://www.afhso.af.mil/shared/media/document/AFD-120803-027.pdf

Mikoyan-Gurevich MiG-23 (Flogger) Fighter-Interceptor Aircraft. (2016). MilitaryFactory.com. Retrieved from http://www.militaryfactory.com/aircraft/detail.asp?aircraft_id=151

Mikoyan-Gurevich MiG-23MLD. (2015). National Museum of the US Air Force. Retrieved from http://www.nationalmuseum.af.mil/Visit/MuseumExhibits/FactSheets/Display/tabid/509/Article/196862/mikoyan-gurevich-mig-23mld.aspx

Montgomery, J. (Ed.). (2000). *Aerospace: The Journey of Flight.* Maxwell Air Force Base, AL: Civil Air Patrol National Headquarters.

Operation Eagle Claw. (n.d.). The Air University: College of Aerospace Doctrine, Research, and Education. Retrieved from http://www.apc.maxwell.af.mil/text/excur/eagle.htm

Operation Just Cause. (n.d.). *Air Force Link.* Retrieved from http://www.af.mil/history/spotlight.asp?storyID=123013656

Phillips, R. C. (2006). *Operation Just Cause: The Incursion into Panama.* US Army Center of Military History. Retrieved from http://www.history.army.mil/html/books/070/70-85-1/cmhPub_70-85-1.pdf

LESSON 5 Global Interventions From 1990

Alex, D. (2016). Lockheed Martin/General Dynamics F-16 Fighting Falcon Multi-Role Lightweight Fighter/Strike Fighter. MilitaryFactory.com. Retrieved from http://www.militaryfactory.com/aircraft/detail.asp?aircraft_id=22

Allison, M. L. (2004). Airmen Use GBU-38 in Combat. *Air Force Print News,* 4 October 2004. Retrieved from http://www.af.mil/news/story.asp?storyID=123008840

B1-B Lancer. (2005). *Air Force Link.* Retrieved from http://www.af.mil/factsheets/factsheet.asp?id=81

B-2 Spirit. (n.d.). *Air Force Link.* Retrieved from http://www.af.mil/ factsheets/factsheet.asp?fsID=82

Bates, M. (2006). F-117: A Long, Storied History That Is About to End. *Air Force Link*. Retrieved from http://www.af.mil/news/ story.asp?storyID=123030185

Boeing/McDonnell Douglas F-15 Eagle Multirole Aircraft. (2016). MilitaryFactory. com. Retrieved from http://www.militaryfactory.com/aircraft/detail.asp?aircraft_id=21

Brubaker, T. (2003). Operation Northern Watch Fighters Say Final Goodbye to Incirlik. *Air Force Link*. Retrieved from http://www.af.mil/ news/airman/0603/world3.html

Chisolm, D. E., Mitchell, N. L., & Roberson, P. Q. (Eds.). (2002). *Aerospace Science: Frontiers of Aviation History* (Second ed.). Maxwell Air Force Base, AL: Air Force Officer Accessions and Training Schools.

Cohen, Z. (2016). Air Force investing $12B in F-15s. *CNN.com,* 2 September 2016. Retrieved from http://www.cnn.com/2016/09/02/politics/us-air-force-f-15-upgrades/

Deaile, M. (2014). The Longest Bombing Run Ever. *On Patrol,* Winter 2014–2015. Retrieved from http://usoonpatrol.org/archives/2014/11/13/b-2-pilot-flew-longest -combat

Dsouza, L. (2007). This is how the F-117A was shot down in Serbia by a SA-3 (S-75) Goa SAM in 1999. *Defence Aviation*. Retrieved from http://www.defenceaviation.com/ 2007/02/how-was-f-117-shot-down-part-1.html

Duff, P. (2006). CAP Proves Worth during Katrina Relief. *Air Force Link*. Retrieved from http://www.af.mil/news/story.asp? id=123026197

Elliott, S. (2004). Roche Unveils AF Hero Memorial. *Air Force Print News,* 9 January 2004. Cited on Arlington National Cemetery website. Retrieved from http:// arlingtoncemetery.net/jachapman-memorial-at-anc.htm

Everdeen, B. (2006). Small-Diameter Bomb Ready for War on Terror. *Air Force Link*. Retrieved from http://www.af.mil/news/story_ print.asp?storyID=123025585

F-117A Nighthawk. (n.d.). *Air Force Link*. Retrieved from http://www.af.mil/history/ aircraft.asp?dec=1970-1980&pid=123006550

F-117A Nighthawk. (2005). *Air Force Link*. Retrieved from http://www.af.mil/factsheets/ factsheet.asp?fsID=104

50 Heroes From 50 States. (2007). Alabama: Chief Master Sgt. Kevin Lynn. US Department of Defense. Retrieved from http://www.defenselink.mil/home/dodupdate/ heroes/50heroes/AL.html

Frontline: The Gulf War. (2007). WGBH Education Foundation. Retrieved from http://www.pbs.org/wgbh/pages/frontline/gulf/maps/2.html

Garamone, J. (2005). General Myers Receives Presidential Medal of Freedom. *American Forces Press Service,* 10 November 2005. Retrieved from http://www.af.mil/news/ story.asp?storyID=123012866

General Dynamics F-16A Fighting Falcon. (2015). National Museum of the US Air Force. Retrieved from http://www.nationalmuseum.af.mil/Visit/MuseumExhibits/ FactSheets/Display/tabid/509/Article/196735/general-dynamics-f-16a-fighting -falcon.aspx

Global War on Terrorism. (2003). *Air Force Link*. Retrieved from http://www.af.mil/ airforceoperationscenter/operationenduringfreedom.asp

Jason Dean Cunningham. (2006). Arlington National Cemetery. Retrieved from http://www.arlingtoncemetery.net/jdcunningham.htm

Keeping Watch. (2002). *Airman,* July 2002. Retrieved from http://www.af.mil/news/ airman/0702/osw.html

Kurle, D. (2006). Predators Provide Eyes in the Sky Over Afghanistan. *Air Force Link*. Retrieved from http://www.af.mil/news/ story.asp?storyID=123021334

McDonnell Douglas F-15A Eagle. (2015). National Museum of the US Air Force. Retrieved from http://www.nationalmuseum.af.mil/Visit/MuseumExhibits/ FactSheets/Display/tabid/509/Article/196332/mcdonnell-douglas-f-15a-eagle.aspx

Mikoyan-Gurevich MiG-29A. (2015). National Museum of the US Air Force. Retrieved from http://www.nationalmuseum.af.mil/Visit/MuseumExhibits/FactSheets/ Display/tabid/509/Article/197174/mikoyan-gurevich-mig-29a.aspx

Miles, D. (2006). Operation Enduring Freedom Marks Five Years. *American Forces Press Service,* 6 October 2006. Retrieved from http://www.af.mil/news/story_print .asp?storyID=123028591

Montgomery, J. (Ed.). (2000). *Aerospace: The Journey of Flight.* Maxwell Air Force Base, AL: Civil Air Patrol National Headquarters.

Moseley, T. M. (2006). CSAF's Vector: Operation Iraqi Freedom Anniversary. Retrieved from http://www.af.mil/library/ viewpoints/csaf.asp?id=223

Noble Eagle Overview. (n.d.). *Air Force Link*. Retrieved from http://www.af.mil/ airforceoperationscenter/operationnobleeagle.asp

Operation Anaconda: A Day-by-Day Guide to the First Week of Fighting. (2002). *Time*, March 10, 2002. Retrieved from http://www.time.com/time/covers/ 1101020318/popup/index.html

Operation Iraqi Freedom. (2003). *Air Force Link*. Retrieved from http://www.af.mil/ airforceoperationscenter/operationiraqifreedom.asp

Paul T. Johnson. (n.d.). *Military Times*. Retrieved from http://valor.militarytimes.com/ recipient.php?recipientid=3546

Stealth Features. (n.d.). *Airman*. Retrieved from http://www.af.mil/news/airman/ 1005/airsb1_txt.shtml

Technical Sgt Tim Wilkinson. (n.d.). *Air Force Link*. Retrieved from http://www.af.mil/ history/person.asp?dec=&pid=123006509

USAFE Unit Debuts Small Diameter Bomb in Combat. (2006). *Air Force Print News,* 5 October 2006. Retrieved from http://www.af.mil/pressreleases/ release.asp?storyID =123028471

Wade, S. (2006). Holloman Airmen Support Operation Noble Eagle. North American Aerospace Defense Command. Retrieved from http://www.norad.mil/newsroom/ news_releases/2006/031306.htm

CHAPTER 6 The Modern Air Force

LESSON 1 The Development of Rotary-Wing Aircraft

Aviation. (2016.) US Forest Service. Retrieved from http://www.fs.fed.us/fire/aviation/

Aviation Program. (n.d.). National Park Service. Retrieved from https://www.nps.gov/orgs/aviationprogram/index.htm

Ball, G. (2016). "Hurricane Katrina Relief Operations." Air Force Historical Support Division. Retrieved from http://www.afhso.af.mil/topics/factsheets/factsheet.asp?id=18651

Bell H-13 Sioux Light Utility/Observation Helicopter. (2013). MilitaryFactory.com. Retrieved from http://www.militaryfactory.com/aircraft/detail.asp?aircraft_id=1139

Bell UH-1 Iroquois (Huey) Multi-Role/Utility/Attack/Transport Helicopter. (2017). MilitaryFactory.com. Retrieved from http://www.militaryfactory.com/aircraft/detail.asp?aircraft_id=42

Boeing/Hughes AH-64 Apache Attack Helicopter." (2016). MilitaryFactory.com. Retrieved from http://www.militaryfactory.com/aircraft/detail.asp?aircraft_id=29

Charles, M. (2011). CJCS presents Bronze Stars to Nellis pararescuemen. *Air Force News Service.* 18 April 2011. Retrieved from http://www.af.mil/News/ArticleDisplay/tabid/223/Article/113587/cjcs-presents-bronze-stars-to-nellis-pararescuemen.aspx

Collins, E. M. (2016). Vietnam War pilot to receive Medal of Honor. *Army News Service.* Retrieved from https://www.army.mil/article/170084?from=moh__news_image

Day, D. A. (n.d.). Bell UH-1 "Huey." Centennial of Flight Commission. Retrieved from http://www.centennialofflight.net/essay/Rotary/Huey/HE11.htm

Day, D. A. (n.d.). Civil and Commercial Helicopters. US Centennial of Flight Commission. Retrieved from http://www.centennialofflight.net/essay/Rotary/commercial/HE10.htm

Day, D. A. (2005). Igor Sikorsky: VS-300. US Centennial of Flight Commission. Retrieved from http://www.centennialofflight.net/essay/Rotary/Sikorsky_VS300/HE8.htm

Day, D. A. (n.d.). M.A.S.H./Medevac Helicopters. US Centennial of Flight Commission. Retrieved from http://www.centennialofflight.net/essay/Rotary/MASH/HE12.htm

Day, D A. (n.d.) Sikorsky UH-60/S-70 Black Hawk Family. US Centennial of Flight Commission. Retrieved from http://www.centennialofflight.net/essay/Rotary/BlackHawk/HE16.htm

Garunay, M. (2016). President Obama Awards the Medal of Honor to Lieutenant Colonel Charles Kettles. The White House. Retrieved from https://www.whitehouse.gov/blog/2016/07/18/president-obama-awards-medal-honor-lt-col-charles-kettles

Head, E. (2016). "Helicopters Respond to Historic Floods." *Vertical.* Retrieved from https://www.verticalmag.com/news/helicopters-respond-historic-louisiana-floods/

Igor I. Sikorsky. (n.d.). Igor I. Sikorsky Historical Archives. Retrieved from http://www.sikorskyarchives.com/siksky2.htm

Igor Sikorsky, Industrialist/Inventor. (n.d.). National Aviation Hall of Fame. Retrieved from http://nationalaviation.blade6.donet.com/components/content_manager_v02/view_nahf/htdocs/menu_ps.asp?NodeID=666001144&group_ID=1134656385&Parent_ID=-1

Sikorsky H-19 Chickasaw Multi-Purpose Transport Helicopter. (2016). MilitaryFactory.com. Retrieved from http://www.militaryfactory.com/aircraft/detail.asp?aircraft_id=128

Sikorsky HH-3E Jolly Green Giant Search and Rescue (SAR) Helicopter. (2016). MilitaryFactory.com. Retrieved from http://www.militaryfactory.com/aircraft/detail.asp?aircraft_id=129

Sikorsky HH-60 (Pave Hawk) Combat Search and Rescue/Military Operations Helicopter. (2016). MilitaryFactory.com. Retrieved from http://www.militaryfactory.com/aircraft/detail.asp?aircraft_id=41

Terrell, C. (2016.) Honor, Respect, Devotion to Duty: Baton Rouge flood rescuers. Coast Guard Compass: Official Blog of the US Coast Guard. Retrieved from http://coastguard.dodlive.mil/2016/08/honor-respect-devotion-to-duty-baton-rouge-flood-rescuers/

V-22 Osprey. (n.d.). Boeing. Retrieved from http://www.boeing.com/defense/v-22-osprey/

LESSON 2   The Significance of Stealth Aircraft

Alex, D. (2016). Lockheed Martin/Boeing F-22 Raptor Air Dominance Fighter. MilitaryFactory.com Retrieved from http://www.militaryfactory.com/aircraft/detail.asp?aircraft_id=20

Axe, D. (2016). Pentagon Kills Its Killer Drone Fleet. The Daily Beast. Retrieved from http://www.thedailybeast.com/articles/2016/02/11/pentagon-kills-its-killer-drone-fleet.html

Alex, D. (2016). Sukhoi T-50 (PAK FA) 5th Generation Multi-Role Stealth Aircraft. MiltaryFactory.com. Retrieved from http://www.militaryfactory.com/aircraft/detail.asp?aircraft_id=782

Chengdu (AVIC) J-20 (Black Eagle) Multirole 5th Generation Fighter Aircraft. (2016). MiltaryFactory.com. Retrieved from http://www.militaryfactory.com/aircraft/detail.asp?aircraft_id=860

Darack, E. (2011). A Brief History of Unmanned Aircraft: From bomb-bearing balloons to the Global Hawk, The Smithsonian Institution: Air & Space. Retrieved from http://www.airspacemag.com/photos/a-brief-history-of-unmanned-aircraft-174072843/

F-22 Begins First Overseas Deployment. (n.d.). Air Force Link. Retrieved from http://www.af.mil/news/story.asp?storyID=123040309

Gibbs, Y. (Ed.). (2016). X-45 Unmanned Combat Air Vehicle (UCAV). National Aeronautics and Space Administration (NASA). Retrieved from https://www.nasa.gov/centers/dryden/research/X45A/index.html

Lendon, B. (2016). China's new J-20 stealth fighter screams on to scene. *CNN.com*. Retrieved from http://www.cnn.com/2016/11/01/asia/china-j-20-stealth-fighter-introduction/

Lockheed-Martin F-22A Raptor. (2015). National Museum of the US Air Force. Retrieved from http://www.nationalmuseum.af.mil/Visit/MuseumExhibits/FactSheets/Display/tabid/509/Article/196040/lockheed-martin-f-22a-raptor.aspx

Majumdar, D. (2016). Russia's New PAK-FA Stealth Fighter Might Have a Fatal Flaw (or Two). *The National Interest*. Retrieved from http://nationalinterest.org/blog/the-buzz/russias-new-pak-fa-stealth-fighter-might-have-fatal-flaw-or-16628

Majumdar, D. (2014). The Russian Air Force's Super Weapon: Beware the PAK-FA Stealth Fighter. *The National Interest*. Retrieved from http://nationalinterest.org/feature/the-russian-air-forces-super-weapon-beware-the-pak-fa-11742

MQ-1B Predator. (2015). US Air Force. Retrieved from http://www.af.mil/AboutUs/FactSheets/Display/tabid/224/Article/104469/mq-1b-predator.aspx

MQ-1 Predator Unmanned Aerial Vehicle. (2007). *Air Force Link*. Retrieved from http://www.af.mil/factsheets/factsheet.asp?fsID=122

MQ-9 Reaper. (2015). US Air Force. Retrieved from http://www.af.mil/AboutUs/FactSheets/Display/tabid/224/Article/104470/mq-9-reaper.aspx

RQ-11b Raven. (2007). US Air Force. Retrieved from http://www.af.mil/AboutUs/FactSheets/Display/tabid/224/Article/104533/rq-11b-raven.aspx

RQ-4 Global Hawk. (2014). US Air Force. Retrieved from http://www.af.mil/AboutUs/FactSheets/Display/tabid/224/Article/104516/rq-4-global-hawk.aspx

Scan Eagle. (2007). US Air Force. Retrieved from http://www.af.mil/AboutUs/FactSheets/Display/tabid/224/Article/104532/scan-eagle.aspx

Shenyang (AVIC) J-31 Gyrfalcon (FC-31/F-60) Multirole 4th Generation Fighter (2016). MilitaryFactory.com. Retrieved from http://www.militaryfactory.com/aircraft/detail.asp?aircraft_id=1024

Spinetta, L. (2016). The Rise of Unmanned Aircraft. HistoryNet. Retrieved from http://www.historynet.com/the-rise-of-unmanned-aircraft.htm

US Navy Halts Funding for X-47B. (2016). UAS Vision. Retrieved from http://www.uasvision.com/2016/02/15/us-navy-halts-funding-for-x-47b/

X-45 Joint Unmanned Combat Air System. (n.d.). Boeing. Retrieved from http://www.boeing.com/history/products/x-45-joint-unmanned-combat-air-system.page

X-47B Unmanned Combat Air System (UCAS), United States of America. (n.d.). Naval-technology.com. Retrieved from http://www.naval-technology.com/projects/x-47b-unmanned-combat-air-system-carrier-ucas/

LESSON 3 The Air Force of the Future

Air Force Association's Cyberpatriot: The National Youth Cyber Education Program. (n.d.). Retrieved from http://www.uscyberpatriot.org

Carr, J. (2016). B-21: Modernizing the bomber fleet. *Air Force News Service,* 20 September 2016. Retrieved from http://www.af.mil/News/ArticleDisplay/tabid/223/Article/950291/b-21-modernizing-the-bomber-fleet.aspx

Daniels, A. (2016). Lockheed F-35 Lightning II Advanced Multi-Role Strike Fighter/Fighter-Bomber. MilitaryFactory.com. Retrieved from http://www.militaryfactory.com/aircraft/detail.asp?aircraft_id=23

The Department of Defense Cyber Strategy. (n.d.). US Department of Defense. Retrieved from https://www.defense.gov/News/Special-Reports/0415_Cyber-Strategy

The DOD Cyber Strategy. (2015). US Department of Defense. Retrieved from https://www.defense.gov/Portals/1/features/2015/0415_cyber-strategy/Final_2015_DoD_CYBER_STRATEGY_for_web.pdf

F-35A Lightning II Conventional Takeoff and Landing Variant. (2014). US Air Force. Retrieved from http://www.af.mil/AboutUs/FactSheets/Display/tabid/224/Article/478441/f-35a-lightning-ii-conventional-takeoff-and-landing-variant.aspx

Harwood. M. (2016). *Internet Security: How to Defend Against Attackers on the Web.* Burlington, MA: Jones & Bartlett Learning.

KC-46A Pegasus. (2016). US Air Force. Retrieved from http://www.af.mil/AboutUs/FactSheets/Display/tabid/224/Article/104537/kc-46a-tanker.aspx

KC-46A Pegasus. (n.d.). Boeing. Retrieved from http://www.boeing.com/defense/kc-46a-pegasus-tanker/#/capabilities

Martin, M. (2016). Air Force reveals B-21 Long Range Strike Bomber. *Air Force News Service,* 26 February 2016. Retrieved from http://www.af.mil/News/ArticleDisplay/tabid/223/Article/673784/air-force-reveals-b-21-long-range-strike-bomber.aspx

Nakashima, E. (2016). Obama to be urged to split cyberwar command from NSA. *Washington Post,* 13 September 2016. Retrieved from https://www.washingtonpost.com/world/national-security/obama-to-be-urged-to-split-cyberwar-command-from-the-nsa/2016/09/12/0ad09a22-788f-11e6-ac8e-cf8e0dd91dc7_story.html?utm_term=.5b0a4ab82565

Nakashima, E. (2016). U.S. government officially accuses Russia of hacking campaign to interfere with elections. *Washington Post,* 7 October 2016. Retrieved from https://www.washingtonpost.com/world/national-security/us-government-officially-accuses-russia-of-hacking-campaign-to-influence-elections/2016/10/07/4e0b9654-8cbf-11e6-875e-2c1bfe943b66_story.html?utm_term=.8197d14a9e15

Nakashima, E. and Zapotosky, M. (2016). U.S. charges Iran-linked hackers with targeting banks, N.Y. dam. *Washington Post,* 24 March 2016. Retrieved from https://www.washingtonpost.com/world/national-security/justice-department-to-unseal-indictment-against-hackers-linked-to-iranian-goverment/2016/03/24/9b3797d2-f17b-11e5-a61f-e9c95c06edca_story.html?utm_term=.45b25bb35c30

Prine, C. (2016). New jet will likely change how America fights wars. *San Diego Union-Tribune*. Retrieved from http://www.sandiegouniontribune.com/military/sd-me-marines-f35-20161021-htmlstory.html

Savage, C. (2017). Chelsea Manning to Be Released Early as Obama Commutes Sentence. *New York Times*. Retrieved from https://www.nytimes.com/2017/01/17/us/politics/obama-commutes-bulk-of-chelsea-mannings-sentence.html?_r=0

Smith, D. (2016). Inspiring the next generation of cyber warriors. US Air Force: 24th Air Force. Retrieved from http://www.24af.af.mil/News/Article-Display/Article/1027057/inspiring-the-next-generation-of-cyber-warriors

Strickland, J. (n.d.). How Web 3.0 Will Work. How Stuff Works: Tech. Retrieved from http://computer.howstuffworks.com/web-30.htm

US Cyber Command (USCYBERCOM). (2016). US Strategic Command. Retrieved from http://www.stratcom.mil/Media/Factsheets/Factsheet-View/Article/960492/us-cyber-command-uscybercom/

Glossary

38th parallel—a line marking the original boundary between North and South Korea. (p. 306)

A

aerial firefighting—using aircraft to dump water or chemicals onto wildfires. (p. 240)

aerial reconnaissance—looking over battlefields from the sky. (p. 18)

aerial refueling—taking on more fuel in flight. (p. 99)

aerobatics—the spectacular stunts, such as rolls and loops, performed in an airplane or glider, or by groups of airplanes flying together. (p. 241)

aerodynamic—designed with rounded edges to reduce wind drag. (p. 84)

aeronauts—people who travel in airships or balloons. (p. 20)

aggression—hostile action against another country or government. (p. 273)

aileron—a small flap on the wing for controlling turns. (p. 42)

airfoil—a wing's profile. (p. 30)

airlift—the transportation of personnel or material by air. (p. 282)

air tanker—an aircraft used to deliver liquids from the air, typically water or fire retardant. (p. 240)

air traffic control—the ground-based system for keeping aircraft safely separated from one another. (p. 196)

airways—the routes that planes must follow through the sky. (p. 196)

all-cargo airlines—airlines that carry freight, not passengers. (p. 215)

alloy—a combination of different metals—or of metal and nonmetal—fused for strength, resistance to corrosion, or other desired qualities. (p. 246)

Allies—in World War I, Russia, France, Serbia, and Britain (later joined by the United States and Italy) (p. 61); in World War II, Britain, France, the United States, the Soviet Union, and China. (p. 129)

altitude—the height above Earth's surface. (p. 84)

amendment—a revision or change. (p. 101)

amphibian planes—aircraft designed to take off and land on either water or land. (p. 84)

angle of attack—the angle between the relative wind (the flow of air) and the airfoil. (p. 30)

annex—to incorporate territory into an existing political unit such as a country. (p. 119)

antitrust laws—laws meant to prevent monopolies. (p. 206)

apprentice—a person who works with a skilled master to learn by practical experience. (p. 93)

appropriate—to set aside for a specific use. (p. 69)

arms—weapons. (p. 275)

arms race—a competition for military supremacy in which each party tries to produce larger numbers of weapons and a better military force than the other. (p. 316)

autogiro—an early, helicopter-like aircraft. (p. 93)

autonomy—independence. (p. 124)

auxiliary—functioning as a branch of another military organization. (p. 110)

avionics—the radios and other electronic systems aboard an aircraft. (p. 232)

Axis Powers—in World War II, Germany, Italy, and Japan. (p. 129)

B

barnstormer—a pilot who travels around the country giving exhibits of stunt flying and parachuting. (p. 80)

bid—an offer or a proposal, with a price attached. (p. 31)

biplane—an aircraft with two main supporting surfaces, usually placed one above the other. (p. 23)

blind flight—the act of taking off and landing relying solely on instruments inside the cockpit for guidance. (p. 95)

blitzkrieg—a war conducted with great speed and force. (p. 136)

bombardier—the person in a military aircraft who controls when bombs are dropped. (p. 166)

bomb load—the total weight of bombs a plane can carry. (p. 163)

bombsight—a device that helps determine when to drop a bomb. (p. 118)

boom—the section of a helicopter that connects the tail with the main body. (p. 390)

bootlegger—someone who makes or sells illegal liquor. (p. 227)

bracing—support strung diagonally between struts. (p. 34)

browser—a program that accesses and displays files on the Internet or World Wide Web. (p. 433)

bush flying—aviation carried out in remote areas, typically not well served by roads or other modes of transport. (p. 238)

C

canard configuration—an elevator that sits in front of the wings. (p. 35)

carbon fiber—a very strong lightweight synthetic material made by heating acrylic fiber to very high temperatures. (p. 262)

casualties—military persons lost through death, wounds, injury, imprisonment, or missing in action. (p. 128)

center of pressure—the focal point of lift. (p. 30)

Central Powers—in World War I, Germany, Austria-Hungary, and Turkey. (p. 61)

circuit—a route that passes through one or more points and then returns to the starting point. (p. 94)

classified—withheld from public knowledge for reasons of national security. (p. 412)

cloud—another name for the Internet. (p. 434)

coalition—an alliance among nations. (p. 359)

cockpit—a space inside the fuselage where the crew sits. (p. 44)

colony—a region under the political control of a distant country. (p. 306)

combined arms—the coordinated efforts of different military branches, such as air and ground. (p. 136)

complacency—a feeling of satisfaction with the way things are, combined with a lack of alertness to danger. (p. 199)

composite materials—materials made from two or more different materials that, when combined, have properties neither has by itself. (p. 262)

configurations—setups for specific purposes. (p. 262)

consortium—an association of companies for some specific purpose. (p. 256)

containment—the US Cold War policy to prevent the spread of communism in the world. (p. 273)

corps—a branch or department of the armed forces having a specialized function. (p. 119)

coup d'état—the overthrow of a government. (p. 339)

cowling—a covering to protect and streamline the engine. (p. 103)

crankshaft—a shaft that turns or is turned by a crank. (p. 46)

crop dusting—the application of fertilizers and pesticides to crops from the air. (p. 240)

cyber—computer. (p. 431)

cybertechnology—computer technology. (p. 431)

cyberwarfare—the use of cyberspace to interfere with an enemy's command and control, disrupt normal economic activity, steal intellectual property or government secrets, and prevent equipment from functioning properly. (p. 439)

D

decertify—to revoke a union's authority to represent its members (p. 200)

de-ice—to remove ice from external surfaces of the airplane using specially formulated chemicals. (p. 258)

democracy—a form of government in which people choose their leaders by voting. (p. 269)

dinghy—a small rubber raft that is used by people escaping from a sinking boat or aircraft. (p. 161)

diplomat—a person who represents his or her country's government in a foreign country. (p. 340)

dirigible—a steerable airship. (p. 18)

dogfight—a battle between fighter planes. (p. 72)

drag—the pull, or slowing effect, of air on an aircraft. (p. 22)

drone—an unmanned aircraft. (p. 415)

drop tanks—external fuel tanks that could be dropped from the plane when empty. (p. 177)

E

elevator—a small moving section attached to a fixed wing to help control up and down movement of the aircraft. (p. 28)

embargo—a legal ban on commerce. (p. 154)

encrypting—converting data into secret code. (p. 435)

enthusiasts—strong supporters or fans. (p. 84)

equator—the imaginary circle that divides Earth into northern and southern halves. (p. 94)

escadrille—a small squadron of planes. (p. 63)

escort—accompany. (p. 147)

expeditionary teams—teams sent for operations overseas. (p. 424)

extradite—to send a person who has been accused of a crime to another state or country for trial. (p. 340)

F

fifth generation—fighter aircraft using the latest technology as of 2016. (p. 413)

firewalls—programs and devices that monitor and restrict communication between computer systems and outside networks. (p. 435)

flak—fire from anti-aircraft artillery. (p. 163)

flame out—to fail for nonmechanical reasons. (p. 185)

flight—the act of passing through the air on wings (p. 5); a unit that has two or more elements. (p. 134)

flight simulator—a training device that simulates, or imitates, the experience and sensation of flight. (p. 96)

flows—the mobile elements of a network industry. (p. 206)

free market—one that operates on the basis of competition and is not controlled by government. (p. 203)

fuselage—the body of an airplane containing the crew and passengers (or cargo). (p. 44)

G

general aviation—all aviation except scheduled commercial airline service and military aviation. (p. 225)

genocide—the attempt to wipe out all members of a racial, religious, or ethnic group. (p. 370)

glider—a light aircraft without an engine, designed to glide after being towed aloft or launched from a catapult. (p. 9)

grades—ranks. (p. 112)

grids—the fixed structures of a network industry. (p. 206)

guerrilla warfare—a type of fighting in which small bands of fighters hit more-powerful forces by surprise. (p. 318)

gunpowder—an explosive powder made of potassium nitrate, charcoal, and sulfur, used to shoot projectiles from guns. (p. 7)

H

hacking—gaining access to a file, computer, or network that you're not authorized to see. (p. 435)

heat-seeking missiles—missiles that track a target by seeking the infrared light it emits. (p. 333)

helicopter—an aircraft that gets its lift from spinning blades. (p. 8)

Holocaust—the mass murder of some six million Jews, mostly in death camps, during World War II. (p. 129)

homebuilding—the construction of aircraft by hand, typically in one's home or garage, rather than on a production line in a factory. (p. 233)

hypersonic flight—flight five times the speed of sound or faster. (p. 264)

hypertext—digital text that contains electronic links to other texts. (p. 433)

I

incendiary bombs—bombs designed to start fires. (p. 157)

incentive—a motivating reward. (p. 102)

incompetent—lacking the qualities needed for effective action. (p. 117)

infiltrate—to secretly enter or join something, such as a group or country, to gain information or do harm. (p. 349)

infrared light—heat radiation not generally visible to the naked eye. (p. 333)

insubordination—a refusal to submit to authority. (p. 117)

insurgent—a rebel or guerrilla fighter. (p. 370)

interdiction—the act of cutting or destroying an enemy's advance through firepower. (p. 137)

integration—including individuals from different groups in society or an organization as equals. (p. 271)

internal-combustion engine—an engine in which the fuel is burned inside, rather than in an external furnace. (p. 19)

international waters—areas of the seas where ships from any nation have the right to travel. (p. 317)

Internet—a system of networks connecting computers around the world. (p. 433)

Islamist—based on a fundamentalist interpretation of Islam that seeks to enforce Islamic values in all areas of life. (p. 340)

isolationist—a nation that does not enter alliances with other countries. (p. 132)

insurgent—a rebel or guerrilla fighter. (p. 370)

J

jet lag—fatigue and sleep disturbance as result of crossing time zones on a jet. (p. 259)

jumpsuit—a one-piece outfit. (p. 52)

K

kamikaze—an airplane loaded with explosives to be flown in a suicide attack, especially against a ship. (p. 172)

keel—a structure that extends along the center of a craft from the front to the back. (p. 18)

kite—a light framework covered with paper or cloth, provided with a balancing tail, designed to be flown in the air. (p. 6)

L

lateral—sideways. (p. 35)

latitude—a line north or south from Earth's equator and parallel to it. (p. 306)

legend—an unverified story handed down from earlier times. (p. 7)

liability insurance—insurance that protects someone from claims arising from injuries or damage to other people or property. (p. 232)

lift—the upward force on an aircraft against gravity. (p. 17)

limited war—a war in which opposing sides try to avoid a worldwide war and the possible use of atomic bombs by fighting with each other outside their own lands and sometimes through troops who aren't their own. (p. 306)

logistics—the aspect of military operations that deals with the procurement, distribution, maintenance, and replacement of materiel and personnel. (p. 124)

loiter time—a combat aircraft's ability to stay aloft near its target while waiting to strike. (p. 421)

low-observable technology—stealth technology. (p. 411)

Luftwaffe—the German air force. (p. 132)

M

Mach—the speed of sound. (p. 291)

machine gun—an automatic rifle that uses belt-fed ammunition. (p. 65)

mainframe—a large, high-performance computer usually connected to several terminals and used by a large organization. (p. 432)

mainstream—the current of most people's life and activities. (p. 95)

malware—harmful software. (p. 436)

Marshall Plan—a strategy for rebuilding the countries of Europe and repelling communism after World War II. (p. 268)

massive retaliation—returning an attack with a large-scale attack, including using the atomic bomb. (p. 269)

materiel—the equipment and supplies of a military force. (p. 144)

medevac—medical evacuation. (p. 394)

mentor—a trusted coach or guide. (p. 79)

metal fatigue—a slow weakening of strength in metal caused by repeated deformation, vibration, or other stress. (p. 249)

milestone—an important event, such as a breakthrough in the advancement of knowledge in a field. (p. 90)

missiles—rocket-propelled vehicles that carry a weapon or warhead. (p. 277)

multiengine plane—a plane with more than one engine. (p. 44)

monoplane—an airplane with one set of wings. (p. 23)

N

National Guard—a military force recruited by each state, equipped by the federal government, and subject to either a state or federal government recall. (p. 270)

neutral—not taking sides. (p. 330)

network—one or more computers linked together physically or wirelessly. (p. 433)

network industry—an industry involving both flows and a grid. The flows are the mobile elements of a network industry. (p. 206)

no-fly zone—airspace enemy aircraft aren't allowed to enter. (p. 364)

nuclear deterrence—prevention of war by convincing an enemy that if he attacks, he will be destroyed by nuclear weapons. (p. 278)

nuclear war—war involving the atomic bomb or the hydrogen bomb. (p. 313)

O

occupation—invasion, conquest, and control of a nation or territory by foreign armed forces. (p. 132)

offshore—away from, or at some distance from, the shore. (p. 232)

ordnance—military supply such as weapons, ammunition, combat vehicles, and equipment. (p. 115)

ornithopter—an aircraft designed to get its upward and forward motion from flapping wings. (p. 9)

outrigger—a frame extending laterally beyond the main structure of an aircraft. (p. 392)

overhaul—to go over carefully and make needed repairs. (p. 118)

P

parachute—a device intended to slow free fall from an aircraft or another high point. (p. 6)

paratrooper—an infantry Soldier who is trained to parachute, often behind enemy lines. (p. 147)

patent—a legal document protecting the rights of an inventor. (p. 23)

phishing—tricking people into downloading harmful software or clicking on harmful links in e-mails or on websites. (p. 436)

pitch—a movement up or down. (p. 35)

playa—a flat-floored bottom of an undrained desert basin that at times can become a shallow lake. (p. 290)

porthole—a small, circular window. (p. 44)

POW—a prisoner of war (p. 320)

precision weapons—guided missiles and bombs. (p. 375)

pressurized cabins—cabins with normal air pressure even at high altitudes. (p. 214)

propulsion—a driving or propelling force. (p. 251)
protocol—an electronic procedure. (p. 433)
prototype—an original or first model that is used for what comes later. (p. 300)
pursuit aircraft—fighter planes. (p. 119)
pylons—tall, thin towers. (p. 52)

R

radial—round. (p. 45)
reciprocating engine—an engine powered by pistons that go back and forth. (p. 250)
relative wind—the flow of air. (p. 30)
reserves—military forces not part of the regular military, but trained and organized for a quick call to action. (p. 270)
retractable—the description of landing gear that folds into the aircraft. (p. 103)
reverse engineering—reproducing someone else's product after taking it apart and studying it carefully. (p. 414)
ribs—the crosswise pieces that give the wings their shape. (p. 27)
rocket—a large, cylindrical object that moves very fast by forcing burning gases out one end of the tube. (p. 7)
rotor—a set of rotating horizontal airfoils (wings). (p. 390)
rotary-wing aircraft—another name for helicopters. (p. 390)
rudder—a vertically hinged airfoil used for controlling horizontal movement of an aircraft. (p. 18)

S

sabotage—the destruction of property by enemy agents in time of war. (p. 128)
sateen—a cotton fabric woven like satin with a glossy surface. (p. 36)
satellite—an object that orbits another object in space, such as a planet. (p. 277)
satellite government—a government dominated politically and economically by another nation. (p. 273)
scheduled airlines—airlines that have flights that depart and arrive at set times. (p. 101)
secede—break away. (p. 378)
self-sealing—able to seal a leak to prevent fuel from leaking or igniting. (p. 185)
signatures—recognizable profiles and characteristics. (p. 411)
skids—long, thin runners, like a pair of skis. (p. 27)
smartphone—a cellphone with advanced computing ability. (p. 432)
social engineering—tricking people into giving out sensitive information such as passwords or credit card data. (p. 436)
social networking—interacting with other people through dedicated websites and applications (apps). (p. 434)
solitary confinement—when a prisoner is held in a cell alone and not allowed to talk to anyone. (p. 322)
solo—to fly with no one else on board. (p. 51)

sonic boom—a pressure wave created when an aircraft flies faster than the speed of sound, heard on the ground as a crack or boom. (p. 256)

sortie—a flight or an attack by a single combat aircraft. (p. 363)

Soviets—the people and especially the political and military leaders of the Union of Soviet Socialist Republics—the official name of the Soviet Union. (p. 162)

spars—the main, lengthwise pieces of the wing. (p. 27)

spatial disorientation—a condition in which a person's sense of direction does not agree with reality. (p. 95)

spectators—people who come to see an event or show. (p. 80)

squadron—an air force unit consisting of two or more flights. (p. 134)

stalemate—a situation in which further action is blocked. (p. 69)

stealth aircraft—an aircraft that can't be detected by radar. (p. 299)

stockholder—a person who owns shares of a public company. (p. 210)

strafe—to attack with a machine gun from a low-flying aircraft. (p. 72)

strategic—designed to strike at the sources of an enemy's military, economic, or political power. (p. 70)

Strategic Triad—land-based intercontinental ballistic missiles (ICBMs), submarine-launched ballistic missiles (SLBMs), and long-range bombers. (p. 276)

streamlining—designing an aircraft to reduce resistance to motion through the air. (p. 8)

stressed skin—an outer covering that can stand up to the push-and-pull forces of flight. (p. 103)

strife—an angry or violent disagreement between two or more people or groups. (p. 378)

strike fighter—an attack aircraft that can also function as a fighter. (p. 309)

strut—a vertical post. (p. 34)

subsidy—government money paid to a person or company that serves the public. (p. 102)

superpower—a powerful, dominant country that has nuclear weapons. (p. 273)

supersonic—faster than the speed of sound (about 770 mph). (p. 255)

T

tactical—involves military operations that are smaller, closer to base, and of less long-term significance than strategic operations. (p. 137)

takeover—the seizure of a country's military and political power. (p. 273)

tandem—two objects with one placed directly behind the other. (p. 44)

theater—a large geographic area in which military operations are coordinated. (p. 131)

thrust—the forward force driving an aircraft. (p. 22)

torque—a turning or twisting force. (p. 390)

transcontinental—coast-to-coast. (p. 93)

transport—a vehicle—aircraft, ship, or other—that carries people, supplies, tanks, and artillery. (p. 187)

treasonable—involving a violation of allegiance towards one's country. (p. 117)

tri-jet—an aircraft with three engines. (p. 252)

tsunami—a very high, large wave in the ocean that is usually caused by an earthquake under the sea. (p. 353)

tumble—roll end over end. (p. 291)

turbine engine—an engine driven by a moving fluid, such as water, steam, or air, that pushes against blades or paddles attached to a central shaft. (p. 250)

twin-float—an airplane with floats for landing on or taking off from a body of water. (p. 106)

U

U-boats—short for "undersea boats," the name given to German submarines. (p. 61)

United Nations—a worldwide organization first formed in 1945 by the victorious Allies to maintain international peace. (p. 275)

unmanned aerial vehicles—unmanned aircraft. (p. 420)

V

variable-geometry wings—wings that can be swept forward for takeoffs or slow flight, or swept backward for high-speed flight. (p. 347)

W

warbird—a vintage military aircraft. (p. 242)

weapon of mass destruction—a chemical, biological, or atomic weapon that can kill large numbers of people in one use. (p. 370)

weight—the force that directly opposes lift. (p. 251)

Western Allies—the United States, Britain, and France. (p. 280)

whistle blower—someone who uncovers and exposes wrongdoing in an organization. (p. 437)

winged gospel—the idealism surrounding flight, especially general aviation. (p. 229)

wing warping—twisting the tips of the wings with a series of cables. (p. 28)

Y

yaw—a sidewise movement. (p. 29)

Index

liability insurance, 232

lift, 17

   Bernouillian, 10

   dynamic, 10

   Newtonian, 10

light beacons, 100

Lilienthal, Otto, 23, 35

limited war, 306

Lincoln, President Abraham, 20

Lindbergh, Anne Morrow, 90, 92

Lindbergh, Charles, 88–92, 193, 225, 442

   contribution to aviation, 90

LinkedIn, 434

Lockheed Martin Corporation, 254, 256

Locklear, Ormer, 82, 86

logistics, 124

loiter time, 421

long-range raid, 70

Looking Glass command centers, 277

Louis XIV, King of France, 17

low observable technology, 411

Lowe, Nancy Harkness, 151, 153

Lowe, Thaddeus, 20–21

Lufberry, Raoul, 64

Luftwaffe, 132, 136, 139, 144, 147, 183, 184

Luke, Frank, 66

Lynn, Chief Master Sergeant Kevin, 371

M

M.A.S.H. (TV series), 394

MacArthur, General Douglas, 306, 309

Mach (speed), 291–292

Mach, Ernst, 291

machine gun, 65, 70–72

Macintosh, 432

Mackay Trophy, 332

Macready, 1st Lieutenant John, 114, 240

Madole, Glenn, 47

mainframe, 432

mainstream, 95

malware, 436

Manjuck, Technical Sergeant Ryan, 402–403

Manning, Bradley/Chelsea, 437

Mannock, Edward, 60

Marie Antoinette, Queen of France, 17

Marshall, George C., 268

Marshall Plan, 268, 273

Martin-Marietta Corporation, 256

massive retaliation, 269

materiel, 144

Maughan, 1st Lieutenant Russell, 114

Maxfield, Lieutenant Colonel Joseph E., 14

McDonnell-Douglas, 252

McNary-Watres Act, 101

Medal of Honor, 97, 117, 127, 133, 161, 319, 320, 328, 330, 331, 369, 388–389, 397

medevac, 394

mentor, 79

metal fatigue, 249

Microsoft Corporation, 432

milestone, 90

military aviation research after World War II, 290–292

military decorations, 369

military reorganization after World War II, 270

Miller, Major Glenn, 145

Milosevic, Slobodan, 378, 380

Minh, Ho Chi, 316

missiles, 277

   air-to-air, 333–334

   SA-2, 334–335

   surface-to-air, 333–334

Mitchell, Brigadier General William, "Billy", 65, 69, 72–73, 76, 110–111, 113–115, 116–117, 267

Moisant, John, 53

Moisant, Matilde, 53

monoplane, 23

Montgolfier, Étienne, 16–17

Montgolfier, Joseph, 16–17

Montgolfier gas, 17

Montgomery, John J., 23

Moon, 1st Lieutenant Odas, 99

Morrow Board, 115

Moseley, General T. Michael, 440

Mullen, Admiral Mike, 403

multiengine plane, 44

Mussolini, Benito, 129–130

Myers, Captain David A., 95–96

MySpace, 434